Record of a Friendship

RECORD OF

FARRAR · STRAUS · GIROUX

A FRIENDSHIP

The Correspondence Between

Wilhelm Reich and

A. S. Neill

1936–1957

Edited, and with an Introduction, by

BEVERLEY R. PLACZEK

Introduction

Wilhelm Reich and A. S. Neill first met in Norway in 1936; they remained friends for over twenty years, until Reich's death in 1957. Though they were separated for most of those years, first by the war and later by the travel restrictions of the McCarthy era, a steady exchange of letters, back and forth across the ocean, kept their friendship alive. These letters stand as the record of a friendship between two remarkable men.

Neill was a Scotsman, a schoolmaster and child psychologist known for his radical views on child education. Reich was an Austrian, an iconoclastic psychoanalyst who had been blackballed by his Freudian colleagues for his unorthodox theories about society and sexuality. When they met, Neill was fifty-three, Reich thirty-nine. Reich, an exile from Nazi Germany, had been living and working in Oslo for two years; Neill had been invited to lecture at Oslo University. On the boat coming over, he had by coincidence been reading Reich's *Die Massenpsychologie des Faschismus* (*The Mass Psychology of Fascism*; there was as yet no English translation) and after his lecture learned with delight that its author had been in his audience. He telephoned and was invited to dinner. "We talked far into the night," Neill recalls. That was the beginning.

What held this friendship together for so long? The two men came from opposite ends of Europe and from vastly different social backgrounds. They were half a generation apart in age. And yet these two could talk to each other as to no one else. Reich: "Please write more often, since you are one of the very few to whom I can talk"; and Neill: "Forgive my grumble, but you are the only one to whom I can write." On the face of it, it was a most unlikely friendship. Opposites are said to attract, and certainly two more different men can scarcely be imagined: Reich, the Central European intellectual, highly educated, enormously gifted, and of driving energy, who moved, thought, and worked always in high gear; Neill, the Scot, intelligent to be sure, even wise, but no intellectual, canny, humorous, patient, and pragmatic. To Reich, who was unstinting in his love for humanity in general, individual people always mattered less than his work. To Neill, people—children and the adults they would become—were the very stuff of his life. Reich, like a magnet, attracted disciples and sycophants, but none could long keep pace with his single-minded intensity or follow his leaping shifts to ever new areas of exploration; time after time, he found himself standing alone at the center of a swathe he himself had carved. Neill had neither disciples nor sycophants, nor did his central concerns ever vary, but some two hundred and fifty people—pupils, past pupils, parents, and friends—shared in celebrating his seventieth birthday, and those who had been children at Summerhill entrusted their own children to him. Reich liked skiing and hiking, and he also played the piano, but his greatest joy was in his work; he could not stand what he called "Gesell-schaftskonversation" (small talk). Neill took pleasure in everyday things, jokes, good talk—preferably over a glass of whiskey—gardening and puttering in his workshop. Golf was his great treat. He understood children intuitively because all his life he himself retained something of the child.

Not only were they unlike in taste and temperament; their origins, too, were utterly dissimilar: rooted Scots-Presbyterian versus uprooted Austrian-Jewish. Wilhelm Reich was the brilliant son of a well-to-do landowner. Born in 1897, he grew up on the family estate in the Bukovina, a province on the easternmost confines of the Austro-Hungarian monarchy, a region where German-speaking Jews were a tiny minority. The father, assimilated and non-religious, was determined to have his son brought up within the German culture: the boy was for-bidden to play with either the local Ukrainian-speaking peasant children or the Yiddish-speaking children of the poorer Jews; private tutors were imported until he was old enough to be sent away to the German-speaking Gymnasium. Reich lost his adored mother by suicide when he was thirteen. Four years later he had to leave school to care for his sick father, and upon his father's death, the seventeen-year-old boy took over the management of the property. It was 1914, and with the out-break of World War I the Bukovina became contested territory. By 1916 young Reich, forced to flee before the advancing Russians, had become an officer in the Austrian army. When, in 1918, Austria and Germany were defeated, the Bukovina passed to Romania; with it went all that remained of the life Reich had known. Alone and impoverished, he arrived in Vienna intending to study law, but soon found that medicine was his real vocation. Throughout his years as a student, he endured cold and even hunger, but he learned quickly, and managed to scrape a meager living as a tutor to less talented classmates. He discovered Freud and the new science of psychoanalysis, married a fellow student with whom in due course he had two daughters, and by the age of twenty-five was himself a practicing physician and psychoanalyst, devoting much time to work in the free mental-health clinics he had helped to establish in the poorer sections of the city. It was here that he came to know at first hand the crippling psychological effects on working-class people of the sexual hypocrisies and suppressions under which they lived. The theories on sexuality and society that grew out of this experience made him increasingly suspect to his psychoanalytic colleagues. In 1927 he joined the Communist Party. Three years later he moved to Berlin, where he hoped to find support for the social reforms he felt were necessary to achieve sexual—and hence mental—health for the workers. At first he was welcomed. Under the aegis of the powerful Berlin Communists, he consolidated and expanded the various Sexual Politics groups into a unified movement that soon counted more than forty thousand members. As time went on, however, the party organizers, embarrassed by a success that undercut their authority, became more and more antagonistic. Then, early in 1933, the Nazis came to power, the German Communist Party was outlawed, and Reich himself was once again forced to flee.

He returned to Vienna. By now he had moved a long way from the mainstream of Freudian psychoanalytic thinking, a divergence that together with other, personal, factors led to divorce from his orthodox Freudian wife and, ultimately, brought about his expulsion from the International Psycho-Analytical Association. Isolated both professionally and personally, he found the situation in Vienna untenable and accepted an invitation to move to Denmark. Within a year, in Copenhagen, he had created a circle of students, was busy with numerous patients, and had generated a Danish movement for sexual politics. When the authorities refused to renew his residency permit, he moved on, first to Sweden, and thence to Norway. Here again, with undiminished courage, he assembled a group to share his work. He made his living by teaching and practicing vegeto-therapy, a treatment of neuroses that combined verbal character analysis with a direct physical attack on the nodes of muscular tension in which, he held, neuroses are expressed and preserved. Leaving active sexual politics to others, he now devoted all his free time and energy to research in biophysics.

In contrast, how straightforward Neill's life appears! Nearly fourteen years older than Reich, he was born in 1883, the middle child of a large family that was barely emerging from the working class; his grandfather and his many uncles on his father's side had all spent their lives as miners, "in the pits." His father was a teacher, the stern dominie of a two-room village school in the north of Scotland; his indefatigable mother, herself also originally a schoolteacher, saw to it that her children spoke proper English—the local dialect was broad Scots—and that in "kirk" they sat through the interminable hell-fire sermons freshly scrubbed and stiffly starched. No one in the family expected much of "Allie"; he tripped over his own feet, forgot his errands, and preferred larking with the village boys to the Latin that his father, implacably ambitious for his numerous children, insisted they learn. Secondary school, it was decided, would be wasted on him; so, when he was seventeen, having failed at a couple of rather menial jobs, young Neill was taken on as an apprentice teacher in his father's school. After four years, he progressed to various minor paid teaching positions. Finally, when he was twenty-four, he passed the entrance examinations to Edinburgh University. Having acquired a very honorable degree in English, he set off for London to work in a small publishing firm. When war broke out in 1914, a severe phlebitis prevented him from enlisting. Instead, he went back to Scotland to become the master of a small school. Here he first began to question accepted educational practices and the wisdom of authority. (His charming *Dominie* books—*A Dominie's Log*, 1915; *A Dominie Dismissed*, 1916; *A Dominie in Doubt*, 1920; followed by *A Dominie Abroad*, 1922, and *A Dominie's Five*, 1924—grew out of the experiences of those years.) Though he was recruited into the artillery in 1917, he never saw action. After his discharge, he taught for a while in a "progressive" school, but even there his views proved too radical and he soon left. During this period he came to know Homer Lane, an American social reformer whose remarkable success with delinquent children Neill had long admired, and who had recently set up as a psychoanalyst in London. Asserting that all teachers should be analyzed, Lane offered to take Neill on—free. Neill accepted. The analysis as such was unsuccessful ("It did not touch my emotions and I wonder if I got anything from it"), but the contact with Lane helped to clarify and reinforce Neill's own developing ideas about freedom for children. By good fortune, he soon found a forum for these ideas in *The New Era*, the journal of the pioneering New Education Fellowship, of which he became co-editor. In this capacity, he also began traveling to Europe to report on advances in European education. On one of these trips he met and became friends with a German architect, Dr. Otto Neustätter, and his Australian-born wife, a woman some years older than Neill. For Neill the year 1921 was the watershed. He gave up his job with *The New Era* and, with the Neustätters and two other friends, opened a school near Dresden which was to offer its pupils that freedom and "creative self-expression" in which the founders all believed. For three years, in spite of the growing disapproval of the authorities, the school managed to maintain a foothold, first in Germany and later in Austria. In the course of those years Dr. Neustätter and his wife were divorced and Neill and she were married.

Tired of constant battles with bigoted officials and hostile villagers, in 1924 Neill and his wife brought their five British pupils back to England and settled them in a rented house in Dorset named Summerhill. When a year later they moved their growing school to a large rambling red brick building in Suffolk, they took the name with them. And so it became the Summerhill School. It was here that, except for the four years of wartime evacuation to the safety of Wales, Neill was to spend the rest of his long active life.

In the winter of 1937–38, almost two years after that first talk "far into the night," Neill traveled to Oslo for a few weeks of study and therapy with Reich. In the long vacation of the following summer he went again, and during the Easter holidays of 1939 was able to make a final trip before Reich left Norway for the United States. All through the war they wrote to each other. And when at last peace came, Neill journeyed from Summerhill in Suffolk to spend ten days with Reich at his new summer place, Orgonon, in Maine. They found that the old friendship was still very much alive. Two days after Neill's arrival, Reich records in his diary: "Several hours of talk with Neill. He is still the same as ever. I could joke with him and be *simple*." A year later Neill returned, this time bringing his young second wife and their small daughter. He stayed for over a month and, when it was over, wrote to Reich: "Hated to leave you"; and Reich, noting that "when you left there was quite a gap at Orgonon," consoled himself and Neill with the promise that "we shall have it again." But in this he was wrong. Two years later Neill's application for a visa was refused without explanation. The McCarthy era had begun. When the ban was finally lifted and Neill could once more enter the United States, Reich had been dead for over twelve years.

For all their differences—of origin, of education, of age, of temperament—Reich and Neill were alike in one way: both were dedicated men. Reich, dominated by a passion to discover the single underlying principle from which all biophysical phenomena could be derived, spent his every spare dollar and every spare hour on research—finally, in 1950, giving up a lucrative practice to immerse himself wholly in his orgonomic work. Neill lived his whole life as a poor man, constantly plagued by financial worry, fighting cagily and stubbornly to keep his school afloat so that "a few hundred children be allowed to grow freely." Their dedication was based on an assumption which they shared, an almost religious faith in the redemptive power of unconstricted, natural development, in what Reich saw as "the inherent decency and honesty of the life process if it is not disturbed." Human beings, they believed, had for millennia been distorted by social conditioning—"structuring" or "armoring," as they called it. To such "anti-life character molding" they attributed all human failings, all human woes. Their trust in the necessary and certain triumph of "unarmored" man was the lode star that made present disappointments bearable and justified every sacrifice.

In this sense, Neill's work was important to Reich. By entrusting real children with real freedom, both social and sexual, in "that dreadful school," Neill was bringing into actuality tenets in which both believed. "The only hope," Reich wrote, "is, I firmly believe, establishment of rationality in children and adolescents," and demanded: "Why should I go into child biology if there are such marvellous child educators as A. S. Neill . . . ?" Also, he appreciated the childlike quality in Neill, noting about Neill's *Problem Family* in his diary: "A very good book written by a child 64 years old; honest, playful; frank; full of love for children."

Neill held Reich to be a genius whose work was bringing humanity closer to the goal of self-understanding and freedom: "Reich, you are one of the great men of our time; I say it as a simple fact without any meaning of flattery or worship." Neill's sense of Reich's greatness was a central fact in his relation to him, even when Reich went beyond what Neill himself could accept or understand. "I never understood your orgone work really; too old, too set, too conditioned," he wrote in 1956, and on reading the account of UFO's in Reich's journal, *CORE*: "If I had never heard of Reich and had read *CORE* for the first time, I would have concluded that the author was either *meschugge* [crazy] or the greatest discoverer in centuries. Since I know you aren't *meschugge* I have to accept the alternative."

Neill's belief in Reich had been laid down in the Norway years; work

with Reich, as his patient and student, had given him a whole new sense
of confidence; it had also, incidentally, freed him from the fierce headaches that had plagued him much of his life. Furthermore, and more
important in the long run, Reich's teachings on sex-economy had provided Neill with a firm theoretical underpinning for ideas he had arrived
at pragmatically and been practicing at Summerhill for years. The continued contact with Reich gave him a sense of sharing in a whole world
of intellectual excitement and discovery; he writes of "the inspiration
you have given me for years," and shortly after his visa had been
refused: "For two years I had looked forward to great talks with you
in Maine, and when that anticipation was shattered, I had no one to
talk to, no one who could give me anything new." And Neill was also,
very simply, extremely fond of Reich: "How could I ever come back to
the States if there was no dear warm friend Reich to greet me?" In
Norway, and again on his visits to the States, he had come to know at
first hand Reich's enormous warmth and charm—something Reich's
letters often fail to convey. (Thirty years later, when I asked her about
Reich, Mrs. Neill's face lit up. She had met him only during that one
summer visit in 1948 and yet she still remembers with affection his
friendly welcome, his directness, and how "easy" it was to be with him.)
It is to this warm and "easy" man that Neill wrote, and of whom he
never lost sight, in spite of Reich's frequent scoldings, his diatribes, and
the general mistrust that darkened his final years. But for all Neill's
loving admiration and his self-deprecatory view of himself as Reich's
"good John the Baptist," Neill, absorbed as he was in his own work,
never got caught in Reich's orbit; he knew that there were two sides to
their relationship, that he gave as well as received. He was distressed by
the refusal of the visa not just for himself but because "I know you need
me in some way . . . and we are separated by a futile suspicion."

Did Reich indeed need Neill? The continuing flow of letters is in
itself an answer: Reich could so easily have let it lapse, unless for him,
too, it was important. Far from doing so, he tells Neill that "it is always
a great thing to have a letter from you," and adjures him over and over
to "keep writing please." He depended on Neill's unswerving friendship,
writing at one point: "I hope you don't mind that I am pouring out my
heart to you." Also, that Neill was preaching Reichian doctrine to
audiences three thousand miles away gave Reich a sense of enlarged
reach and impact. Though he often scolded Neill: "I am cross that you
don't follow my advice . . ." or "Why can't you see, Neill . . . ?" or "It
is of the utmost importance that you revise your basic attitude . . ."

he respected Neill's independence of mind and his honesty: "I know no one in Europe who could listen better and understand better what is at stake at the present time in the development of our work," and wrote appreciatively of Neill's "unique position, being in the orgone fold but at the same time independent."

During the 1950's, as the pressures on Reich increased, he became mistrustful even of Neill, but it is a measure of his real affection that, as late as 1956, the year before his death, he wrote to Neill: "It would be splendid if you came to the U.S.A. this summer. You could stay at my summer house as my guest. Though things have greatly changed since 1950, and much new has happened, I am certain we would get along." But the ban still stood; Neill could not come.

Even had he been able to accept Reich's invitation, it is doubtful whether, for all Neill's steady good sense and even-tempered realism, he could have influenced the course of events that finally destroyed his friend. Reich's passionate intransigence made him unable to accept advice and left him perilously exposed to his enemies.

For a number of years after his move to the States, things had gone well with Reich: he had remarried, had established the Orgone Institute and the semi-independent Orgone Institute Press, which put out a journal and published his books; he had acquired a beautiful tract of land in Maine, intended as the future center of orgonomic research and teaching; his practice flourished and he had attracted a considerable following of student-physicians and supporters. Then, in 1947, the hostility which, time and again throughout his life, his theories had aroused came to the surface in America. An article by a freelance reporter, Mildred Edie Brady, entitled "The Strange Case of Wilhelm Reich," appeared in a respected periodical, *The New Republic*. Widely quoted and repeated, this clever mixture of half truths, snide distortions, and suggestive misrepresentations came to be accepted as fact by all those who found Reich's views on the primacy of orgastic fulfillment objectionable. Some righteous citizens alerted the Federal Food and Drug Administration to the possibility of fraud in the claims which, the article alleged, Reich had made for the orgone accumulator. From then on, for ten years, the FDA pursued its investigation of Reich with relentless zeal. Finally, in 1954, having failed to uncover the vice ring for which the Orgone Institute was purportedly a front, the agency succeeded in persuading the attorney general of the federal court in Maine to issue a complaint against Reich and the Wilhelm Reich Foundation, as a first step to banning the sale or rental of accumulators.

Reich, arguing that no jurist was competent to judge matters of science, refused to appear in court to challenge the complaint; thus, the terms of the injunction obtained by the FDA were extremely broad: accumulators on hand were to be destroyed and, on the grounds that the literature of the Orgone Institute Press constituted "false labeling" of these devices, its publications were also ordered destroyed. Having procured the injunction, the FDA, temporarily, left Reich in peace.

Some months later, however, an event occurred that was to be decisive for the outcome of the agency's dogged resolve to get Reich. During the winter of 1954–55 Reich spent some time in Arizona on a research project. A young associate, Michael Silvert, was left in New York to deal with routine administrative matters. In Reich's absence, and without his knowledge, Silvert had some books and accumulator parts sent from Maine to New York. The questing agents of the FDA got wind of this shipment and, asserting that it constituted "interstate commerce" and hence violated the terms of the injunction, demanded that Reich be indicted for contempt of court. In the spring of 1956, hearings were held—and this time Reich did appear to present his views. However, in the trial that followed, a jury found him guilty, and he was sentenced to two years in prison. The sentence was postponed pending appeal. In the interim, the FDA saw to the destruction ordered in the injunction. The few accumulators and the relatively small number of Orgone Institute journals on the shelves at Orgonon were duly burned under the supervision of FDA agents, after which a much larger operation of the same sort took place in New York. Huge quantities of journals, pamphlets, and books were removed from the Foundation's warehouse, loaded onto a truck, and carted off to the incinerators of the City Sanitation Department, where they were burned.

By the following spring, it was clear that Reich's year-long effort to have the verdict of the Maine court overturned had failed. On March 11, 1957, in Portland, Maine, after a last desperate effort to have the sentence reduced or suspended, he was led out of the courthouse in handcuffs to begin serving his prison term. Less than eight months later, on November 3, 1957, in the federal prison in Lewisburg, Pennsylvania, he died of heart failure. "I came to think in all earnest," he had once written to Neill, "that almost all heart diseases are originally heartbreak diseases."

Reich kept all Neill's letters, and copies of his own. With rare exceptions, Neill typed all his letters, but he never made carbons and frequently repeats some piece of news or asks "Did I tell you . . . ?" this or that. Usually, Reich noted the point he intended to take up—or, it may be, his reactions to what Neill had written—directly on the letters themselves: passages are underscored, vivid exclamation marks dot the page, and here and there, particularly in later years, a large "NO" or "LIARS," "SCOUNDRELS," or the like, will be scrawled in the margin, the very vigor of the marking suggesting a shout.

In all, there are close to five hundred letters. Spread over the twenty years of their friendship, this would average a letter from each man every month. But that, of course, is not how it was. There are few letters until 1938, when Neill went to Oslo to study with Reich. By then both men knew that war was coming, and there is much discussion about the protection of Reich's microscope slides and the possibility of his moving to England. In 1939, Reich emigrated to America. And here some crucial letters are missing, the first he wrote from the States. We know they did exist, because in September of that year Neill writes: "It was good to get your letter saying you had arrived"; and again, in October, "I got your long letter"; and finally, on January 5, 1940, "I got your two letters by the same post." How fascinating it would have been to read those first impressions! Though through the war the mails must have been uncertain, the flow continues with seldom a pause of more than a few weeks. Plans for Neill's visits of 1947 and 1948 fill the letters of those years; then, in 1950, when his expectation of joining Reich was thwarted by the ban, more letters went back and forth than in any other year: more than one a week! (It is quite startling, incidentally, how quickly a letter could get from Rangeley in Maine to Leiston in Suffolk: some letters are answered a mere three days after they were sent.) From 1950 on, as the realization grew in Neill's mind that he would probably never see Reich again, the number of letters diminished. In 1955 we find only one letter of Reich's, though from Neill's responses, it is clear he wrote more often.

Despite the enormous differences in background and outlook between the two men, despite separation and the pressures of a censorious society and their own sharply defined personalities, the letters they wrote to each other through the years glow with their affection and the enrichment each brought to the life of the other. Each was intensely interested in the other's thoughts about the things that seemed important to them both. Discussions of how the world should be run recur: Reich believed that the world of the future would be governed by what he called "work democracy"; although Neill agreed with the ideal, he doubted its practicability. Surprisingly, they seldom comment on actual events except in personal terms—even the end of the war is mentioned only as it allows Neill to return from Wales to his beloved Suffolk. In the 1940's, both men became fathers and thereafter exchanged constant bulletins on the progress of their children: Reich's son, Peter, born in 1944, and Neill's daughter, Zoë, born two years later.

The tone and content of each man's letters are as different as the men themselves. Neill's are variously humorous, speculative, penetratingly realistic, and deeply depressed—often all these simultaneously. He fills them with everyday things, concrete activities, news of friends. He talks of his unceasing efforts to make Reich's work known in England, always responds at length to the publications Reich sends him, and faithfully passes on any comments he may have gleaned. When the school is evacuated to Wales during the war, he writes about the narrowness, the overcrowding, the cold, and the damp. He frequently asks Reich's advice about psychology, how he might best use what he has learned on behalf of individual children. In later years he confides his worries—over the nuclear threat, the school's financial situation, and his daughter Zoë's future: "Well, Reich, bless you, I think of you often especially when I am in trouble and want to talk to someone who will listen." And always he wants to hear of Reich's doings, plying him with questions about his work and his life. In contrast, Reich's letters seem curiously impersonal. He speaks, always in general terms, of the many people who believe in him, of the growing success and acceptance of his ideas—"My social and academic standing in the U.S. is very strong"; and "Our literature here still sells like warm bread"—and of his current theories and interests. Frequently he inveighs against the scoundrels who deride him or, worse still, who distort his meaning and ride to wealth on his efforts. As the years went by, he moved further and further to the right politically: the hand of Moscow was behind every disappointment, every harassment, behind even the FDA and McCarthy. Occasionally, his proud optimism is shot through by a premonition of his coming tragedy: writing to Neill as early as 1946 that "there is only one thing I still fear. That is, some crooked frameup, some abysmal *Gemeinheit* [meanness] which may hit me in the back and destroy my work"; and elsewhere, comparing himself to a "fiery horse racing over meadows enjoying a sunny morning in the spring," describes how "a small stick of 20 inches brings the horse to a fall. It breaks its neck."

Sometimes there were arguments, as when Neill demurred at Reich's attempts to justify the United States' refusal of travel visas—"of late you have appeared to me pretty close to the Americans who are witch hunting"—or took exception to Reich's growing tendency to attach the label of "red fascist" to any person or action of which he disapproved. But these disputes were always ultimately set aside, as when, after an increasingly discordant exchange, Neill writes that "all this dispute between us never gets us anywhere. It just tires us and saddens us"; or when Reich affectionately suggests that "two glasses of good whiskey soda would suffice to clear up our disagreement." Only once, in the autumn of 1956, did Reich allow suspicion to blind him to Neill's stubborn loyalty. During the preceding summer Reich's son, Peter, had stayed for a while at Summerhill. Some of his talks with Neill, when later reported to Reich, led the latter to believe that finally Neill, too, had failed him. Reich expressed his feelings of betrayal to a mutual friend. This was more than even Neill could bear: "So our long friendship has come to an end because you consider me unreliable"—ending his letter: "Goodbye, Reich, and bless you." But the friendship did not end. Reich disregarded the reproach and the farewell, only telling Neill not to "worry," and a few weeks later begging him to "be patient, please, if I keep silent or do not reply promptly. I am extremely busy." And Neill responded, damning "this 3000 miles separation," and then, writing of his concern at the turn events were taking: "Reich I love you. I cannot bear to think of your being punished by an insane prison sentence. You couldn't do it and you know it."

How right Neill was: though Reich had committed no crime, a few months later he died of the punishment.

Sixteen years later, just before his own death in September 1973, Neill summed up his feelings in his autobiography: "A great man had died in vile captivity. I think that Reich will not come into his own as a genius until at least three generations from now. I was most lucky to know him and learn from him, and love him."

We too are fortunate that now, with the publication of this eloquent record of their friendship, we can come to know these two extraordinary men in their full humanity.

BEVERLEY R. PLACZEK

New York
December 1980

All the letters published here are taken from Reich's file. Very few of Neill's letters appear to be missing, but the file contained only carbon copies of Reich's letters, and many are missing. A remark of Neill's may explain this: "Now that Ilse has gone, you seem to have to write by hand"; when that was the case, Reich would, of course, have made no carbon. Neill signed all his letters just plain "Neill." None of Reich's carbon copies are signed, but Mrs. Neill tells me that "Reich signed his letters in a variety of ways: sometimes just WR or Wilh. Reich and sometimes just REICH or W. Reich."

As far as possible, Reich and Neill have been left to speak each in his own voice. At the start, Reich's English was uncertain, but I have altered it only where the sense was unclear; and in translating the few letters he still wrote in German, I have tried to maintain their flavor. Though Reich never lost his accent, he was always highly articulate, and his command of the written language improved steadily. Neill talked directly into his typewriter: he used slang when it suited him and dotted his letters with German words and phrases; his abbreviations are idiosyncratic, his punctuation and capitalization irregular, and, of course, his spelling is British. All this has been left unchanged.

In preparing so large a body of letters for publication, some abridgment was essential. If some letters appear abrupt, it is for this reason. I have deleted repetitions, redundancies, and passing allusions to people who play no part in the story. I have also somewhat reduced Neill's descriptions of his health problems: Reich, as well as being his friend, had also been his doctor. On the other hand, I have retained every sentence that might shed light on any aspect of the life, the thought, or the personality of either man, even such as perhaps in themselves seem unimportant or trivial.

The people mentioned in the letters, unless identified in the text, are identified in footnotes, as are events, current and important at the time, that may not be clear from the context.

I am most grateful to Mrs. Ilse Ollendorff Reich for generously allowing me to include a long, important letter she wrote to Neill in 1952, which contains a description of an event not covered elsewhere.

My very warm thanks go to Miss Mary Higgins for her unfailing help in elucidating obscure points and tirelessly searching out relevant material.

B.R.P.

Record of a Friendship

1936-1939

Summerhill School
Leiston, Suffolk

March 22, 1936

Dear Reich,

You remember I mentioned a Mrs. Tracey who wanted to come to you? I would be very grateful if you would take her on for analysis. She is a parent here and I tried to analyse her myself, but found her emotional attitude to me made it impossible. She wants if possible to go to Oslo about May 10th, and as she is very unhappy and having ghastly dreams I am hoping you can find time to analyse her. She has a dream of dealing with children analytically later on.

Let me know as soon as you can. Best Wishes.

◆◆

Oslo, Norway

March 26, 1936

Dear Neill!

Before I can decide myself to start an analysis with Mrs. Tracey, I would like to have entire information through you or by herself about her difficulties, her age etc. I am rather occupied and would have to reserve an hour for her. Besides I am rather expensive, that means my circumstances don't admit to take low prices. My *minimum* fee is 20 norv.Kr. for the hour. If that would be too much a character analysis with a lower price, about ten norv.Kr. would be possible by one of my pupils. I could guarantee for a very good one.

Please let me know about what Mrs. Tracey is going zu decide.

3

I hope you are doing well. You will get my new book *Sexualität im Kulturkampf** very soon. Best greetings.

—◆•◆—

Oslo, Norway

December 17, 1936

My dear Neill!

I did not write you so long, that I have to apologise. I had to go through a lot of very hard accomplishments personally and in my work. There happened a very lucky turn in my investigations: I succeeded to compose microscopic things† which behave just like protozoa. It was demonstrated the last week in Copenhagen in the Rockefeller-Institut and Albert Fischer the biologist, took it first with fun, but then when I made the experiment before his eyes, he became rather serious. I have to do now a lot about it, to prove it to the most compulsion-neurotic scientists.

It will interest you to hear that Mrs. Tracey has made a big step forward: She succeeds really to solve her tremendous muscular tensions especially in her face. I think she will write you herself.

Please let me know if you are doing well and how you are getting along with your fine work.

You will get soon a reprint about the first part of my latest experimental work. Please send me reprints if you got some new ones.

With my kindest greetings.

—◆•◆—

---

* *Die Sexualität im Kulturkampf*, 1936 (*The Sexual Revolution*, 1945; in a new translation, 1974). Reich's critique of prevailing socio-sexual conditions, based on his studies of sexology and on his experience as a physician working in the free mental-health clinics he had founded in Vienna and Berlin.

† Reich later came to call these vesicular forms "bions."

Summerhill School
Leiston, Suffolk

October 4, 1937

*Dear Constance,**

I am coming to Oslo probably about the New Year. Ask R. if he can find time to give me a few talks at of course paying rate. Elsa† asks me to be her guest but I am telling her I want to be entirely on my own, with no feeling of duty or responsibility to anyone except myself. I'll be able to have a fortnight in Oslo and will bring my ski boots in case there is a chance of a few falls. R.'s latest book is fascinating, but so difficult for me to read that I want to get it in English from him.

Mrs Lins‡ is also fascinated with R.'s book; she wanted to come too but I said I must get away alone to get some perspective. She has gone stale also, and we carry on with too much effort. Both get so discouraged by setbacks. Uphill work pioneering.

P.S. Arrange with R. I'm not writing him because he has as little time for letters as I have.

———◆·◆———

Oslo, Norway

November 9, 1937

My dear Neill,

Constance gave me your letter which you wrote to her. I shall reserve one hour§ for you after Christmas. Of course it cannot be guaranteed that I shall accomplish much in this short time. Neither is it sure that my permission [to remain] in Norway will be prolonged. But I hope we shall find the opportunity to discuss through a few of your difficulties entirely. I believe I know where they are rooted: in the contradiction between the tremendous pioneer needs and the complete

---

* Constance Tracey.

† Elsa (also Else) Lindenberg. Although never legally, she was effectively Reich's second wife. They had met in Berlin, where she was a dancer with the Berlin State Opera. When he moved to Copenhagen in 1933, she joined him; they lived together until Reich left Norway in the summer of 1939.

‡ Neill's first wife, an Australian, born Lilly Lindesay—whence the nickname "Mrs. Lins," by which she was generally known.

§ That is, one hour each day. During his two-week stay in Oslo, Neill probably had ten or twelve psychiatric sessions with Reich.

hopelessness of our great time under which we are suffering. That works hard upon the poor mistreated human structure. Don't mind my being busy. I shall surely have time enough for you.

———————◆•◆———————

Summerhill School
Leiston, Suffolk

November 21, 1937

Dear Dr. Reich,

Sorry for delay in answering; I have been in Scotland burying my old father. I am delighted at the prospect of coming over to study even if for so short a time with you. There is a growing body of opinion in scientific circles in this country that you have made the greatest advance in psychology since Freud began the psychology of the Unconscious. I am taking steps to get your books translated into English, for they are full of new ideas and a completely new technique. As you probably know I am called the most advanced child psychologist in the country, but I realise that I can learn much from you, and I think it splendid that you are giving me the opportunity to come and do so. Your *Character-Analyse** is the finest thing I have come across for many years.

I shall come as soon after Christmas as possible and can stay until the middle of January.

———————◆•◆———————

Oslo, Norway

November 24, 1937

Dear Neill!†

I shall expect you sometime around Christmas. I am most grateful to you for the things you say. In this terrible time you are a great support in the fight. Freud once said to me, in connection with the analytic concept of "cultural repression": "Either you are on

---

* *Charakteranalyse*, 1933 (*Character Analysis*, revised English edition, 1945; expanded edition, 1949, 1972). A psychoanalytic investigation of the various character structures that grow out of the need to preserve repressions against release and recognition, and of the socio-economic forces that promote them.

† Translated from the original German.

entirely the wrong track or you will have to carry the dreadful burden
of psychoanalysis completely alone." As to the latter, I wish he had
not been proven so right.

Do please let me know in good time the day of your arrival.

*[In the three months between this letter and the one that follows,
Neill traveled to Norway as planned and worked with Reich. He
also came to know some of the people who were working and
studying with Reich.]*

———— ◆•◆ ————

*Summerhill School
Leiston, Suffolk*

February 22, 1938

My dear Reich,

So far I am dead. No sex, no interest in work or play, just
dull and depressed with frequent headaches. But already I feel a change
coming, and hope to give you a more cheerful report soon. Depressed
about my work. The boy bedwetters all hold back their abdomens and
are stiff,* but I can only observe that and feel depressed at not being
able to do anything for them. *Habe Sehnsucht nach Oslo* [I am yearn-
ing for Oslo].

Helga† was on the boat but I had no interest in her at all. *So eine
Geschichte!* [What a business!] Am reading *Bione*‡ slowly but again depressed because too scientific for me.

But there are good signs. Less afraid of the wife, and more decided
about making up my mind. Very conscious of the Narcism [*sic*], and
able to smile at its signs when they appear.

Thanks for much. I long to return again.

———— ◆•◆ ————

* While in Oslo, Neill had learned from Reich to see this as a sign of repression
and tension.

† This is not the lady's true name; we have used the pseudonym Neill himself
used in his autobiography.

‡ *Die Bione*, 1938 (*The Bion Experiments*, 1979). Reich here documents the
series of experiments he carried out in Oslo. These, he held, opened the way to an
understanding of the origin of life and provided the basis for all his later work with
cancer and orgone biophysics.

Oslo, Norway

March 5, 1938

*Dear Neill!**

Please forgive me for answering your letter only today, but as you know, my time is always far too full.

The things you tell me are on the whole encouraging. I remind you again of what I have said to you repeatedly, namely that in four weeks I cannot effect a cure. I also told you in advance that at first you would be depressed by what you experienced with me. It is not pleasant to come back to the school and suddenly to see that all the children have stiff stomachs. But what is one to do about it? Do please give yourself time and rest to digest the whole thing.

Please write again. Let me know in plenty of time when you want to resume, as I have to arrange the hour.

With warm greetings.

———◆◆———

Summerhill School
Leiston, Suffolk

March 16, 1938

Dear Reich,

Austria and Spain seem so terribly important† that it sounds silly to write about myself. We are all furious about Austria and still more furious at Chamberlain and Co who are really Fascists.‡ I don't know how you stand now, but unless you are German you have no nationality. I hope your girls§ got out in time. One thing is sure, that the great war isn't far off now.

Apart from my pessimism about world events, I feel better than when I wrote last, more *Arbeitsfähig* [able to work] but not enough yet. No

---

* Translated from the original German.

† Just that week Austria had been annexed by Nazi Germany, while in Spain Franco, with the help of Hitler's Germans and Mussolini's Italians, was clearly winning the Civil War.

‡ Neville Chamberlain, the British Prime Minister, had made no attempt to intervene.

§ Reich's two daughters, Eva (born 1924) and Lore (born 1928). After Reich and his wife, Annie, were divorced, the girls had remained in Vienna with their mother. Mother and daughters did in fact emigrate to the United States some months before Reich himself.

sex at all. The chief difference is a more positive attitude to life and people. I still get bad headaches. Nearly always beginning on a Friday, *Gott weiss warum Freitag* [God knows why Friday].

Tell me, can I do any harm if I make the bedwetters, boys of 8 and 9, lie down and breathe? I can't think that there is any danger in it, and they are both as stiff as Hell in the *Bauch* [stomach], I am sure that the Orgasmus Reflex would be the cure.

I have just reread with pleasure and profit your *Sexualität im Kulturkampf*. But the Bione book is so difficult for me, not knowing any science.

I'll come over in July if Europe isn't by that time a hell. It might be wise to take the whole school to Norway, but since Norway is a part of British Capitalism, I suppose she will be brought into any war. The general opinion here is that war will come very soon.

My regards to Elsa.

———◆•◆———

Oslo, Norway

March 24, 1938

*Dear Neill!**

I can write to you today only very briefly. The situation is mad, and it is quite impossible to foresee the outcome.

In answer to your question whether it can do any harm to release the orgasm reflex† in children with stiff stomachs, it is hard for me to say anything certain, because I have no experience with children. By all means, try, but please be very cautious. Don't force anything; one can easily bring about serious vegetative reactions. Also, it is not easy to do such work without involving the natural reactions such as defiance etc. which then set in.

I shall probably not be here in July. If you wish to work with me again, I would advise you to take May or June or, if that is not possible, September.

———◆•◆———

* Translated from the original German.

† Reich described this as "a series of involuntary total body contractions," fundamental to the full "discharge of biophysical energy" in the orgasm, and possible only where no muscular rigidities are present. Neill often abbreviates the term to "o. reflex."

Summerhill School
Leiston, Suffolk

April 24, 1938

Dear Reich,

I have been to Scotland motoring. You say you will be away in July. May or June are impossible for me, for the school is in session. We close end of July, so that I could spend August and the first two weeks of Sept in Oslo. *Geht es?* [Is that all right?]

I hope so, for I am still dull and without much interest in anything.

I never hear from Constance now, but suppose she is still with you.

———◆◆◆———

Oslo, Norway

April 29, 1938

*Dear Neill!**

I am agreeable to having you work here in August and the first weeks of September. Only we must be prepared that at this very time the official International Commission to check on the bion research will probably be working here. But that will not disturb our work.

Please do write again with news. Very warmly yours.

———◆◆◆———

Summerhill School
Leiston, Suffolk

May 6, 1938

Dear Reich,

Gut, Anfang August [Good, beginning of August]. Helga has been down here for a holiday and I find myself as much in love with her as ever, and she with me. I have a wife and a school: she has a husband and a child. Hell! *Was kann man machen?* [What can one do?] I know that if I were free inside I should know *was zu machen, aber* [what to do, but] . . .

Saw Stekel† last night. He said: "Reich is the most brilliant analyst

———

* Translated from the original German.
† Wilhelm Stekel, Viennese physician and early adherent of Freud, who had moved to England when Hitler took over Austria. Some years earlier, Neill had been his patient for a few weeks.

Freud has produced." He is coming here for a weekend soon, and I'll ask him what he thinks of the Orgasmus Reflex. He goes in two months to settle in California.

I hope my stay with you this time will get me much farther on. I fear that my stomach isn't now so loose as you made it.*

———◆◆◆———

Oslo, Norway

May 16, 1938

Dear Neill!†

I should like to ask you to plan for the middle of August, not for the beginning, because probably in the first two weeks of August there will be a public demonstration here of my bion experiments . . . which will take up my time.

———◆◆◆———

Summerhill School
Leiston, Suffolk

May 22, 1938

Dear Reich,

All right, middle August. That will give me only about four weeks in Oslo, for my wife is going to America and won't be back when the school reopens middle September, and I'll have to be there to do it. But of course what Europe will be like in August no one knows. Today's news of Henlein and Co‡ might mean war at any moment, and in that case my breathing and orgasmus reflex become very minor things in society.

---

* Reich held that parents force their children to repress their natural sexuality and in so doing incur the hatred of the children, which is also repressed. These repressions create anxiety, which is held at bay by a stiffening primarily of the stomach muscles. These in turn remain stiff until the repressions and the concomitant anxiety are removed. Reich explained in *The Function of the Orgasm* that it is by holding their breath that children are in the habit of fighting against continual and tormenting conditions of anxiety which they sense in the upper abdomen; they do the same thing when they sense pleasurable sensations in the abdomen or in the genitals and are afraid of these sensations.

† Translated from the original German.

‡ Konrad Henlein, leader of the Sudeten-Germans in Czechoslovakia; his escalating demands eventually led to the Munich crisis.

I read your typed news*blatt* [sheet]. Your enemies are fiercer than ever . . . *ja, und dümmer* [yes, and stupider]. If your genius had expressed itself in inventing an explosive more powerful than any other, you would have been received as a national hero long ago. To invent material dynamite is allowed, but your moral dynamite is far more dangerous, and your diehard psychiatrists know it.

I have had an attack of my old pyelitis again (the psychic conflict gone physical). Not believing in drugs and doctors I went on a fast for five days. Result a complete cure. Interesting that after a fast ordinary food is disgusting. On the other hand a fast increases sex desire greatly.

I don't know why I tell you all this, for you aren't interested in fasting and food. I can only guess it is my old trick of patronising that poor man Reich . . . "Yes, yes, Reich, but your orgasmus reflex isn't everything."

At the same time I know that if my reflex were working properly I wouldn't be getting pyelitis again. I am really curious to know why a fast cures all the same. If pyelitis is caused by lack of sex why should lack of food cure it? Same old Neill—always asking questions! Which Reich never thinks of answering.

Cheerio. If Oslo does make it too hot for you we'll work hard to get you safe in England or America. Freud is also coming to London.

———◆◆◆———

Oslo, Norway

May 26, 1938

*Dear Neill!**

Thank you very much for your offer to help me in moving to England or America. I am taking advantage of it at once, although the danger that I shall have to leave here is not acute. Still, I believe that I must already start preparations. Please initiate whatever steps may be necessary to get recommendations and support, and let me know to whom you have turned. My move to America would be inseparable from moving my laboratory equipment and two or three assistants. The main point is that I am not a poor emigrant soliciting entry into America as a favor; rather, that it is the honest opinion of reasonable people that my work is necessary and that pity would here

---

* Translated from the original German.

be entirely out of place. I am also writing to Malinowski* on this same matter. In August an American physician, Wolfe,† will be here from New York, whom in fact you will probably get to know. He is coming here to study vegeto-therapy.‡ It is possible that I shall already be able to take you at the beginning of August, but we shall be in touch about that later.

———— ◆•◆ ————

Summerhill School
Leiston, Suffolk

June 1, 1938
Dear Reich,

It is difficult to *vorbereiten* [prepare]. It is impossible to make any application to the government unless you are certain to be put out of Norway. It is useless for me to tell people that Reich is a genius and ought to be allowed to come to England (or America). No English government department would care a damn what Neill said. They never heard of me. The only way is for me to try to get your work known here. I am asking Professor Haldane§ if he would read your *Bione* book. It is possible that if you could get an article in English on the *Bione* and *their possible application to disease,* I could get it published in *The Lancet,*** for the editor has a problem son at my school. To be invited to a country you must be known, and because your books aren't translated into English you are known only to a few. I dined with Stekel last week at Flugel's†† house. I asked him what he

---

* Bronislaw Malinowski, the social anthropologist.

† Theodore P. Wolfe, Swiss psychiatrist now established in the United States. A year later, he was instrumental in bringing Reich to New York and thenceforth remained closely associated with Reich and his work. Although English was not his native language, he became Reich's first translator; he helped set up the Orgone Institute Press and edited its journals.

‡ A method of treating neurosis by direct physical attack on the nodes of muscular tension which, according to Reich, represented and sustained early, primarily sexual repressions. The repressed material set free when these tensions were broken down was then analyzed in terms of character structure. "Vegeto" is an abbreviation for "vegetative"; i.e., pertaining to the autonomic nervous system.

§ J. B. S. Haldane (1892–1964), British biologist and geneticist.

** The most important British medical journal.

†† J. C. Flugel, Freudian psychoanalyst and friend of Neill's; an early member of the British Psycho-Analytical Society and for some years co-editor of the *International Journal of Psycho-Analysis.*

thought of your theories. He replied: "I don't understand them." I found that Flugel knew scarcely anything about your work, and another psychoanalyst there, [Millais] Culpin, had never heard of you. Hence I say that the first thing necessary in England is publicity. At the present moment I think it would be possible for you to enter England with all your instruments, but to bring your assistants at the same time would possibly be impossible. That could be done I fancy only if some university said your work was essential for them. That's why I am approaching Haldane now.

It will be good if you can take me at the beginning of August.

———— ◆ ◆ ————

Oslo, Norway

June 4, 1938

*Dear Neill!**

I do beg you to be extremely cautious in making any propaganda for the bion book as far as "authorities in the field" are concerned. Imagine if I were to send one of your excellent books, for instance, to William Stern or Charlotte Bühler† by way of propaganda. I would achieve the exact opposite.

For the time being, there is no question here of my residence permit being refused. So give yourself plenty of time to look around. I think it will be possible for me to take you already at the beginning of August. So make your plans accordingly.

That the psychoanalysts do not understand my basic concept is a story that is already 16 years old. Please don't even try to persuade them. Please write again as soon as you know more.

———— ◆ ◆ ————

* Translated from the original German.

† Stern, a well-known German "authority" on youth psychology; Bühler, one of the first women professors at the University of Vienna, lecturing on child psychology.

Summerhill School
Leiston, Suffolk

June 8, 1938

Dear Reich,

You are really a most difficult man to help. You seem to think that we are all a lot of damn fools. You mention Stern and Bühler, but so far as you are concerned, most people here are Sterns and Bühlers. Until you do something to have your ideas translated into English you are unknown here. It is useless to approach the Freudians in London. The old-fashioned psychiatrists are worse. There only remains the younger group of scientists of the Haldane–Bernal* class. They are all modern in politics and more open-minded than the psycho-analysts here.

I grant that my ignorance of science is a handicap, but what I can't grasp is this: if a scientist like Haldane cannot read and understand *Die Bione*, who can? Where can one find a scientist who is a specialist in biology and also in psychology? You seem to me to have a phobia that you will always be misunderstood, but why then write books if everyone is to misunderstand them? I feel that one of your main aims now should be to have *Die Bione* and your *Orgasmus Reflex* translated into English. But as I say, you are so indefinite and fearful of publicity that I don't know how to help you. It may be that living among a crowd of little Norwegian enemies you are out of touch with the English world. The arrival of all the Viennese analysts in London will make psychology very important, and now is the time for Reich to be known in England.

I hope to be in Oslo *Anfang August* [beginning of August].

———— ◆•◆ ————

Oslo, Norway

June 10, 1938

Dear Neill!†

You are right, I am an incorrigible pessimist, since I do not believe in the good will of academic authorities. Still, I do beg you not to let that influence you, and if you can do something toward the publication of *The Bions* or its distribution, I would be grateful to you.

---

* J. D. Bernal, British biologist and teacher, friend of Neill's.
† Translated from the original German.

My book, *The Orgasm Reflex*,* has already been translated into English by Constance and is available for publication at any time.

————◆•◆————

[*Neill was in Oslo between June and September and worked with Reich as planned. The following letter was written by Reich in answer to one from Neill that is missing. The original is in German.*]

Oslo, Norway

September 16, 1938

Dear Neill!

      Now an urgent request: I am at present getting everything ready for the evacuation of my laboratory and its safekeeping. In this, my primary concern is to ensure that the only existing proof of the soundness of the bion research, namely the cultures I have on hand, be taken permanent care of in the event of war and disaster, so that they can reemerge unchanged. I am writing in this matter to Stockholm, to the French Academy and to you. Please ask Bernal or whomever else whether there is a biological or bacteriological institute that would be willing to take care of the bion cultures; I would include an exact description of how they are to be cared for. Only some ten glasses [i.e., retorts] are involved.

      I do beg you to comply with this request of mine as quickly as possible and to let me know who in England might be considered for this.

      I am very glad that you are feeling so well. I really do believe that this time you have accomplished a great deal.

      With my very warmest greetings to you and your friends.

————◆•◆————

---

* *Orgasmus Reflex,* originally published as a monograph; later included as chapter 8 in *The Function of the Orgasm.*

Summerhill School
Leiston, Suffolk

September 19, 1938

Dear Reich,

You could send the glasses direct to me and I could find a safe lab for them, either through Bernal or someone else. The difficulty there would be the Customs people, who might suspect a new way of smuggling in cocaine or drugs, and who might play hell by trying to analyse the stuff themselves.

One difficulty here may be that Bernal is a prominent member of the Communist Party and for all I know may be prejudiced against you.* But I am sure that he would arrange the safety of your glasses.

Looks as if Chamberlain and Co are to throw C. Slovakia to the wolves. The people here are only concerned in not going to war. But C.S. will fight, and everyone will be in it.

Best wishes to self and Elsa.

———◆•◆———

Summerhill School
Leiston, Suffolk

October 3, 1938

Dear Reich,

Bernal writes that if you send your cultures to Dr. E. T. C. Spooner, The Pathological Laboratory, The University, Cambridge, they will be taken care of. I don't know Spooner myself.

But why think that your work will be safe here? Chamberlain's criminality to C. Slovakia will make us more easy to attack in the future and the chances of Cambridge or London being bombed to hell are worse than those of Oslo. I am seeing the man [Barnes] who wrote about translating your books this week. Constance thought him a good man. He has an Austrian wife.

In the great *Angst* [anxiety]† of last week I was surprised to find that

---

* During his years in Berlin, Reich had become suspect to the Communist leaders, who felt that with his Association for Proletarian Sex Politics he was luring people away from the single-minded pursuit of the party's goals. He was finally expelled from the party in 1934.

† The threat of imminent war, postponed by the Munich Pact.

I had none. Reich's *veg. Therapie* was the cause. But I have not settled the big question of my sex life yet.

Constance sends her love to you and Elsa. *Ich auch* [Me, too].

———◆•◆———

Oslo, Norway

October 6, 1938

Dear Neill,

If the Pathological Laboratory in Cambridge would really take the Bion-Cultures, it would mean a great help, and I would have to thank you very much. I am doing it already now for all the troubles you had with it. Please tell Bernal that I am now preparing everything to send over the cultures. Also that the French Academie of Science in Paris had proposed to publish my results. The reason to transport and depose the cultures is not, as you seem to believe, that London would be safer from bombs than Oslo. But London has no fantastic *fremmedkontor* [alien registration office] which only waits for the right moment to get rid of me, whatever the way would be.

Chamberlain will cost us all tremendously much. But as long as people allow the Chamberlains to take care of them, the matter will remain unchanged. There is only one hope: that it will become completely clear to everybody that there is no choice between "Democracy" and "Fascism." There is only a third way out: only those who work and suffer can decide!! All right—an interesting time we are living through.

That your *Angst* was gone was a good thing to tell about. I hope we shall also settle all the rest of it.

I'll write you when I am sending off the Cultures. If I only knew how much I can tell about them without being choked.

———◆•◆———

Summerhill School
Leiston, Suffolk

October 16, 1938

Dear Reich,

If you simply want your cultures to be stowed away in a safe place it is easy. But if you want Spooner to investigate your *Bione, das ist etwas anders* [bions, that is another matter]. I think you should risk asking him to investigate them.

On second thought I have a better idea. I'll write to Spooner myself today and sound him on whether he is interested or not, and shall let you have his reply in a few days.

Everything points to England's going Fascist now, and I fear that soon freedom of the press will go. Then there will be no country worth living in.

P.S. Stekel writes me: "I am coming down next weekend to see you. I want to hear about Reich. No man should be too old to learn from another, and none of us have all the truth."

———◆•◆———

Oslo, Norway

October 19, 1938

My dear Neill,

Many thanks for the troubles which you are taking about my cultures. I hope someday it will pay you back. I send you a few fotos for Dr. Spooner as a first orientation. You understand how dangerous it would be to believe that those cultures and the way I got them could be understood instantly by scientists who *have* officially to deny and to laugh at the idea that living substance could arise from dead stuff. They are all waiting for proof of this simple fact, but at the same time kill it. It is strictly forbidden, against God. Meanwhile those cultures prove to be identical with products of the cancer process. I never expected it— simply met it.

Be please also cautious with Stekel. The so-called vegeto-therapy, simple as it is, needed nearly 20 years of hard work and fight, is based upon a very strict theory of life and sex—psychologically, and biologically as well as sociologically. To let anybody simply take up a few technical principles and test them on patients could only harm its fame. Furthermore, the technique needs much study and improvement. Stekel never could wait for the results research work brings only by and by. I don't want to harm Stekel, but I want to protect my work. The vegeto-therapy cannot simply be added to the usual psychoanalytic theory and technic. Mostly they are opposite.

I hope you feel all right. Let me hear please about it, and how you are getting along privately.

———◆•◆———

Oslo, Norway

October 22, 1938

Dear Neill,

You see, I had a good and correct feeling about Dr. Spooner. I am not in despair as far as the future of my work is concerned. But I don't much trust the loyalty or scientific reliability of most of the so-called scientists. It did not appear probable that a bacteriologist would be interested in the *Bione*. Meanwhile I get cancer after cancer on mice. Well, I could wait, if the fascists would not press on. What are you going to do in England? Is there some sincere countermovement?

Did you get the pictures which I sent before I knew that Spooner said no? Now I send pictures and *preparata* [microscope slides or cultures] to the States. I shall flood them with pictures and *preparata* as long as I can until they have to listen and to look.

How are you? Let me hear please from you very soon.

———◆•◆———

Summerhill School
Leiston, Suffolk

October 24, 1938

Dear Reich,

I am enquiring about the Lister Institute before I write to them for information about storing bacteria. I fear that they also will be without interest.

Had Stekel *und Frau* [and wife] for the weekend. He didn't after all ask much about you, but spoke about your books in a very complimentary manner. His one criticism was that he does not like your imitating patients in your *Characteranalyse*, but gave no reason. Don't be afraid that I shall give a wrong impression of your work. I say very little.

I am in a bad mood myself. Full of hate, hating my wife and feeling ashamed to introduce her to visitors because she looks so old, and then feeling angry at myself for feeling ashamed. Then one or two of my older *Problemkinder* [problem children] make me feel hateful and murderous, for I never get away from them. I saw Helga in London and wasn't sure of my attitude to her. We were on the streets all the time and had to talk only. But this sexless life is going to destroy me if I don't settle it soon. I am constipated and for weeks have had conjunctivitis of the right eye. And I haven't any enthusiasm for my work. I need more Reich yet, I know.

I shall store the photos and the table you sent in the meantime.

P.S. I see nothing before us now than a Fascist France and England. I fear this generation is doomed, that it will have to go through fascism before it becomes conscious of what is going on in society. You were right about workers being castrated; they are oxen with no life in their eyes and souls.

———— ◆·◆ ————

Summerhill School
Leiston, Suffolk

November 20, 1938

Dear Reich,

    I got the slides and am trying to see a friend, Prof. Wright of the Pathology Department of Guy's Hospital about them. He is a decent fellow and will help us if he can. The general attitude of the Bernal group is that your discoveries are nonsense. I daren't try any more of them.

    Barnes has sent me the first chapter of your *S. im Kulturkampf* in English. Quite well translated. One difficulty in translating from *Deutsch* [German] is that you all write more fully than we do. I have told you often that I can say in a page what you take three pages to say, and that is no merit of mine: it is the difference between the two languages mostly.

    Have just been reading your *Charakteranalyse*, and feel depressed about my own work. I feel like never trying to analyse anyone again, for I have no system as you have. Yet I wonder why most of my past patients improved so much.

    You ask me to tell you how I am, but my last letter told you this and you don't seem to have read it. I can't get rid of my conjunctivitis, and am going to London to see an oculist.

    I wish I could give up the school for a year and come back to you. I have no sex life and feel damned discontented and often hateful. I have a dozen problem children whose parents send them here because of me, and if I took even three months off duty they would object strongly. *Eine schwere Lage* [A difficult situation], Reich.

    I am sending Elsa my new book, the children's story I wrote in Oslo.*

---

* *Last Man Alive* (London: Herbert Jenkins, 1938).

It is in easy English and will be good for her English study. It is a good study of my Sadism disguised in humour.

Your stomach theory is completely proved by the stomachs of the children here. The repressed ones have stomachs like wooden boards, but children begin to loosen up very quickly, and at once begin to be hateful and savage. They kill off their enemies (family ones) eagerly in the form of cushions and dolls, and I feel sure that their analysis should be only the active one of doing things without any attempt by me to make unconscious things conscious. The things that matter are outside the school's control. Some kids I can do nothing with because the home is impossible.

Now don't get alarmed that I am dangerously experimenting with Reichism. I have learned much from you but have a million things to learn yet. Now that Chamberlain is being beaten slowly by the elections here, war with Hitler seems nearer, and I dare not even think of coming back to you in summer. If you can have me at Easter I have four weeks then.

———◆•◆———

Oslo, Norway

November 23, 1938

Dear Neill,

I got your letter. Hope Prof. Wright is not the physiologist who told me in 1934 that I was crazy, because I said that skin surface shows electrical phenomena which it may be possible to measure. I thank you very much for all the things you are doing for me. Now I have sent off slides to five different places in the world. Something must happen now—at least contradictory statements. While great men are declaring my thoughts to be nonsense, I cannot keep up with the investigations which my cancer mice compel me to. But among the slides I sent you are a few which cannot fail to be recognized for what they are. You certainly oppose my distrust toward scientists. But you will see, it will become still worse. Did you read the history of the Curies?

Why should reading my *Character Analysis* disturb you? Psychotherapy is a rotten business, as you state yourself, mentioning the parents and other circumstances. My "system" is nothing but something to hold on to.

Of course I read your letter entirely. But I know how matters tend to change, and therefore I asked again.

I was very glad to hear your statements about the stomach attitude of children. Here I am sure is the future of Therapy and Prophylaxis. I would like to be in your place, to work with children and not with grown-ups. Would you please write down your observations for our *Communication* of the Institute? It would mean much. I am starting to discover that I have discovered something important, and am ceasing to believe that everybody always knew about it.

Write please again. At Easter I shall probably interrupt my work for about 8 days. If that will not disturb you, I should like to go on with you.

————◆•◆————

Summerhill School
Leiston, Suffolk

November 26, 1938

Dear Reich,

Failure again. The professor asked me to dinner and then looked at the slides under the microscope, obviously without interest. "They show some inflammation by bacteria," was all he said. He had never heard of your work and when I told him in my unscientific way what you were doing, he said what Bernal said . . . infection from the atmosphere. God, Reich, these men are children. They aren't really interested in science. This man Wright is a very nice fellow, kind, broad-minded in politics and in everything except science. I fear you will get no help from the orthodox scientists. *Zu klein* [Too small]. They all seem terrified to commit themselves to an opinion. I'll try once more with Haldane this time. Next time I go to London I'll ask him to see me, and will keep the slides till then, unless you give up English scientists in despair and ask me to send the box back.

Today I have a letter from the big publishers John Lane saying they would like to see the translation of the *S. im Kulturkampf*, and I am sending on the introduction and the first chapter that Barnes sent me. I told Lane that you were the only man who had given us something new and valuable since Freud. I am not entirely pleased with the translation. One phrase, "disorganisations of the vegetative harmony," means nothing to most people. You should really make some sort of explanation of your terms, for the word vegetative is unknown to most readers.

Most people unconsciously associate it with vegetarianism. With a few simplifications it would have a better chance. If this book is taken I hope you'll let *Charakteranalyse* be the next one to be translated. It is a lovely book, full of the most important things to any analyst.

I am writing Lane now warning him that he must not ask any Freudian for an opinion on your book. The biggest medical publisher, Kegan Paul, has Freudian readers who refuse to pass books that aren't according to the *Verein* [Society].*

About myself . . . I am always depressed. I want only Helga but that is impossible. She has now got a sense of loyalty to her husband and child. *Nichts zu machen, aber das Leben für mich ist sehr sehr leer* [Nothing to be done, but life for me is very, very empty].

———◆•◆———

Oslo, Norway

November 29, 1938

My dear Neill,

I am answering your letter immediately to prevent great mishaps. Those "scientific" chaps are as you say: without any interest in science and, I would add, without responsibility. Your Wright will now perhaps run around saying that he has "controlled" my cancer work and that it was nothing but "infection." Among the slides which I sent you are three which have as much to do with infection as I with Hitler. It's all nonsense. But with their "authority" they can spoil everything for me perhaps for ever.

Your depression is apparently not completely irrational. Your real situation has to make for depression. The question is only how much support it gets from irrational things and how far you succeed in fighting real situations without disturbing your work. Don't please forget that we cannot give certainty of pleasure, only the ability to enjoy it when it happens to offer itself.

———◆•◆———

* The British Psycho-Analytical Society, and orthodox Freudian psychoanalysts in general, whom Neill sees as forming a closed society.

Summerhill School
Leiston, Suffolk

December 14, 1938

Dear Reich,

I hear that you have got your visa for America and are going this Spring. This alarms me, for it means no more *Stunden für mich* [hours for me]. Tell me about it, if it is true and if so when you will be going. For your sake I hope it is true, for America is wide and has a future.

I haven't had the chance to do anything more about the slides.

Very busy with plays for the end of the term dramatic evening.

Oslo, Norway

December 19, 1938

Dear Neill!

It is true that I got the visa for the States. But I am not leaving before July or August. So you will have the opportunity to continue. How long would you like to stay and when? I have to know in time to arrange the hours.

Don't worry about the slides. Send them back please. I have already got a cancer diagnosis in one of them. They will give more when the time passes on.

Oslo, Norway

January 19, 1939

My dear Neill,

Please don't take on the burden of translating the *Bion-Communication** into English. It is already done. I shall send you a copy as soon as possible. Meanwhile there happened something important. Without knowing it I had microscoped for about four weeks a new bion culture which apparently is radioactive, that means, it behaves like radium. It makes the skin red through glass and penetrates the

---

* *Bion Experiments on the Cancer Problem: Abstracts of a Lecture given to the Norwegian Society of Medical Students in Oslo, June, 1938* (Sexpol-Verlag, 1939).

cover of foto-plates and darkens them. I paid attention to it first when my eyes started to ache. They became very sensitive against light, but the doctor says nothing serious is to be seen yet. I continue the tests and am trying to get in touch with Niels Bohr, the physicist. If the matter holds, then there will be radium to be had for nearly nothing for everybody. These Bions kill cancer cells promptly. You can see it in the microscope. If only nothing bad has happened to my eyes. I have had to stop my work now and am waiting until the eyes get better.

Write me please if you made sure the possibility to publish in this medical magazine [*The Lancet*]. I would not like to get a rebuff. I had enough of those dirty tricks. I shall write you again when the matter is definitely affirmed.

———— ◆•◆ ————

Summerhill School
Leiston, Suffolk

February 8, 1939
Dear Reich,

The lecture went off quite easily. Stekel was there. Haire* was my Chairman. I spoke quite a lot about Reich and I could see Stekel didn't like it. He got up later and spoke, saying that it was pure phantasy to say that capitalism had anything to do with sex repression. Later we all went to Flugel's house for supper. Then I learned the real truth about Reich! Oh, Haire was bitter about you . . . you have a rebel complex that compels you to destroy everything you touch . . . *z.B.* [for instance] the Freudian *Verein*, Communism, Sex Reform League. "Reich has done more to destroy sex reform than any man living." Nasty man, Norman, isn't he?

On the other hand quite a number of people came to me after my lecture and asked me where they could get your books, and if they were translated into English.

I am to have lunch with H. G. Wells soon. You know him and his books? He wrote the *History of Science*. Possibly the most powerful man in English science. I feel he would be interested in the *Bione*. Now, Reich, can't you send me a clear account of *Bione* so that I can at least explain them to Wells without of course giving away the inner secrets? I suggest something short . . . how *Bione* are made, how they react to

---

* Norman Haire, British sexologist, headed the Sex Reform League.

other organisms, if they can make cancer or destroy it, also the mice *Geschichte* [business], what happens when mice are *geimpft* [inoculated], what they die of when they do die after inoculation, etc. I want enough to interest a man like Wells. I tried to interest Prof. Haldane of London University Biometry Dept. "Too unorthodox," he said. I never knew before how little these great scientists are.

Now do send me the short history of the *Bione*. I could do it in two pages if I knew the facts. German will do.

———— ◆•◆ ————

Oslo, Norway

February 10, 1939

My dear Neill,

I had never expected a better and nicer compliment than this Haire gave me. I only hope that he is right in saying that I destroyed the Sex Reform. Just that was the purpose when I started to fight against it 10 years ago. And what Stekel said are very old *Kamellen* [tales] as we Germans used to say. I am glad that people came to you and confirmed the conviction that there are other reasonable people in the world. We are flowing in a stream, which took hold of the whole social process since Hitler came to victory. We have to carry on.

About the *Bione*: I shall send you a copy of the communication which I sent to the French Academy. (They won't publish it but will deposit it in the archive.) In it you will find the latest general results summed up. You can give him [Wells] a copy of the *Bionbook* too. And a general review of the Bion field is to be found in the pamphlet *Der dialektische Materialismus in der Lebensforschung* [Dialectical Materialism in Biological Research], which was printed in the same issue as the *Orgasm Reflex*. You have got it. I have had a few copies of books sent to you.

It's fine that you feel good. I am glad about it.

Write again please. Also about Wells. Very soon you'll get the English translation of the new pamphlet about *die natürliche Organisation der Arbeit.**

———— ◆•◆ ————

* *Die natürliche Organisation der Arbeit in der Arbeitsdemokratie,* 1939 (The Natural Organization of Work in Work Democracy). This was never published in English.

Summerhill School
Leiston, Suffolk

February 13, 1939

Dear Reich,

Thanks for description. I am trying to translate it with the help of an Austrian teacher. Even he cannot translate all the terms. I must get a science dictionary Eng-*Deutsch*, for your words are not in the ordinary dictionary.

I could easily get what you sent published in *The Lancet*, but you don't want that, do you? In your place I should do it, so as to have printed proof that the *Bione* was your discovery. You will find that other men will steal your ideas and publish them. I told you that the *Lancet* is the high-class medical journal of England. And such a publication would very likely be of great value to you if you were to seek entrance into England, or even to America. What do you say? Overcome that anti-publicity complex of yours.

———— ◆•◆ ————

Summerhill School
Leiston, Suffolk

February 25, 1939

My dear Reich,

Congratulations on your latest discovery, but I am worried about your eyes. Is there no protection that will keep out radium rays on the microscope? You must find one.

I got an answer from the *Lancet* asking me to come and see the editor when in London. I shall be going up next week for I must consult someone about my eyes. The conjunctivitis gets worse and worse daily.

Wells has been in Australia and has just come home. I hope to see him next week too.

I can find no English translation for *Zeitraffung*. Slow motion photo isn't the translation and there is no word for the opposite. Also *Rasenförmig* is unknown here. My Austrian lad says "shaped like turf or lawn." It is hell trying to translate scientific German.

I'll be able to say soon if I can come over to Oslo at Easter. Much depends on my eyes. I have no faith in specialists who simply give drops to suppress the disease, and I may consult the people who cure eyes by exercises, blinking etc. Only I hate doing exercises of any kind. I hope to hear from you that your eyes are O.K. by now.

———◆•◆———

[*With the previous letter, Neill had enclosed a draft of an English translation of the paper on bions. It is to this that Reich now alludes.*]

Oslo, Norway

March 3, 1939

Dear Neill,

I don't believe that they will take the Bion paper, but I am sending it [back] to you anyway. Maybe you have luck. I corrected the ms. as well as I could and enclose some pictures. They are very important. The translation seems all right.

My eyes are better, but I don't dare do any work with those bions on the microscope. It aches immediately. The radioactivity is quite sure now. I am trying to get a physicist to measure it out. But what is wrong with your eyes?

Rasenförmig means growing like grass on earth naturally. *Zeitraffung* means taking up only one picture in a while, so that the movement becomes very quick.

———◆•◆———

Summerhill School
Leiston, Suffolk

March 4, 1939

My dear Reich,

Once more I have nothing to report but failures. Ethel Mannin the novelist was arranging for her and me to go to Wells for lunch. Suddenly I got a letter from her saying she had had a violent quarrel with him because she had criticised him in a book. So the lunch never came off.

Then I went to see my friend the editor of the *Lancet*. He began thus: "Before you tell me about Reich let me show you a letter I had from our correspondent in Paris to whom I wrote asking if he knew anything about Reich." He handed me the letter. It said in effect that you are mad, that your discoveries are nonsense: the writer said: "I asked three of the best biologists in Paris what they thought of *Bione* and they said the *Bione* were worthless, and that R. should stick to his own subject analysis. The letter was signed J.L. I asked who he was and was told he was a doctor of broad mind.

I handed back the letter and said: "Then there is nothing more to discuss." I feel so angry with myself for putting you in this position, yet it is of value to know what is going on behind the scenes. It is good to know that the fight against you has reached England. I fear that your only chance now is America. Europe is dead to new ideas. I fear now to try to approach any other person in England. You are an outsider to them all: that's the main point. What right has a psychoanalyst to dare to even talk of biology? That is their attitude. I can't find one scientist broad enough in mind even to try to find out if you are a fool or not.

I hate to have to write thus: I thought at last I could help you in the *Lancet*. I feel that I want to write a bitter article on British scientists calling them the narrowest men in the world.

Thanks for all the literature. The booklet on *Die Arbeit* [Work] is brilliant.

Tell me how your eyes are.

———— ◆•◆ ————

Oslo, Norway

March 13, 1939

*Dear Neill!**

I am sending you herewith a summary of my observations on the radiating bions—for your own use only. The matter is now being examined in Holland, quantitatively and qualitatively.

Please write whether you were successful with the work [presumably the translated bion paper].

Then I should also like to know whether you are coming over at Easter, so that I can reserve an hour for you in good time. I shall

---

* Translated from the original German. Reich had not yet received Neill's letter of March 4.

probably be away shortly before Easter, but only for a day or two, if I have the money.

With warm greetings.

———◆◆◆———

Summerhill School
Leiston, Suffolk

March 17, 1939

Dear Reich,

I shall arrive in Oslo by boat on the 6th April if Hitler hasn't taken Norway by that date. I am glad your eyes are better. Your latest bulletin is of great interest. I have stopped trying to interest anyone here, for it is so sickening always being rebuffed by the narrow fools.

Let me know if you will be back in Oslo by the 6th, for there is no good my coming if you are still away in the country.

———◆◆◆———

[Neill made his last trip from England to Norway and spent a few weeks working with Reich in Oslo. Then, in the late summer of 1939, Reich left Norway for the United States. On September 3, war was declared.]

———◆◆◆———

Summerhill School
Leiston, Suffolk

September 19, 1939

My dear Reich,

It was good to get your letter saying you had arrived.* You got away from Oslo just in time. You ask if we have evacuated the school. No, we are going to stay here. Our children are not afraid. I was glad to note that I have had no sign of any neurotic attitude to the operation† or the war. But it isn't easy to concentrate on psychology at a

———

* Neither that letter nor any other from Reich to Neill between March 1939 and April 1940 survives.
† Neill had recently undergone minor surgery.

time like this when one is apt to concentrate on essential primitive things like eating and safety and sex.

You were so right about Stalinism,* but the future does not lie with Stalin or Hitler; as you said it lies with the people who do the world's work. In this country there is a pretty grim determination that Hitlerism must be destroyed.

From now on I guess I shall have to devote more time to planting and digging than psychology. Also I am going to teach mathematics— a subject I like so much that I spent many hours in hospital working out problems.

It doesn't seem likely that I shall be able to come to visit you for a long time. My daydreams of a lecture tour in the States must remain daydreams in the meantime.

You ask what you shall do about the loan I made you. I don't know what the new financial laws in England are, only that one can't send money abroad. But it is possible that a debt made months ago can be paid into a New York bank in my name. In such a case it would be very useful if later I came to study further with you. In any case, you need not repay me until you are sure of a good income from your work . . .

Write me from time to time, and for God's sake don't develop an American accent.

———————◆◆◆———————

Summerhill School
Leiston, Suffolk

October 23, 1939

My dear Reich,

I got your long letter. About the money, you should not pay it in monthly instalments because that is too complicated for me.

No, we are not overworried about the war so far. God knows what the end will be, for history is doing in a week what it took many years to do long ago. There never was such a tempo. I can't write about the war because I don't know what the censor passes or blacks out, and in any case I am tired of discussing it. One thing is clear, however, that during such a time one lives fully and alertly. My regret is that I can't

---

* The Hitler–Stalin Pact had allowed Hitler to invade Poland. This, in turn, triggered England's declaration of war against Germany.

come back in 100 years to see what a damned fool humanity has made
of things.

My own affairs go fairly well. My reflex is not so good as it was,
possibly mainly because I have not "love" to perfect it. Here again
censorship is difficult . . . when a man wants to write about himself to
his psychologist, he hesitates to say so much as he would say in ordinary
peace time. All the same I do not feel one bit neurotic: I can work, but
unfortunately I prefer digging and building bricks to analysis. *Gott*,
I wish I could come over to you and have some more therapy all
the same.

I get no news from Oslo. I wrote to Elsa Backer* and the letter took
14 days to reach her.

When I was in hospital my surgeon took your booklet on Cancer to
read. He said he could not follow it because he was not a pathologist,
and could he lend it to the pathologist at Ipswich Hospital? I said yes.
The pathologist returned it saying that he did not understand it *but it
was all wrong!* They are all schoolboys really.

The school is full, although we are getting less money now. But
money I do not worry about so long as I can work.

Tell me what is happening with you, and send me every paper
you print or stylograph [mimeograph]. Take twenty dollars off your debt
as a subscription to Sex Pol.

Well, well, Reich, enough for the present. I am always glad to get
your letters, and if and when peace comes it will be great to meet again.

---

* A Norwegian friend and Summerhill parent.

1940

Summerhill School
Leiston, Suffolk

January 5, 1940

My dear Reich,

I got your two letters by the same post. They had taken over three weeks to come over. But in neither letter did you say how the work was progressing.

I don't know what to say about myself. After my operation my Reflex seemed to disappear. I found an attractive friend, but my reflex is never good enough, usually too early and unsatisfying. It is very disappointing. So with my work. I realise that I was not long enough with you to see the end of the treatment. With the war likely to spread to a world war I see no chance of ever completing my analysis with you. I keep hoping that my poorness in reflexes is due to the exhaustion after the operation. And I know that I am infinitely more relaxed and less afraid than I was before I went to you. My headaches have gone away completely. I believe completely in your method and will carry on with it till I come back to the great feeling of power and potency I had when I returned from Oslo in summer.

Is anything Sex Pol* being published in U.S.A.? I long to see something new. Judith† says they are to publish a magazine twice yearly in Oslo, but as it will be in Norwegian it won't help me.

---

* Sexual politics, Reich's term for the effects of political pressures on sexual attitudes and behavior and hence for any examination of the interconnection between the political structures of society and sexual-mental health.

† Judith Bogen, a kindergarten teacher who had been studying and working with Reich in Norway.

My school goes on as usual. Finances so bad that I am having to go
back and take in real problem children who can pay enough to keep
the school going, thieves etc. That makes me sad, for I had almost
given up that kind of pupil. I had many years of having my money and
tools and clothes stolen by young crooks, and to begin all that again
makes me tired and hopeless. However I'll see what Vegeto-Therapy
will do for young crooks.

I often think how lucky you were to get away from Europe. Oslo
that seemed so peaceful is now getting towards the danger centre. It is
not easy in England for those who supported Communism. The Party
of course has it own line which each member accepts without thought,
but the many Left Wing people who looked to Russia as to a new
world, are very depressed now. Left papers like the *New Statesman* now
say more bitter things about Russia than the old Conservative ones say.
But I won't discuss politics: I want to forget them and get on with
life's work. Write again soon and SAY WHAT YOU ARE DOING!!

———◆•◆———

Summerhill School
Leiston, Suffolk

April 10, 1940

My dear Reich,

I have interesting news about your books. Herbert Read, a
well known writer on art and philosophy, is a director of Kegan Paul
and Co, the best psychology and medical publishers in England. He
read my *Problem Teacher** and wrote asking me if your *Kampf der
Jugend*† was to be published in English as I had hoped in my book.
I wrote to him and told him not yet, and he replied that he was interested in what I had written about Reich and if I could lend him a few

---

* *The Problem Teacher* (London: Herbert Jenkins, 1940). Describes the problem teacher as one who hates the child in himself and loves the hateful disciplines
that rob the child of freedom and happiness. Children, Neill writes, must be entrusted only to those who believe in life; the problem teacher believes in subject
matter.

† *Der Sexuelle Kampf der Jugend* (Berlin: Verlag für Sexual-Politik, 1932) (The
Sexual Struggle of Youth). Addressing himself primarily to the young, Reich discusses the processes of maturation and the socio-political purposes of sex repression. He sees social revolution as a prerequisite to sexual liberation. This work
was never published in English.

of your books he would read them himself with a view to publication. I suggested to him that it would be best to bring out *Charakteranalyse* first with an appendix of the O. reflex, but said I would like to hear his opinion. I told him that I approached his firm two years ago trying to get them to take your *Fascismus** book, but had no success because then their advisers on publication were the Freudians. It is fine to have a man of Read's importance taking an interest anyway.

I feel guilty about not writing you earlier. Perhaps it is because the war has changed my occupation, for I am no longer a child psychologist: I teach maths and dig in the garden. Today I have dug for seven hours and my back aches. I still have a few "cases," but my difficulty is that through the therapy they lose their cramps and complexes without my seeing what is happening. That is, they breathe and fight and bite me etc., but no memories seem to come out as they did with me. That is very disappointing, and I feel that it must be something wrong with my technique.

Constance is alive and happy. She telephoned me tonight in great distress about our friends in Oslo. It is unbearable to think about. Judith wrote me at the time of the Finland crisis asking if I would invite Philipson† to England. Then the Russo–Finnish peace came and I did not write the letter. I feel bad about it now that Norway has been invaded, so much so that in my dream last night P. was at Summerhill. I thought the danger to Scandinavia was over, and as I say, I don't know how I could have got him over with wife and child. I feel guilty about it because if it had been Elsa L[indenberg] or someone I liked better than I did him I would have tried all ways.

Where is it all to end? Holland will be next I fear.

I sent you my book.‡ Several people have written me wanting to know where your books can be got. I have great hopes of launching the Reich ship on the English public.

I won't be so long in writing next time. I feel well and good, and any

---

* *Die Massenpsychologie des Faschismus*, 1933 (*The Mass Psychology of Fascism*, 1946, 1970). Discusses fascism as an expression of the unsatisfied orgastic longings of the masses, which for millennia have been suppressed and distorted by authoritarian social structures. Reich argues further that people whose characters were formed by an authoritarian society would be incapable of creating a free society. This contention led to his expulsion from the Communist Party in 1934.

† Tage Philipson, Swedish psychiatrist, student of Reich, who became the leader of the Reich group in Scandinavia after Reich left Norway.

‡ *The Problem Teacher.*

stiffness I have now is due to digging I fear. I would love to see you again. I often wonder if we shall ever meet again in this weary world of today. I'd like to live to see the better world that must follow this present insane one.

————◆•◆————

Forest Hills, New York

April 28, 1940

My dear Neill!

Your letter arrived yesterday together with the offer of Mr. Read. I shall send a copy of the *Jugendbuch* [youth book], but I doubt whether it would be wise to have it published at first in England. Dr. Theodore Wolfe from Columbia [University], whom you remember, is translating another book of mine which had not been published before.* It deals with the fundamental problems of Sex-Economy,† presenting them according to their development within the *IPV*‡ beginning in 1919 up to the present. It is much more simply written than my other books, and I think it would suit the purpose of introducing my work into English countries best. It contains in the first part the controversy with Freud, and in the second the autonomous development of my clinical work. If you get clear whether Kegan would be interested in this book first, I shall send you a copy as soon as it is available. After this the *Jugendbuch* will be accepted much more easily.

I was glad to hear from you. We had terrible days when Norway was invaded, and are still worried in spite of a telegram from Raknes§ saying that "friends here all well." I try hard to find out how I could manage to get Else and some others out and over here. I fear the worst. Could you help somehow? I am afraid not. But how to get in mail touch with them? It is dreadful. As soon as you hear further details write please or wire.

---

* *The Function of the Orgasm* (published as Volume One of *The Discovery of the Orgone*, 1942; republished in a new translation, 1973). Describes the development of Reich's work on sex-economy and his discovery of the emotional functions of biological energy.

† Reich uses "economy" in the sense of management or regulation; hence, "sex-economy" denotes the regulation of sexual (biological) energy within the organism.

‡ Internationale Psychoanalytische Vereinigung [International Psycho-Analytical Association].

§ Ola Raknes, Norwegian psychotherapist and lifelong supporter of Reich.

Somehow this war will be over as the first was, and life and work
will continue. Question is, who will survive. We are informed here
very well about the main events.

I have read your book, and gave it to Wolfe. It is I think very good.
The only thing I may mention is that you don't show clearly enough the
difficulties which would arise immediately if rational thinking were to
get hold of affairs.

I wish you all the best and hope to hear from you soon.

———◆•◆———

Summerhill School,
Festiniog, North Wales

August 2, 1940

My dear Reich,
What a time we have had evacuating the school from the
East Coast to the mountains. We are all delighted with the scenery.

I have read your Biography* with joy; it is to me the most fascinating thing you have written, and in better times I'd myself translate
it into English. I may do it in the dark nights of winter.

Herbert Read wrote again saying that his firm couldn't bring out
your books in war time with the shortage of paper. Later perhaps is all
the hope we have from that source.

I have no word of our friends in Norway. Someone saw Else's sister
in Stockholm, but I hear that Elsa Backer and family could not
get away from Oslo in time. I can get no news of the others, and fear they
couldn't get away, otherwise they would have written you from Sweden.
Of course there is no way of getting news out of Norway now that it is
under the brutal heel of the Nazis.

We carry on with the school and will carry on as long as we can. I
played with the idea of trying to take it to America, but something inside me was against the idea, some objection to running away from
danger I suppose.

I arranged things with my wife about having a free life and thanks
to you and your treatment have ways and means of having a full life
with full satisfaction, although, alas, not with full love as I could have

* The German version of *The Function of the Orgasm,* which Reich had sent
him.

had with Helga. I am continuing my Vegeto work this winter, but have so much to do teaching English and mathematics that the analysis will have to be done in the evenings. As this is an isolated place with no temptations to go out I shall find work pleasant.

Did you know that Stekel killed himself lately? Poor old Stekel. I had a soft spot in my heart for him, for behind his childish egoism there was something very warm about him. In these days of war interest and paper shortage he got hardly any notice from the newspapers, and his final "Message to England" was only published in brief in one paper. The individual isn't news in these times unless he is a blackguard like Goebbels.

Let me know if you hear about Elsa L[indenberg].

———◆•◆———

Forest Hills, New York

September 4, 1940

My dear Neill,

Your letter of August 2nd has just arrived. I hope that you could arrange yourself somehow. We are absorbing eagerly every word of the radio about the success of the English resistance.

I had word from our Scandinavian friends which are safe. Elsa is in Norway and is married.

I expected your coming to America, and I wonder whether it would not be wise to carry through this idea. The struggle for new education is great in this country in spite of many old-fashioned obstacles.

I did not know that Stekel killed himself. Apparently he belonged to the people who were not prepared for taking new disastrous changes. I did not like his "Message to England." I read some of Wells and think he is talking too much.

I would love to hear from you very soon again, and about your children, etc.

———◆•◆———

Summerhill School
Festiniog, North Wales

October 2, 1940

My dear Reich,

Just had your letter. I still think it would be a mistake to begin Reich's English and American reputation with the *Kampf* [struggle] book. If you get known as the serious scientist of the *Charakteranalyse,* etc. then you can come out as the champion of youth. Here I have experience. When my *Problem Child** appeared in New York (McBride and Co) about 1928 a paper said it was an obscene book, and McBride got frightened and stopped advertising it so that the yearly sales were about two copies.

Little to tell you about life here. We are away from the war so far, but are in a smaller house and haven't room for everyone. We are even using passages for sleeping in, and I have to refuse new pupils daily, much to my sorrow. It isn't easy for us here, for Wales is a very narrow religious place and we are looked on as atheists and sinners. I never yet saw a religious community that wasn't filled with rotten hate and spite. Must be many stiff stomachs round here I fear.

I was glad to hear from you that Elsa was safe, but not so pleased to think that she possibly had to marry for safety. I haven't heard a word of the Backers and your group. I expect the new Sex Pol society has been broken up by Hitlerism.

I am troubled because I don't seem to get on with any psychological work now. From morn till night I am kept busy teaching maths, doing all my own secretarial work, mending doors, planning for food, interviewing officials (who never heard of me and bother me about regulations). Add to that that our Central Heating is broken and we can't get it repaired. We had to wait for 8 weeks to get electricity in and lived with candles. Life is so much more primitive, and all of us have to cook and clean rooms, that is do the necessary things first in order to live. That is not the whole truth; much sadder is the fact that since the war I haven't been able to concentrate on the individual psychology of anyone. The individual has become to me relatively unimportant. I hope the interest will come back to me.

I can't see how I can come to America. It would mean breaking up the school here, leaving children and staff who have been with me for years. And as America is likely soon to be in the war, conditions there may not be too good for new education.

Constance seems to be still in London braving the bombs. She always writes saying how well she feels since her analysis.

---

* *The Problem Child* (London: Herbert Jenkins, 1926). Neill shows how unhappiness arises from coercive upbringing, and maintains that all crimes and hatreds, and hence all wars, can be traced to unhappiness. Freedom, on the other hand, "does not make children good, it simply allows them to be good."

You never mention your own kiddies. Does the mother keep them away from you? The one certainly needs you.

———◆•◆———

Forest Hills, New York

November 7, 1940

My dear Neill:

I have your letter of October 2nd. I was very glad to hear from you.

It is good that you seem pretty safe in the place where you are, and are still able to carry on the work. You can imagine how closely we watch events over there. The re-election of Roosevelt seems to me of tremendous importance. I learn more and more how this so-called bourgeois society, in the course of 7 years under capitalistic rule, has done more in the field of social security than any communist in Russia would dream of getting. This is only to indicate that, being quite firm in all my scientific convictions, I feel myself completely confused and inclined to revise most of the things I ever learned in Europe about what Socialism should be. I can only hope that the roots of my special work will prevent me from becoming reactionary. If you hear socialists and communists who have come over here claiming that Roosevelt is a dictator or a fascist, then your stomach simply turns around. I have started to hate them. They seem to me a complete nuisance in their lack of any ability to think a thought to the end or to do any kind of work. But it may be that a part of this feeling is mere disappointment.

You are quite right that the personal matters come more and more into the background in order to make place for the social matters, but that should not mean that you forget the personal matters, but that you look upon them as expressions of a definite social situation.

Elsa is still in Norway and striving hard to come over here, that means to accomplish a matter which she could have had easily a year and a half ago.* But this comes from the misinterpreted *Selbstständigkeit* [independence].

As to the new kind of education, I can only say that the people here

---

* Reich means that she could have come with him, presumably either as his assistant or as his wife. They broke up shortly before he left Norway for the United States.

seem to be much more in the dark but also much more open to the natural point of view.

I think you will be glad to hear that the mother of my children fails so completely in her attempts to pronounce me crazy and to detach my children from me that I am beginning to pity her. Eva has turned over to me completely without my doing anything to achieve it except that I kept quiet and waited and helped her when she began to ask my advice. Here again was a proof that compulsory authoritarian behaviour has to fail in the end if real freedom in the well-understood sense is maintained.

I want to hear from you very soon about many good news.

1941

Summerhill School
Festiniog, North Wales

February 5, 1941

My dear Reich,

I got your letter just as I went on holiday to my old school in Suffolk. You did sound a little reactionary, for America can't be a Paradise with so many unemployed and so many millionaires. But I am not going to write a political letter.

We had an Xmas visitor, a refugee woman scientist, biologist. She read *Die Bione* and said she would put her criticisms on paper for me so that I could send them to you. She has not done so yet, but her argument is that your sterilisation is weak all the time, that no one knows that all life is killed in incandescent heat, etc. I suppose you have had the same argument from many of them. If she sends the criticism I'll forward it to you at once.

I am at present spending my valuable time teaching maths, but am trying to get a teacher so that I can get back to my other work, for which I feel ready now. Of course the uncertainty of the future makes it all so difficult. In the coming world what place will there be for freedom in education? We are moving to State Control of everything, and after the war the middle class may not be able to send their children to private schools. All schools will be State ones, and I can't see myself in a State school with control from above. It is queer that only under Capitalism have I been able to be a pioneer in education. I know what Nazism would have done with me, but what would a Communist State do with me? I couldn't make children sing the Red Flag or study Marx.

No, Reich, the future is dark for my work, but I carry it on and will do so as long as I am allowed to.

I am glad that you are in touch with the children.* That must be very comforting. I often think how lucky you were to get away before Hitler marched into Oslo, and I smile when I think that Elsa Backer wanted me to bring my school to Norway "for safety." I can get no news of other folk in Oslo, but fear that moderns like Sigurd Hoel† and Raknes may be having a bad time under the devilish heel of brute force.

I had a most pleasant dream last night. I was in N.Y. with you and it was most realistic, for you took me round N.Y. and showed me all the best sights, but I know that old Reich wouldn't waste his time taking me to the top of the Woolworth Building in real life.

My wife is done out now, unable to do anything in the school. It is very sad to see one who has been so active become like a child again.

I wish I could have a few more hours on your sofa.

———————◆•◆———————

Forest Hills, New York

February 24, 1941

My dear Neill:

You are quite right, it sounded rather "reactionary" what I wrote you about America, but I think it is true. I am sure you would not find either in Russia, nor under any socialist government in Scandinavia or in Germany such honest and widespread efforts to acquire a spirit and a general way of looking at things as I found here. But, of course, all the evils are here too, and nobody knows which of the two forces will conquer the other in the course of time. You know very well, what I believe is that the problem of true democracy is rooted much deeper in history as well as in the biological roots of the human structure than any politician, socialist, administrator, statesman, etc. knows or would like to believe. That sounds very depressing, but at the same time it is the only hopeful knowledge that we have. I believe neither in state capitalism nor in state socialism. I believe only in the possibility that the international disaster will swamp up to the surface deepest natural intentions and ways of thinking in the human beings themselves, which would be a real basis for a real reconstruction. I mean work democracy, based upon science, work, and natural love.

The "criticism" of your German biologist is a very usual one and often heard. I am tired of it, and prefer to treat my cancer mice with orgone radiation. I met here Einstein, told him the whole story. What he said was that the whole thing is phantastic, but he did not reject it and understood very well that the connection between the bions and energy being dissolved from matter is the real thing. The discussions still go on. Bacteriologists as well as pathologists and biologists will, I am afraid, have to rebuild their thinking as well as their acting. The first book about "Living Matter"* is translated completely into English, and I hope that it will appear soon.

I understand your worries about where your school could find a place in the future, but do not worry; if your school will not be able to find a place in the new world then nothing honest and decent will.

Write again and more often please, and give my greetings to Erna,† Constance and all the other friends.

———— ◆•◆ ————

Summerhill School
Festiniog, North Wales

                                        March 4, 1941
My dear Reich,
        You may have noticed in my letters how vague I have been in mentioning psychological matters. I was held back by the thought that my letter might be read by some conventional young lady in the Censor's office, and I didn't think it fair to have the strong meat of sex psychology placed before one who most likely is unaccustomed to the terms and ideas we use in writing and conversation. I wrote to the Chief Censor and he asked me to send any such letter via him.

I have been reading your books again with more and more admiration. I feel, however, that your Orgasm Reflex is too egocentric, too

---

* *The Function of the Orgasm* (Volume One of *The Discovery of the Orgone*).
    † A young refugee pianist whom Reich had befriended and to whom the Neills had given a home in Summerhill.

individual. Your point is that, given freedom from repression and muscular cramping, the Reflex should be perfect. I agree, but not on all occasions. But perhaps you believe that it depends on the partner. Yes, you hold that without love the Orgasm Reflex will be incomplete. My point is, taking the point of view of the man, that unless he meets a woman with the power of attracting strongly his sex impulse, his orgasm will be unsatisfying. In other words a man can be without sex repression, but unless he meets the girl whose touch thrills him, his satisfaction will not be nearly complete.

I can count on my fingers the number of girls I have met in life whose touch even when shaking hands gave me a tremendous thrill. Sex appeal isn't nearly so common as the film fans would have us believe. You would say that, given absence of repression and wrong moral ideas, everyone would have this sex appeal. I believe it, but in a world of unconscious hate of sex there are so many without the sex appeal that gives out, that it is difficult to find a true mate. You remember how you always said: "Give yourself, let go." Sex repression keeps the great majority of girls (and boys) from giving out anything.

All this simply amounts to this: that to be sexually free in an unfree world isn't so easy as it sounds. You are so right in your attitude to promiscuous sexual intercourse: it couldn't live in a free sexual education.

I wonder what you think of the age question. At nineteen I could have been promiscuous. At 57 I wouldn't want to go away for the weekend with the most beautiful film star, unless of course I knew her and was much attracted to her. The temptation isn't likely to arise, but I am curious about the effect of years on the sex impulse. My own experience is that the pleasure does not lessen; what lessens is the phantasy side and the frequency.

I have a theory that in a war the soldiers should have their women with them at the front. Since starved sex so easily turns into anxiety, wouldn't an army fight more bravely if its sexual urge was satisfied? An old pupil, now on a ship, was telling me how the lack of sex affected a crew, how some got introverted, others irritable and so on. This aspect of war is important. Millions of men cooped up in barracks with only their own sex. The old idea was that women had no place in danger, but with the bombing of towns that idea no longer holds. Think of what the clerics would say if some bold man proposed that the army should have its women with it!

I am afraid that our friends in Oslo may be having a bad time under the Nazis. From Sweden I hear reports that the Norwegians are fighting hard for their independence.

I wish I could have a long talk with you about the war, not the military aspect, but the future. I feel strongly that the war won't be won by military means alone, that we can win only if we can get the millions of Europe on our side. I feel that we aren't doing enough to get this. It is useless to say that we are fighting for freedom and democracy unless we can get the men of Europe to agree with our idea of freedom and democracy. Churchill is a great man, a man of the Elizabethan tradition, another Sir Francis Drake, and all Britain relies on him. But do the peasants of France and Germany, Austria and Poland feel the same about Churchill as we do? They don't want a big man; they want a big plan, and I say we haven't got one, at least no one has published one. Hitler has a plan, a plan of slavery and hate and death to all decent men. If we are to smash him we need tanks and planes certainly, but an idea is greater than these. We want something bigger than Communism as we know it. Here your idea of a nation, a world run by the workers comes in, meaning by workers every man who does a job, and excluding every damned politician in the world. It would be a new socialism, but I can't see the privileged in the world giving up their power and profits. In your last letter you praised Roosevelt, saying that there was more socialism in U.S.A. than in all Russia. Having been to neither I can't say. But so long as anyone in U.S.A. is making profit out of armaments and the people's needs, how can you talk of socialism in America? If Churchill or Roosevelt could get up and say: "There will be no profit in the new world after the war," the millions of Europe would rise against Hitler.

But I could go on on this theme for pages, and I have work to do. Next letter I hope to tell you how I am getting on with child analysis. Write soon.

———◆•◆———

Summerhill School
Festiniog, North Wales

March 20, 1941

My dear Reich,

Yours today. The difficulty in that New World of yours is this: workers like you and me don't want to govern, because governing is an inferior brand of creation, and the second-rate fellows will want to run our civilisation for us as politicians or bureaucrats. Take your own line of the moment—cancer research. Any State will want to organise this; and any State will put men above you who know how to add up figures, but know nothing about cancer; and you will be too busy in your lab to bother about the organising. I simply can't see a solution of the problem: how to run a State without the bureaucrat. After the war it is probable that there will be no private schools in Europe. Already the big schools like Eton and Harrow are appealing to the government for support. What hopes, therefore, for small schools like mine? They will either be closed or will come under govt. organisation, and that means that I have to treat children, not as I know how they ought to be treated, but according to the ideas of a Minister of Education or his subordinates. That would be death to free experiment.

You see I am taking men as we know them now; I am not postulating a new race of men who will be great enough to allow freedom to the scientist or artist. Yes, under your universal natural love and work and science it could be done. But, Reich, we have to face a post-war world in which stupidity won't have been killed by bombs, I mean an immediate post-war world. The Left people are just as retarded as the Right. After all, I wouldn't ask Karl Marx or even Einstein how to run a school.

I am so glad you met Einstein. I do hope that his interest is aroused and that he investigates the thing for himself. Be sure to send me everything you publish in English; even the smallest pamphlets.

My letter of a few days ago, sent via the Chief Censor, was not exactly what I meant it to be; for knowing that another man will read a letter is enough to inhibit the writer more or less. But what I said fits into what I am saying in this letter, viz. that in a world where sex is bound it isn't easy to love or rather to find love. So in occupation. You and I are both ahead of our time (you more than I) and we find so much difficulty in a truth-inhibited world in advancing our ideas, for sex and truth are both badly inhibited.

I still think you don't give enough credit to the Communists in spite of their great mistakes. Maybe I give too much importance to the mere abolition of profit,* of exploitation by private employers, but I think that the abolition of profit was and is a tremendous step forwards. Without it I can't see how your own idea of the future State can come about.

---

* In the margin of this letter, Reich wrote: "Not abolished."

I'd like to hear your comparison between the democracies of U.S.A. and Norway. It may be that you are finding New York more tolerant than Oslo because it is bigger, and you are left much more free from local silly criticism. Move on to a small town in the Middle West and you will find narrowness enough. In East England we were free to do what we liked. Last Sunday here we were gardening when a local religionist came and lectured us on profaning the Lord's Day. New York versus any Main Street.

Your English is vastly improved, but it hurts me to think you are possibly talking with an Ammurican accent now: can't think that you call a "bird" a "boid."

I have got back my interest in analysis again, but have also a great interest in mathematics. Last weekend I travelled to the east of England to lecture to a big meeting of teachers, a day's journey. I spent the day working out maths problems.

Well, well, Reich, goodnight. I long to see you again, but in a different way from before, for I have no wish to lie on the sofa and be the Emperor or anyone else; I just want to see you and hear all about what you are doing. I am convinced that your name is the successor to that of Freud. I hear little of the analysts now; most of them are out of London. Apparently bombing has not made more neurosis. One doctor wrote that it had lessened it.

———————◆◆———————

Bion-Cancer Research Laboratory
Forest Hills, New York

April 1, 1941

My dear Neill:

When I read your letter of March 4, I was struck again by an experience which I have made over years and years, that is, how it is possible that so many people, good, clever, honest people, still, only after years of their own experience get in touch within themselves with the problems I describe. Then for the first time they understand the problem as well as its details. Then they reread those books and come to understand my headaches. Quite a similar thing happened several weeks ago when I received a letter from a physicist in Zürich who had followed my work since about 1930, and who now for the first time, 10 or 11 years later, seemed to have got into contact with the real problem of human life, apart from reading my books. He wrote that matters are developing quickly and hopefully in Europe and that if the great breakthrough comes, my ideas would become of great importance. When I read such things and compare them with my everyday life and struggle then I am confused. How is it possible, I ask myself, that, as I know, I have given birth to a very great knowledge and that on the other hand all the many people whom I learned to know during the past 15 or 20 years and who know what was accomplished, *do not do* something about it. There is a great gap between the understanding of the people who encounter my work and the practical influence exerted by all those people together. Very often I phantasy that if all those who came and have gone or are still there would cooperate and act as usual political party members do, then I may frankly say, the greatest and most efficient political movement which the world has ever seen would be at work and would bring about with perfect certainty all that Churchill wants, as well as Roosevelt and every man in this world who honestly tries for the best—and [even] more than that. There is a gap between the fact that every single living human being in this world knows more or less clearly that the real life process is running on a quite different line than the apparent official process which is called diplomacy and politics. Still, the gap is there and somehow all those millions and millions do not seem to be able to find the proper form and organization for their knowledge of the real life process. Very often I felt the temptation and even the responsibility "to do something about it," that means to organize our knowledge as the political parties organize their nonsense. A definite consideration, or rather a feeling, always kept me from doing so. The feeling was that the first real step into a party-like organization of real knowledge, truth, decency and straightforwardness would kill immediately knowledge, truth, decency and straightforwardness. That is because these activities of the living matter are not to be organized, they are alive, and life which is productive, and swelling and acting and moving and making mistakes and correcting them and so forth, cannot be organized.

One of my students here told me once a story: "The devil in Hell had heard that human beings had found the truth, the real truth. His advisers were shaken with terror. But the devil told them: 'Don't be afraid, go there amongst them and let them organize the truth they found.' " This is a very good and true story. I don't know any answer to this greatest of all problems. You can organize gangs, crooks, profit-makers, a railroad, a war-machine industry, you cannot organize life and truth.

The way how my own thoughts and publications have become understandable to others and are affecting them is a very peculiar one. I had to learn that this knowledge about life and its laws cannot be conferred, as you confer the knowledge of the technique of an injection. Somehow every one has to refind it himself amidst the varying life process. He cannot learn it, he can read and understand what is written, but he does not understand it really. There are very few only at this time who have gone through our famous mill and have found themselves in the reality that I have found first about 18 years ago. You know, for instance, and they know too—and many others know it without being able to formulate it—that real true work democracy is going to come. I would not call it socialism because this word has been dishonored by politicians. Why not call it "Work Democracy"? But *we* cannot bring it about; it will be the task accomplished by those who will have to build up and to secure it, that means: no political party and no special organization apart from the work and the consumers organizations.

I have tried to work out some ideas and phantasies about a possible outcome of this war into work democracy. But I would like to emphasize, as I often did, that I do not have the ambition, and that I even hate the idea of being looked upon or regarded as the one responsible for, as you call it, the new socialism.

Now to your questions: You are quite right saying that the orgasm reflex brings about the problem that so few partners can be found if you are perfectly healthy. But just that was the point which made me break through into the field of sociology and sex politics in 1927. It was the fact that a sick world is fitted for sick human beings and not for healthy ones; that healthy ones are lost in this world and very often despised and condemned. Your suggestion about the difference in the sexual structure in the adolescent and the grown-up is also correct. The problem of women being in the army is very difficult. It is quite clear that, as you write and everyone can observe, the army spoils the character because of sexual starvation and the roughness of the soldiers. Women in the army would settle the problem, but, on the other hand, every militarist will tell you that women in the army could mean a hampering of the most characteristic habit of the army and that is automatic, mechanical discipline. Here again, the incapability of life to be mechanized or organized hits against an institution in the mechanized civilization which is based (and by necessity) upon stiff stomachs, retracted behinds, high chests, rigid musculature.

The essence of all those things is a belief that the natural life process has broken through in our age, striving for release and creating new forms of life and confusing all human beings. The old forms have brought society into the abyss of war and destruction. The new forms are not yet born and nobody knows what they will look like. But one fact is clear: the perversities and lunatic happenings which were brought to the peak by Hitler can only be conquered by life itself. I think we can only try to understand and help as much as we can. There is no authority born yet in this field and should an authority once be created, then I am afraid a new setback would take place.

I had very good news from Copenhagen. They are working, and more and more people are beginning to trust them and to help them. Please write again soon.

Bion-Cancer Research Laboratory
Forest Hills, New York

April 2, 1941

My dear Neill:

Your letter of March 20 arrived today, a few days later than your first letter. I was very glad to have it. You ask a very important question based on a very correct statement: How to run a state without the bureaucrats. It is my deep conviction that perhaps not the state in the usual old sense of the word, but human society can be run without bureaucrats, and even better so. It is my deep belief that bureaucracy is not necessary, but is to be compared to a cancerous growth on the body of the society which works, searches for truth, improves living conditions, and suffers from the bureaucrats. Today, the social process is run in two ways: by the real working process of its own, and by the bureaucracy which imposes itself upon this working process. In the future it may be that the first, the working process which exists and works today, will administrate life quite on its own.

I, personally, would never, happen what may, submit to any minister of education or any minister of anything who is not a specialist in the field and does not know more than I do.

What you call the immediate post-war world will be either a work democracy, a society based upon the rational working process carried on and cared for by the people who work in all the fields which are necessary for sustaining life—or it will be a pre-war world with a new war within the next 10 to 20 years. I do not think there is any other possibility. I do not believe in state capitalism, nor in state socialism, nor in any isms any more. This world will crash with all its nonsense, hypocrisy, bureaucrats, diplomats, politicians in such a deep abyss that, in order to preserve life itself, the working human beings of all professions will simply *have* to take care of the social process.

I do not worry how my ideas of the future society can come about. I wish to state this, and I do not want to make any secret of it. There is and exists a definite kind of power which is beyond all limits and not accessible to any crook or any kind of politicianship, and I even want them to know it:

1) I have in my hands and I dispose of the orgone radiation which exists in the earth and in the atmosphere, and nobody but I knows how to handle it.

2) I have the knowledge how to determine the weather before any barometer in the world can do it. They will need it, and badly so.

3) I possess the secret of cancer, rheumatism, tuberculosis, neurosis, psychosis and many other diseases which devastate social life and even bring about wars. Nobody but I can handle this field at this time.

4) I have definite proof that it will be possible not only to fight many of these diseases, not only to direct the radiation, but there are many indications that the radiation which I have discovered will be indispensable for science as well as for every aspect of technique.

5) And finally, I alone dispose of the formula and the experiments which give mankind power over the raising of living substance from non-living substance.

I have known this for several years, and I did not publish a word about it. I spoke and have written about the radiation and cancer only to Einstein. My dear Neill, that means *power*, and be sure I am going to use it against every one who will not prove clearly and unmistakably that he is ready and willing honestly to secure human liberty and decency. I shall not cooperate in any way with any organization, be it political or otherwise, which is not thoroughly democratic and which does not mean what it promises or says. What could they do to me? Nothing. Put me in jail, hang me, or what? I am not afraid of them. I know them too well because I have worked with them for many years. I hate them and despise them, to the deepest bottom of my being.

I do not dream or phantasy ever doing to them what they did to human beings, to my work, to refugees, to Jews, socialists, children, and so on. But they simply will not get what is in my hands and depends solely upon my own free decision to do with it what I want. The U.S.A. patent for some devices to operate the orgone radiation is applied for since a few months. It is a great thing to fight for and I shall fight for it. And do not worry please, my dear Neill, about whether some bureaucrat or ignorant politician will try to destroy free research, free education, individual initiative and happiness. They will need it when this war will begin not only to impose death upon several thousands of people, but when death and illness and epidemics, etc. will harass hundreds of millions of people. Then they will need it, be sure of that.

And I repeat, I am not willing to give it unless human liberty and security of life and happiness are granted. I would stress and repeat what Roosevelt said the other day, that the administrators of today are to be the servants of the population and nothing else.

Bion-Cancer Research Laboratory
Forest Hills, New York

June 2, 1941

My dear Neill:

My experiments with cancerous human beings are doing well beyond any expectation. I think you and your colleagues will hear about it in detail in the course of next winter. I am going to write down the whole story this summer.

We are following here eagerly every bit of news from Europe. This does not mean, of course, much help, but at least an important contact is there.

Summerhill School
Festiniog, North Wales

June 6, 1941

My dear Reich,

It is some weeks since I had your most interesting letter, full of hope for the future of your work. I long to hear about it all in detail, and anticipate the day when it will all be in English print. People keep writing me asking when you are going to be read in English.

I have had a spell of not very good health. The Welsh air is not so bracing as that on the East Coast, even though it is a mountainous country, and none of us feels so energetic as we did. The appalling thing, Reich, is that I have completely lost all interest in psychology. It is possible that my analysis with you, by giving me freedom in the reflex, destroyed a complex which had been expressed in trying to cure the other fellow. I can rationalise that with my wife's breakdown in health, with shortage of staff etc., I have too many things to do, but I know it is only a rationalisation, that if I were keen, I'd find time for veg.-therapy.

I find I am happiest in writing, but here again, with paper shortage, it is almost impossible to have a book published. And also life has become so much more primitive in many ways. I spend hours digging to produce food, and so do the children. And thank God, I think I have more interest in the children than I ever had. They are grand and clever and lovable, and I know that this system is the only one of any value in the world. They don't seem to need any therapy of any kind, and that is the ideal education—to educate children in such a way that they won't need therapy later on.

I hear little from Sweden, no word at all of our old friends.

Two years ago I had just come back from Oslo. No, it wasn't two years ago; it was two thousand.

All the best, Reich, and the moment you publish anything send it to me.

P.S. I keep wondering if there is any connection between your cure by *Bione* and the Naturopath's cure of cancer by fruit and raw greens, for he cured a lady doctor I sent to him of cancer of the breast six years ago. Are the same sun rays in *Bione* and fresh grown vegetables? Or do both have a vitamin not yet known? The Nature Cure people talk of a cleansing diet (fruit) but they are all so moral that their idea of eliminating the "poisons" from the body has a strong link with their wish to eliminate the moral poisons too. They are nearly all very anti-sex.

———◆•◆———

Summerhill School
Festiniog, North Wales

July 1, 1941

My dear Reich,

I am late in replying; felt run down and went off for a golfing holiday, and now feel fine.

For some reason I cannot trace, I can't do any psychological work at all. I am full of energy in my work; I believe more vitally in what I am doing, and I rejoice to see the result in the children, but I cannot bring myself to do individual analysis. Is it that you destroyed my saving Christ attitude? Is it that the O. Reflex gave me a satisfaction that I was trying to find in assisting others? Or is it that I didn't go far enough with you? I don't know, Reich, and it all troubles me. On the other hand I have an intense interest in your work, and long to read your journal in my own language. And the time I had with you has changed me much. The effect is seen on the school. The atmosphere is happier because I am happier. I can take decisions easily now, but still can't be aggressive.

I feel I have let you down; that I am not fighting in the front line for the new psychology. I have tried to face the question: Is my apathy due to not really believing in Reich? I think the answer would be: If I didn't believe in Reich wouldn't I seek the truth in Freud or Jung or Stekel or Adler or anyone else? I have no interest in any of these gentlemen now. Whatever the cause, I am not worthy to be the representative in England of your Veg.-Therapy. Best to expel me from the Society.

Like most people here now I am greatly interested in the Russian war. Even if U.S.A. stays out I can't see that Hitler has any chance to win, for even the German army can't keep down 180 million Russians. Look at their difficulties even in Norway where the people are fighting back. And what do the five million Germans who voted for Communism in '32 or '33 think of this new war?

One feels a desire to live for a thousand years to see what is to come to pass. I am no longer satisfied with the explanation that it is purely an economic war for profit and imperialism. The slowness of the masses is very disheartening . . . the army of Japan after all these years of fighting China should have demanded to know what it was leading to for each man personally, each man facing destruction, sex starvation, total lack of creative life. Yet the Japs still follow leaders blindly. How much of any army is conscious? Soldiers complain, but mainly about the small things—food or absence of leave, etc. When will all the soldiers of the world ask the big question: What is all this leading to? For they are the men who will build the new world. We see now the result of what we called education, which was mere learning about things that didn't matter. The education of the emotions was entirely neglected when it wasn't deliberately repressive. Hence the easiness with which a Hitler can get his millions of emotionally-starved men to let out their feelings in blood and cruelty. What should have come out as love comes out as hate. In this connection it is interesting to hear my old pupils. They are all in it, fighting, on ships, in the army, the navy, in the air. They do well, but they are conscious of the inner meaning of it all. They are not fighting with any hate at all; their attitude is: here is a job that must be done and we must do it, but they see beyond the German soldier, beyond Hitler, beyond the war. They are all intensely interested in the life to follow the war, and if they live, they will do well in the reconstruction. They feel the tragedy of having to destroy when all they want to do is to build. I wonder how the German soldier feels? What future does he hope for? Surely not a Gestapo one. How does he see the new German State? I wish they would ask one to write the propaganda they drop over Germany. I would get at their hearts not their heads.

When shall I be able to cross the Atlantic to see you again? It is a great wish, one that can't be fulfilled for a long time, I fear.

Oquossoc, Maine

August 5, 1941

My dear Neill:

In the main statement [in the letter of July 1] you are, of course, completely wrong. Your breaking away from psychology and your turning over to nature is completely in accordance with our own way of thinking, being and working. I myself am digging more and more into the field of biology, and we can expect many enlightening results for psychology from this realm. So you don't have to be "expelled" from the Society and I privately believe that you have done more for the matter of sex-economy than many others in the field.

All your remarks about the slowness of the masses and the expectations of the young soldiers are very true. If only someone could be found who would connect and organize all those forces, then many of these problems could be easily solved.

Did you receive my latest private pamphlet about "Work Democracy"? I worked fine now for a few weeks in a little place on a lake which I bought a year ago. The experimental work is counterbalanced properly by working in the woods. So you see, I am not far from where you are.

Summerhill School
Festiniog, North Wales

October 10, 1941

My dear Reich,

I had your last letter when I was in Scotland. Not feeling well. I went up to Thomson's Nature Cure home in Edinburgh for five weeks. Well, well, Reich, I feel better and can work better, although my interest in analysis is still weak. Constance and I are translating your *Arbeitsdemokratie* [Work Democracy].

I had a letter from Tor Raknes who is in the Norwegian Air Force in this country. He writes: "I don't know much about my father now, but when I left Oslo, January 20th, he had quite a lot of patients and up to my departure he didn't have any direct trouble with the Nazis except for an article where he was accused of 'spoiling the Nordic race.' The article also referred to Dr. Reich as 'a swindler' and so on."

Tor came here about May the First, so that if he left Oslo in January he must have come a long roundabout way. Like you, I am completely cut off from Norway and now Sweden too is impossible to write to or get letters from. Reich, how are we to get rid of that bloody poisonous thing Fascism early enough for you and me to go on working in freedom? It must die just as the monsters of primitive times died, for like them it has strength but no head and brain. I am impatient to live to see it slain.

Constance and I talked about your references to Stalinism in *Arbtsdem*. Do you want them kept as they are, or does the war modify your opinion of Russia? I suppose that to you Stalinism would be better than Hitlerism naturally. We can discuss this when the booklet is translated anyway.

I long to read of your *Bione* work and its results. I hate the fate that prevents our being able to meet again. God knows when anyone will sail from here to N.Y. on a pleasure cruise. In the new world it will be all building up and there will be no room for pleasure ships I fancy. If I were young I'd take up architecture as a profession. Think of the wonderful opportunities there will be to build great cities. The half and half men, the compromise architects will get the work to do, I fear, the men who stick to brick and cement when the future is possibly one of glass buildings or bakelite [plastic] or rubber or what not.

Well, Reich, let me hear from you again.

99-06 69th Avenue
Forest Hills, New York

November 3, 1941

My dear Neill:

Your letter of October 10th arrived several days ago. It was good to hear from you.

I could not, of course, change my opinion about Stalin and Stalinism because of what is going on now. The fight of Stalin against Hitler does not prove that his system is not a hitlerite one. The blame for the outcome of this war so far is still on Stalin who betrayed the Czechs in 1939, who cooperated with Hitler in Poland, who opened all doors to everything that happened since. Of course, he fights now because he has to, but you don't doubt, I think, that he would have preferred much more to be able to fight on Hitler's side against the democracies. The bravery of the Russian army is not his but the people's work, as is the bravery of the German people. It is not a question whether the one or the other is brave, but whether the basic and main issue of this war will come forth and be fought for with the same bravery as they fight today for no reason at all. No reason, I mean, is given for first messing up all the people of Europe in irrational politics, then creating a Hitler, then helping Hitler along, consciously or unconsciously, in most of his early victories and letting down and betraying the former allies, then finding out what one could have known years before if one had not unconsciously admired Hitler, and, finally, holding back what everyone knows and wants, namely the fact that the people are fighting for an order which, if you want, you may call work democracy. What would you tell a mother who has messed up her child in education? You would say you should not have done this or that to begin with. Once a situation is messed up, I do not think that things can be improved within the framework of the mess. Stalin carries 80% of the guilt for the form and present status of this war. We have to fight against Hitler and against Hitlerism everywhere, but we have not to fight for Stalin and we should not hide what we have learned in these dreadful years. To hide this now would mean nothing but to create new Stalinism later. You may leave his name out if you want from the description of the dictators and their function, but please do not leave out Stalinism. And I don't think Stalinism would be better as a framework for our work than Hitlerism or Chamberlainism.

You want to know about our work here. Well, the situation here now is the following: We have a small group of about six physicians and a lawyer. Some of them are already practicing Vegeto-therapy. The publishing house has been built up again. Dr. Wolfe, who has turned out to be one of our best and most reliable workers, has taken in his hands the editorship of our new journal, *International Journal for Sex-Economy and Orgone Research*. The first volume of my book, *The Discovery of the Orgone*, is in print now and will be issued in about 6 weeks. This first volume contains the history of the orgasm theory and of my work since 1919 up to now.

Regarding this book and the journal, I would like to ask you whether you could arrange for their distribution in the Empire. We also expect from you papers for this journal. I think you will enjoy it as I do.

To come back to our Institute. The American group of the Institute is organized now. The name is Orgone Research Institute. We have broken through completely into the realm of experimental application of the atmospheric Orgone radiation to different diseases, especially cancer, with some amazing results. I think that this natural biological energy will play some role in the coming deterioration of human health in the course of the war. I only don't know how to get at the respective authorities in the health departments of the English speaking world, so as to make clear to them what a worked-out Orgone treatment would mean as a help in the war effort. I would appreciate it if you have any ideas. I am willing and ready to show them everything that I have got and accomplished. The American group also has bought a house for the laboratory and me to live in. You will find this new address on the letterhead. So finally I am not depending any more on any landlord who could throw me out when he wants to.* I hope to see you once in this house.

This is about all the important news I can relate about our work here. I hear regularly from Denmark, but not from Holland or Norway. Several of our friends are in jail, but the clinical and educational work is going on and the population has confidence in us. Let this letter be read by Constance, Erna and whomever you want. Please write again and soon, especially about the distribution of our literature in the English Empire.

---

* Reich had in fact earlier been "thrown out" of the house he was renting because he kept experimental mice in the basement.

1942

Summerhill School
Festiniog, North Wales

January 18, 1942

My dear Reich,

Thanks for your long letter of Nov. 3rd. I am late in replying because I went to Scotland for a few weeks.*

I am delighted at the idea of your work appearing in English. I shall help all I can on this side to get a publisher. One great difficulty is that all publishers seem to have Freudian readers to decide about publication, and then there is the shortage of paper. I think that any new publication needs a government license. Any issue on this side would have to be financially independent of U.S.A. No profit could be sent to you, but as there won't be one and as you don't think of that side, that will be O.K. Send me as many copies [of the book, *The Function of the Orgasm*, published in the United States] as you can spare and I shall try to get them distributed among the people who matter. I long for the day when I can help to introduce you to England.

We shan't argue about old Joe Stalin. New things are moving and all will be changed. All I meant was that the British public at the moment would not take kindly to anything printed that lumped Stalin with the other two as dictators. The enthusiasm for Russia here is tremendous at present.

How will you stand as an alien now that the U.S.A. is in the war? I hope you can continue your cancer research work, for that is more important than war work that any doctor could do.

---

* The rest of this paragraph was deleted by the censor.

I am looking for a larger house. I am turning away dozens of new pupils and could have a large school now. The school goes well. The kids are great, and when I lecture I get bigger and more enthusiastic audiences.

The war looks like being very long now. I fear it will be some time before we meet in New York.

My wife fails fast and is most pathetic to see now. Paralysed partly, and conscious of what it all means. It is a grim life to see one who was energetic and capable go downhill like that.

I seldom practice psychology now. I have become a teacher of maths and English because men are scarce; an office boy half my time because my secretary is in the army. My whole life is changed, but since I no longer take in problem children, the school runs happily with freedom alone. My own love life runs smoothly and happily.

I hear that a little girl I had for a short time is a refugee in N.Y. and has been treated by a Reichian. I'd like to hear about her, for she was a most introverted little thing with a stomach like iron and a hate like steel.

I am not writing any books now. Most of the stock of my old ones has been blitzed, and there are no copies of *Problem Child* and *Problem Parent** left. I have no desire to write; things change so rapidly that what one writes today seems out of date tomorrow.

Odd thing, I have a postcard from a British Air Officer, a prisoner in *Oflag* [officer's camp] IV, saying he had my problem books sent out to him and could I recommend other books on psychology. Queer, isn't it, for my books are strongly anti-Hitler. I wonder why they allow them to enter Germany.

What's the future? I feel it belongs to Russia, China and India. They have the great masses. The days of empire seem to be shortening rapidly. I'm afraid that our rule by one class hasn't been too successful.

Well, goodbye for a time, old friend. I think of you often and Erna and I often say: "Pity Willi Reich isn't here tonight."

---

* *The Problem Parent* (London: Herbert Jenkins, 1932). Neill argues that even the most difficult child was probably made so by parental mishandling. He describes the various ways in which parents stifle and distort their children's natural healthy development.

Forest Hills, New York

March 18, 1942

My dear Neill:

I had your letter of January 18th at the end of February. It was good to hear that things are quite all right with you.

Our *International Journal* and my new book are just coming out. You will receive enough copies through Dr. Wolfe. It would be very important and useful if you could provide our journal with typical and significant descriptions of children's behavior under the circumstances of freedom and non-freedom. We shall print them gladly and I think that it would also help your cause to have them printed. I believe the most important task would be to elaborate the problems which arise in children who were brought up in a more or less disguised authoritative manner and who encounter for the first time freedom of movement, thought and utterance. We always agreed upon the one point that it is not so much the content of a free life, but the fear of freedom which concerns all of us. There would, without doubt, be no dangerous problems in freedom if the people and the children were not afraid of it and if they did not long for the guidance of authority.

Which chapter of which of your books would you like to have reprinted in the journal? Let us also know, please, to what extent you succeed in distributing the journal and the book. So far, the journal is being received here with great appreciation.

Please do not fail to keep in touch with me and write as frequently as possible. My regards to Erna and all the other friends unknown.

Summerhill School
Festiniog, North Wales

April 28, 1942

My dear Reich,

Number 1 of the journal has arrived. I must congratulate Wolfe; it is splendid. Some of it is above my head . . . no layman can grasp words like parasympatheticotonia, but I feel strongly that one need not know anatomy and physiology to grasp the essentials of Vegeto-Therapy. To see them in English when I am unconscious of the language is truly delightful. Reich, the magazine is full of dynamite; it impresses more and more on me what I have long felt—that you are the only successor to Freud. You alone among them all have something new and great . . . makes me feel quite conceited to have "discovered" you!

I hope more copies are coming. I'd buy a lot but as you know I can't send money abroad. I want the whole of psychological Britain to see the number. But how? I could send copies for review to the P[sycho-] A[nalytical] Review, but then only an Ernest Jones* would review it and, of course, damn it. I could get my friend the editor of the *Lancet* to get it reviewed, but naturally he wouldn't guarantee a sympathetic review. The scientists—Haldane, etc.—know nothing of psychology, and the educational journals know less. I'll write a review and send it to the *New Statesman* or *Spectator* but there again they have so little space these days. But I'll try them. I am writing a new book on Education† as it should be in the coming socialist world, and I shall gladly write about the I.J. [*International Journal for Sex-Economy and Orgone Research*] there. It will appear this autumn, I hope. You will have much more opposition than Freud had. His "danger" was to the patient in the consulting room: your "danger" is to society. It will be a long hard fight but you will win, and I want to live to see the day that you are acknowledged to be right.

If I have any criticism of the journal it is that it is too scientific for the layman, too much written for the specialist. Clever members of my staff read it and fail to grasp the essentials, but when I try to explain, as one who went through the treatment (partly, alas) they begin to understand the words. Your method will succeed only when it by-passes the doctors and gets understood by the ordinary people who will feel its truth without needing a professional knowledge. One psychoanalyst here when I told him about V.T. said airily: "There is nothing new about it; it is all in Freud, and the Freudian analysis automatically frees all tensions." That is the type you want to by-pass, the man with a set system.

I am in the best of health, full of work energy and not conscious of any tensions or anxieties, somatically functioning well, too. Of course in these days there is the big anxiety about the future and the present.

---

* Leading exponent of Freudian psychoanalysis in Britain.

† *Hearts Not Heads in the School* (London: Herbert Jenkins, 1945). Pleads for an education of the emotions aimed at producing balanced rather than learned individuals. Bottled-up emotions tend to explode in destruction; if emotions are free, the intellect will look after itself. "Nothing," Neill writes, "will keep a healthy child from learning."

I think myself that Hitler won't last long although the pathological fellow will be the death of many yet. The spirit here is aggressive and the popular demand for action and a second front is strong. The great problem is why did Hitler attack Russia? If he hadn't we would have had a most terrible time. Whatever our view of Russia there have been no Quislings [traitors] there.

I can't get news of our Norway friends. Elsa Backer got permission to visit Oslo for three weeks (from Stockholm). She saw J. [Judith Bogen] who still has her Kindergarten, but the kids all are thin and much underfed. All adults in Oslo look thin, she says. I see in the *Times* that the Gestapo has arrested Per Krogh the artist. I knew him well, nice chap with no politics. I think they are arresting all the well-known men as hostages. They have guts in Norway.

Let us be hopeful. Let us phantasy a little . . . daydream that Stalin is right and that Hitler will be smashed in '42. Japan can't stand alone long. Then in summer '43 a bloke called Neill crosses to New York to have a long talk (and a long drink) with old Reich, a talk about the new world and the work to be done in it. I am now 58 and hate the idea, for I want to go on working for many many years. So just scrap your cancer research and find a few *bione* that will make me live to be a thousand.

Write soon. Send as many mags. as you can afford, and we'll start the vegeto ball rolling in this island.

———◆·◆———

Forest Hills, New York

May 19, 1942

My dear Neill,

I just received your good letter of April 28th. I do not think that we can avoid or that we should avoid the scientific physiological terms. You cannot do without them for they mean definite facts. I also believe that in a true democratic way we should not try to free the layman—a teacher is not quite a layman—from the responsibility to acquire a general knowledge of physiology and biology. For many years I have been trying to see how a better world could set up microscopes and charts about the body functions in public parks, instead of the foolish and useless lotteries they have now. The vegetative function of vagotonia and sympatheticotonia appears very simple if you present it

in the form of an opening and closing hand. The opening is the vagotonia and the closing the sympatheticotonia.

Your letter was most encouraging. We know here that we hit the
nail, but we never know whether the others also realize it. I think you
should not worry about whether the Joneses will write a positive or
negative critique. My experience is that a negative critique in our matter
mostly hits back at the critic. I would suggest that you send out as many
journals as possible to educational, psychiatric, psychological and
cultural institutions. We think it important that every reader gets the
feeling that the biophysical experiments and clinical observations are
and remain the core of all our psychological, educational and political
statements.

I wrote you already to ask you to write an article for the third
number of the journal. We would appreciate practical instances of how
children behave, especially when they come to the school from unfree
environments and how they adjust themselves to self-regulating* behavior. This problem is, I believe, the most important problem of
education and will be so in a truly free society.

My book† is being sent this week to you in many copies. I think that
the people who have not gone through the mill will understand the
journal better if they have read my book, which, according to people
who read it, is very easy to understand in spite of its scientific subject.

I was glad to learn that you changed from pessimism to optimism.
You remember that you looked upon me as a kind of utopist when I
said that the irrational in society cannot last for ever.

We had very encouraging word from Europe. I look forward to
seeing you in New York, and I mean it. You will not believe it, but my
orgone accumulators are far enough advanced to charge up living bodies
and I want you to have one. A long drink and a good long talk to go
along with it, and my European longings will be satisfied for a while
at least.

Did you receive the English translation of the *Work Democracy*? I
wonder what you think about it. Wolfe wants to publish it in the third
number of the journal. About 500 copies of the journal's first number

* Self-regulation, a way of rearing children which gives the child freedom to
develop without the imposition of adult demands or adult prohibitions. Summerhill
was run on self-regulation principles.
† *The Function of the Orgasm.*

went into the world. There is a funny kind of quiet around it. It is as if the people who avoided the main issue up to now are stunned that it is possible to dare to present the core of the plasmatic function and of sexuality.

When you read my book I ask you very much to write me about what you think is lacking in it. I myself think that the problem of adolescence has not been dealt with extensively enough; but having written a special book on youth, somehow I did not feel it necessary to present it extensively again. Or was it that I am growing older?

It was so good to hear that you are in good health. I have heard that Constance is in troubles, but I hope she stands them well. Why don't you take her as a member of your staff for some special work? I think she ought to be helped along in order not to be alone.

* * *

Summerhill School
Festiniog, North Wales

July 4th, 1942

My dear Reich,

Thanks for the signed copy of your book. I had to neglect my work to read it through at almost one sitting, and it struck me as being true all the time and all the way. It all seems so obvious, and it seems so clear to me that yours is the only post-Freud psychology to be considered. Thence, when this morning I get a letter from Rickman, Editor of the *British Journal of Medical Psychology*, thanking me for sending him a copy of the journal, I feel disturbed and angry when he writes: "It seems to me very poor stuff, and to take a narrow view of psychiatric problems, but it is young and may broaden out. But although I wish he would not talk in such old-fashioned sex jargon, he must express himself in the best way he can." The only other reply I have had was from Flugel. ". . . am finding R. most interesting reading. He is certainly an amazing fellow with an astonishingly wide outlook and a most useful power of synthesis. Orgone excites my curiosity a good deal. Walter Frank's article on Veg. Therapy I found particularly useful and it put me au fait with a lot of things, though I think he ought to give some credit to Cannon who in his book said substantially the same things but some ten years earlier." . . . I am sending out the mags. rather slowly because so many journals have been blitzed and have new addresses that it is hopeless to send to old addresses. And I fear the Rickman point of view will prevail.

I wrote to George Allen, of Allen and Unwin who are well-known publishers and modern, telling them about your *Orgasm* book and suggesting that they ought to consider publishing the book and being pioneers for Reichism. [Neill here discusses the journals that might review the first issue of Reich's *Journal for Sex-Economy and Orgone Research.*] The editor of *The Lancet* had a boy at this school and two years ago when I wanted to interest him in your *Bione* book he was sceptical and would not review it. No, Reich, you can expect nothing but hostility from established magazines, and your progress must come from your own group and its own magazine. You can't ask Jones, Flugel, Rickman to approve of you and thus confess that their life work has been wasted. That would be too great an optimism.

My "lay" staff (i.e. teachers untrained in science and psychology) are all fascinated with your magazine and eager to learn more, while the profession is hostile and arrogantly critical.

If I can find a publisher for the *F. of the Orgasm* have I your permission to make a deal with him? My only aim is to let England know of your work, and I guess that is all you want also. Your book is so patently original and wise that I am sure it would make history if published here even in wartime.

To come to my own affairs . . . life isn't easy. Troubles with staff. Most good teachers are in the war in some capacity and I am limited to Conscientious Objectors or old pensioners. The former all seem to have some limitation, some negative quality . . . I am sure they all have stiff stomachs. Your suggestion of giving Constance a job isn't practical so long as Suzanna* is a pupil, and to tell the truth I think that C. would not fit into a community life easily. I feel she tends to the autocratic in life and would clash with the system of majority rule, but maybe I am wrong.

Enclosed sheet isn't so much of a criticism as a query. I can't criticise much of your book because it is beyond my training and knowledge, and indeed many pages make me feel that I haven't been educated at all.

All the best and let us hope that Veg.-Therapy is to grow on both sides of the Atlantic.

* Constance Tracey's daughter.

Questions.

(a) The sign of cure in the adult is the reaching of the O. Reflex. But what is the criterion of cure in a child who is in the pre-orgastic stage? I suggest a happy face and a loose tummy?

(b) In the journal, I want to see an article: Why is Man a Moralist? by W.R. (I know he became one the first time he held his breath, but why did he hold his breath anyway?)

(c) Is sex repression by moral training enough? I ask because a stallion cannot perform the sexual act without the assistance of the keeper (*wer muss das Glied führen* [who should guide the member]). In domesticity the horse has no moral training, but his sex function apparently deteriorates. Why? Artificial food, housing, ventilation? And if so with domestic animals, how with domestic humans? Wrong food, clothes, beds, bad air in rooms, tobacco, alcohol, coffee, chairs and w.c.'s that give unnatural sitting? In short, can there be a universal natural orgastic life when the rest of life is unnatural? Trobriands may be fine fellows, but they don't have the Kultur that makes bombs and poison gas, prisons and politicians.

(d) The book throws more light on the adult than on the child. I feel you are afraid of children and avoid them.

———— ◆◆ ————

Summerhill School
Festiniog, North Wales

July 9, 1942

My dear Reich,

This letter looks hopeful.* Send me permission to negotiate with them. The Reich ball has been set rolling over here, and your books published here would sell well.

———— ◆◆ ————

---

* Enclosed was a short letter to Neill from the publishing firm of Allen and Unwin saying that they would be glad to have an opportunity of studying the psychological works of Reich and of examining the volume to which he had referred.

Orgonon
Rangeley, Maine

July 20th, 1942

My dear Neill:

I suppose that you have received several copies of my book meanwhile. I would appreciate it very much if you would let me know how it was received and which suggestions have been made as to its elaboration in the second edition. You will also receive very soon the second issue of the journal which brings some excerpts from your book *The Problem Teacher.* I would like to remind you again how useful it would be to have stories from your school related in our journal. But somehow, I don't seem to be able to penetrate your armor concerning such articles.

Before I left for Maine, I was visited by the vice-director of a New York State Hospital who has read the book, liked it and suggested that I begin to apply the Orgone on patients of different types at the hospital. I don't know if something will come of it, but if it does, there will be rapid progress. By the way, did you build an Orgone Accumulator for yourself according to my description? I want you to have it. It does a really good job in building up strength and killing bad stuff in the blood. You have only to build a closet to sit in with inner metal lining and an outer wood lining and cotton or wood shavings or sawdust or earth in the space between the two linings. Such a closet can be used to fight colds, sinus troubles, flu, anemia and similar things. It is not dangerous in any way and it really helps. You may trust me, in spite of the fact that I am the inventor.

By the way, when do you come over to New York? It would be a marvellous idea.

I shall ask Dr. Wolfe to send you some more copies of the journal which you will perhaps be able to send over by plane to Sweden.

P.S. I was just about to mail this letter when I received yours of July 4th. I was very glad to have it. Now to every single important point:

1) I am happy that you like the book. I only wonder why honesty gives one so much stomach ache in the process of production. I guess it's rational cowardice.

2) Don't mind Rickman, he always was and is the type of psycho-analyst who escaped the Freudian primary truth. Well, they will hear more from me about sex and orgone. As to Flugel, I think his attitude

is fair. I shall find out whether he is right in saying that Cannon said "the same things ten years ago" So, please, convince Flugel of my deep sincerity concerning quoting from others.

3) It is a pity that the Orgasm book should be reprinted in England when 3000 copies have been printed here.

4) You are completely correct in saying that we can rely on no one but ourselves, that we alone are responsible for what happens to our science. Edison would have been a fool to expect the acknowledgment of the electric bulb by the manufacturers of the gas lamps.

5) You have, of course, my consent, to have published in England whatever and however you wish, as long as no publisher succeeds in censoring what I have to say.

Now to your questions, which are very significant and important. You are not right that I am afraid of children. Children like me very much and I like them. But I do not know enough about children, not having worked with them and only knowing them through the reflection of my work with grown-ups. Why should I go to child biology if there are such marvellous child educators as A. S. Neill, etc. who can apply orgone bio-physics to children much better than I could. And (b) "Why is Man a Moralist?" is being dictated just in these days after many sleepless nights and stomach convulsions [spasms] which filled my wife with fear for my future and the outcome of my brain development. I have once tried to answer this question in my book *Der Einbruch der Sexualmoral** on the basis of the influence which is taken upon the human organism by socio-economic processes. Still, the answer why the human being is a moralist, i.e. afraid of the nature within himself, was unanswered. In *The Function of the Orgasm* some answer is given by working out the function of the pleasure-anxiety which is created by muscular spasms in the pelvis, on the background of historical economic processes. But still the answer is not complete. Maybe man held his breath for the first time in order to choke his orgastic feelings when the first mother, subjugated for the first time by her husband, who had been subjugated for the first time by his economic chief, in turn for the first time subjugated her child when this child masturbated. That leads up to your question,

---

* *Der Einbruch der Sexualmoral*, 1932 (*The Invasion of Compulsory Sex-Morality*, 1971). Reich's first attempt to explain the origins of sexual repression and their connection to neurotic disturbances.

whether training alone is enough to explain sex-repression. I would think yes. No wild stallion needs the assistance of any keeper. The domesticity of animals is entirely a moral training, because the natural sex function is not lived any more according to natural rules, but according to the opinion of man as to when a young horse or a young calf should be born. All the things you mention, wrong food, clothing, etc. are in their last meaning nothing but evasion of nature, and of course, there can be no universal orgastic life if the rest of life is unnatural. And as to the value of culture "that makes bombs, poison gas, prisons and politicians," I believe it is destroying itself and the level of the life of the Trobriands will be back soon—and happily.

Write again, Neill, you are not only the only important European connection, but more than that, you are an honest good friend, and I am proud that you are a member of the Institute.

———— ◆•◆ ————

Orgonon
Rangeley, Maine

July 29th, 1942

My dear Neill,

Your letter of July 9th concerning the publisher, has just arrived. You have, of course, my permission to negotiate with them, and also to make the contracts. The main point in such a contract would be that

(a) the publisher has no right to censor, to change or to leave out anything of the text without my consent.

As to the translation, I think that it would be sufficient if they translate the book and if you revise it. I would only like to stress the following points:

a) The fascism book* was written ten years ago, when I still had some confidence in the Marxists. The book contains therefore many Marxist expressions, expressing my own viewpoints. Words like communism, communistic, proletarian, socialistic and so forth. These words have meanwhile lost their meaning completely. Not only because of the behavior of the Marxists, but mainly because of the new formulations of our work-democratic concepts. The word "worker" does not mean the

---

* *The Mass Psychology of Fascism.*

handworker alone in distinction from the intellectual. "Work" means all branches of labor, which are indispensable for the process of society, a physician in this sense, or a teacher, is not less important than a machinist. All such words should be eliminated and be replaced by the simple word revolutionary, revolution, etc. When I shall hear from you that the deal is made then I shall go through the book and shall add footnotes at the places where it is necessary to bring the book up to date. But the text in the whole should, out of historical reasons, remain unchanged.

b) To cover the development of our social knowledge up to date, I believe it would be advisable to have an appendix printed which would contain either my pamphlets about "Work Democracy" or a summary of these pamphlets. To bring out the book about fascism would be rather useful. I know that it is read all over Germany and Austria in the underground movement. People like it, and it is more true today than it was ten years ago.

The second issue of our journal has just come out and you will receive many copies.

I am writing an article for the third issue and have spent the last four weeks worrying tremendously about how to handle the incapability of the masses to govern themselves. This incapability was entirely overlooked by all free social movements, and the result was that social freedom was crushed again and again. You can't tell the people that they are incapable of freedom and be liked. I am afraid I shall have to choose the truth instead of being liked. It is a tough problem. And don't look please upon it from the standpoint of your school. Look at this incapability for freedom from the standpoint of 2000 million people on this earth and you will see what I mean. Object sharply, if you have objections. I tried to find objections to my statement myself.

———— ◆◆◆ ————

Orgonon
Rangeley, Maine

August 6, 1942

My dear Neill,

I have looked through the second German edition of *Die Massenpsychologie des Faschismus* and become convinced that it would be very bad to publish it as it is now. The book is permeated with Marxian slogans which lost their meaning completely meanwhile. For instance, I am speaking about the bourgeois human, but meanwhile we learned that the so-called proletariat is in its structure not less bourgeois than the bourgeois. I have to replace such words by other words which reflect the real meaning in a better way.

I don't want to be taken for a Marxist any more, in spite of the fact that I have a higher regard and a better understanding of Marx's achievement than I had then. And I cannot subdue the insights of our new biological findings to old and wrong concepts. I believe that the elimination of the empty slogans and the addition of the new bio-psychological and work-democratic facts, will bring the book up to date without changing its factual content. I am going ahead with the adjustment of the book and the publisher will obtain a copy of the manuscript in case he decides to publish it.

———◆•◆———

Orgonon
Rangeley, Maine

August 20, 1942

My dear Neill:

This letter is to ask your opinion about an idea which I had lately in connection with the further development of our work. I have encountered some uneasy feelings about describing the actual political and social tasks in plain language as I was used [to do] in Europe. You must understand that—in spite of the fact that American democracy is, due to the American Revolution, far more free of traditional thinking than the European world, and much further advanced in dealing with the "common man"—there are besides that still prevailing attitudes which don't like to see heavy scientific stuff brought forth together with actual social policy which never lacks the taste of the "soap box." I myself have the feeling that a pamphlet about "Work Democracy" which has been translated in England is too political in its nature to be quietly accepted together with the findings about the orgone. Yet they are closely connected; but not for the feeling of the average individual. I don't wish to yield to conservative views, but we have to be flexible where flexibility does not hamper our truth. In short: What would you think of editing a special journal in English within England's borders called, say, Work Democracy, Journal for the Social Evaluation of Depth Psychology and Orgone Biophysics. It would train specialists in social work; it would explain what work democracy is, its history, different work-democratic trends in different places in the world, as for instance, the new work democratic Labor-Management Committees which begin to function in America; the natural existence of work democracy in primitive society; the difference of formal, parliamentary from natural work democracy, and so forth. I believe firmly that we should weigh the idea and prepare for its possible realization. Please tell me whether you would be willing and capable of directing the issuance of such a journal under the auspices of the Institute, with the help of your co-workers in England. I expect your advice as quickly as possible.

Did you receive the second issue of the *Journal* yet? And did you receive enough copies? The *Journal* and the book are received very well here: in a Westchester, New York, newspaper I was proclaimed again, as in France and in England, as the successor of Freud. I only hope that this honor will not make people forget that the succession of Freud's discoveries has been added to by a new, decisive discovery of its own. I would like to hear more about you personally than you have let me know recently.

Did you have an Orgone Box built for yourself? Why not?? Give my best regards to all friends over there and also my best wishes for the future.

———◆◆———

Summerhill School
Festiniog, North Wales

August 24, 1942

My dear Reich,

I have just got your long letter. At the moment I am in Edinburgh having a Cure with Thomson the naturopath. All summer I have not felt well. Always tired. Having no faith at all in the ordinary doctor with his drugs, I am trying the only alternative offered me. I shall return to wet Wales unwillingly, for there is little chance of exercise there. Also the work is full of difficulties these days. The kids are as always delightful; it is the adults who give trouble. My original staff left to help the war, and the children whose fathers and mothers are all in the war don't like the pacifist attitude.

I see I am telling you all this partly to explain why I have not done enough about the magazines. I sent out copies to the well-known psychological mags, and only Rickman replied. I am keeping my eyes open for reviews. I can't see how I can send any literature to Sweden or

Switzerland. The law here is that only the publisher or a recognised bookseller can dispatch books abroad.

I still don't know what to do about distribution. I show the journal or the book to the ordinary reading man—teacher, doctor, etc. He is delighted with it, wants to know more about your work. The big man, the man with a name, doesn't even reply thanking me. The big man in any line hates to hear of another's good work.

No, I never made the Orgone Accumulator because material is impossible to get, especially metals. I can only spend one pound a month buying wood. Also, I forget about my own health until I break down. But I wish I could set one up. You know how ignorant I am of science. In my ignorance I don't understand the cage as you describe it in your letter, and I don't recollect your ever telling me how to make it. If in a letter, it must have gone down.

I don't like to hear about your stomach convulsions. You must live another 40 years, friend. I want to live long enough to see you king of the new Trobriands, so to speak. This cursed dependence on the body is so tiresome. I want to work and forget all about the damned body, and then the body has its revenge and stops the work. If the span of life were 150 years or so, a man could do something in his life. I feel bitterly about the body at present. The pleasure went out of the Reflex two months ago, and I have been sexless since then. I can't decide which is cause and effect. Or how much an age of 59 affects the world of desire in general.

Well, I shall wait and write more cheerfully when I get some health back. I have no news from Stockholm.

————◆•◆————

Summerhill School
Festiniog, North Wales

September 25, 1942

My dear Reich,

Your letter came today just as I sat down to write you. I am touched by your concern and most grateful for your advice re: the BOX. I am not clear on a few points. (1) Must I sit in it naked, or does the Orgone work through clothing? (2) Wood is most difficult to obtain. It is severely rationed. Would a small room lined with tin sheeting do? Behind the sheeting would be brick or wood and plaster. I am trying to buy a moveable wardrobe or cupboard which I could line, but do tell me if tin will do. After all, tin is thin iron sheeting dipped in molten tin.

Reich, I have so complete a faith in your genius that when you tell me the box is the "goods" I believe you, and I accept it without requiring any proof. Your Journal No. 2 convinces me entirely, and it by the way is much better than No. 1 in my estimation.

I returned from Thomson's much better. I think his "theory" all bunk, but his practice certainly is good and gets results in physical *but not in psychical health*. It does not release the orgastic reflex, indeed nature cure is anti-sex and Calvinistic and moral. I go to it simply because it does not treat bodily symptoms. I should think that this "cleansing" diet plus your box should keep a man alive to the age of 150 or so.

Smoking I still keep off but as to drink I have no intention of keeping off it. With whiskey at over £1 a bottle and wine almost unprocurable I guess alcohol won't be any problem during this war anyway.

Life is more complex with me now. War conditions are not easy. True we are safe from bombs in Wales, but it is always wet and relaxing and far from all culture and companionship. I can't get teachers or if I can they are usually inferior—mostly conscientious objectors to military service, negative folk who won't face reality. Then with an invalid wife I have a double load to carry, having to do a thousand things I never had to do before . . . food, servants, children's clothing, etc. And settling the differences of opinion among the female staff who all want to have things their own way. But in the main things are tolerable. So far the children haven't suffered for lack of good food, but they suffer for lack of good exercise, for in this mountain land there isn't one flat field for hockey or football, and the snow is never good enough or lies long enough for winter sports.

Of late I have taken up in an amateurish way scientific agriculture. Here the land is very poor and no good farmer will sell manure. My problem was to feed 100 people on home-grown veg. and fruit. I have the same attitude to inorganic artificial manures that I have to drugs in medicine; both are dead things, and artificial manure can never make the first essential to growth—humus, which must come from decayed organic stuff. Hence my problem has been to compost all veg. rubbish so as to get good manure. Unfortunately grass, nettles etc. will not make a compost without animal manure, but I was lucky enough to buy 20 tons of mule dung, and have some fine heaps now. I am most interested in the ideas of Sir Albert Howard* who says that all spraying of trees with tobacco, mercury, etc. is wrong, merely treating symptoms. He traces all plant diseases back to poor soil and manures, and says that in India he had cows on grass artificially manured and they took foot and mouth disease, but in the next field he had cows on naturally manured pasture and they rubbed noses over the fence with the infected cows but none of them contracted the disease. The trouble is that an editor of a *Gardener's Weekly* can't easily condemn artificials when so doing would lose an advertisement worth £2,000 a year, say. This may be boring to you; it only shows how land-minded the war makes us all. You will guess by all this that the war has converted me from a psychologist into a damned farmer . . . not much difference between the two, for both waste time dealing with muck, yet it is better to fork farmyard muck than to sit and listen to psychic repressed muck.

Well, Reich, I shall end this rambling letter. Do answer the main questions . . . . must one be naked? Is stone suitable instead of sawdust, etc?

P.S. A thought: That cancer case in No. 2 Journal. Danger . . . unskilled men will put their cases in the Box, cure the cancer, or rather reconvert it into sex repression and not know how to deal with it then. Probable result, too much suicide. How to cure what causes it. Another thought: A parent, expert in radio, says: "I sit in a Faraday box† for hours at a time, testing apparatus. Neither I nor anyone else in the profession have ever noticed any difference to health or skin. Ask Reich why the effects of an F. Cage hasn't been discovered by the many engineers who have used one." He says that the cage can be of copper wire netting of one inch mesh. That sounds odd to me.

———◆◆◆———

* *An Agricultural Testament*, by Sir Albert Howard (London: Oxford University Press, 1940).

† Better known as a Faraday cage. An electrostatic shield made of wire mesh or a series of parallel wires.

[1942]

Forest Hills, New York

October 17, 1942

My dear Neill:

I have just received your letter of September 25th. I am glad that you are ready to use the Orgone Accumulator and I am hurrying to answer your questions. The outer walls can be of stone too, but it would be better if you would fill the gap between the inner metal lining and the stone wall with, say, newspaper. The main point in the functioning of the box in regard to the organism is that the inner metal lining should not be at a greater distance from the body than six to eight inches. If your closet has the dimensions of *about* five feet high, three feet deep and two feet wide, then it is all right. That answers your thought concerning the radio operator within the Faraday cage, who did not observe any effects. A Faraday cage has too big holes in the metal wall, also the metal walls are too far removed from the body. Well, I want you to make all the experiences quite by yourself, but you have to use the Orgone accumulator every day once or twice for about a half hour and for weeks and months in one stretch.

I want you to do that also for another purpose. The longer the war will stretch, the more diseases will arise, the more the value of a cheap and highly effective biological energy will be appreciated by the common people, and I want you to have the experiences gathered by then.

Your discourse on manure and *Maul und Klauenseuche* [foot and mouth disease] was a great help. I understood suddenly from what you told about Howard's work, that the chemical industries are not only not curing diseases, but more, they are creating diseases, and I am going right ahead to clear that question. Thank you for your suggestion.

It is better that you are naked than with clothes on within the box, and please, watch your temperature, whether it rises when you are in the box for some time and how much.

Your suggestion regarding the danger of easy cancer cure is very true. I had it myself. But let's see later, first we have to put the boxes into action. Write again soon and much.

———◆•◆———

[1942]

Summerhill School
Festiniog, North Wales

November 9, 1942

My dear Reich,

I have been expecting to hear from you for weeks now. Failing to get anything out of psychological journals here, I suggested to Constance that since there were so few copies of your works in England, the best way would be to form a circulating library. I advertised that your books were on loan from Constance, at so much a time, just enough to cover expense of advertising, postage, etc. The enclosed letter shows that some people are interested. This is well; unknown folks read the books and slowly your ideas spread. Barnes, the man who tried to translate one of your books, writes that he would like to start a journal popularising your theories. I didn't encourage him, I said that since you were sending out the journal, the best way would be to use that as the central authority. What do you think?

I am still working away amid difficulties and wet weather . . . N. Wales is the wettest part of the island, I believe. But the war news on N. Africa has made me feel much more cheerful. I can't see that Hitler has the least chance of winning now. The Allies will smash Germany and Italy; they will surely go red, and what then? In my *Problem Teacher* book, finished just as the war began, I wrote: "The war is fundamentally a class war." I still hold that is so, and fear greatly that when it is won humanity will split up again into for and against socialism.

Write soon. I miss your letters now.

My wife gets frailer and her mind is infantile. I am trying hard to find a Home for her. It is pretty awful to see her now and most depressing.

P.S. I am smoking again!

Later. Your letter just arrived. I want to make that cage, but how can I here? A house without central heating to save coal and coke; every room very full of people; material impossible to buy except for national importance work. It will have to wait till I can do it properly.

Had lunch with Rickman. Impossible to talk to him about Veg.-Therapy. Gets worked up and bitter about it all . . . "It turns on what is a real orgasm. R. can't prove that his idea of an orgasm is better than any other man's." It is uphill work doing anything here owing to shortage of paper so that reviews are cut down to a minimum. I simply can't get any editor to allow a review of the *Function of the Orgasm*. The growth is slow, but the people who are reading your work here, though a small group, are those who at least have an open mind for something new.

I am glad that you seem to think that drugs are as evil as artificial manures. It must poison a body to dose it with mercury or tar products and all the artificial nostrums of the big drug combines.

———— ◆•◆ ————

Forest Hills, New York

November 24, 1942

My dear Neill:

I did not hear from you in a long time and I wonder why. This letter is to ask you about the nature of the "Progressive League." I am wondering whether the events of the last 10 years have taught the Huxleys, Russells, Wells, Wests, Burts, Flugels, etc. such a lesson as to make them more ready to accept and to propagate a sex-affirmative and sex-economic point of view in education and social action than ten years ago.

Two weeks ago I was approached here in New York by a group of people who are working at sociology departments of universities, in birth-control clinics and organizations etc. who asked me to attend a meeting in which they try gropingly to build up a sex-political organization. Though I have not much time now, being very busy with students and research as well as writing, I would like to take up again the Sex Pol work which I have done in Europe. Therefore I would appreciate if you would kindly give me information about the actual activities and the factual sincerity of this English organization. The main question is: Are they ready and willing to enter the fight for sex-economic affirmation of the natural love life of children and adolescents within the frame of the present fight for a new world; the substance of which everybody knows but nobody likes to call by its proper name.

Do you think it feasible to organize an English branch of the Orgone Institute Press, in order to make the distribution of our literature more easy in the United Kingdom? Could you provide the necessary money for it as we do here? After a certain length of time the publications pay back by income and directly by sales. We have met here, so far, with very great interest and appreciation.

Some days ago I received a manuscript of Raknes from Sweden. They are working there very bravely and intelligently. Let's hope the time is not too far away when we shall all be together and concentrate upon the many questions which are in our mind concerning mental misery . . .

Please write me about yourself too, whether you are using the Orgone Accumulator and what kind of experiences you are making with it.

———————— ◆ ◆ ————————

Forest Hills, New York

December 22, 1942

My dear Neill:

I received your letter of November 9th some days ago. The physicist whose letter you sent me is a typical mechanist who uses words where understanding is lacking. I don't mind his saying that I do not know much about physics because the cosmic biophysical energy, Orgone, was discovered by me and not by him, and I am ready to leave the physical knowledge to him and to solve the problems of the Orgone by myself, even if "without knowledge." To illustrate his complete confusion of thinking, I refer to a passage in his letter where he writes that "the twinkling of stars is caused by strong currents of cold air flowing in the upper layers of the earth's atmosphere." If you put together 100 physicists and one phenomenon, then you will hear 100 different kinds of words and interpretations of one and the same phenomenon, pronounced with the greatest dignity of pure science. I am glad to have rid myself of the respect for this kind of science. To illustrate that I am justified in doing so: A week or so ago I visited the New York Planetarium with my wife. Even our physicist will admit that in such a planetarium there are no layers of air in great heights and yet the artificial stars were twinkling. I am sure he will have a different explanation for this phenomenon in the Planetarium. He also overlooked the experimental reproduction of the twinkling of the stars in any orgone accumulator, by simply drilling a few holes into the walls and looking at them in the dark while a dim green light is shining inside. The task of natural science for thousands of years was always to reduce hundreds of thousands of different facts to one and the same principle and not, what most of the so-called physicists do, to explain one and the same fact with hundreds of thousands of words. In short, the attitude of your physicist is deeply irrational and identical with the irrationalism in all mechanistic and metaphysical science.

Why do you try so hard to convince the Rickmans? They are quite unimportant and I don't believe that it is useful even to try. Other younger, more daring and better thinking people in the coming generations will come and take up our matter and carry it to social consequences. I am not worried about that.

I am very glad and thankful for what you are doing to spread knowledge about my work. Good things do penetrate, but only slowly. I don't want you to get disappointed.

I would not object to a magazine popularizing our knowledge if it were to be done well.

I am cross at you that you don't follow my advice to have an Orgone Accumulator built immediately and use it. There is some kind of resistance in you against it if you permit me to be quite frank. I assure you that it would do you much good.

I wish all of you there a pleasant New Year and much success in it. My wife is joining me in these wishes. We have sent you a small package with some, not much, useful things in it.

————◆◆————

Summerhill School
Festiniog, North Wales

December 29, 1942

My dear Reich,

Many thanks for your Xmas gift. The coffee is *wunderbar* [wonderful] and the chocolate better than our own here. It was kind of you to think of it. I am just off to Scotland to lecture and if possible play some golf if it doesn't snow. I have tried to think out how I can build an Accumulator, but in war time you have no idea how difficult things are. Even things like nails and screws are impossible to get in some places, and sheet metal can't be bought. Then there is the question of heating. This year I have no central heating—to save fuel; but if I could make one, I could at least use it in summer. Is it possible to make a bed enclosed in one? That would solve the question of heat and also the question of time. But if a whole night of Orgones would be good for health I don't know. I haven't heard recently from Constance as to how the Library is going. I find it uphill work trying to interest people, handicapped as I am being so far from the centre of things. My latest attempt was to send the book and journals to Dr. Harry Roberts who writes of medical and psychological things in the *New Statesman* and *Nation*. The Freudians are going to *tot-schweigen* you [kill you by silence] and they have so big a say in journal reviews these days. Then there is the uprooting from the war. The psychologists are all scattered, in hospitals, the army, etc. Private practice has almost ceased in London. I sent out journals to Harley Street* men and question if they ever got them. How are you being received in U.S.A.? Where do you get the capital to carry on printing and research apparatus? There must be good people who are interested and helpful.

I am well but never really happy in exile in Wales. The climate, the Calvinism, the difficulty getting staff, they all get me down. I long to get back to the east coast. So many little pleasures have gone. I have no car now and have to queue up for buses that are always overcrowded. Whiskey is £2 a bottle. I have no golf, no recreation except dull digging in the garden. This isn't a grumble; millions are much worse off; it is only an attempted explanation. But next term I am going to return to treating kids psychologically and teach less. What troubles me is that I can't write now. I began a book on the future of education, wrote three chapters . . . and stuck. First time I ever stuck with a book. I require a few months on Willy Reich's sofa. I long for the end of the war and a crossing of the Atlantic.

---

* Where fashionable London doctors had their offices.

1943

Forest Hills, New York

February 10, 1943

My dear Neill:

I have your letter of December 29th. I get the impression that you are still preoccupied with the idea that the Freudians and other psychologists should embrace us. You will be disappointed all the time if you won't accept your own judgment, which you expressed some time ago, namely: The ones who are losing ground in fact and in theory cannot be glad about work which just shows them what they are omitting. Please stop trying so hard to convince psychologists. I personally don't try to convince anyone, but simply present the facts as accurately and truthfully as possible.

Some of my students like your books very much. They are distributing them and many discussions are held about your viewpoints.

Our work is proceeding slowly, with many difficulties, but surely; and more and more people take notice of it and like it. But I have reconciled myself to the idea that in our lifetime the pestilence* will apparently go on devastating human life. It is, of course, understandable that we would like to see what we hold true become true also for everyone else, but I have no illusions about that for the next twenty years at least. It is very

---

* Also "pest," "emotional pestilence"—i.e., "emotional plague"—which Reich defines as follows: " 'Emotional plague' is a strictly scientific term to denote evil social action from irrational motives with irrational evil results" (October 7, 1951). Elsewhere, he calls it "an endemic epidemic of much larger dimensions than cholera and typhoid" (February 9, 1945).

87

painful to realize the situation as it really is and to see the deep fear the human being has of his own possibilities.

———————◆◆◆

Summerhill School
Festiniog, North Wales

February 23, 1943

My dear Reich,

Your letter came and today No. 3 Journal which I have read with great pleasure. I shall sell the journals and books that Constance doesn't need for the library. So far, I have not done this because the buyers would almost certainly be the wrong people . . . partly the rubber-necks who always seek what is new and forget it at once. But it is the only way. I think I can get permission to send out the proceeds of sales. The money I gave you when you emigrated before the war was a gift towards your cancer research.

Do not be annoyed at my not making an Accumulator, for you have no idea of the position here. Food we have enough of, and clothing, but one can't buy wood or metal without a government permit. I have tried for months—in vain—to get wood for necessary repairs and for the children's woodwork classes. I can't buy a short rod of brass and sheet metal cannot be obtained unless one is helping the war effort. Again, you have no idea of the housing question. We are 100 people in a house built for 20. Children even sleep in passages sometimes. The staff has no staffroom. Domestic servants are called up for the army or munitions, and we all have to work. I spend much of my day mending windows, stoking furnaces, sifting cinders, gardening, and no longer can give nearly as much time as I should give to the children. Luckily, they are all normal now. I tell you, Reich, that I should welcome an Accumulator where I might retire for health and peace for a bit daily.

I have had to send my wife away to a Mental Home, and that is not a pleasant duty. And within two days I have news of deaths of old boys [former pupils], one of them Elsa Backer's boy killed flying in Canada. It isn't easy to feel optimistic with all this sorrow around. To see youth die for the mistakes of all of us is never pleasant. Must the Son always be crucified?

You took the criticism of the radio man too seriously. He is only mechanical and was quite sincere in his criticism. He devours all you write and is a Reich enthusiast about Sex-Economy.

I am trying to get on with my new book, the one on the Future of Education. So many people are writing rubbish about it that I feel I ought to contribute my share of it also.

I am out of touch with the Sex Societies you mention, being buried in the country as I am, but at Easter I go to London and will enquire. I fear London Sex Societies. Used to lecture for Norman Haire's one and found that audiences were mostly neurotics, betraying their interest when Norman became pornographic. I fear that such societies attract the voyeur, the repressed homo, etc. But there must be good people in them who should be approached.

You tell me I shouldn't bother about the Rickmans. I do because they control publicity in the psych. magazines. There are "popular" magazines but it would be unwise to be taken up by them, for they, by necessity, must be guarded in their statements about sex.

I feel a little guilty about not doing enough to get in contact with these societies, even though I know that I have far too much work and worry here. For one thing, most energetic people are in the war, and societies tend to get filled with pacifists and cranks. I have nothing against pacifists as pacifists, but I have had a succession of them as teachers (one can't get anyone else) and I am fed up with their incompetence and dreaminess and negative attitude to life. Indeed my staff exhaust me much more than the pupils do, and visitors often ask: "Why do you have such normal children and such a neurotic staff?" I don't want to give the impression that I have only grumbles. Rather call them difficulties. No playing fields for children, too mountainous. No wood, etc. for them to make things with, no good teachers. Result, they do destruction, not from hate, simply from boredom. And the Welsh church protested because they played hockey on a Sunday. *Mein Gott!* You can understand my wish to get back to England. On the optimistic side, the demand for Summerhill is so great now that I have a waiting list of 80 pupils I can't find room for. I am not making money because I did not increase the fees with the war, but the money side never worries me . . . Scots don't think much of money.

My o. reflex has returned and that part of life is fine.

I am just about to write the chapter on Sex of my book, and if it seems good I'll send it to Wolfe for the next No. of the journal.

That is about all my news this time.

P.S. The journal gets better each time. I wish we could get it circulated and appreciated over here. Tell me how America receives your work.

———————◆◆◆———————

Forest Hills, New York

April 1, 1943

My dear Neill:

I am writing in a hurry and thus this letter will not be very long. I received your February letter. I am so sorry that you have these worries with your wife, but for the rest I feel that you are getting along fine. We are waiting eagerly for your article for the 2nd issue of the journal this year.

The orgone research is making slow but steady progress. Just two months ago I succeeded in demonstrating the biological pulsation function of the orgone in a purely physical manner; that means a great deal.

I am glad that you like the journal. We hope to improve it still more. Our work is accepted in the U.S. very nicely. First of all, there are only very few pestilent reactions to it. Second, some journals have reviewed our publications objectively and kindly. About 26 Orgone accumulators are already distributed amongst students and lay people. My publications are widely read at universities; some sociologists especially are very much interested and I have received some rather encouraging letters. I wait eagerly for the moment when we shall be able to meet again either here or in Europe in order to organize the international set-up. I mean organize in our way, the free way, and not the bureaucratic way.

Your books are spreading slowly but surely among our students and their friends. I already see you lecturing here sometime. A small kindergarten group is slowly forming. I firmly believe that sex-economy will mainly be in the hands of educators rather than physicians, and rightly so.

My wife and I are working very hard to build up the Orgone Laboratories in Maine. The Institute has acquired a farm of 160 acres, beautifully situated.* I hope to concentrate all the research and teaching

---

* In Rangeley, Maine. Reich named this property "Orgonon."

up there in the course of the next few years. Even money seems to loom on the horizon.

I still want you to have the accumulator built. You simply have to. It will give you strength and will build up your blood, and you will enjoy it.

———— ◆◆ ————

Forest Hills, New York

May 14, 1943

My dear Neill:

I am enclosing a preliminary draft of our [by]-laws [for incorporation of the Orgone Institute in the United States]. You know that I hate such formalities as much as you do, but the more the influence of the Institute grows—and it does grow—the more necessary are provisions to safeguard its existence and functioning against the diverse influences of the emotional pestilence.

I want you to know that the orgone research has cost me $24,000 out of my own earnings since 1939. My wife and I are living on about $200 a month, i.e., much less than a worker in a war factory receives. This is only to explain the formula contained in the by-laws. It means only that I would get back the money which I have put in. The discovery of the orgone has been donated to the International Institute.

The students of our Institute here are reading your books with the utmost interest and benefit. Your name has spread very far in educational circles.

Our work is continuing unhampered and with some recognition in many parts of the U.S. as well as in South America and Palestine. When the big crash will come again I don't know; but this time I have decided not to keep quiet, as in Oslo, but to fight back with all our knowledge and influence.

I would be glad to receive a letter from you as soon as possible about everything worth knowing. My best wishes to you and all friends over there, and for a quick finish to this chaos.

———— ◆◆ ————

Orgonon
Rangeley, Maine

July 5, 1943

My dear Neill,

I did not hear from you for months, and I cannot make out what the trouble is. This letter is only a short note to remind you that we are still existing here, and that we wish to be kept informed constantly about you personally, your work, your troubles and joys, and about everything worth knowing.

I assume you received already Dr. Wolfe's letter in which he suggests that you send to Sweden regularly copies of the book, *The Discovery of the Orgone*, and issues of the journal. We cannot send them from here because of transportation difficulties.

With my best wishes to you and all.

———————◆◆◆———————

Summerhill School
Festiniog, North Wales

August 3, 1943

My dear Reich,

I haven't written you for a long time. I wonder why. Mainly because of a sense of failure and frustration in making your work known over here. Journals and books came by post, and I had no clear idea what Wolfe and you wanted me to do with them. I sent copies to various scientists and publicists, and either got no reply or an adverse one as I got from H. G. Wells, who read the 3 journals and wrote me: "You have sent me an awful gabble of competitive quacks. Reich misuses every other word, and Wolfe is a solemn ass. There is not a gleam of fresh understanding in the whole bale."* Then the idea of a

———————

* To this letter Neill replied:
Dear Wells,

I can't understand why you are so damned unpleasant about it. I considered you the man with the broadest mind in England and sincerely wanted light on a biological matter I wasn't capable of judging myself. Your Black Out letter might have been written by Colonel Blimp. I hoped you would give an opinion on bions and orgones, whether they are a new discovery or not, and all I got was a tirade against Reich. You apply the word "quack" to a man whom Freud considered brilliant, a man who has slaved for years in a lab seeking truth.

I grant that I asked for it. I intruded. I apologise and . . . being a Scot . . .

lending library seemed a good one and Constance did nobly here, but again the sense of failure, in that the borrowers were *unbedeutend* [insignificant] neurotics seeking a personal salvation. Lately, I approached the biggest medical library in England, and they agreed to try to sell the Book, but would not have the journals. They have sold 8 already.

Then I had to fight doubts in myself. When the new number came the other day, No. 1 of Vol. 2, my doubts seemed to fade out automatically, but, being so uneducated in science, I haven't been able to judge the pros and cons for myself. Scientists said Reich doesn't know enough about electricity or physics or what not, and all I had to counter that was my faith in your genius. My only defence was the thought: R. is right about psychology, and he can't then be a fool about biology. So I have had to face two attitudes: the common man who reads you and says, This is damned interesting, but of course I can't judge its value; and the scientist who says: False premises, unprovable assumptions (orgones), no good. The common man cannot help you because he is ignorant, and unless the trained scientist accepts you, I don't see how you are to succeed. Cannot a man like Einstein give a definite opinion that would settle all the little scientists? No. 4 Journal is fascinating. Makes me long to try the Accumulator which I can't possibly build before peace comes. Which makes me ask why you don't give each mouse its own Acc[umulator] made from a cocoa tin in a wooden box?

My own news now. Wife still in a Home costing more than I can afford. Money a great worry now; school losing owing to high prices and taxation. Over 100 pupils waiting to come into the school but no room for them, and the present ones can't pay high fees. Outlook for pioneer schools not bright. The big unions of teachers, trade unions, etc. all demand the abolition of the private school, and certainly it cannot live very long now, and under the State, socialist or otherwise, there can be no real freedom to pioneer. Most Communist Party members have disapproved of S'hill, even those whose children were pupils here.

---

refund your postage . . . But this is no quarrel, and I won't bother you again with Reich or anyone else. Yours sincerely, etc.

To be answered in turn by Wells:

Dear Neill,
    No, I decline your stamps, but this business is quackery. You call me a Blimp, I call you a Sucker. Bless you, H. G. Wells.

As a body, the C.P. is totally ignorant of psychology, and worse still, considers it a bastard science.

I have finished my book* and it is in the press. I shall send on a proof for Wolfe to see if he can fit it into the journal. You ask if I can send copies of your book and journals to Sweden. I can't. I enquired and only letters and postcards are allowed by air mail—the only mail to Sweden.

The structure of the Orgone Institute seems o.k. to me. It looks foolproof and proof against exploitation. I don't yet know how I can stand financially to it, for at the moment my income is less than my expenditure. The dollars I lent you in peace days I do not want repaid; they are my small contribution to the good work.

School goes well. 150 waiting to get in if I had room. No solution to the sex question. Most parents want the status quo. My article will show how little advance I have made.

Just off to Scotland for a few weeks. Have let myself get run down. I wish I had an Accumulator.

———◆•◆———

Orgonon
Rangeley, Maine

August 19, 1943

My dear Neill:

We don't understand your keeping silent for so long. Keeping contact now seems to me of the utmost importance, since in a few months or a year or so we may face very huge and responsible tasks. We can operate only very badly if no contact is kept. It is personally unpleasant as well as factually. I hope you don't mind my frankness, but I am not only speaking for myself, but also for some teachers who are eager to learn more from you and even to try to get you over here for lectures, or, maybe, for good.

———◆•◆———

---

* Probably *Hearts Not Heads in the School,* not published until 1945.

Orgonon
Rangeley, Maine

August 27, 1943

My dear Neill:

Your letter of August 3rd reached me yesterday. I had felt all the time during the last two months that something had gone wrong. I am glad that you told me about your doubts. Now I want to meet your frankness, and be frank myself. You remember that I wrote you several months ago, asking you not to bother yourself with convincing people and getting support from so-called specialists who have nothing whatsoever to do with Orgone biophysics. I firmly believe it is your own fault that you got a sense "of failure and frustration" in making my work known. I really don't care whether my work is known or not, I only care about whether what I described is true. I want you to believe what I am saying: I don't care. So please, do not send any journals and any books any more to anyone. Let people come to you if they wish to.

As to H. G. Wells: You ought to have known that this man is a philosopher and a representative of just the kind of mechanistic science which brought this world to the verge of ruin, and which incited the press campaign in Norway against my work. I know Wells: He is a big balloon, blown up with nothing-gas, who is in danger of bursting any time out of mere conceit and good-for-nothingness. You should have understood why he became so unpleasant. Some years ago he wrote a book about natural science. So when he met orgone biophysics, he sensed no doubt that he was an ass to have written a book about natural science about a decade or two too early. If you care, you can let him know what I said just now.

As to yourself: I do not understand why you wish to confirm my biological theory. The main thing is whether it makes sense to you. If it does not, why care? If it does, why not rely on your own impression? You say that you are not educated in science. But nobody in this world is as yet educated in orgone biophysics. I really wish out of our old friendship, that you would not add the troubles of the pioneering work in orgone biophysics—which has nothing to do with electricity—to your own worries in the field of education. I would not like to have our friendship clouded quite unnecessarily. The matter of orgone physics and biophysics is not a question of belief or disbelief, it is a matter of observation and experience. As to the physicists, I have not only lost all the respect I had for physics, I regret to have to say that I would never have dared imagine how bad their thinking is, how conceited and fruitless their efforts, how wrong their statements are. It is true, they can build bridges and machines, but they don't know anything about the most primitive questions of life. I don't hesitate to express my utter bewilderment about the silliness within natural science—with only a few exceptions—which I find to be ever greater the deeper I penetrate into my own and their field of work with my experiments. You will hear more about this in a year or two, when the inconsistency and lack of logic in physical theory is revealed. The same way as I revealed the prejudices and the cowardliness in the thinking of the psychoanalysts. Do you really believe that this world would look as it does look if it were not so?

And now the Communist Party. I think they have revealed themselves fairly thoroughly by now. Did you hear the latest news? They have abolished the principle of co-education in Russia. It is quite clear why they hate psychology. They could not act as they do if they did not hate it.

We had very good news from Sweden and other countries. Our friends are working, writing and fighting. We are preparing a convention in the U.S.A. of all workers of the Institute as soon as the War ends.

I have faced the same experience which you face: Neurotics are the ones who are reading the literature, but not *only* neurotics. And why do you want to eliminate neurotics if 80% of humankind is biopathic?* That is just the trouble: the disaster is the result of the general biopathy, and a new world, if at all, will have to be built by neurotic individuals. Again: If that were not so, things would not look as they do.

I am glad to hear that your school is going all right. Unluckily, you are right: Pioneer work will have a very difficult stand against state regulation of civilian life. That is the reason why the work-democratic principle is so important and the only hope we have.

I received the book of Nathan.† I did not know that you sent it. He is one of the many who see things about Fascism which should have been seen and which I saw around 1930. Even if Nathan had known my book about Fascism he would not have mentioned it because of a principle that the natural love question must not enter the realm either of psychoanalysis or of politics.

---

* Reich defines biopathy as "disease processes caused by a basic dysfunction in the autonomic life apparatus."

† *The Psychology of Fascism,* by Peter Wilfred Nathan (London: Faber and Faber, 1943).

If you can get hold of several square feet of tin you can use it by putting it under the bed-cover while you lie in bed. I saved the life of a cancer patient who was lamed in his legs by that simple measure. Again a fact impossible and unbelievable for the big-shots with twisted brains.

Please write again and often. We are all eager to hear from you.

———— ◆•◆ ————

Orgonon
Rangeley, Maine

September 6, 1943

My dear Neill,

There were two points in your last letter which I did not answer in my letter to you. The one point is concerning the money which you have lent in peacetime and the other is Einstein. I shall proceed with the second first.

When I wrote you that the great respect I once had for physicists had vanished completely, it is due to a great experience with Einstein. I don't know whether or when it will be necessary to publish this experience; anyhow, I want it to be on file in a letter to you, so that no future biographer may miss it. Here is the factual story, according to notes in my scientific records of nearly two years ago:

In July, 1940, I discovered the light phenomena, i.e., the orgone in the atmosphere. Several months later I constructed the accumulator. Soon after that I found that the temperature, measured by thermometer above the top of the accumulator, was continuously higher than the temperature in the surrounding air and within the accumulator. I knew from physics that such a fact is unbelievable and of tremendous importance, because according to physical law, all temperature differences equalize. If they don't equalize, then there must be some source of energy which creates heat. This temperature difference was not only continuous but it changed exactly with the weather. When the sun was shining it was high, up to 2 degrees, and when it was raining it disappeared completely. The curves I obtained were completely in accordance with electroscopic measurements of the energy concentration within the accumulator. The electroscope, too, showed strong concentration in sunny weather and a great diminishment in rainy weather. I realized the exceedingly important quality of this finding. I wrote to Einstein to have a talk with him. He answered that he would be glad to discuss it. I went to him one day in January, 1941, at 3:30 p.m., and we had a rather exciting discussion about the orgone, lasting continuously until 8:30 in the evening. I explained to him the main features of the bionous disintegration of matter, and the discovery of the orgone radiation, first in the SAPA* bions and then in the atmosphere, as reported in my articles in the journal. Not only was every single fact new to him; but he became increasingly interested and excited. Otherwise he would not have listened for nearly five hours. I did not tell him about the temperature differences, which I knew was an unbelievable fact for a physicist, until I had shown him the rays in the orgonoscope which I had brought with me. And now, please be attentive: We put out the lights in the room and I gave him the orgonoscope and showed him how to use it. We waited about 20 minutes to accommodate the eyes. Then he looked through it, through the window, and he exclaimed amazed: "Yes, it is there. I can see it." He looked again and again. We put on the light again, and he said: "But I see the flickering all the time. Could it not be in my eyes?"

I was a bit astonished that he withdrew, because the orgonoscope shows the rays in a delineated gray circle, distinguished from black surroundings, and his exclamation was quite genuine and true. In my article about the discovery of the orgone, I had discussed at some length the question of the objectivity of the rays, which are both in the eyes and outside the eyes. The objective proof for the objectivity of the rays is, as I explained, the fact that you cannot magnify impressions in the eye, but you can magnify objective rays. Einstein asked me what else I had observed. Then I told him that I hesitated to tell him about another phenomenon I had observed, because he would not believe it. And I told him about the existence of the continuous temperature difference between the air above the top of the accumulator and within the accumulator and the free air. To that he exclaimed: "That is impossible. Should it be true, it would be a great bomb!" (verbally). He got rather excited and I too. We discussed it sharply and then he said that I should send him a small accumulator and if the fact were true, he would support my discovery. Before departing, I told him that now he could understand why people were saying that I was crazy. To this he said: "I can understand all right."

I had a small accumulator especially built for him and brought it over about 2 weeks later. We agreed to observe the fact of the tempera-

---

* SAnd PAket (sand packet) bions, so-called because the culture that showed a radiation effect was obtained from ocean sand heated to incandescence.

ture difference immediately. We put the accumulator up in his cellar, the accumulator being on a table, and a control thermometer hanging about 3 or 4 feet away in the air. After some time he and I could both see that the temperature above the accumulator was higher by about 1 degree than the temperature of the surrounding air. We were both very glad. He wanted to keep the accumulator for about 2 or 3 weeks and then write to me. He said he wished to observe the continuity and the average of the temperature difference. After about 10 days he wrote me a letter. The letter stated: He had observed the existence of the fact of the temperature difference on the accumulator for several days. Please remember that he, as well as I, thought such a fact to be quite extraordinary—according to his words "a bomb in physics." So he had observed the fact and affirmed it, but now comes that which I have experienced with physicists and other natural scientists again and again: First they deny the fact. When I demonstrate the fact and they cannot deny it any longer, then they try to explain it away by some wild interpretation. That happened, not with Einstein but with his assistant. I stress again the fact that the possibility of a continuous temperature difference without any visible source of heat seemed impossible to Einstein. Well, now it comes: The assistant, apparently some wise guy, knew all the answers. He told Einstein that in cellars there is a "convection of heat from the ceiling to the table top," and that this must be the cause of the phenomenon which could no longer be denied. Now, it is a law in scientific research that, when you have to confirm a fact and you propose a different explanation of that fact, you are obliged to control your own objection. Einstein's assistant did not do that. He simply "objected" without proof. Einstein took the trouble, as he wrote in his letter, to take the accumulator apart and he discovered that there was a temperature difference between, above and under the table. The fact, mind you, had not been known to Einstein. It seemed to confirm the objection of the assistant, but there were only two ways of finding out whether that objection was correct or not.

Now I shall pause for a moment. The answer is in the next few lines. I want you to think for yourself what you would have done in order to find out whether the temperature rise on the accumulator was due to heat convected down from the ceiling or not.

Here is the experimental answer:

a) You simply take the control thermometer which was in the free air and put it above the table at the same height as the thermometer above the accumulator. If the temperature difference is still there, it cannot be due to the warmth from the ceiling. This is true. I had measured with both thermometers above the table for months, and the temperature difference was always there.

But this experiment is still not pure, because the ceiling of the room is still there. Thus we have the possibility

b) to arrange the experiment in such a way, and to measure the temperature above the accumulator in such a way that no ceiling interferes. In February, for two whole days, I put an accumulator into the soil in the open air. The ceiling was eliminated—and thus also the argument of the assistant. I measured the temperature of the air above the accumulator, in the surrounding earth and in the air. Not only was the phenomenon still present, but more: In the closed room the temperature difference, as confirmed by Einstein, was several deci-degrees—3–6 or 7 on an average. In the open, the difference climbed up to 10 degrees and more in the sunshine, and 20 deci-degrees i.e., 2 degrees, in shade and cold. The ceiling was not there anymore, but the fact of the temperature difference was still there. So these physicists had not thought, after having confirmed the fact, to control their own objections, whereas for more than two years now I have eliminated the ceiling and have still been able to demonstrate the fact. I wrote the whole story to Einstein, feeling uneasy about this great physicist not having thought of the simple measure, namely to control the fact in the open air himself. Einstein did not answer to this clear-cut elimination of the objection.

In the beginning, Einstein's whole procedure was correct, but when I had eliminated the objection it was not understandable. I can only assume that some crookish friend of mine from Vienna had, through the rumours put into the world about me, destroyed this great chance. We all had the impression that Einstein wished to wait, and not expose himself.

This experience shattered my confidence not only in practical knowledge but also in the ability of physicists to think, act and behave correctly where "bombs" in physics are concerned. Einstein and I agreed that this one phenomenon, especially in connection with many others, could not only shatter a great many concepts of physics but that, in addition, it would also lay open a great many black spots in astronomical and physical science to correct answers. So they sit there quietly and are watching, without taking responsibility, my deadly difficult struggle to put these things across. When, after a decade or two, I shall have succeeded and be worn out from frustration, human disappointment, and economic and psychic strain, then they will come— I am sure of that. But I doubt whether I shall accept them then. Einstein is very cautious. I do not doubt that he knows that I am right. He saw the radiation in the orgonoscope and he saw the temperature difference in his house, and he was informed of the much greater creation of heat in the open air, without a ceiling. He well knows that it is a bomb. He also knows about the results obtained so far in cancer.

Now you understand my attitude toward physics and physicists in general. I want you now to join my standpoint that there are no authorities in orgone physics anywhere; that the fight is hard, and that I am on my own. But the facts are coming through slowly, thanks to the conscientious and extensive proofs I have given, most of which are not published yet. The matter is especially hard and difficult because the discovery of the orgone overthrows a great many wrong assumptions and emergency theories in the physical world. The four and one half hours of this intensive discussion with Einstein made him make the remark in the end, when I told him that I was originally a psychiatrist: "What else are you doing?" He had thought that I was originally a physicist.

Well, that is the story. It would be very painful and regrettable if I had to publish it. The temperature difference which meant a bomb to Einstein has been observed now for nearly four years, constantly and in all kinds of variations. It is a bomb because it explains the heat of the earth which was not understood until now, and it explains the immense quantities of heat of the sun, which had not been understood until now either. They become simple through an understanding of the fact that when the orgone particles which are everywhere are stopped in their motion, they create heat. The body-temperature and body-heat have not been understood either. They constitute one of the greatest riddles of biology, which is admitted by leading scientists. We don't have to consider the chatter-utterances of the small lice in science, who know everything by putting a label, a word, undefined and unundestood, which means nothing, on every phenomenon.

Now as to the money. I don't feel that it would be correct to accept your offer. Your institution is your own worry economically, and you are contributing your part as a member of the Institute by sustaining your school. I would suggest that we discuss this problem at our next meeting.

My best wishes.

————◆•◆————

Summerhill School
Festiniog, North Wales

November 18, 1943

My dear Reich,

Your double letter most interesting, especially the Einstein one. I can't understand that incident. As you know, the psychologists are divided into two lots . . . Lot A considers you a genius, Lot B a madman. If Einstein thought that your discoveries were sound and new, no talk by an enemy would affect him. So that apparently he rejected your whole concept of life and science. OR FEARED IT.

Re journals etc. sent to me. You complain of my attempts to have you appreciated here, but what was I to do when Wolfe kept sending me journals and books? Sell them? I tried, but no bookseller would take them. Lewis, the biggest medical booksellers, took a few books and sold about seven. I had no idea what you wanted of me. True, Constance's lending library was good and still is good. But from this desk I see about two dozen No. 1 Journals on a shelf, and I still don't see what I was supposed to do with them if not to send them to likely people who might learn from them. One mother of a child here is in a publishing office. She borrowed a book to read and showed it to her firm. They asked a well-known non-Freudian analyst to read it. I got his report, but am forbidden to mention his name. He wrote:

"The last 100 pages is a most valuable account of R's new therapeutic technique which is based on his recognition of nervous disorder. I found this unique and a most valuable contribution to our knowledge and I regard it as a most important statement with which I am in full agreement, from the standpoint of my own theory and practice which I have arrived at, of course, independently. If the whole book were as sound and constructive as the last 100 pages I would unhesitatingly recommend its publication here."

He then gives quotations.

Page 73: "only one thing wrong with neur. patients—lack of full and repeated sexual satisfaction." Page 70: "prognosis depends on establishment of full genital satisfaction." Page 106: "The neurosis is the expression of disturbance of genitality."

He then goes on:

"These quotations are open to much misunderstanding and to dangerous abuse, although R's own technique is so thorough that it does apply some of the necessary safeguards. R believes that the sexual act is the end, and only requires fulfilment and that there is no other problem. Some who see the moral justification for unlimited selfish indulgence will of course be glad to use such a treatise for their own dubious ends. If you are prepared to risk an immense amount of well-deserved objection on sexual grounds, the book is worth publication in England because of what it does to our new bio-electric theory. That in my opinion is the coming trend of scientific process in psychological work. In its present form I regard the book as highly dangerous in spite of its being a most valuable contribution to psychological process."

Reich, I guess that you know this line of argument already. Still the man doesn't think you suffer from dementia-paranoia as another analyst thinks you do!

Now about myself. I am not very fit. I wish I could have an Accumulator, but even if I had, I couldn't use it easily in winter with no central heating and cold rooms. Your idea of a tin sheeting on the bed makes me hopeful even though, so far, I can't find a way to get the metal. However, I'll get it before I write again. Many worries. Older girls of 16 or so taken away from school because of the danger that freedom logically leads to sex freedom, so that any man who sets out in England to carry out the R. theory of sex freedom would be likely to end in being a martyr and a martyr only. Do you realise this point?

My book is being printed. I shall send Wolfe the proofs of the sex chapter for the journal if he wants it. I expect them daily.

I don't write often enough, I know. This time it has been that I haven't felt very cheerful lately. I don't think I shall till I get back to my dry climate in Suffolk when the war is over. I was 60 recently and wish I were 20 again with no painful arms.

P.S. I still don't know why the orgones can't work if I lie under the tin with clothes on. Also, I wonder what effect the old armour of the middle ages had on bodies which were almost completely encased. Interesting speculation.

———◆◆———

Forest Hills, New York

December 23, 1943

My dear Neill:

This is only a short answer to your letter of November 18th. I do not believe that Einstein was so much afraid of it (though he was afraid, too, as every other mortal), but more likely some of the pestilent rumors had apparently reached him and obviously he wanted to be careful. I cannot judge this interpretation of mine. I am usually inclined rather to try to understand the actions against me than to be suspicious. I wish I had much more of the paranoic qualities of other fighters who smell an attack before it comes.

I hope and I wish that you would write more often. It is important to keep in touch. You probably realize that your teachings are making quite some headway in the United States, thanks to our journal.

To use the orgone under the cover with clothes on as you suggest means that the clothes are taking away much of the orgone which otherwise would reach the body directly unhampered.

Regarding the possible martyrdom of people who are representing my teachings, I very often feel like withdrawing in order not to endanger others. But, as I used to say, "I did not make it!" It is not my fault, but rather the fault of the whole set-up of thinking and education that endangers our people. It is left to the consideration of every single one to decide whether he wants to confront the emotional pestilence or not. You can be sure that I have never forced any one, and that I shall never force anyone to represent my teachings as a politician would do.

I wonder whether there is some motive in you which inhibits your succeeding in finding some metal to have an accumulator built. I shall not be quiet until you have managed it.

Would you kindly let me know how you liked the last issues (Volume II, No. 2 and 3) of our journal. Give your opinion.

My best wishes to you and all our friends for a happier 1944.

1944

Summerhill School
Festiniog, North Wales

January 18, 1944

My dear Reich,

Your letter today. I have just had a fine holiday in Cornwall getting some sun, and have come back full of energy. During my holiday, I read your latest journal, Vol. II, No. 1. It reads like a stirring romance, one that has to be read to the end at one sitting. It sounds sincere and modest, for you make no claims, and only seek truth. I was most interested in your trouble about the eliminating organs being unfit to deal with so much elimination when the cancer breaks down. If a layman can have a theory, let me give you this one. If your patient has fasted for, say, a week or more before you give the Akku treatment, his organs will have eliminated everything and be free to deal with the cancerous rubbish. It seems obvious that a patient can't go on eating, thus giving his organs work to do, and at the same time eliminate your brown cancerous poison.

I have at last found a way to get enough metal for the cage and am having it sent on. I say again that you don't realise my difficulties here. Overcrowded in a house that is always cold and damp, with central heating that I cannot use because of the expense of coke and the difficulty in getting fuel. How am I going to find a room hot enough to sit naked in the cage I don't yet know, and I dare not try heating the cage with electricity. But I shall find a way.

About writing more often. It must be the war and evacuation to this damned Wales. Life is an *Ersatzleben* [substitute life] all the time—constant worries about getting staff . . . worries about money and a landlord who hates my ideas and keeps trying to make me pay for damages etc. In Cornwall I was a different person, free and happy. I lectured in London to a most enthusiastic audience (hundreds couldn't get into the hall) and felt happy and useful. It is the exile in a strange land of rain and cold and a foreign language that gets me down.

I keep hoping to have a lecture tour in U.S.A. when the war is over . . . if it is over in time, for I was 60 the other day [October 17, 1943] and want to see U.S.A. before I am too old. Sadly enough I had hoped to see my wife's first husband, Dr. Otto Neustätter in Baltimore, but he died the other day. I loved him and he loved me.

I still don't understand the Einstein affair. Pestilent rumours will not or should not affect a man's attitude to truth. I find quite a few who say: "Reich is right; one fears he has got the truth about psychology and sex and cancer, but he spoils his case by saying controversial things about rubber gloves and twinkling stars which scientists seize on and then dismiss his fundamental and great discoveries as bunk." My friend Prof. J. D. Bernal, the leading and most original scientist in Britain, simply says that you haven't produced enough evidence of your discoveries. Haldane dismissed your *Bione* as "too unorthodox" which is about the silliest thing a scientist could say. So that it isn't only a case of Einstein. But knowing you as I do, I am convinced that you are right and that in time you will be acknowledged as right.

Have you any connection with that magazine *Sexology?** It reads well and seems to be sound on fundamentals. But, oh, this sex business, Reich! The logical result of S'hill freedom is of course sex freedom, but I find of the parents only one, Zero, is ready to believe so. Parents of boys, yes, but of girls, no. So that one cannot simply go far ahead of public opinion. Martyrdom for a cause isn't good enough, for it destroys other causes at the same time . . . i.e. the freedom from fear and moulding in small children.

My new book deals with education, demanding that emotion must come first, and that if emotion is free the intellect will look after itself. I hope to write again soon.

All the best, Reich. I believe in you and hope to live long enough to see the world do so also.

———— ◆‧◆ ————

* An American journal, still published; it was one of the first to deal openly and seriously with sexual issues.

Forest Hills, New York

February 7, 1944

My dear Neill,

I was glad to have your letter of January 18th.

I am also glad that you finally decided to make the effort to obtain the metal. Build the accumulator so-to-say around your body, so that the inner walls are not further than 2–3 inches away from your body. If you have enough metal, then you can make a single or double extra layer around the accumulator, 2–4 more side walls and 1–2 more back and top walls. This increases the concentration of the Orgone within the accumulator 2–3 times, and decreases, of course, the time you have to sit in it. You feel it better and the results are obtained more quickly. In case you do not obtain enough metal for the box, then build a simple sheet to put under the bedcovers, so that it covers you on both sides and on top of the body, by simply bending the metal. Then again you have metal inside and organic material outside. The effect is not quite as good, but it is near.

Now a few words on the general situation: Please be sure that I understand your situation as far as the school is concerned thoroughly well. Not only because I know your work and the world in which it has to operate, but also because I find myself in a quite similar situation. As you have troubles with the [character] structure of your teachers, I am often in complete despair concerning some of my assistants. Very often I wonder whether it would not be wiser not to teach at all and not to produce any followers at all, in order to prevent superficiality and disastrous sloganism. This is the sort of thing that happens: The patent application for the Orgone Accumulator has been filed now for more than two years. Lately, the Commissioner of Patents in Virginia told my patent lawyer that he would not grant the patent "*no matter what proof I would bring forth.*" "Do you think," he said, "I want to go out on a limb and to make myself ridiculous."

Well, that's that. People are enthusiastic when they read my book or the articles in the journal. But I know that they do not understand it really. The more convinced I become that my basic findings concerning the human structure and its consequences in the social set-up are right, the greater becomes my despair, because there is nothing I can do about it besides sticking to the truth and thus exposing myself to great dangers. There cannot be any doubt that the average human being, whoever he may be, fears nothing more, dreads nothing more terribly than realizing himself and the truth of his deeds and thoughts. He is ready to die for somebody's else's ideas, if somebody tells him it is necessary; but he is not ready to take the least bit of risk for his own sake and ideas. There is not one voice to be heard in this noisy world of today who would dare to show the common man how he really is thinking, acting and feeling according to the education he suffered, though all the voices are shouting: This is the age of the common man. But if the common man is going "to take over the rule," then the first condition would be that he sees the truth about himself, and that he corrects himself. Everybody keeps reminding everybody else that the truth must be said, but nobody really makes any attempt to this end. It is the same whether you deal with workers or union officials, whether you deal with doctors, educators or scientists. Your Haldanes and even Bernals have been expecting what I actually have discovered for several centuries. Now it is there. I have given more proof than any scientist ever did about his discovery, and I have more to come. But the only honest man in the crowd was that Examiner in Virginia who said, "nothing doing, he may give as much proof as he wants." This is the hidden and real attitude of every single one of them.

We have good reason to worry about the near future of decent truthful work. There is a possibility that we shall have to keep quiet for decades, and to write only for our desk drawers. And the core of the whole matter is the sexual orgastic anxiety of the animal Man, and nothing else. Everything else is consequence and not cause of this one central fact. I am afraid that the cannons will keep on thundering— with short intervals—for centuries, maybe longer. They will not stop thundering unless man finally discovers and learns to appreciate that he is really nothing but an animal, a piece of living plasma which wishes nothing more fiercely than to discharge energy by a few involuntary contractions from time to time—besides food and housing. Well, that's that. A rather unfriendly outlook. I really hope you will be able to sustain and to develop further your good work. There are few things in the world which are as badly needed as good and honest education.

In the next number of the journal we are also publishing the factual things of the Einstein affair.

Please give my best regards to all good friends over there and extend my hope that circumstances will permit that we meet soon.

Forest Hills, New York

March 15, 1944

My dear Neill,

You find enclosed in this letter two (2) registered letters. They contain two scientific documents of the utmost importance, legalized in the offices of the lawyer, John P. Chandler, on March 14th, 1944.

Please keep these documents somewhere among your precious things. I honestly hope there will never be a time when it will be necessary to use the publication of these letters in connection with this, still ununderstandable, attitude of Einstein. You may receive, sooner or later, a letter urging you to make the contents of my registered letters public. I would like to emphasize again that these documents are of decisive importance for the further development of natural science.

◆•◆

Summerhill School
Festiniog, North Wales

March 28, 1944

My dear Reich,

Yours [of February 7th] this morning. My "unconscious" reaction at once was: Ignore Einstein. Do nothing to antagonise him. Unlikely that you can now be reconciled. Make out a complete statement of your discoveries. Put them in the Safe Deposit of your bank and get a receipt saying what date the packet was deposited, so that, whoever writes an article or a book later claiming or explaining anything to do with Orgones, you can publicly prove that you deposited the whole *Sache* [thing] before the date of their publications. After all, Einstein isn't the universe. Hence my advice is: Carry on as if you had not had contact with him.

My metal has not come yet. It will have to be the bed cover, for apart from the impossibility of getting wood for a real Akku, this house is never warm enough to sit in a cage naked.

You still did not answer my suggestion of fasting to clear all organs for the elimination of the cancer.

Re—my sending you an article: things move so fast that writing is not easy . . . what I wrote six months ago so often seems to me out of date.

Next time you write, tell me what you think of *Sexology*. Some of it isn't bad, but when the editor tells a homosexual to cure himself by will power, I have my doubts. And the gaudy cover makes it look cheap and vulgar.

To return to Einstein . . . I feel it would be an error to make anything public at all. You don't want to compel people to take sides. Einstein versus Reich. But you must face the fact that E. doesn't believe in you or your work. I can think of no other explanation of his attitude. I say, What the hell! Don't forget that a great physicist can have complexes that may blind him to any science that touches emotion. That of course is the greatest drawback in having your discoveries recognised.

———————◆•◆———————

Orgonon
Rangeley, Maine

May 2, 1944

My dear Neill:

I received your letter of March 28th. I agree with you in regard to Einstein. I firmly believe that you overestimate his influence. I have sent out and distributed several documents which secure my priority in the discovery of the cosmic energy. I wonder whether you received the one I sent you. Please keep it simply among your documents.

As to your question of fasting to clear all organs for the elimination of the cancerous material, I don't have any opinion, but it is possible that it could help. On the other hand, to make a cancer patient fast, who is so much inclined to lose body substances, seems rather dangerous to me.

I do not believe that what you wrote six months ago is out of date today. You may say it is not timely, but it won't be out of date for decades to come. Your writings will live as Pestalozzi's* writings are alive. But our species, *homo sapiens*, is a funny creature. He admires most what he understands least, because he despises himself. And if he has the choice between a good library and a baseball game he will surely choose the baseball game because it does not require as much of him as the library. And he loves most what gives him the least re-

----

* Johann Heinrich Pestalozzi (1746–1827), Swiss educational reformer, whose theories laid the foundation of modern elementary education.

sponsibility. Your pedagogy means responsibility, but what he wants is orders. Therefore, your things are out of time, but they are never out of date.

What I think of *Sexology?* I think it is far from what it ought to be. And yet, when I started out in sexual mental hygiene nearly 20 years ago, a monthly journal like *Sexology* was unthinkable. Then you had only pornography, and *Sexology* means, in spite of all, a definite step forward in making the mass of the people accustomed to the fact that they are basically sexual animals. In about 500 years, maybe, the mass of inhabitants of this earth will recognize the fact that if they kill the natural sexuality in their children, and if they don't let them act according to natural laws, the tissues and mental capacities of these children will surely be choked. For several months I've carried the idea around with me to write a long open letter to the so-called little common man, not excluding myself, telling him a bit of truth about himself. You know, it is funny, everybody speaks today of the coming age of the common man. If an engineer is about to build a bridge, he is bound first of all to make a survey of his skills, tools and shortcomings, but nobody seems ready or willing to make a survey of the skills, tools and shortcomings of the so-called common man, who is just around the corner of obtaining power. Nobody dares to criticize him, least of all he himself. Why? Because everybody wishes that he remain ignorant, boasting, inclined to accept every kind of leadership but never his own responsibility. I am deeply engrossed in mathematical and orgonometrical studies, but still, I am going to write this open letter to the common man.

You did not tell me what you thought about the sociological articles in Vol. II, No. 2/3. It is important for me to have your opinion.

My name, and the subject of sex-economy and orgone biophysics, have at last been taken up among the natural scientists officially in the Who is Who of natural science "American Men of Science," and in the World Almanac. First swallows! Now, of course, people who know damn little about my work will trust me more. It is their shame and not mine. What a world! What an education! What a structure! What a civilization! Make a big noise, boast, make propaganda for yourself, and you will amount to something even if you have to say nothing. Live on the other hand quietly, do a good job, let things speak for themselves, and everybody thinks you are a charlatan. Again, what a world!

I wonder whether you know that I became the father of a third child. It's a boy, called Ernest Peter Robert, a husky strong little fellow, 4 weeks old, with a strong will, serious in his facial expression; just discovering the world around him and developing together with his mother very nicely. I assure you that after 25 years of intensive and extensive psychiatric work I am discovering for the first time, like a new student of psychiatry, the real nature of a new-born baby. It is amazing and frightening how little this high-boasting psychiatry knows about the most primitive things of human life. I hope sometime to be able to write down what I learned during these last 3 months. Would you ever have imagined that an unborn baby will stop kicking in the mother's womb when it hears good music; that after birth the same baby has real oral orgasms with twitchings of the face muscles, rolling of the eyes, twitchings of the tongue after a good exciting feast at the breast? I am very happy in spite of the fact that the little fellow has upset my whole schedule, that, for the meantime at least, the quiet to which I was used while working at problems of natural science is gone. I can only hope that we shall at least succeed in making the next war happen not within the next 25 years but after the next 50 years, so that this boy won't have to die for liberty but will be able to live for liberty.

I am always happy to hear from you. Please, write more often. I really hope after 5 years of separation to have an opportunity soon to have a good and long personal talk with you.

———◆◆

Orgonon
Rangeley, Maine

May 18, 1944

My dear Neill:

I read in the *New York Times* that your wife has died.* Though I did not know her personally, I know what she meant to you since she had participated in the hard struggle for Summerhill School. As you probably know, I am very bad at making long speeches on such occasions, but you know that I am in deep sympathy with you. I really

---

* The first paragraph of the obituary notice in *The New York Times* (May 4, 1944) read: "Mrs. Alexander Neill, co-founder of the famous 'do as you like' Summerhill School, where students were permitted to smoke, swear and, inner urges demanding, even kick out windows, has died at a nursing home in Wales, it was announced today."

hope that you can take a rest soon from all the worries you have gone through lately, and keep yourself going on the highest level possible. Did you receive the note which appeared in the *New York Times*? It was a rather funny mixture of admiration and poking fun at you out of self-defense.

Don't you think that you should write something about this slogan "Do as you like" which they apply to your school? As a matter of fact your boys don't do as they like in the sense of our enemies, but they do as they like in our sense, which is a completely different matter. And they are made to do as they like in our sense, because your authority can make them do as they like in our sense and not in theirs. I really hope to get an opportunity soon to talk the matter of the dangers of freedom over with you again. Do you think it would be possible to transfer your educational principles to a society of 130 million people with about 30 million children? We should discuss such a problem right now. Please let me know what you think about it.

Did you hear anything from Sweden? Let me know if you did.

———◆·◆———

Summerhill School
Festiniog, North Wales

May 22, 1944

My dear Reich,

Your telegram [Reich had wired condolences] and letter arrived; the latter today. Thanks a lot for the former; how you knew I can't guess, unless the *Times* goes to N.Y. by air. It was a relief in one way, for life to her was a misery for three years, but I felt the parting keenly. Made me feel so much alone. You can't work closely with a woman for 24 years doing the same important work without feeling a strong bond. There is a big question in this relationship to women. To have the ideal love mate and ideal companionship and co-working in one woman is almost a rarity. And in the days of Helga I had this conflict most strongly, for the real interest in the work wasn't there, so that today I can meet H. without having any special interest now that passion has died. I suppose it is that now I am 60, and the glands are slowing up, companionship becomes more vital than other human relationships. I find that I give more energy to work, whether cutting grass or writing or dealing with kids. Ambition sinks into the background. Fame? What is it but a soap bubble? But it is good to see the young making good. We have a new art master with a genius for teaching and he got such marvellous work that we had an Exhibition in Bond Street, London. It was crowded out daily and the talk of the town . . . the joy was to see how happy the kids were with their success. I felt keenly that my wife hadn't lived to see it.

No, laddie, I think you are wrong. My name is writ in water. I don't really care if my name lives or dies. What I do care about is the *Tatsache* [fact] that S'hill has influenced countless parents and teachers all over the world.

Congratulations on E.P.R. [Reich's baby son]. But a word of warning . . . don't let anyone ever mention the word psychology to the little chap, nor allow anyone to deal "psychologically" with him. I've suffered lately by having a few teachers in the school who were amateur psychologists, and if a child of 4 picked up an earthworm they began to suggest it was a phallus . . . the fools. I've got rid of them luckily. Your observations of the kid are going to be interesting, and I expect that in six months time there will be a new Reichian discovery to shock the world.

Worried about finance now but I have opened a branch junior school nearer London which I think will pay its way. So the work expands . . . until the day when the State suppresses schools like mine. Under socialism I'd simply be classed a bourgeois school and shut down.

Slowly your ideas permeate Britain. Quite a lot of people know your work already, but not the scientists and doctors, only the searchers after truth.

Letter from Elsa Backer. She says it is terrible in Norway, hardly any food, children thin and weak.

I have begun to analyse a girl of 17; Veg. Therapy technique of course. Difficulty is time, for I have to teach and organise and mend water pipes and plant potatoes and all the time interrupted by 75 kids wanting nails or string or to know the time.

Weather still very cold here. It is never too warm in Wales . . . but I am tired of telling you how difficult it would be to use an Akku here.

Well, Reich, that's about all my news. A separation of 5 years is a long one, but it will be great to meet again. But I won't come as a patient next time. Too old now, but I did get a hell of a lot from you, a greater personal freedom, a wider outlook, best of all a warm friendship. I have written of my wife that she belonged to tomorrow. We all do who are in the work.

My blessings on you and wife and the kiddie. Let's hope that by the time he is of military age the war will be against poverty and ignorance only.

[*Neill included with this letter a page of his notes on two issues of the Journal (of Sex-Economy and Orgone Research), Vol. II, nos. 2 and 3, which Reich had asked him to comment on.*]

Deliberately put off reading it fully in case it should influence the book I was writing.

You make a splendid case for Work Democracy. Analysis of politics most masterly; I agree with all you say about them. But I criticise the style. May be partly the translation, but I feel you are over-explanatory, using a page to rub in a point that might be tersely put in a sentence. More important criticism is that you leave it all so vague. You want no organisation, but when your doctor and plumber and teacher in the village want to discuss a new water supply you are in danger of bureaucracy at once, for some fellow with a gift for talking will get up and say: "You guys, you leave this to me. I'm a teacher with short hours and have more time on my hands than you do. I'll take on to organise the bloody thing." And when you apply that to the State and a new housing plan is put forward, someone resembling the politician of today will be commissioned to carry it out, and all your teachers and tradesmen will be too busy at their jobs to watch him and see he does what they want. The politician today does in his way represent workers . . . You will always require executives to carry out national work and laws, and the moment they are tempted to serve even secretly a vested interest they will become politicians. So that your W[ork] Dem[ocrac]y postulates first the public ownership of all means of production, that is socialism. True, we see the Soviet abolish co-education, but on the other hand isn't Russia a country without politics? Yet without its politicians why does it regress? Because as you say, the people are not ready for democracy. The men who started the 1917 revolution are now old, anti-youth, anti-life, and that is a problem not yet faced—the father role which becomes conservative, timid, safety-firstish against youth.

I can't see any practical Work Demy until schools like S'hill are many and powerful in influence. Today your electrician after a hard day's work goes to his local political meeting *as a relaxation* . . . same as I play golf and you ski, or as I love to talk to an engineer about lathe work rather than talk to a fellow teacher about kids or psychology. And are you right in saying that the political man is always against? They are only against the guys who have another opinion. Politics are only the voice of interests, and until you get a Utopia in which all workers will have nothing to kick against, you'll have grumbles and men to air those grumbles—the professional politicians.

By a miracle, loosen all the adult stomachs of the world and you can have Work Demy. Until that happens, what? Only the slow process of education. But of course if this war forces the pace, condenses 100 years into five as far as movement is concerned, the masses may come quickly to your truth that the Caesars and Hitlers of life leave nothing behind. But already the reaction forces are very busy preparing to keep the status quo of 1939, to keep the old world alive on the same basis of rich and poor, worker and drone.

Rest of journal good. Feel proud and humble to see my name quoted so often as an authority.

On the whole every journal is a bit heavy. You have got something new and fine and it ought to be dished up in the best way. I spent two years of my life editing an encyclopedia* which had to be condensed in one volume, and got into the way of using as few words as possible. [James M.] Barrie said to a young writer: "Cut it down by half, leaving nothing out."

I know it is difficult to make translation run easily. Why don't you write in English? Your letters to me are perfect English.

———— ◆•◆ ————

Orgonon
Rangeley, Maine

June 24, 1944

My dear Neill:

I was glad to have your letter and your note on the subject of work democracy some time ago.

The objections which you bring forth in regard to the practicality of W[ork] D[emocracy] are the same as those I have put up against myself when I realized the existence of the natural W.D. interrelationships of working human beings and the babylonic tower of ideologies and messy institutions of the same species. As you have well understood,

* Neill's first job after graduating from Edinburgh University. In his own words: "The work was extremely useful in one way: it gave me a dread of superfluous words."

W.D. is an existing fact, and not a political program. Not being a politician, I have no answer to the question as to how to clean the natural W.D. from its irrational entanglements and political mess. As to the ability of a socialistic regime to carry through this clean-up, I have my well-founded doubts. Maybe that I am wrong, but experience and consideration both leave no hope in regard to socialism, this word understood in its everyday meaning. The only hope I see is a sudden, rational upheaval of the greater part of the people who carry the burden of work and social interrelations upon their shoulders. It is interesting to note that it is just the socialist leader who is most averse to such a turn of events.

In spite of all, I have the definite feeling that once the fact of natural W. Democratic interrelationships is revealed and has entered the arena of human thought, it will not disappear again and will possibly develop its own course of logic. It is beyond me to feel responsible for this development. But I may add that the organization of the existing working groups of our Institute proves that a work-democratic orderly functioning, without politics and red tape, *is* possible.

I was impressed by your remarks about what the Summerhill School means to the world and the way it is not mentioned by plagiarists. People are stealing progressive ideas and revolutionary knowledge not in order to carry them through and defend them. If that were the case, they would gladly and with the humbleness of the decent worker mention the origin of their information. If they do not do so, it is for the sole reason that they take the raisins out of the cake, and leave the dirty work and the dangerous statements to the pioneer, not caring whether he or his work live or die. Thus the thief has all good hope to survive any change of social structure, to sneak in with his irresponsible thievery into any kind of job, in order to determine the course of society *backward*, just in the reverse direction which you showed him, i.e., forward. In that way he appears modern and revolutionary without danger. The Russians now acknowledge the fact that it is the masses who make Hitler and not vice versa, a fact which they fought like devils 15 years ago, on the basis of higher proletarian values. But in acknowledging this fact, finally, they leave out the main thing, namely the question why the masses are Hitlerian. The fact that it is the rotten sex-economy of the masses which renders them capable of submitting to every political crook. Some psychoanalysts stole my principle of character-analysis without mentioning me, because to mention me as the originator of the character-analytic technique would mean to defend the orgasm theory, and to stand the blows which follow in its path. So they have thrown out the orgasm theory, and are taking over a kind of ghost, which does not mean yes or no, black or white, mah nor bah. You are helpless against such procedure on the part of the so-called common or little man, who grabs without being punished, and pays tribute where he is treated in an authoritative manner. Take, hit and run is their motto.

Don't worry, no "psychologist" will enter the life-sphere of my boy during the first five or six years of his life. What I said before about the politicians applies naturally to the psychologists too. They took the wrong and superficial in Freud's theory and left out the dynamite.

About my boy another time. He is a great joy, but also a complete upset of my routine, quiet remote life. For months now I could not do much except routine work. But I shall cope with all that. I discovered first of all that a baby is a fully developed being and that we great biophysicists etc. know damn little about what a baby really expresses. Second, I found out that the baby is born without a trace of irrationalism. It always has a good reason when it cries, never cries without a reason, whether we understand it or not. He is very curious, studies whatever crosses his field of vision.

Write again and soon. My congratulations on the success of your school. I am dreaming of getting you here.

———◆·◆———

Summerhill School
Festiniog, North Wales

June 18, 1944

My dear Reich,

Odd that since my wife died I have had a burst of creation. Have written a play and finished my book. Have given up teaching and am doing only veg.-ther. analysis. The more I see the results with adolescents the more I consider that bloody man Reich a great man. But why haven't I done it till now? Some *Hemmung* [inhibition].

Did I ever acknowledge the two registered letters you sent? Sorry if I didn't. I am keeping them in my safe meanwhile.

I haven't any special news at present. Will let you know how the veg.-ther. goes. Marvellous why patients weep so easily when lying on their backs. Some do so the first *Stunde* [hour]. Why?

At last I expect to get enough tin to make if not the Akku, at least the bed cover. Buying today isn't easy; so many things are controlled. I can't even get enough wood for the school, and no brass nor iron at all. Thank heaven our food is good. My own theory is that rationing has improved health, for so many can't now eat too much.

Well, Reich, all the best, and let me hear from you soon. The last journal I had was the Work Democracy one. I have sent it on to Herbert Read, the art and philosophy writer, well-known here; he is a director of the great publishing firm of Kegan, Paul and Routledge. Meant to send him my copy of *The Function*, but as usual someone has taken it from my bookcase. Quite a few people in England now know of Reich, and some are sending direct for the journal.

I'll be interested in that kid of yours. I still have a little fear that the raised voice of the father when he gets angry will be dangerous to it. That man Reich may be a genius but he ain't got too much patience!

———◆◆———

Orgonon
Rangeley, Maine

July 1, 1944

My dear Neill:

I am enclosing a few photographs of "the family." I think you never met Eva. She is twenty now. I also want you to meet my wife and Peter.

Would you kindly inform me whether the rumours about my "lunacy" are still around, or whether they have died out. The other day I had a letter from a co-worker in Palestine, to the effect that he had clamped down on the Palestine Psychoanalytic Association for its rumour-mongering with great success. I never wrote you the story of the origin of this rumour. I shall do so extensively very soon, "in order to have things on file."

———◆◆———

Orgonon
Rangeley, Maine

July 9, 1944

My dear Neill:

I just received your letter regarding Mrs. K. [an acquaintance on whose behalf Neill had written to Reich]. She can rent an accumulator for prophylactic purposes, and she can visit me when I

shall be back in New York by the end of September. A breast operation
always means cancer, and since the removal of a breast does not touch
the rotting process in tissues and blood, the use of the accumulator is
indispensable to prevent reoccurrence if possible.

I would like to hear more about your vegeto-therapy experiences.

My baby is doing very well. My voice is going high only if I meet
stupid emotional-pest reactions and when I feel helpless to cope with
them. Else, I am known as one of the most patient of human beings.
But I can shout all right if necessary and if there are no other ways of
settling things. (If you think the father is impatient, just wait until you
meet the son. His voice is even higher than his father's when he gets
impatient. This is written by Ilse Ollendorff Reich.) Don't you think I
have shown tremendous patience in waiting for nearly 2 decades now for
people to understand the most simple thing in the world which I am
teaching.

----◆·◆----

Summerhill School
Festiniog, North Wales

July 15, 1944

My dear Reich,

Many thanks for the photos. I take back what I said about your
being a dangerous father whose voice might give the kid fear . . . the
photo convinces me that *he* will be the danger, and I see a fearful father
hastening to obey his commands. He is a splendid kid, with most ex-
pressive eyes. All I get out of Ilse's picture is a great pride in what she
is looking at. You are two lucky ones, and I hope I live long enough to
see Peter and watch his career.

Your query about lunacy means nothing to me, for I don't know
what is behind it. Of course a few Freudians dismiss you as *meschugge*
[crazy] but that sort of thing is a compliment from them.

I am veg-therring 4 girls and 4 boys, adolescent. Often I wish I could
run to ask your advice, but feel it is better that I can't. With a girl of 17
it goes easily and quickly, but with the others I am in the middle of
strong resistance, which brings in a difficulty. I am analyst AND headmaster. In spite of the fact that I am not a feared headmaster, I can see
the old difficulty arising. Suppose a boy has been stealing from me, or
ruining a workshop tool of mine. His resistance to my knowing it goes
over to everything. One boy of 14 sent to me two years ago as a bad

bully and thief is going to be difficult and dangerous, for when his hate begins to come out I'll have to fight for my life!

So much for the difficulties. I find the method a million times more pleasant (for me) than the old, in which I sometimes nearly fell asleep listening to dull dreams. And the children like it better and come regularly, which they seldom did in the old days.

Lewis's Medical Library has just informed me that they have sold a dozen *Functions*. I am telling them to apply direct to N.Y. if they want more.

I get quite a few letters from N.Y. now. Your journal has given me some publicity there, and it looks as if I'll have to arrange a lecture tour the moment the war is over . . . if it is over by the time I am 80 or so. It should be a great event to meet you again. By your photo I see you haven't changed a bit. You must send me a photo of Ilse, one in which her eyes can be seen.

At last I am within sight of an Akku. Two weeks ago an Indian physicist came on a visit, read your journals and was most interested. He said he could get a cage made in his lab and would send it on soon.

It is almost impossible to make contact with people in the war period. Many are in the forces, doctors and teachers who, in peace time, might be interested in veg.-ther. The leading scientists are all on war work. Reichism will have to await the peace days.

Well, Reich, all the best, and may your loving study of Peter add new knowledge to your whole philosophy of life.

———◆·◆———

Orgonon
Rangeley, Maine

August 6, 1944

My dear Neill:

I have your letter of July 15th. I am glad you began to do vegeto-therapy, and especially that you tried with adolescents. Since all grown-ups are more or less hopeless, as far as basic change of structure is concerned, the only hope is, I firmly believe, establishment of rationality in children and adolescents when the biophysical reactions still can be molded.

The term "resistance" is still valid, but in quite a different way than used in psychoanalytic technique. If a patient "resists," it means that you did not find the correct words and actions on specific places on his body, which correspond to this specific emotional situation. For instance: You may have released a bit of the mask-like stiffness of the facial expression. An impulse to bite may be on the point of breaking through. To this biophysical emotion the patient may react, by way of protection, with a withdrawal in his shoulders, a kind of holding back. Now you cannot get out the biting impulse in the mouth unless you release the auxiliary muscular armouring in the shoulders first, by bringing the shoulders forward. It is always a matter of observing the patient in such a relaxed manner that you learn to realize where a muscular defense (which is of course identical with the character defense) appears anew when the muscular defense on which you are working is just about to yield. This substitution of armouring mechanisms may take place anywhere in the body. Another instance: If there is a withdrawal tendency in the right arm due to a blocked impulse to hit; you let this arm move and the hitting impulse wants to break through; the patient may, in order to avoid hitting, arch his back very strongly. If you recognize the connection, and you release the arching of the back, you have destroyed the auxiliary muscular defense, and the hitting impulse cannot help but come through.

I would be glad if you would care to let me know from time to time how you are getting along with adolescents. The main thing in all vegetotherapy is to know unshakably that the main obstacle to progress is always a tremendous fear of yielding to involuntary uncontrolled motion and emotional currents. There is always destructive energy blocking love emotions.

I am glad you finally will get your Orgone accumulator. Do you have it built with double layers and close around the body? You will enjoy it very much, I am sure. You should have also smaller accumulators for your boys and girls.

Peter is prospering. He is absolutely healthy, happy, eager, curious and interested in everything. I never would have guessed how little we know about newborn babies, how completely developed they are biophysically, and, accordingly, how stupid and preposterous this whole educational set-up of our society appears—now even more than it did already ten years ago. I am learning very, very much and many important things. I hope to be able to present them at a later date in a useful and helpful manner.

Every day Ilse or I take Peter into the Orgone Accumulator for 5 to 10 minutes. It does him very good. I urged his mother to be in the accumulator every day while she was pregnant. Somehow I cannot get rid of the feeling that the liveliness, health and quick maturing of this boy is somehow connected with the fact that orgone was applied from the moment he was created. I can assure you that I feel most humble and very much like a religious man might feel in connection with what he calls religious experience, when I watch and enjoy this absolute perfectness of an animal organism, still unspoiled by education. I could not trace a single irrational attitude until now in this boy, and I have, as you probably know, a very sensitive organ for irrational neurotic or biopathic behaviour. I cannot help getting more and more convinced that our views on education of children and on what follows in consequence are 100% wrong and upside down. This experience after 25 years of psychiatric work is very great. I had even to correct some of my own basic assumptions, that means to correct them in the sense that I was not true enough nor courageous enough to stand for what I thought with all vigour at my disposal. I feel now that I had a bad conscience, that I was inclined to compromise, that I was hanging on too long to theories which, deeply in myself, I knew were wrong. I should not have wasted nearly 14 years with psychoanalysis and its sublimation and false child-psychology. You may be astonished, but a baby of 3 months is not autistic whatsoever. It has its interest in its surroundings fully developed. I have to assume now that the contention of the psycho-analysts of the autistic character of the baby is an artifact. This artifact is apparently due to the armouring of the analysts which does not permit them to develop a full and natural contact with a newborn baby. The baby on its part, if it does not find natural response to its outgoing feelings and emotions, in other words if it is not understood emotionally in a simple manner and responded to, has to shut itself in. A baby of only a few weeks senses emotional blocks and unnatural behavior in grown-ups with absolute certainty. A baby will not take a dead mother's nipple, it will begin to cry when a cold armoured person wishes to play with it. We easily forget that a child has millions of different emotions and desires, but only one way, in the beginning, to try to make itself understood, namely crying. It took me several weeks to learn to under-stand what the boy wanted when he cried. I did not apply any scientific knowledge—the more I did so, the less I succeeded. The only thing that worked was identifying myself with his expression and then I knew what he wanted. What psychoanalysis calls identification seems to be rooted very deeply in what I might call the contact of the orgonotic system of a grown-up with that of the baby. Animals, if not domesticated, show this emotion-language very clearly to me now. It is a very vast and most important field of human life, which I have just begun to look into. My greater worry now is that I might make some mistakes due to my own difficulty which might spoil the further development of the boy in the direction in which he is moving. Would you believe that a child of three months, or even two, does not like to be all the time in his crib, where it cannot see things move and change their position. But it is true. When it does not sleep, it wants to have things happen, and it rewards you with the most moving thankfulness if you give it the opportunity to see things happen around it. During the first few weeks for instance, I could not get to work because the boy cried when he lay awake in the crib. Then we learned that we could work, my wife could type and I could dictate even very difficult stuff, if only we put the crib close to the typewriter, so that this boy could watch mother's fingers move along the typewriter.

Well, these are only a few examples about the course of study I am going through now.

I hope you are all well. Write again soon, and if I can be of any help to you in your vegeto-therapy work, I shall be only too glad to do so.

————◆◆————

Summerhill School
Festiniog, North Wales

August 30, 1944

My dear Reich,

Your latest letter to hand. Your description of the biting and hitting defence makes me feel I have a hell of a lot to learn.

Just off to Scotland to play golf, after a distressing time of disunion in the staff. Section against the lady in charge who happens to be very near to me in all ways. Tired of dealing with women; feel like having a male staff only!

My long awaited Akku is again off. Physicist who promised to make one says he can't get it done in his lab; the reason no doubt is that unconsciously he thinks it mad. When I say that I can't buy a tin funnel for petrol in England you may realise my difficulty in getting metal and wood too. But is it not possible for you to send me one? I'd rather have one made by an expert than trust to luck and the village carpenter.

Sex Econ is spreading fast among the young here, but the scientists still explain away all your orgone work. Curiously enough, they never seem to pick out any specific points and say that you are wrong; they just dismiss the whole thing as pseudo-science. I want to know how science reacts to you in U.S.A.

Your observations on your son are most interesting. So far, no one has solved the problem of why kids cry so much up to 3 years old. I look forward to a book Babies, by W.R. Much needed. So far the only good one I know is Homer Lane's *Talks to Parents and Teachers*, 1925. He was an American and my first analyst. America never discovered him.

I have just come back from a branch S'hill I founded in Essex,* and when I return to Leiston I think of taking a house halfway between the two schools and having a bit of private life in my old age. Perhaps have a family, although it is a bit late at 60 perhaps.

Thanks for the photos of mother and child. I look forward to meeting them both.

Orgonon
Rangeley, Maine

September 11, 1944

My dear Neill:

I have just received your letter of August 30th. It is too bad that you cannot provide the metal, and that I am unable at present to send you one of our accumulators. But I promise you to keep three accumulators—one for grown-ups, one for 6–10 year-old children, and one "shooter" for healing wounds—in readiness, to be sent off to you as soon as it is possible.

You ask about the reaction of science in the U.S.A. It is far better than in Europe; though they are still keeping silent, I know that they listen very attentively to what we have to say. Some, of course, are very fiendish, but other groups are expressing their admiration. A palpable indication was given when I was asked to join, together with my laboratories, the register of "American Men of Science" which registers only experimental natural science. But I would suggest that we do not wait for any approval, but simply go on with our work. Recently, I was informed by a medical doctor in Palestine that he has built an accumulator and has achieved already some very amazing results on sick people.

---

* Named "Kingsmuir," it was in the charge of Lucy Francis, who had been the nursery-school teacher at Summerhill. Elsewhere, Neill refers to her as "my infant mistress."

To keep mentioning, however, and to make known that Orgone physics
is registered under experimental natural science in America would induce
many "scientists" to change their minds.

I look forward to you having a child. You owe it to humanity.

Why don't you gradually replace your staff by people who went
through our work? I believe it would ease your task tremendously.

My best wishes to you and all.

———————◆◆———————

Summerhill School
Festiniog, North Wales

October 7, 1944

My dear Reich,

If you think this article fitting for the *Journal* please hand it
on to Wolfe. Even if you disagree with some of it!

I have just had another adverse criticism of your work. A biologist
from the Rothamsted Experimental (Agriculture) Station came last
year to see us and took your *Bione* book and three journals with him.
He returned them yesterday with a letter . . . "I have passed them on to
various biologists and biochemists here. The general result is, the value
of the psychology we don't know, but the biology and 'science' are
hopeless. Reich's microscopic descriptions show that he knows nothing
of microscopy, and it is probably all a lot of rubbish." I hope to live
long enough to write him saying: "How do you feel now that Reich has
been proved right?"

Your photos all convince me that you have got a great kid and a
most pleasant-looking wife. I hope it won't be long until I see the three
of you.

Meanwhile I am going through a most difficult stage. Section of staff
very much against my secretary who means a lot to me in every way.
Constance has come down for a few weeks to help solve the problem,
and is giving the staff breathing.* But living in a community is not her
nature and she says a month or so will be all she can bear. At the moment
the school is all divided, and the rebels talk to old pupils and parents

———————————————

* Exercises which Constance Tracey had learned while she was Reich's patient
in Norway; they helped to relax the abdominal muscular tensions that contributed
to maintaining neurotic inhibitions under repression.

giving their side of the matter, and I have got to be careful lest S'hill goes to hell.

My new book* was almost ready but today I get a letter from the publishers enclosing one to them from the manager of the printing firm. He has just read the ms. and refuses to let the book go out unless I cut out some things I say against religion and sex. My answer is: Go to hell. I shall not tolerate censorship by any printer. *Ja, lieber* [yes, dear] Reich, life isn't always easy for the pioneer. But I feel in a fighting mood.

I'd like to tell you lots about my personal problems, but I don't like talking about my own psychology when a censor is to read it. I guess the censorship won't be necessary for long now.

I wish you would go into the question of fasting I suggested to you. I feel that the medical complex about "keeping up the patient's strength" is wrong, for every animal fasts when ill, even if cats and dogs do eat grass. If your cancer patients have to eliminate cancerous stuff as well as beef and carrots they don't get a fair chance. I always told you you neglected the food side too much.

Maybe if I can do it, I'll write an appreciation and criticism of the journals for publication. Here I give you a few passages from a letter to me from Herbert Read, director of Kegan Paul's publishing firm, and famous here as an anarchist writer on art. He says: "Work Democracy . . . Here Reich expresses truths that are fundamental to what I call anarchism which is essentially anti-politics. Not being a scientist I can't judge the Orgone theory. I shall look forward to Reich's book on Work Democracy." By the way, he is one who criticises the heavy language of the journals: "Germano-American jargon."

———— ◆•◆ ————

Forest Hills, New York

October 10, 1944

My dear Neill:

I do not like to intrude upon private affairs of other people, especially when they are good friends. But I had for some time now the feeling, aroused by indications in your letters, that there is some trouble going on or developing at Summerhill School, a trouble of sex-economic

---

* *Hearts Not Heads in the School.*

character, or in other words, the danger of an attack of the emotional pest on decent living. I assure you again that I don't want to interfere, but I feel that it is proper to tell this: I had many encounters with the emotional pest during the past 30 years. My experience taught me that the *only* way to get through in this terrible fight is to stand up fully for one's own way of life, no matter what public opinion thinks about it. My experience tells me further that you endanger yourself when you appear uncertain and that you gain a great following and admiration just when, in a simple and frank manner, you proclaim that which you think right and true. When I was still working among the suppressed masses in Germany, I had the typical experience that the police never touch the one who was walking calmly among them and who would face them in a simple natural way. You can beat the pest to its death if you show up the falsehood and if you stand up for the inner laws of decent human behavior as against the outer compulsory laws. That is all I can say.

———◆•◆———

Forest Hills, New York

November 8, 1944

My dear Neill:

I liked your article very much, although I cannot agree with everything you say in it. It goes to print, of course.

I still wonder why the opinions of the various biologists are so important to you. Is that not an expression of your own insecurity in the matter? The Orgone work is being acknowledged here more and more.

I hope you were able to clear the situation in your school. It is sometimes very bad to permit co-workers to mingle into private affairs. It is none of their business.

As to the question of fasting: I have nothing to say, because I am lacking experience in this field. But I can imagine that it could do some good.

When you write the next time to Herbert Read, it would be wise to tell him to drop the expression "anarchism" which means to the feeling of the average man the absence of any kind of law and order.

As to the heavy way of saying things: I do not believe that this is my fault or that of the translator. There are definite scientific matters which cannot be described the way you describe a football game. And why

should the so-called little man be spared the trouble of taking his time
and thinking a bit? It won't harm him to think things over.

———◆•◆———

c/o Constance
124 Wigmore Street, London W1

November 24, 1944

My dear Reich,

Your short letter fearing I was having difficulty certainly was
right. Not easy to say what it has all been about. Much better now that
I announced to the staff that I was to marry the young lady who is my
secretary. I explained the situation; that I don't believe in marriage as
it is today, but that professionally I would be in danger of extinction if
I lived without marriage. During a war all the stiff-stomached people
seem to flourish with their so-called moral and religious self-satisfactions,
so that in the recent parliamentary discussion on the new Education Bill,
most of the time was devoted to religious education which is to be
applied to all schools now. This shows the tendency during a war when
so many lose their loved men and grasp the hopes that a religion, almost
dead in peace time, has to offer. So that I fear that any cheap newspaper
has the power to damage any professional man who is "immoral" in not
believing in marriage.

The situation isn't perfect. The love one, yes, but my wife has to be
more than a success with herself and me . . . she has to succeed with
herself, me, and the work, and here she is most capable, but she expects
too high a standard of work, and says so and gets disliked. Her ambition
is to go to New York and have a Reichian analysis as soon as she can
get over.

We hope to return to our own home this summer. I am trying to find
a cottage near the school where I can have my own domestic life (which
I've never had before), and, most vital of all, have my own workshop
from which tools won't be borrowed or stolen.

Someone told me with surprise that your *Function* book is in
Cambridge University Library.

Am trying to stop smoking, not on moral grounds, no, I find that I
always oversmoke, from morning till late at night, one pipe or cigarette
after the other, up to an ounce daily. Result always a bad throat, cough,
bad tongue, lack of energy. I find I want about two hours less sleep

non-smoking, have a better appetite, but feel the lack of something to do when I am working. I am not optimistic (or pessimistic) enough to burn my pipes yet.

All suffering from a sunless summer. We stored no orgones . . . the land here lacks lime and for four years we have drunk water as soft as rainwater, lovely to wash in but lacking in all salts. Welsh children with their soft water have bad teeth; so in parts of Scotland.

This is a dull letter. The sun doesn't shine at all. I hope to hear more of the son and his mother.

———————◆◆◆———————

Forest Hills, New York

December 22, 1944

My dear Neill:

The most important thing in your letter of November 24th seems to me the question of what has to be considered a "marriage." Time and again, I and many others working in our field of endeavour are meeting not only the difficult problems of social sex-economy, but, in addition to that, also wrong concepts which have been adopted from a dying world by the very same people who profess to change this world.

You write in your letter: "I explained the situation, that I don't believe in marriage as it is today, but that professionally I would be in danger of extinction if I lived without marriage." I am sure you won't mind if I object to this statement, not as a person but as the representative of a definite type of work which tries to abolish social ideologies without basis in facts. *You are married when you live married, and not when you possess a certificate of marriage without being married.* In almost all of the states of the United States the fact of factual marriage is acknowledged in the form of the common-law marriage. The same is the case in France and was the case in Germany and Austria.

It is not a matter of "believing" in marriage or not. It is a matter of correcting the irrational and pestilent notions of sick people about what marriage is and what marriage is not. The pestilent ideology that you are married when you possess a certificate of marriage and that you are a criminal when you are *really* married but don't possess a certificate of marriage has been spread for decades and centuries by sick people, all over the world. It is not the opinion of the healthy average man. The piece of paper called a certificate has under present conditions only the function of protecting the woman in case the man does not wish to acknowledge the child. But a certificate in itself does not constitute a marriage. There is nowhere a law which forbids actual marriage without a certificate for adult persons. And giving in to pestilent public opinion in such matters means to counteract yourself if you fight for human health. Furthermore, not the law but the marrying people declare whether they marry or not. The certificate only certifies this decision of the marrying people.

We do not force anyone to live married without a certificate, but, taking human freedom deadly seriously, we have to object most severely to the pestilent attitude of some kind of people to force married people to take out a certificate if they don't want to.

I firmly believe that if we do not take the principles of freedom deadly seriously, we shall not accomplish anything, and all the talk about democracy will remain idle chatter. The essence of the matter is that you were actually married to your wife when you felt married. Whether you take out a certificate or not is of no importance at all. And if you live practically and functionally married, then you believe in marriage whether you acknowledge it or not. I regret not to be able to be at a meeting in your school and to shake the conscience of those teachers of yours who did not take the trouble to think a matter through.

I wish you all good luck for the New Year, much success and as much joy as you can gather in these times of disaster.

1945

Summerhill School
Festiniog, North Wales

January 13, 1945

My dear Reich,

We seem sadly enough to be drifting apart on what are fundamental questions. Let me try to be elementary about this marriage business. I think you will agree that there are certain outer forms that we "respect" when we don't believe in them. I see no use for royalty, but when the band plays "God Save the King" in the theatre I stand up with the rest. On the street I sometimes raise my hat to a woman I don't like nor respect. In short, one has not the time and energy to protest against everything one disapproves of. We all try to keep from compromising on the big things while we compromise on the minor matters. To me the big thing in life is my work, and I shall compromise always enough to keep that work from being stopped. If an enemy wrote to the Ministry of Education saying that a head of a school was "living in sin" I think that his work would be in great danger of suppression. You rightly say that a certificate in itself does not constitute a marriage. but your idea of a marriage or my idea is a *Nebensache* [minor matter] when those in power have the right to kill our work. And my work is not primarily sex reform; it is work with children from ages of 4 and 5 upwards to adolescence. The new Education Act is making Private Schools come under the State, to be inspected and closed if inefficient. The other day the Education Minister in a speech said: "If a head of a private school were a drunkard we should close his school." He might have said: "If the head of a school is an immoral man, etc."

What you say about marriage I agree with, of course. When I wrote

133

you that I didn't believe in marriage (certificate etc.) I simply meant that there must be no legal binding for an emotional union, that indeed the very binding is dangerous as every chain is dangerous. I have no intention of getting married on their terms; any marriage for me will be on my own terms, and I can use the word in my own way while they can use it in their certificated way. But again to the point . . . to publish MY version of marriage to all and sundry would mean the end of my work. If you say: To hell with your work; it is more important to be a martyr for the cause of free marriage, then we differ much. But I don't think you do. What you don't know is life in England. Last generation two able politicians had to give up their parliamentary careers because of their sex life . . . Sir Charles Dilke and Parnell, both brilliant men. It is the same today. A banker here sees his wife go off with another man. He says he dare not divorce his wife, and I ask him why? "Because I shall lose my job," he says. "What!" I cry, "but you are the innocent party." "Makes no difference," he says. "To the bank I am mixed up in a divorce and that is enough to get me fired out." That is in Scotland. We are ruled by the 11th Commandment . . . Thou shalt not be found out, and a man can remain a great public figure if he has a dozen concubines . . . and keeps the fact dark. So that when I shall introduce a lady as my wife I shall be o.k. because the outer forms are satisfied, whereas if I boldly introduce a lady as "my lover" I am in danger of disaster. But enough of this.

You are a big puzzle, Mister Reich. You complain because I want scientists here to be interested in your work, but why the hell did you let Wolfe send all the literature? Dozens of journals and books. What did you expect me to do with them? Sell or give them to shopkeepers or to educated men? You suggest I give them to biologists because of my own lack of faith. *Aber, Mensch* [But, man], it isn't so easy as that. Some of it is just infantilism . . . "Here, you guys, look what a friend of mine has discovered! Clever of me to have such a friend, eh what?" I hope you aren't going to get solemn in your old age, Reich. You won't be successful until someone has made a joke about Orgones: then you will know that they have arrived for good.

Letter writing is so unsatisfactory. Let us wait to talk it all over later. All good things this year including peace.

Forest Hills, New York

February 9, 1945

My dear Neill:

I have your letter of January 13th. You agree with me in the main points, yet you state that we are drifting apart on fundamental questions. I don't think so. I would not compare the paramount question of factual and formal marriage with standing up in the theater when some hymn is played. The latter does not inflict severe psychic and organic diseases on millions and millions of people and does not interfere with your private life. I wish to state that I am not a sex reformer but a research physician who discovered the biophysical emotional background of biopathic diseases and who has to fight these diseases just as you have to work with children. Other physicians before me who discovered that cholera and typhoid were caused by bacteria in infected water etc. had willy-nilly to upset the old rules and to create new rules in order to abolish epidemics. I had the bad luck to hit upon an endemic epidemic of much larger dimensions and much more devastating effects. I mean the emotional plague. What you describe about the hypocrisy in social life in England is a part, a consequence, and a cause, of this general disease. I cannot bow to it without giving up my work. Please understand my point of view as well as my social task. I don't force anyone else to think as I do, but I refuse to be forced to think according to viewpoints which are wrong, sick and devastating.

I feel that you were a bit annoyed at me and I understand that I should not have mingled into the affairs of your school. And, of course, I never thought of "to hell with your work."

After 26 years of hard work and building up one group of co-workers after the other, I find myself again alone. This whole job is, I understand now, too much, too hard, too strictly against the established ways of thinking. I don't feel that I am a big puzzle. The big puzzle is in reality the fact that social non-sense of such dimensions as we both know can exist for centuries and millennia, go on and go on in spite of the hard and dangerous struggle and endeavors of many good and honest men. I am not resigning, but I am facing more and more the deep abyss which separates honest natural science from the political life of the masses of the people. I did not create this abyss, I suffer from it most severely and I realize to my deep sorrow that I cannot expect or demand that others should stand against the tide and endure it for decades as I did. If I had a school as you have, I would have to take the attitude of the

Education Department as you have to take it. I know how you feel about
it. And I understand more and more why so many men who were forced
or preferred to stick to the principle of some truth had to withdraw from
social life completely. I am afraid that will be my fate in the end too.
But please, don't blame me for that. As my friend I ask you to understand the position I am in.

In the meantime, my work in the laboratory goes on quietly, and
brick is added to brick in the understanding of the tremendous puzzle
of life. I don't care when and how many others will know it too. I can
wait 200 and even 500 years. When you succeed in drawing biological
energy from earth into water, testing it on an exact instrument; when
you filter this highly charged water clean of particles; when you autoclave* it to make sure that no bacteria are alive; when you then freeze
it and let it thaw again and you see life matter in that orgone water,
then I beg you to understand, you have the right, more, the duty, not
to care, because that amazing experiment explains how life originated
on this planet. No other reward can compete with the satisfaction of
decent and honest insights into the origins of what has been talked
about for millennia in dark, mystical terms of poetry and philosophy.

Some weeks ago some biochemists of a famous research foundation
visited my laboratory to see the bions. Their amazement, their humbleness and at the same time their fear of getting in touch with the life
process showed me again where I stand and where my way is leading.
Sex-economy of human beings, to be frank, has become rather unimportant, compared with the steady progress into the realms of the
origin of life.

I really hope that we shall see each other soon and talk things over.
A talk of a few hours will do away with many a misunderstanding.

———— ◆•◆ ————

Summerhill School
Festiniog, North Wales

March 14, 1945

My dear Reich,
          Your letter of Feb. 9 plus *Journals* to hand. Excellent number.
I seem to see in this number an optimism, a "having arrived" sort of

---

* Autoclave, a strong, pressurized, steam-heated vessel used to establish special
conditions for chemical reactions, for sterilization, and for cooking.

feeling, although in your letter you sound not so optimistic. And don't you go telling me lies about your being willing to wait for 500 years! You aren't willing; you want to see it come about NOW in your lifetime. Why not?

Our little argument about marriage was hopeless. One can't express oneself in letters especially when a censor is to read them, at least I can't. We shall clear all that up in half an hour's conversation. And even when we do differ it cannot touch the warm regard we have for each other. Our main difference is that you are more of a Brand* than I am; you demand All or Nothing and are brave enough to stick to that demand. I cannot as long as I have a school.

Here I have sad news for you. I find that I have lost interest in curative psychology, even the Veg. Therapy. Maybe after thirty years of it I want to live my own life in the few years left to me, for my life has been one long living for others—*Christus Motif, ja, aber* [the Christ theme, yes, but]—I find my interest is in creative work now. Drama. Wrote a four act psychological play which no theatre will look at here. We acted it ourselves (I act well, by the way) and it was a great success locally. I want to create in my workshop, nothing special, just playing with a lathe and tools. Want to dig my garden and experiment with manures etc. That with a satisfying love life. Also with the children I find myself always joying in the creative side . . .

It is sad I say. I get many letters from parents . . . "My boy of 15 is stealing and you are the only man in England who can cure him." And I can't any longer, for curing such meant having no life of my own, having my tools and clothes sold by crooks, my furniture damaged. I did it for many years but now younger men ought to be doing it.

We hope to get back to our own house this summer, and that will be a great delight. The place will have to be remade after the military use of it, and that will be good work, for it is my own house and anything I do is mine, not a landlord's as it is here. I plan to build a small house outside the main school and have my own private life at last. And a joy will be to get golf again. I have had none for five years and I love the game as much as you do skiing.

But I am not retiring from educational work . . . nay. I have much to give yet, but I want to give it to normal kids, not the misfits of life,

---

* The central character in Ibsen's play of the same name, who sacrificed all to principle.

who after all seldom come to much. Once I thought and said that the problem child was the one with originality and guts, but I was wrong. He is mostly the super-egoist, the player to the gallery. I have had dozens pass through S'hill but I can't think of one who later showed brilliance in work. I feel and have felt for years that it is better to concentrate on the normal ones who are worth the trouble.

U.S.A. education sounds to me in a bad way. I get letters now from well-known American teachers, all progressive, but again compromisers on the main things, timid of freedom, moral about sex. I look forward to having fun when I meet them over there.

Constance. *Etwas* [Something] wrong with her. Unhappy. But what is the answer to the fact that a woman of her age does not attract lovers? She came down to help me here for two months, but I found her almost supporting the malcontents among the staff.

Your boy looks a wonder child. With the same post came the photo of a boy the same age, son of a late girl on our staff. Your lad looks twice as intelligent and alive. Another Willy Reich—poor kid! . . .

Well, Reich, all my best wishes to you and your Frau. Sad to hear you say friends have drifted away in the war years. Perhaps not. When human contact begins again it may be like old times; the touch of the hand, the glance, the laugh can't be kept fresh by letters. I know that when we meet over a bottle of the best we'll pick up the threads of life where we dropped them.

Forest Hills, New York

April 2, 1945

My dear Neill:

This will be a short letter. I understand very well your desire to get away from curative psychology. For a few months now, I am bothered terribly by the same wish to escape the world of the neurotic and to make *Schluss* [an end] with my psychiatric nuisance work. I am trying to find a way to secure my living somehow, and to give all my time to the investigation of living matter. I would only continue to restructure educators who are dealing with nursery schools. That is justified by the only hope we have, which is in the new-born babies.

I agree with your judgment on U.S.A. education. But there are great possibilities here for a break-through, but also, of course, for being hanged for the break-through.

Our research has for nearly a year now dug deeply into the problems of growth of animals and plants with amazing results.

My boy is a living proof of the inherent decency and honesty of the life process, if it is not disturbed. I am quite sure that all children could be that way if they were left to themselves during their growth and if no neurotic relatives were around.

Summerhill School
Festiniog, North Wales

June 6, 1945

My dear Reich,

I got married in the usual way three weeks ago. The other way too difficult when my main fight is for education, and any other fight—for reform in marriage, etc—would weaken my position re education. To fight too many battles is to lose the lot. Marriage agrees with me, for I have gained so much weight that my trousers won't button on me now. I begin to look like a successful pork butcher. Have been east seeing my own school and we hope to move back this autumn at latest.

Philipson's idea of a Sex Econ. Conference* at S'hill is fine, yet perhaps it would be better in London where it would get a better chance of interesting people outside.

Flugel's new book *Man, Morals and Society* mentions you five times quite kindly, but does not grasp your fundamentals.

Philipson seems to say that the Norway crowd has disintegrated. A sad comedown from Veg. Ther. to shock treatment indeed. Can't think in what way old Raknes has gone off the lines. Most odd that he was allowed to practice for over four years in Oslo, isn't it? The world is going to be very interesting now that the first phase of the class war is over.† The real fight between fascism and socialism is next on the programme, and there will be some great events in Europe in our time. For myself I think that the next era will be communism leading slowly to universal liberalism without profit. A queer situation here in which

---

* Neill enclosed a letter from Tage Philipson, suggesting an international conference.

† Surprisingly, this is the only reference either Neill or Reich makes to the end of the war in Europe, an event to which both men had looked forward for so long.

the official labour movement seems to hate communism as much as it does fascism or maybe more. I take no part in politics at all and take a narrow view that under any system I shall be unfree to be an educational reformer.

It is good to hear of your Peter and his progress. But whether he is born to carry a rifle twenty years hence depends on you and me and other fighters. That is the only cause that really matters at this time in history.

Well, Reich, all the best. I like to hear that you also are tired of neurotics. I've had 25 years of them (including myself) and feel that my tiredness of them means that I am no longer one of them!

———— ◆•◆ ————

Orgonon
Rangeley, Maine

June 15, 1945

My dear Neill:

It is difficult to say what happened in Scandinavia with our co-workers. They seem to be in great trouble, and mutually antagonistic. Such an interruption of contact as that which has been caused by this war is always bad. Philipson himself behaved very peculiarly. I had sent several manuscripts to Sweden and did not receive any answer. We shall have to wait until Raknes, Nic* and others write, in order to know what is going on. According to my opinion no congress could take place, unless preparations had been made. I think you will agree with me that, first, messages from all concerned should be awaited. I am expecting an answer from Philipson. You don't seem to be enthusiastic about the idea of a convention in Summerhill. I can understand that you would not like the disturbance.

Did you have word from Hamilton,† of the Hamilton School in New York? They like your books, and are enthusiastic about the sex-economic standpoint in education. How about a trip to New York, my dear Neill? I think that you will like Hamilton very much. He is going through vegeto-therapy with me.

---

* Nic Waal, Norwegian psychiatrist, friend and student of Reich's in Oslo.

† A. E. Hamilton, known as Tajar, and his wife, Eleanor, known as Ranger, together ran the Hamilton School, first in New York and later, as the Hamilton Farm, in Sheffield, Mass.

We are putting up a $4000 building on Orgonon for experimental work.

Your suggestion of the possibility of a future liberalistic social setup without profit sounds very probable.

You should not feel too bad about the marriage license. We took one out ourselves after 6 years of marriage, in order to satisfy the worries of the naturalization office about our moral status. Do you think the moralistic pest will ever vanish from the face of the earth? It seems like an important asset to have-nots.

Summerhill School
Festiniog, North Wales

June 25, 1945

My dear Reich,

Yours today. Also one from Philipson who seems to be most anxious to get out of Scandinavia now.

Re conference. Don't know what inner objections I have to having one at S'hill. I haven't got back to Suffolk yet and when I do (this autumn I hope) it will mean a long time of hard work to build it up again. That incidentally will conflict with my wish to lecture in U.S.A. A conference run by you yourself would be most welcome to me in S'hill at any time. But even then I'd want at least a lecture by you in London where there are people who know of you now.

Tell you what I feel, Reich. That the Scandinavian group narrowed down your teachings too much. They saw it too much from the curative point of view; their horizon was the patient. Mine is the life of a child, eating, playing, learning, sexual, fighting, striving. I think your disciples tend to lose perspective just as Freud's did. Disciples are a damned nuisance every time. Let's abolish them! Most boring letters I get are from fans who look on me as their inspiration or leader. *Mein Gott! Nein*, Reich. Still I see that a Conference would help disciples to get back their perspective. S'hill is open for YOUR conference any day.

Exchanged a few letters with Hamilton. Maybe winter of 1946. No use coming in summer for no lectures will be on then, and I must make some money if I come. Am losing all the time now, with high prices and poorish parents. I wish I had some trade or business to support the school. May try market gardening, for my land in Suffolk is rich.

P.S. I'm 61 now and have had S'hill 25 years. I wish I could have another 25. Why is life so damnably short? You are just beginning to learn about life when it is time to put your toys away and go to bed.

———————◆•◆———————

Orgonon
Rangeley, Maine

July 2, 1945

My dear Neill:

If you don't mind, I would like to bother you with an organizational matter, an issue arising from the fact that the contact between me and the Scandinavian workers of the Institute has been disrupted for so long. Here is the trouble:

When I left Scandinavia, Philipson automatically by his skill as a teacher took, so to speak, my place in the Scandinavian organization. But he did not succeed in keeping this organization together, and, as you know, great troubles arose with the Scandinavian group. I decided to write to Philipson and to ask him what happened. To that I received a nasty letter. He and other members of the Institute are of the opinion that I at once disavow anyone who attempts to work on my theory. He assumes that I would sabotage or prevent a congress. (After I had suggested it myself.) He mistakes the work-democratic principle as the abandonment of any necessity to keep each other informed, in other words, co-operation is not necessary. I am supposed to have the responsibility for the international work, without having the right to expect that a scientific worker, who is leading a national section, keeps me informed of where he lives, and what is going on in his section. I hate to be a director, but I must know how things stand. You are in a far higher position than he is, and I too, and yet you were kept informed by me about the progress of the work here, and though I did not see you for more than 6 years, I know from your letters roughly how you stand and what your school is doing. Such co-operation is so matter of course that I regret to have to point it out.

To be frank, and I am sure you will understand my viewpoint, I refuse to play organizational politics. I refuse to be a director. I can exist, and I really believe even better so, without any organization apart from the organization needed to carry on my research. I am far beyond the state of development of 1939. I am ready and willing to give my advice if somebody wants it, but I am not ready to do all the dirty work, and to suffer all the dirty attacks, and to give at the same time the one for whom I work and who became famous through my work, the freedom to behave badly against me. I would like to suggest, therefore, that we find out whether this International Institute of 1939 still exists or not, and to dissolve it in case it did not stand the test of the war crisis. The work is organized anyhow locally in the American Orgone Institute, including sex-economy, in your school, in Palestine and in other places. I am engrossed deeply and with all my heart in orgone physical research which will keep me busy for the next 30 to 40 years.

July 12

I gave myself several days' time to let matters sink in. Now, after re-reading my letter to you I think it is right to send it, and I would like to add a few more things about my standpoint. I am ready to work in a factual, rational, work-democratic set-up of co-operation. It seems as if the principle of politics to unite easily and smoothly for war, but to be incapable of unity for practical rational peace aims, applies already to the old Institute of 1939. I am ready to give freedom to everyone to do what he wants, but he cannot spit on my table when he wants to and still expect me to relinquish my right to freely accept or refuse his spitting. We know from spoiled children how easily they mistake real freedom for licence, and how easily they think they are behaving freely when they are only behaving badly. Freedom in my life and work and concept of living does not mean that you can do whatever you want, but that you can choose among numberless free possibilities to do what is best toward a definite goal.

I cannot judge how far apart the members of the Institute of 1939 have drifted from each other. If you can do something to correct the situation in the sense that there is rational co-operation and not in the sense of licence, I shall appreciate it. I would appreciate your true opinion and advice.

———— ◆ • ◆ ————

Orgonon
Rangeley, Maine

July 13, 1945

My dear Neill:

I had just mailed a very thick letter to you yesterday when I received yours of June 25th, and I am hurrying to answer it. I wish to thank you most heartily for offering Summerhill for a conference. But I am afraid much time will have to pass—according to a rough judgment at least one to two years—before such a conference could be held. We cannot have a conference without having prepared it properly together with all concerned. I want you to accept my invitation to stay at our home in Forest Hills while you are in New York. It won't be too comfortable because four-fifths of the house is full of instruments and laboratory stuff, but it can be arranged, and will be more convenient. I am sure that Hamilton will be only too glad to arrange all the lectures you wish to give.

The letter I sent off yesterday confirmed in advance what you wrote about organization and disciples. But it is not an easy matter to decide. It works as badly with as without disciples, and we have to find our way. I regret that I had to bother you with this Scandinavian affair, but I could not do otherwise.

I have an important suggestion to make as to the support of your school, but about that when you are here.

————————◆•◆————————

Summerhill School
Festiniog, North Wales

August 6, 1945

My dear Reich,

Sorry for delay in answering you. In the middle of packing up to move back to Suffolk, and working about 25 hours a day.

Don't know what to say about Philipson. His letter is most neurotic and suggests to me the "beloved disciple of the Master" psychology . . . —"I, Dr P, am the one and only disciple who understands the New Christ who is being betrayed by the other Judases." In any case his letter is absolutely subjective and therefore unanswerable in logic and reason.

A young man called Barbikan, or some name sounding like it, came here for a week from London. He began at once to attack me. He knows all your works and your work is the centre of his world. He went away saying that he is to write you a full description of S'hill, proving that it is not working according to Reich Sex Econ. I told him the school isn't a Reich school. He is quite friendly and honest and wants to show me any letter he writes to you. Faint resemblance to the

P. affair. They introduce personalities instead of the work. Tiresome when I have to concentrate on moving pianos and books all day long.

If my article hasn't been printed in the journal ask Wolfe not to use it. I don't like it now; I always feel like that about writing; by the time it is printed I've thought of another way. Yours in haste and worry.

———◆•◆———

Summerhill School
Festiniog, North Wales

                August 22, 1945

My dear Reich,

      A short letter because I am moving my school and am very busy. Many thanks for your two books.* You are a wonderful man, Reich. I read you and realise that I know nothing of psychology.

And shall I try to get a London publisher for your two latest books? I think I could now that the war is over.

My own new book† isn't out yet, and I hate its appearance, for much of it I don't like now. A book written during a war is bad; things change too quickly. I didn't see the turn to the Left in politics here.

What of the atomic bomb? How does it connect with your Orgone? Death versus Life. Inorganic versus Organic. Death always seems to win in science.

P.S. How is Peter?

Had a wonderful dream last night in which I came to N.Y. and saw you in your lab. It was a disappointment to awake. How I am to come over in reality I don't know. I have just been over to Suffolk and there is work there to restore the place, years of work, for the land is all weeded and I'll have to become a gardener for at least a year.

———◆•◆———

---

* *Character Analysis* (1945) and *The Sexual Revolution* (1945).
† *Hearts Not Heads in the School.*

Orgonon
Rangeley, Maine

September 10, 1945

My dear Neill:

Many thanks for your kind letter. I would like to have my books published in England. But why reprint them if they are here in English already? Would some publisher in England sell them on commission for our Press? They are selling my stuff quite strongly now in the U.S.A.

We have finished the laboratorium building in Orgonon. It cost about $3000 more than expected.

Send me your book as soon as it appears.

I had several enquiries regarding the relationship of Orgone to the atomic bomb. Orgone is, as far as I can see, sub-atomic energy in its natural form out of which chemical elements arise. The atomic bomb energy is obtained by smashing matter. We are gathering the cosmic energy naturally. I don't believe that the mechanists will ever succeed in slowing up the process of smashing up matter to such a degree that the energy could be used beneficially. Somebody said the other day that the Orgone energy is the only real counteractor to the deathly atom bomb energy.

———◆◆◆———

Forest Hills, New York

October 29, 1945

My dear Neill:

I did not hear from you in a long time. I wish to present a problem to you and I hope you will co-operate:

We are stopping the publication of the *Journal* in its present form, but it will continue to exist as an archive under the title "Archives of Orgone Biophysics," which will publish the "heavy" natural scientific stuff. Now, I am pondering a plan of issuing a periodical of much smaller size and much less pages, and on a much more popular basis, under the possible title of "Living Matter, New Ways in Education." If you have a better title, please let me know. This popular journal would be edited by all educators who on principle agree with our viewpoint. It would be fine and very encouraging if you would agree to sign as one of the editors, and second, to contribute regularly to this journal out of the material of your school. I hold that this plan is of the greatest practical importance to promote the development of public opinion which would confirm the natural life functions of the child from before birth until it is grown up. Please give me your suggestions on that idea.

Did you succeed in establishing at Leiston again? How is it going? We are functioning full blast again in our lab, but I am so burdened with administrative work that I cannot get time for thinking and theoretical research.

———◆◆———

Forest Hills, New York

November 24, 1945

My dear Neill,

We had quite a bit of discussion here concerning the further upkeep of the *Journal.* We now developed the following idea: We would not have to stop the publication, and it could be broadened considerably, if you and others would be willing to take care of your specific field of work, editing your specific material. I hope very much that you will be interested enough to help along. I imagine that educational material, gathered from your school and your co-workers, as well as material about the status of education in England in general, would be interesting enough for you to be taken care of by you. Please inform me how you feel about it, and whether you would like to do this job together with your co-workers for England.

I would take care of the natural scientific, orgone biophysical field.

I am conducting at present a seminar with about 16 educators from various schools, about the problem of how the new-born child is met by armored parents, nurses, etc. It is quite exciting what that does to life.

I hope very much that you find time for rest while building up anew your old beloved school. Here are a few photos of my son.

———◆◆———

Summerhill School
Leiston, Suffolk

November 28, 1945

My dear Reich,

I have sent you my book. You will see by it that I have still one foot in the old camp of Freud etc. and one in the Reich camp. In short, I have not grasped all your message, possibly because I got it too late in life. Put it in this way: I have added a little of Reich to S'hill whereas to make S'hill a complete orgonotic-orgastic school would mean a new basis entirely. So that when you ask me to take part in the new journal editing, I get a little afraid that I am not the one to propagate sex-economy views with complete sincerity. Some of my self-distrust comes from my experience of veg.-therapy with adolescents here. One by one as things got nearer to vital repressions they stopped coming. Don't know how much I was to blame, but therapy must be desired by the patient every time obviously. But I can see that your new journal will not be a therapeutic one; it will be creative for the future rather than trying to clean up messes from the past. That sort of journal I could of course help with. Let me know what plans you all make. *Ich werde mitmachen* [count me in]!

We came back here in Sept. and it was a big task, an exhausting one too. But it is so delightful to be back again that all the trouble is forgotten by now. Much has to be repaired after 5 years of army occupation. At Christmas we celebrate our Jubilee, for it was Xmas 1921 that I began in Hellerau, Dresden. 25 years of kids is a long time, but I am still fresh, although I am not so patient of their noise as I used to be, and have had my part of the house partitioned off for quietness.

Wood is still severely rationed, but I can buy one pound's worth per month, and now see my way to building an Akku.

P.S. Like you I am burdened with work that doesn't interest me. A popular Sunday paper had picture of S'hill and I had 150 letters mostly from working people asking if I'd have their children. I had to answer every one myself. They don't ask me to broadcast now but when I did I spent weeks answering letters. That and interviewing government officials, builders, gardeners, etc. fills too much of my day. Just an office boy I am.

———————— ◆ ◆ ————————

Forest Hills, New York

December 19, 1945

My dear Neill:

Yesterday I received your new book *Hearts Not Heads*. I began to read it immediately and found it, contrary to your opinion, not only extremely interesting but *very important*. I agree with you on nearly every step you take, but there is a great But which not only concerns you and your attitude but also my own work: I learn to see more and more how deeply rooted and how complicated the distortion of the human soul has become through the maltreatment of many thousand years. That is a point where the answer to the question, how in heaven's name the masses of the people should actually and practically seize the rule of *true* self-government becomes lost in misty fogs. It is all well and good to clamor for freedom, to fight the suppressors of freedom, but I feel that all of us miss the point in that we do not give any practical answer to the question how and whether the streetcars will run, and the streets will be cleaned and the coal mined and the mail distributed and the countryside policed, and the subways engineered, if there is no authority from above. I am only throwing back the burning stick you once threw into my lap when you cooled me off by saying rightly that administration will tend to become bureaucratic and authoritarian. Do you remember that hot potato? I don't see anything about it in your book, and I have been deeply disturbed for the past few months, because I cannot arrive at any practically sound conclusion in regard to the administration of such an intricate mechanism as our society. And to say "*responsible* freedom" instead of only "freedom," does not solve the problem. The more you learn about the emotional pest in the depth of the human being, the more hopeful I become as far as the distant future is concerned, but the more hopeless the situation looks in regard to the near future.

The other day I received a letter from the International Mark Twain Society telling me that I have been elected Honorary Member of this society. I suppose I deserved it, but I am haunted by the terrible fear: I am holding 3 honorary memberships by now; if I get 2 or 3 more of this kind, I shall not be able to write a true line any more. So I have to hurry up before it is too late.

I hope you will succeed in living through a peaceful Christmas with rest and joy. We are taking it easy too in these days.

◆◆◆

Summerhill School
Leiston, Suffolk

December 27, 1945

My dear Reich,

It is kind of you to say what you do about my book. *The* [London] *Times* in a long review calls me a genius and then proceeds to

show that I am not one. Also I have been honoured by being chosen
as one of 16 contributors to a memorial book of essays to celebrate
Bernard Shaw's ninetieth birthday. What with your honours too, we are
both becoming far too respectable. Does it mean we are both out-of-
date? I wonder.

Group of young men in London want to start a Sex Econ. journal.
I know two of them, Eastmond and Day. Day has been my maths
teacher and has a very wide craps✝ of all your work including the
Orgone side. They want it to be independent of the U.S.A. work. They
are writing to you about it. I see the snags in it although I am all for
their getting to work. I hope you will let them work, for they are keen
and in Day's case very clever. Their journal might exchange articles
with yours.

Note: Mark ✝ above. I meant to write "grasp." I wrote "craps" which
in slang means faeces! I hope the Freudian error doesn't betray my real
opinion of Mr. Day.

I don't quite grasp your fear that no one will bring the coal or sweep
the streets. Why not? Given short hours and good pay in a new
civilisation. I am spending most of the day making gravel paths, heavy
work wheeling barrows and using a pickaxe. I like it, and wouldn't mind
being a navvy every morning if I could do something else afternoons
and nights. No, the problem I can't solve is who is to direct the coal
heavers and post men. The desk blokes? Yet I feel that, given education
such as you and I demand, the *Stimmung* [mood] among people will do
much to solve all these questions. I feel that today there is a race
between socialism and the atomic bomb; that is the immediate question.

Another problem. You hold that Stalinism is no longer socialism.
Then why is the capitalist world so hostile to Stalinism? Why are so
many diehards openly anticipating the Russo-American war? Why the
fear that Russia is bolshevising central Europe? I don't know the
answers; am just puzzled. I'd hate to live in a Communist state as we
know it, yet I always find that my "feelings" are with Russia against
the Imperialist idea. And, Reich, whether we like it or not Communism
is the next step, and if we and the International Labour Party and the
Anarchists and the Social Democrats don't adapt ourselves we can do
nothing, for we are a small minority. And once Communism is set up
we won't be allowed to differ; we'll be liquidated. Most confusing and
perplexing. Certainly no Communist state would tolerate S'hill and my
work.

We have just celebrated the 25th birthday of S'hill with many old pupils and parents down dancing till 6 a.m. The only snag was that we couldn't get any drink to celebrate with, and this is the first Xmas in years when I didn't have wine and whiskey with my Xmas dinner. Sad, but a few million were worse off in Europe.

Constance is working hard to raise money to feed the starving kids in Europe. It is a question that one is apt to repress all the time. I find myself doing so sometimes.

Your son grows fast. I like his looks, brave and curious. Ena my wife does not seem to get pregnant. I want her to see a specialist at once. She hates specialists, *aber* . . . We are very happy together, and both have the fullest in love. But she hates it when my female fans come along and want to talk to me at length.

This fan business is tiresome . . . I often daydream of a quiet life in the country with a garden, a workshop and some hens and no post and no visitors, but I know I'd soon tire of that.

Well, Reich, every good wish to you both . . . to you three in '46.

1946

Summerhill School
Leiston, Suffolk

January 10, 1946

My dear Reich,

I hear that The Freedom Press, London, is wanting to publish your books over here. I think this would be a great mistake. It is an Anarchist Press, disliked by diehards and communists alike and by liberals. If they publish you then your public will be limited and the big public will be suspicious. No, your books should appear with the name of a respectable publisher . . . any of them, but not a narrow sect. Some anarchists are claiming you as one of them already, so be careful.

My book selling like hot cakes. Getting good reviews, but one or two bitter and hostile. *The Times* in first paragraph calls me a genius, and then in the rest of half a page shows that I ain't.

Re that proposed trip to U.S.A. on a lecture tour, I begin to think I am too old.* U.S.A. with its hustle . . . lecturing in one city on Monday night then flying 300 miles to lecture next night sort of thing would kill me. No, I'd like to come as a visitor and maybe give a few lectures leisurely to help pay my fare and expenses. To face a long tour with a fixed timetable would be appalling. In the meantime of course *es kommt nicht in Frage* [it is out of the question] for I have much to do here and can't get the right teachers and have to worry a lot when I want to have an easy life.

---

* Neill was sixty-two.

153

All good fortune to you and Ilse and Peter in 1946. Lang may your lum reek . . . get a Scot to translate that one.

———————◆•◆———————

Forest Hills, New York

January 12, 1946

My dear Neill:

This is to answer your letter of December 27th. First of all, I would like to discuss the project of Eastmond and Day. It is a tough proposition to decide upon. I am a bad police dog, and I don't like to supervise. I would say, let them go ahead and let's hope for the best. There is only one wish I would insist upon being fulfilled. They should not use the words sex-economy or orgone biophysics in the title of their journal, unless they are ready to cooperate with the Orgone Institute very closely, as Dr. Hoppe* in Palestine and others in other countries do.

I believe you are still adhering to an old antithesis of capitalist world and socialist world, which is a dead past. You say your feelings are with Russia against the imperialist idea. I wonder why you don't see that Russia is as imperialistic as any capitalistic country could be (see Iran, Finland, etc.) and that the American government has divided up the big estates in Bavaria. I also believe that you underestimate the truly democratic trends and forces in the U.S.A., the hate of imperialism and dictatorship. I wish we had time to discuss these things thoroughly.

Take my belated congratulations to the 25th birthday of Summerhill. I wonder whether you know how important Summerhill is, and how much more important it will become in the future. I don't believe that there will be a communist regime in the whole world. It is not honest, and will die out just because of that.

Please write soon again, and let me have a snapshot of yourself and your school.

———————◆•◆———————

---

* Walter Hoppe, German physician who had immigrated to Israel.

Forest Hills, New York

January 21, 1946

My dear Neill:

A few days ago I received a letter from Eastmond concerning their plan to issue a periodical *Work Democracy*. Of course, I like their idea and I said so. They can have all my support. But the danger is that not working practically on sex-economic educational and social problems, they may slip into ideological, or still worse, political talking of the old type.

Now I must take your time for something else that concerns not only me, but everybody who is in touch with me and my work: a meeting with a federal judge at the office of naturalization in Brooklyn. It brought again to my consciousness something of which I have been aware for a long time: that my life is swinging back and forth between police actions on the one hand and honorary memberships and future Nobel prizes on the other hand. It is a rather interesting, though dangerous mixture.

When I received the document that conveys upon me the honorary membership of the International Mark Twain Society, I felt like the criminal Huckleberry Finn. I felt that I had done wrong in accepting or receiving this document of honor, that the illustrious gathering of well-known names on the letterhead would soon feel embarrassed about this new and strange honorary member.

I have to confess that I am not what is called a solid member of good society or a "good citizen." My name, though beloved in some quarters, is hated and detested in others. When I see a policeman, my heart beats faster, as if I had just stolen silver spoons, or as if I were a boy who had just punctured the tires on the car of the older brother of a bad friend.

The other day I stood before the bar of a judge in Federal Court of the Naturalization Office of the U.S.A. I felt afraid and spiteful. The judge, a young ardent officer of the law, eager to gain his spurs early, recriminated me for certain books which have been seen or found in my library; books by Lenin and Trotsky. "And what has politics to do with biology?" he asked. I could not tell him that if you are a writer on human affairs and conflicts, you must have read the writings of these two bad citizens of the world! I felt guilty because the offense was my silent thought that a judge of the Federal Court of the U.S.A. should not ask such silly questions.

To be short: I am an embarrassing fellow. I might not turn out to be the Honorary Fellow to some after all.

Imagine a fiery horse racing over meadows enjoying a sunny morning in the spring. It jumps over high bushes and broad brooks. It overcomes seemingly unsurmountable obstacles. But behind a small bush far in the corner of the field, well hidden and protected, a small stick of 20 inches brings the horse to fall. It breaks its neck.

That's the course of life. Imagine now the honorary colleague of Einstein and Eisenhower breaking his neck in such a manner! To fall over a small, ambitious judge of a small court who does not know what a library is used for.

Honored and esteemed in the highest terms in many circles, the danger of a new mess-up of things, emigration, homelessness, is on the horizon again because the word communism is associated with emotions which cannot be handled medically in a court. To explain to the average mind the difference between the intended true democracy of Lenin and the sham democracy brought about by the irrationality of the masses is, I think, quite beyond present possibilities.

Maybe that my life, spent hitherto in about 10 changes of domicile, makes me look at things in this manner. It is not the troubles of life but the irrationality of procedures which I cannot overcome and which takes my guts.

Summerhill School
Leiston, Suffolk

January 26, 1946

My dear Reich,

Yours yesterday. I had often wondered what was happening about your naturalisation, and feared difficulties, but kept saying to myself: "When the world acknowledges the Orgone, R. will be safe in any and every country as a famous discoverer." I have become impatient waiting for your public success, and I confess that sometimes Mr Doubt would whisper in my ear: "Perhaps Reich has got hold of the wrong end of the stick with his new physics." But the doubt never lasted more than a moment or two.

What puzzles me is how the learned men of U.S.A. come to reward you with their gifts of membership of exclusive societies? It means you are known by the few who have no political influence. I think of my own case. I am known to the intelligentsia of this country; recently a few well-known newspapers have called me a genius. But if I had to appear in court on some or any charge, financial or criminal or what not, I'd be "a schoolmaster Alexander Neill etc." The judge and jury wouldn't know my name, and if the enemy counsel quoted from my books they would certainly not be in sympathy with my views. I take it the case with you is similar. Any hostile person can condemn you out of your own mouth as seen in your writings. It sounds insane that any judge should challenge a man for having Lenin and Trotsky books in his house. A wise judge would say that these two authors cancel each other out! You say I am out of date in my opinion that the old set-up Communism versus Capitalism is still alive. If it is dead why does your judge see danger in your library? Odd that your judge should fix on the political side, ignoring the fact that your sex-economy views are of greater moment than mere political set-ups.

After six years in N.Y. have you no friends at the top? It is usually easier to deal with a lord than with his butler. A way must be found. You can't go moving to another country which will get all your dossier before you arrive. I here admit a daydream . . . maybe after all Reich will come to live in London. I wish you could, but not as a compulsory expelled man from U.S.A.

Forest Hills, New York

January 29, 1946

My dear Neill:

I just received your letter of January 10th. I am, of course, strictly against my books being published by political organizations. That does not mean that I have anything personally against anarchists, communists or even individual fascists. You find useful and useless ones in all camps.

I am glad that your book is selling well. It deserves it.

Re your trip to the U.S.A.: I would suggest that you hook up with the Hamilton School in New York which could arrange a leisure-full lecture tour in the U.S. I would advise very much against the typical American touring. I am still longing for a good long chat with you.

Forest Hills, New York

February 4, 1946

My dear Neill:

I have yours of January 26th. You are absolutely right in what you say. Only one remark does not seem clear: You write that the people with whom I am associated now have no political influence. Is it possible that the generals Marshall, Mountbatten, Pershing, Eisenhower, Nimitz, Alexander, the scientists Einstein, Wells, the statesmen Churchill, Hoover, Camaccio [Camacho], Mackenzie King,* have no political influence? They have, but I am afraid that as it happened in Norway, a small judge of a small court, or a small little fellow in a police court, is stronger, much stronger, than the knowledge of the few and even the power of the few. It is a dark and terrifying picture.

As I learned directly from this judge, a document was sent over apparently from Norway to the FBI before I came to this country, and as he said, "they knew all about me." But I don't know what "they knew about me." My social and academic standing in the U.S. is very strong. And yet, I am deeply worried. Though I know the working of the emotional pest fairly well, I am still helpless to cope with it. Even power would be of no avail here. All this has nothing to do with Communism versus Capitalism, but only with the deadly fear and terror of the armored men of living plasmatic functions which I happened to discover. And the orgone is in that respect still much more dangerous to the pest than sex-economy. Sex-economy deals "only" with the moral issues, but orgone biophysics deals with God himself, having shown that what people call god is identical with the cosmic energy which really is everywhere, penetrates everything, created the world, constitutes the emotions and religious feelings, governs life, etc. etc. It is a very tough and straining job I am doing, Neill. My brain works at high speed day in, day out, and very often through the nights. The more I learn to understand the perversity of human reactions, the more desperate I become, even though the picture of a final solution of the social tragedy of man becomes clearer and more definite. I wish I had you here to talk things over . . .

———◆•◆———

---

* These were all men listed as Honorary Members of Societies of which Reich had himself become a member. As he took membership extremely seriously, he considered them his associates.

Summerhill School
Leiston, Suffolk

February 12, 1946

My dear Reich,

I wrote to an old friend, a lady in New York, asking her if she could help a friend of mine in being naturalised. Today I have her reply . . . "I have a friend in the State Department in Washington and one in N.Y. in the Office of War Information who would know ways and means." I don't know if you care to use influence in this way, but if you think it important I'll give her the information.

Two Danish teachers here for a month, friends of Leunbach,* etc. . . . One of the Danes is being analysed by Philipson who is back in Copenhagen.

My book has had a good reception here. *The Times* in a leading article in the Educational Supplement says I am right, and a professor of education at London Univ. praises me a lot, comparing me with Rousseau and Pestalozzi. Changed days when my books were sneered at. But the price I pay is heavy . . . scores of visitors who make me very tired with their questions. I lectured to Cambridge Univ. two nights ago with a crammed full hall and a tremendous enthusiasm from the undergraduates. They asked about sex a lot.

———◆◆◆———

Forest Hills, New York

February 18th, 1946

My dear Neill:

I hurry to answer your short note of February 12th, in which you suggest help at the State Department in Washington. It is not advisable at the present time to use any such measures. My standing in the U.S.A. is very strong, and either I shall get the citizenship in spite of all fiends or, if not, we shall be able to fight it through at the courts.

I am very glad about your success, and would like to add that I regard you much higher than Pestalozzi.

We are waiting for a new article from you for the *Journal*.

———◆◆◆———

* Dr. Joyce Leunbach, one of the leaders of the Danish Sex Pol movement; his wife, Buddha, was a member of the group around Reich in Oslo.

[1946]

Summerhill School
Leiston, Suffolk

April 30, 1946

My dear Reich,
I have been long in writing to you. Am on holiday, and after a busy term with too many visitors I feel tired, and spend the day painting walls and mending the property, which is the best way of taking a holiday. The army left the place in such a mess that there are years of work to do on it.

Not much chance of my coming for some time, I fear. Ena is having a baby in October, and that means no travel this year for me.

I don't seem to have much to write about this time. My thoughts wander to golf, and I am prouder of my improvement in the game than of my fame as a teacher. Golf is to me what skiing is to you I guess.

I am trying now to begin to get material to build an Akku. Self-interest wasn't enough, but now that Ena is pregnant and is having a bad time with sickness, I want one for her.

When are we to have a book devoted only to the scientific side of the Orgone? I'd like to give one or two to scientist friends.

No more to say. I am resting, knowing that summer will be one long talk to hundreds of visitors . . . *Gott*, how tired of them I get, for they all ask the same questions.

I am lecturing to the University of London Psychological Society in May.

———◆•◆———

Forest Hills, New York

May 8th, 1946

My dear Neill:
I have your letter of April 30th. First of all, I would like to tell you how glad I am that you have joined us in having a child. That's a marvellous thing. Please do not fail to have Mrs. Neill use the accumulator very regularly. We have very much good evidence now that regular use of the orgone accumulator helps the mother and the child to a very great extent before and after birth. Another great help is the direct irradiation of the nipple when the child starts feeding. It prevents any soreness of the nipples, and is easy to apply with the pipe and funnel. Please, don't fail to send me a photo of yourself, Mrs. Neill and the little one, when it comes.

Your question in regard to a book on the orgone is very timely. After a long struggle, and in spite of being at a peak in my psychiatric work and earning, I decided to restrict earning money to two hours a day, and to devote all the rest mainly to writing down the story of the orgone as far as it goes up to now. It is very important to have a summary of these things published. But the writing alone will take about 2 years, so that the book won't be here till another 3 years have passed.

It will interest you that my old foes of 1938 in Norway are still at work. The other day, one of my students here from Norway showed me a letter from her father in which he says that the hereditary biologist Luis Mohr of the University of Oslo has told him that I am a swindler and that he is ready to say so in public. I am going to write down and publish the whole fight for biogenesis which I have had to put up since about 1926. In spite of having gone through it myself with heart and blood, I am still astonished and amazed at what people are capable of doing, saying, pesting, and so on.

Now a remark as to "free" sex. In order to distinguish ourselves from the damaging pornographic concept of sexual activity, we got used, and found it very helpful, to using the word healthy or natural instead of free. When suppressed people use the word free, they invariably mean fucking around indiscriminately.

Summerhill School
Leiston, Suffolk

June 19, 1946

My dear Reich,

By this time Barakan will have met you. He is a clever lad and mad about your work. You may find him as I did, a bit of a *Besserwisser* [know-it-all] but not an objectionable one as so many can be. I could think of no special message to give you via him, and all I asked him to do was to bring back a detailed method of making an Akku.

Ena gets big with child. Australia offered to pay my expenses if I went out to a conference there in October, but I refused because I can't be away when she is having the child. I don't know what to say about a trip to U.S.A. Ena wants to come with me, and she won't be fit to travel for some time. I don't want to come by air if I can help it, especially now that fatherhood lies before me, and flying isn't too safe yet . . . which is most likely a rationalisation. I have noted in recent years a fear of death connected with S'hill. When at any time in London I happened to be in a Blitz, my first thought was: If I am bumped off what will happen to S'hill? Which means of course the old silly idea that no man can do our job if we depart. All the same, I can't find any man I'd like to carry on S'hill after my death. It doesn't matter though, for any man would change it, and if he didn't he'd show he was a nobody.

I long to see you and talk with you. So many things I want to ask about. O. reflex—I am now 62½ and naturally there must be a gradual process by which sex desire lessens. Or should it? I find I can go longer without wanting any sex. Is that normal or a legacy from my Calvinism? I'm not worrying about it; only curious.

I am doing no psychological work at all. Can't get staff and have to teach maths myself, but waste so much time entertaining visitors. We had 60 teachers at one time last week, and another 30 come next weekend. Good for them, but hard work for me, for I have to give them a long talk every time (free of charge, too, damn them).

Buddha Leunbach is coming for three weeks. She is translating my books into Danish. Apparently she is the girl who sat outside No. 110* summer '39 with too little on, much to your annoyance at the time. But she writes sensibly.

Orgones are still outside scientific language here. How long till they are recognised?

All the best to self and wife and kid. I want to see him. And *die Frau auch* [the wife too].

P.S. Latest story here: Young soldier fell in love with the regimental goat and was sent to a psychoanalyst.
Analyst: "Let me see now, is it a he-goat or a she-goat?"
Soldier (indignantly): "A she-goat of course. You surely don't think I'm neurotic, do you?"

———————◆◆◆———————

————————————
* The street number of Reich's address in Oslo.

Orgonon
Rangeley, Maine

[late June or early July 1946]

My dear Neill:

I have your letter of June 19th. The things you say about one's worries in regard to the future fate of one's labor are so very true. I can understand them perfectly, being in a similar position. One's disciples are apt to split their head mutually over who is the best follower. It often happened that it was just an apparent opponent who really carries on . . . but his way, and not mine or your way. I believe your school as such will not continue. But it will stand for all times as an example of what education should be. And that is more than the walls and the kids in it. As to Orgonon, I intend to establish a scientific research foundation carrying my name (it seems vain but the name promises stability to certain central ideas!!), a foundation which will house the whole archive and will be devoted to Orgone Science. Should my son grow into it, all the better. But otherwise my children should build up their own lives.

On May 28th I became an American Citizen "with the privilege to vote and to function as a juror." I told the officer that I hope to be of more important service by taking the constitution *wörtlich* [literally]. I am glad to have a passport again.

Barakan came. Seems quite a clever fellow, but I shall have to clean up his soul quite a bit too.

I want you to come over here by all means. So much has to be talked over. It should be possible, shouldn't it?

The Org. Refl. diminishes of course in later years. But so also the desire, and all is calm if the life was and is running fully as yours. The Org. Accum. will do to you what it did to Hamilton: make you tanned and give you pep. Now you are sure to have one and to use it by autumn.

I had a nasty letter from Philipson again. The man mistakes lack of respect for freedom. The whole Scandinavian situation is a mess. I am learning more and more about the lack of ability in people to function freely and cooperatively, to the point of despairing of human freedom.

I would like to get away from psychiatry of sick messed-up people. They are hopeless. I prefer to work with Bions and Earths and life energy and seeds, that is, with undistorted life. As to the Orgone: It is too early for people to write about it. It upsets the second law of thermodynamics and does away with too many wrong assumptions and theories of mechanistic science. I am looking calmly into the future and hopefully too. There is only one thing I still fear. That is, some crooked frameup, some abysmal *Gemeinheit* [dirty trick] which may still hit me in the back and destroy my work. But we are all alert and watchful. This time I think the science of living matter, so often frustrated in the past, is bound to come through.

———◆◆———

Summerhill School
Leiston, Suffolk

July 2, 1946

My dear Reich,

Am trying to pick up threads in Vienna. Karl Baer, with whom I founded the Dalcroze Schule, had my letter returned marked *Abgereist ohne Adresse* [Left without forwarding address]. Poor Baer; never realised till Erna told me that Baer is a Jewish name.

Your work and mine can be destroyed only if life itself is destroyed by atomic idiocy. It is incredible that people are talking openly about an atomic war of east against west. The atomic bomb has arrived a few hundred years too soon, at a time when an emotionally uneducated world seems likely to destroy itself. It is an appalling situation.

I advised Barakan to have as much veg.-ther. as he could. I must tell you that I gave him the Reich letter file to read, a file I kept for the future to read. I kept out of it any letter I thought personal.

I am so glad you have got your citizenship. Must relieve your mind a lot. Re our coming over. We'd both like to come when the child is born. S'hill is like a prison; it is so difficult to get away from it, for I can never find folks to leave in charge.

Your remarks about the O. Reflex are good. I can never understand the ageing men who try frantically to recover their potency with nostrums and exercises; as you say, the lessening of the sex urge should be naturally accepted. Such men must have had no other interest in life.

Tired, awfully tired. Had 40 visitors last night all asking the same old damn fool questions. I wish I could shut them all out, for the kids hate them and the staff are weary of them, but I suppose a pioneer school must pay this publicity price all the time. When I see a stranger walk into the grounds I feel like murder now. And ten Indians come this weekend, students. They will be deadly *ernst* [serious], want to ask about teaching methods . . . God, teachers are a lost tribe. I flee from them when I can.

My best wishes to Ilse and the laddie.

———◆◆◆———

Orgonon
Rangeley, Maine

July 17, 1946

My dear Neill:

We are making inquiries about how to get an accumulator, built here, over to you right away. You *must* have it. It will release much of troubles. Barakan is in charge of settling *this*.

I am all for your coming over next month if possible. I can assure you, having been a father of three newborn babies, that a father is nothing more than a nuisance around a nursing mother, if the mother is well and has some help. Please make up your mind quickly like the young man you really are and jump over this ocean by plane. August would be good for you to see Orgonon, the Lab., the working unit, the Kindergarten a few miles away, the marvellous country, and—last not least—to REST a bit, far away from your routine Summerhill. Well, how about it?

It would be grand to have some real talks as in old times.

———◆◆◆———

Summerhill School
Leiston, Suffolk

July 23, 1946

My dear Reich,

I'd love to see you all, but not now. The baby is due in mid-October and I won't leave Ena in her present state. The money question also complicates matters, for the school is paying so badly that we are having to take paying guests all August, and I can't leave her to face the worry and work alone. No, Reich, it isn't yet time to come. I want to bring her and the child when I come.

Leunbach's wife, Buddha, here for three weeks. With a Swedish woman also a patient of Philipson. He seems to be an autocrat with patients and I can see that both women are afraid of him. Buddha is having sex talks with our girls, but I am sticking to my point that I must have their mothers' consent before I have them fitted with cervical caps.

I always fear some neurotic mother will turn round and blame me, for three years ago when I asked the mothers for consent, only one, Constance, agreed. Two other mothers whose girls had been at S'hill from 4 to 16 took them away in fear. So that I must always put S'hill first and not be led into any conspiracy that might harm the school. I am too old to take risks now. Old and cowardly.

It is wonderfully kind of you to try to send us an Akku. Ena is overjoyed about it, and I certainly shall use it with hope.

In Denmark the strong Communist Party is very hostile to your people I hear. And previous admirers of my books now in the C.P. won't have them because I believe in that awful man Reich. Your circle over there has gone all to hell.

———— ◆·◆ ————

Orgonon
Rangeley, Maine

August 4, 1946

My dear Neill:

I was sorry to hear that you won't be here this summer. But I think after all that you are right in awaiting your child. We shall arrange it sometime between October and next summer. All right?

Philipson is quite a problem, and I do not know how to go about him. He "improved" on my technique without informing anyone what the "improvement" consists of, as is usual in scientific matters. He is out of contact since 1939, and still thrives on the authority in psychiatry which he received from me. I have withdrawn completely from all old organisational ties and have restricted my sphere of strict influence to a few physicians, teachers and research workers who are my personal assistants, my helpers. I do not want any international organisation of which I would be the "boss." I am a very bad supervisor and police dog. The rotten degeneration of so many great thoughts through their own organisations, in which I partook for many years, has warned me not to let any such organisation grow. My influence is widely spread without any association. I have to let life take its course also in the realm of my own creation. The old international Institute with its Scandinavian "members" does not exist any more. Ph. does not know that he is no member of anything. Please, tell this to the Danish people who are with you. It is no secret. I know that Ph. is far off the track and a track far behind even Freud, too.

I don't care whether a few scientific thieves are mentioning where they got their wisdom from or not. Here in the U.S.A. they do the same thing. They don't last long, because work based on dishonesty cannot prevail. [Reich then describes the plans for a new journal, *Annals of the Orgone Institute*, which is to replace the journal published heretofore.] If you wish to publish gathered material about your school separately in a special issue I would be glad if you would do so. I think it would be interesting and of great importance to have an issue picturing your school; articles written by you and your co-workers about principles and single cases. I would appreciate your comment about this matter.

To be thought badly of by the communists of today is only a compliment. I would feel rotten if they would love me. If there is any group of living humans who can claim to top everything else in evasion of the truth and in high politics, it is the communists. The Christians held on to their principles for a few centuries. The communists did not manage to stick to theirs for even 5 years after Lenin's death. It is a long sad chapter of human character structure.

We hope to get the Accu through to you as soon as possible. It would help Mrs. Neill quite a bit. I am happy that you will have a child of "your own" (to use this capitalistic expression). To see it grow from the first day through the first two years is quite an experience!! Later on they grow away on their own, but the memory lasts. My daughter Eva who is 22 years now and married, also studying medicine, is living at Orgonon this summer and works at the laboratory. She overcame the terrible conflicts of some years ago nearly completely and I love her as a good friend rather than as a daughter.

The third edition of my *Mass Psychology* is coming out now in a few days. I'll send a copy. All the other publications are sold by many hundreds each month. Many state libraries and universities are among the consumers. Physicians are pouring in for study and patients for treatment to such an extent that we are unable to place them.

———◆•◆———

Summerhill School
Leiston, Suffolk

August 28, 1946

My dear Reich,

I am longing to see Barakan to hear all about your work and family. My brat may come about the end of Sept. the way Ena looks now. I fear it will be a boy for I'd rather have a daughter. My work is my son.

Spending the days painting doors, making walls, etc. and feel I never want to see schools or think about education again. My life is one long GIVE and it is a joy to me to do something that requires no thought. Laying bricks I find most soothing. The sad fact is that people tire me much more now than they did. And 133 local teachers want to come in October to see S'hill . . . come at one time!

I think the international situation depresses us all. Science has invented the atom bomb, but science of living can't control it, and I have the nasty fear that the fools who control it may blast us all to hell before education can control the world. But I want to visit you before that happens. My main hope now is that Russia and China and everyone will discover how to make the bomb, and then each will be scared to use it. A poor hope indeed, but what is the alternative? The politicians have all the power. No statesmanship visible, no hopeful outlook (why did Roosevelt die?); all squabbling for things that should be dead—security, empire, power, oil, trade. The war against Communism has still to be fought, and it is so difficult to know what to think and do. I'd hate to live in Russia, but if the alternative is living under oil kings and empire builders, what can one do? For the alternative isn't your *Arbeitsdemokratie* [work democracy] or liberalism. It is *entweder oder* [either or]; when the time comes I have to ask myself the question: Do I fight for what Stalin wants or for what capitalism wants? I don't like either, but what then? How easy it is for the simple ones in life who can take a side wholly.

I am looking forward to seeing Barakan again to get all the news. I wish you would make the trip to Europe yourself to see what mess they are making in Scandinavia, and of course to see us here.

———◆•◆———

Orgonon
Rangeley, Maine

September 4, 1946

My dear Neill:

This letter is to tell you about Barakan. You were right in saying that he is a very intelligent and capable fellow with a scientific future in front of him. I think he can be trusted with work with adolescents, but I would not advise, and I told him so, to do anything with grown-ups beyond 25 years and with biopathies.

During the past years, we developed here a very strict attitude against pestilential reactions of people. We have no time and no desire to get involved in complicated attempts at convincing, or bringing to our side people whose negative behavior is clearly rooted in their biopathy, that is, in their fear of life. We are only a few, and the prevention of biopathies in children seems much more important to us.

There is also the other danger, that the London group* may try to work like a political party. I told Barakan explicitly that we are not a political party, and that we do not want too many followers. On the contrary, a nucleus of a few selected workers seems the best guarantee against a too early dilution of the core of our work.

I am expecting Raknes here today or tomorrow, and I hope to get a clear enough picture about the situation in Scandinavia to be able to mend the damage which was caused by the interruption of our contact for 7 years.

I sincerely hope that everything is all right with you over there, and that a meeting in the not too distant future will be possible. I think it would be of great importance.

One more thing: Barakan received a loan of $330 from the Orgone Research Fund which he promised to pay back to you in the course of 2 years, beginning this autumn, on account of the $600 which the Fund still owes you.

Please don't fail to inform us of the arrival of the baby!

———◆•◆———

Orgonon
Rangeley, Maine

September 14, 1946

My dear Neill:

It was good to have your letter (Aug. 28, '46).

About our social dilemma: When there was only the choice between the Austrian and the English King in 1918 we chose a THIRD thing, the Republic. The same applies now: When today there is the choice between capitalistic and red imperialism I choose the THIRD thing, the govern-

---

* The group around Eastmond and Day with whom Barakan was associated.

ment of love, work and knowledge. These political systems are bogged down fully and without any hope in political rigmarole. If human society is to survive (I fear that our present society will NOT survive!!!) neither capitalism nor communism must exist. But there is no doubt whatsoever that the chances, the possibilities of thinking and talking things over and preparing for the future are there only in the Western countries and not in Russia. You don't get killed in U.S.A. if you publish about work democracy, but in Russia you do.

The main problem is and will probably be for another 500 years the Little Man and his ways of thinking and acting. I just labored hard and painfully on a 60-page "Talk with the Little Man"* which is unpublishable.

Did you receive my *Mass Psychology of Fascism*? I sent you a signed copy. People say that it's good but I am far away from it.

According to Raknes, our work stands well in Norway. Its representatives are regarded highly and they live well. Raknes saw the Orgone in its different forms and is going to take all back to Norway.

Good luck for the great event you expect. Good luck! Write when it happens. You will see it's different to have a child of your own—it's "capitalistic." Give my regards to Mrs. Neill!

———◆•◆———

Summerhill School
Leiston, Suffolk

October 4, 1946

My dear Reich,

Your *Fascism* book is too good; it is like a rich Xmas pudding, and taken in too large doses is indigestible. I mean it seriously. I found that after reading three chapters I felt I had to rest and think. Your point of view is easily the most important of all views today, for you are the only man who is viewing society from the Sex Pol point of view. But reading you makes me pessimistic; I say to myself: "How the hell can Reich, who is so obviously right, get across to the man in the street?" What is needed is a book called "Reich without Tears," one

---

* *Listen, Little Man!* (Orgone Institute Press, 1948; new translation, 1974). Originally written as a private formulation of Reich's outrage over what man (the Little Man) does to himself and to the great men who try to help him.

in simple language that Tom, Dick and Harry can read. Men who have most to say too often are difficult to read . . . Freud, Reich . . . but smaller men write simply, a man like Stekel whose language is easy to follow, or a man like Neill who writes journalese. I say I get pessimistic about it because time is so short, and the after-war mood and psychology is so lost, so opportunist, so atomically dangerous. Bad also is the increase of church power during and after any war. I want to be quick, to fight all that, or rather to see your message fight it so that the village shoemaker can read it and understand it. I want my friends Bill the painter and Ted the plumber to get your message.

Ena expects the child in about 14 days. Her pregnancy has been rather difficult and we are both longing for it to cease.

P.S. Statistic? U.S.A. is said to have 2000 atom bombs. How many Sex Pol members to balance that figure?

———◆•◆———

Forest Hills, New York

October 14, 1946

My dear Neill:

I just received your letter of October 4th. I find that you are in the same terrible mood as I found myself in already for months. You are quite right, there is no use in writing good books, true books, if the Stalins have the ways and means to keep the man in the street in their power and pocket. I would only correct the following: I don't think that the *Sexual Revolution,* or the *Function of the Orgasm,* or even the *Mass Psychology* are too difficult for the man in the street. I think we should begin to look at the man in the street more closely and to see him as he really is. We must ask why he listens to trash rather than truth, to fanfares rather than to sensible things. That things are not so simple and become rather complicated is, among other things, due to the little man's unwillingness and inability to sit down and think things over. After 4 years of belly-ache, I finally succeeded in writing down my *Speech to the Little Man.* But I won't dare to publish it. I just cannot step out and tell the little man in his own language what he is, how he looks, how badly he thinks, how cowardly he is, and how he promotes all the rot in the world. You simply cannot do it, though you ought to.

The problem of organization and keeping things in check is one of the toughest I ever met in my whole 30 years of experience. I confess that I don't know whether to organize or not to organize, how to control the process which I have put into the world. I feel so badly about it because, though being a good worker and organizer of my own work, I feel that I am a very bad police dog, and that there is no way to keep people in check, with the millions of irrationalisms they are falling prey to every single hour of the day.

By now, I guess, the baby is already here. I hope all went well. Please hurry to inform me of the event.

———————— ◆ · ◆ ————————

Summerhill School
Leiston, Suffolk

October 18, 1946

My dear Reich,

Yours today. The babe hasn't arrived yet . . . I was hoping it might come on my birthday yesterday. Ena longing to have it appear.

I think I find your books difficult to read because I am 63 and have too long a load of repressions behind me. You write for the new generation. I get tied up—I can't grasp why patriarchy ousted matriarchy and when. Your view that religion stems from sex is a deep thought which I feel to be right. But again, historically, I can't see why it had to do so or why primitives always had certain sex taboos. I am sure I have psychic blindnesses coming from my own history. Yet in my work I seem to be going your way, which means that as a thinker I am a nobody, but as a doer quite important.

But that man in the street . . . no, I can't agree with you. He hasn't the basic chance. Here we have domestic maids from the town, girls of 15 to 20. Their ignorance is appalling; they have no culture of any kind. They are incapable of reading anything better than a washer-woman's weekly. And the State schools are producing a million such. I feel guilty that I have 72 favored kids who get a real education while the millions don't. My own books, said to be easily understood, mean nothing to the average worker. I question if ten workers in Leiston have read one of them. So that the approach by means of books may be quite the wrong one. Your Vienna and Berlin Clinics showed a better way.*

---

* In the 1920's Reich had established mental-health and sex-hygiene clinics in working-class districts. In Berlin he had also founded the German Association for Proletarian Sex Politics.

I don't get your refusing to publish your Little Man speech. Why don't you?

Troubled about the terrific amount of hate among my Communist friends. They seem to have so vindictive a strain about them. I always feel that any Communist friend of mine would sign my death warrant without emotion if the Party required it.

In your *Fascism* book you strike me as being too optimistic about American democracy, but then I am not on the spot. Hardly one of the many G.I.'s I spoke to during the war was conscious; he could tell me how many miles of bolts were in the Brooklyn Bridge, but on life itself he was a baby. And so many were Roman Catholics. I blush to say that one of my old pupils married an R.C. and took his religion in U.S.A. But she came to me at 14 or 15, said he lamely. Your books have made me conscious of my cowardice in replying to lecture questions about religion. I shall now fight the questioners boldly.

Though I hear Barakan is back he hasn't come near me nor phoned nor written. Nor has the child arrived but it can't be long now. The doctor says by its pulse it is a boy, and I wanted a girl and so did Ena who has a boy of 13.

Are you doing anything about having an English publisher? Kegan, Paul are bringing out a new complete edition of Jung in English, but it is often so; the man who has nothing to say in 40 volumes gets published. If you agree I'll try some of the other well-known firms. I am impatient to have England read you.

[*In a handwritten scrawl*] 2nd Nov. A girl ZOË SUTHERLAND, healthy and big. Ena doing well.

———— ◆◆ ————

Forest Hills, New York

November 9, 1946

My dear Neill:

It was a great joy to hear that your babe is here. Good luck, Neill, to you, your wife and the little one. I know what it means to you!! I hope you will bring your family over next summer to enjoy Orgonon and to finally get at those talks we are both longing for. Please send photographs!

You have put forth many basic questions in your letter. I have to limit my attempts to answer them:

I don't think that you have difficulties in understanding my books. You only seem to grope too deeply into the maze of human relations, thus proving that you are as good a thinker as a doer. Your questions are entirely logical. The one for instance regarding the WHY of the replacement of natural matriarchy by the unnatural patriarchy is one of the most complicated questions of human history. I have tried to find some of the answer in my book *Der Einbruch der Sexualmoral** (1932). It hasn't been translated yet. It is one of the most tragic events in the history of the human race: The core of all the misery seems to have developed when the first mother forbade the first child to experience love naturally. The reasons were of a *social* nature, most probably the meeting of strange hordes of human beings. It is too much to be expounded here.

I feel that we did not reach bottom yet in understanding the full amount of mental misery in the human masses. It is constantly obfuscated by the talk of the politicians about the "Common Man" and "his age." The human sickness is deep-rooted not only in social institutions but also in the stiffnesses of the bodies. I wrote my *Speech to the Little Man* mainly for my own clarity, in a desperate attempt to free myself from my sympathy and my loyalty to the little man, from my disappointment in him, and for the sake of becoming more objective in evaluating fully the chances of a future true self-governing society. I hesitate to publish because it puts even to my own mind the little man into clear focus in regard to his sickness of the character. And . . . there are also many little men, including myself, in my surroundings.

This funny world of ours has promoted me "overnight" from the status of a schizophrenic charlatan to that of a "big Man," a "Genius." They change opinions like shirts, don't they? To be affiliated with me, being a disgrace up to a short time ago, is now not only regarded as a great honor, but more than that: IT GIVES MY STUDENTS A TREMENDOUS AUTHORITY in the eyes of this public. The responsibilities become more involved and bigger each passing day, and only a very few can accept them. The problem of organisation has become a burning one. We cannot let everything run its own course because of the abysmal lack of knowledge and often responsibility in the workers who were trained by me. When I try hard to make an educator APPLY WHAT HE LEARNED WITH ME IN HIS OWN FIELD, he mistakes it for license to open an office, receive patients and ask for 10 or 15 dollars per treatment like a physician on Park Avenue. I am a bad

---

* *The Invasion of Compulsory Sex-Morality.*

police dog, and I do not know what to do. I would suggest the formation of a separate professional organization, apart from the Orgone Institute. I wish to remain free from the influences of the organization with all the aunts and grandmothers who worry about their daughters' decency. I also have still much to fight and to pull through. Therefore I would like to be my own master in my Institute as you are in your School. I would only have personal assistants who help me to perform my studies and work. I would love to have your opinion on this matter. You were the one to warn me of organization and pupils. But doctors are streaming in for training. The doctors who are trained already are asked to give lectures on my work. People are streaming to the few seminars and lectures that are given by some co-workers. But also envy and mutual hatred, together with greed are raising their heads. Can you help clarify?

I would like to warn of the Communists. I don't believe them to be basically human or truth-loving. They would kill me and you at a blink of a Stalinist eye. And I am not sure that they won't do it actually, when the influence of this work becomes socially powerful. They are capable of everything. I know them well, too well, for more than 20 years now.

I am not overestimating U.S.A. But the chance for development of the life principle is *here*, and not anywhere else.

It would be good to have my books published in England. If it does not annoy you to get refused and to waste time, try, if you like. I feel they will be ready to publish me very soon.

Write soon again, esp. about Zoë and Mrs. Neill and about when you will come over.

Summerhill School
Leiston, Suffolk

November 15, 1946

My dear Reich,

Many thanks for your good wishes for Zoë. She is a pretty kid without a blemish on her skin. So far I don't feel possessive about her, and won't until she begins to take notice. Luckily Ena agrees with me that timetable feeding is the devil, and is very likely the cause of so much modern thumb-sucking. I have two boys of 16 who have sucked their thumbs since they came here at 5. And I wonder if there are any statistics of malnutrition among timetable-fed babies, for during the compulsory wait the hunger and sex components accumulate libido, so that when the babe comes to the breast there is an orgasm of sex-pleasure outlet which makes him stop sucking before he is fed. The fashionable London birth clinics all have this timetable feeding plus weighing all the time, and the poor mother has to watch a clock to see that baby gets so many ounces only, and hastily snatches him off the breast when he gets his prescribed ounces. Zoë is making her own time-table I notice.

Someone in N.Y. sent me a book by a Russian . . . *I Chose Freedom.** Dunno who sent it. It is horrible reading and sounds sincere. Must humanity always have a police state? The book frightens me.

Have been away lecturing at various towns. I find it most exhausting, and if I didn't need the money wouldn't do it. True, I get hundreds of eager listeners, but the long railway journeys, the hotels . . . and worse still the hosts who ask me questions till past midnight, these make me weary.

Elected President last Saturday of the Progressive League, London. Elected at end of a two-hour meeting. I made my first speech which began: "I want to resign. I've listened for 2 hours to hear one word indicating progression, and all I heard were empty words about nothings. You argued for an hour whether freedom should go *in* the school or *within* the school. Folks who have minds like that shouldn't be in a progressive league." Said also that personally I don't need a Progress League, for I live and work in one.

Yes, we must try to come over in summer, and that leads me to thank your good wife for her sweet little note. If she does come this Spring she must make S'hill her home.

I was invited to stand as Socialist candidate for the Scots Universities by-election. I refused of course, saying that I couldn't leave my valuable work to sit and listen for hours to speeches in the Westminster gas works.† But I have a little regret that I couldn't be an M.P. and say living things about Education.

I wonder who your pupil is who has set up at 15 dollars a time. I wrote in one of my books: "It should be the prayer of every man that he has no disciples."

———————◆•◆———————

* By Victor Kravchenko (New York: Scribner's, 1946).
† The Houses of Parliament meet in Westminster.

Forest Hills, New York

December 16, 1946

My dear Neill:

I don't understand why Barakan did not turn up at your place yet. I heard from Constance that they are building accumulators in London. It may be that he is very busy with his newly acquired practical knowledge.

I hear that your baby develops marvellously and that you enjoy her. Please accept my heartiest and best wishes for Christmas and the New Year for yourself, your wife and your daughter. One could enjoy it more that "peace" has returned, if one didn't have the sure feeling that, due to lack of ability to fill peace with peaceful action, they are running headlong, unconsciously, against their own will and intention into a new and this time the highest type of war, atomic war. I am listening sometimes to the UN meetings. It is the deadliest kind of corpsy formalism. I don't understand it and I am afraid of it. It is not the future of the world.

Summerhill School
Leiston, Suffolk

December 20, 1946

My dear Reich,

Yours today. I have not had a word from Barakan and can only conjecture that for the moment he has some neurotic grudge against or indifference to me. Sad, for I wanted to hear all about you from him.

I wrote to Allen and Unwin who are one of the best London firms, telling them that you were the only original voice since Freud and they would be fools if they didn't try to publish you. Your books should come from a good firm of publishers who will sell them.

Your atomic pessimism is like my own. Humanity isn't evolved enough to have atom bombs, and the stiff-stomached rulers of all nations will use it and get the Church to tell them they are waging war for truth. I have no confidence in U.S.A. which is ignorant, superficial in its education, moral in the wrong way, outside world opinion. The alternative, a Soviet world, is also unwelcome. How powerless you and I are. A few military or political idiots can destroy our new children and we can do nothing.

But this is Xmas time and I ought to be merry . . . not so easy with nothing to buy but weak beer.

Constance comes to us for Xmas. Must ask her about accumulators in London. I should like to see Ena sitting in one. Like me she hates doctors with their drugs and injections.

P.S. Zoë flourishes and already is trying to bully us both at seven weeks. God help a poor father.

———— ◆•◆ ————

Forest Hills, New York

December 29, 1946

My dear Neill!

I just received your letter of Dec. 20th . . .

The world gets worse and worse. The logic in the downfall of our civilisation is appalling. There is nothing we can do at present except save all the archives and the bit of knowledge about the human animal for better times to come. For months I am at work to pile together the history of my work, the correspondence, the archives of the discovery of the orgone. I am preparing in all earnest to save what can be saved. A concrete cellar will be built at Orgonon to deposit the important material—several thousand tightly typed pages.

Our literature here still sells like warm bread. About 4–500 copies a month. Many thanks for your kind endeavours to have my books printed in England. They will start to print my stuff when it will have ceased to be new, when it will have become commonplace, that is, when no more danger will be involved in standing up for it.

The communists have attacked my *Mass Psychology* here in *The New Republic*, calling it "psychofascist." What bad consciences these fellows have!!! What a nightmare of politiciandom!!! They are toppling everything they have fought for honestly only 20 years ago.

I still believe that you underestimate U.S.A. But the wave of militarism and imperialism is growing stronger by the week.

Ilse has reservations on the Queen Elisabeth around 6th of April. How do you feel about a visit to U.S.A.? It could be arranged easily with the help of the Hamilton School.

I would like so much to hear more about Zoë. Does she let you sleep peacefully at night?

1947

Forest Hills, New York

January 19, 1947

My dear Neill:

I am worried about Barakan's behavior. Some students of the Institute told me that he had made bad, disparaging remarks about me, just as he did to me about you and Wolfe and others. It will be important to learn what he is doing under the authority of having studied at Orgonon. Please let me know about it as soon as you have news.

Ilse is going over to England in about two months. She will be able to give you all the data about the orgone, and also all the details about our situation here. This situation is good and bad at the same time. Good, because my work broke through on a wide front in the U.S.A.; bad, because I have to switch from having been in opposition for 25 years to a most dangerous position from now on. I know that such successes are apt to soften the acuity of sharp, uncompromising attitudes in science and social matters. My doctor students have discovered that much money can be made by Orgone therapy, and this is very bad for the work and for them. Since the amount of money you make is the measure rod for your greatness here as everywhere else, I find myself in the awkward position to ask horrible fees if I don't want to risk to fall behind. I am actually earning less than some of my students who work 10 hours daily with patients, because I am working only 3 hours daily with money making, and the rest with study and writing. I see the whole question of prevention of the biopathies going to hell, and I see already fear in the eyes of the workers to deal with the social structure which opposes healthy living. You don't mind I hope that I am pouring out my heart to you. Our work, yours as well as mine, is caught right in between

179

money and madness and political frenzy. People live their lives in ideologies, and are avoiding the realities evolved in honest pioneering. I see for instance educators raving with enthusiasm about your writings, but in reality taking no steps to fight the misery of children all around us. What is the use of all this struggle, if the common man, teacher or physician, spoils the fruits of hard work when he touches it? Do I exaggerate? Am I pessimistic? They call me a damn optimist, and yet there is reason to be desperate in view of this flattening out of everything that is meant to change our lives in a rational manner. They hail me now because I introduced the understanding of the Character. They say it is accepted everywhere, but I know that no one who is not under my immediate control is actually doing anything practical about the core of the problem. They still don't mention the issue: Healthy sexual living of children and adolescents!!!!!

Did you get your Orgone Accumulator already? I want you and your family to have its benefits.

January 21

I wonder, my dear Neill, whether you are still the great *Menschen-liebhaber* [lover of humanity] you used to be? I have the impression that you withdrew from them to some degree.

———◆•◆———

Summerhill School
Leiston, Suffolk

January 25, 1947

My dear Reich,

Your letter came just after a visit from Barakan. He is in a bad way emotionally. He says that you will stand no criticism at all from any co-worker, that you get into a fury and throw them out if they dare question your rightness in anything . . . your physics, electricity, maths.

I listened. All I said was that you and I have criticised each other for years, and have remained the best of friends, but his answer was that that is different, for Neill isn't working under Reich nor Reich under N.

This loyalty business is hard to be wise about. B. hadn't been ten minutes in S'hill on his first visit before he started to tell me it was wrong, that I was swindling myself, that I wasn't really on the child's side at all, that S'hill shouldn't have any failures etc. Yet I took him on as a teacher, knowing that he would continue to criticise me. (True, teachers are so scarce that I couldn't get anyone else for maths and physics.) But although he went on with his criticisms he was loyal in this way, that he didn't ever speak to the kids about me. I sacked him, telling him that although he taught well he was too much of a luxury for S'hill, for outside his 4½ hours daily teaching he never mended a chair or sawed firefood or played with the kids, in short as a community man he was useless. I was not honest enough to add: "And also you are sacked because you tire me to death with your endless *Warums* [whys] and talk."

My own view is that he needs much more veg.-T. although I wonder if his deadly serious attitude to life is beyond mending. I can't like him. Can't laugh with him, there is something calculating in him that baffles me. I think of all his neurotic mystery-making with his assumed name etc. A lot of *Verfolgungswahn* [persecution mania] in him I feel. Asked him about the Akku. "Hasn't one been sent from Orgonon?" he asked in surprise. I said no, and he said O.K. we'll make one for you in about 3 weeks, double ply of metal and wood. Price £12. I said O.K. for we need one badly.

B's photo snaps were fine. You don't look a day older, man, and Ilse looks the kind of woman it will be good to meet, while the kid looks just grand, although nowadays as a father of a girl I rather despise mere boy brats of course.

This money *Frage* [question] is most tiresome. Shortly I have to make four long tiresome journeys to the north of England to lecture, just to make some money. I have just had my report from my Accountant for last year. The loss is £1100, but that is partly due to expenses of moving from Wales, extra repairs etc. Still the dead loss is over £400 and that can't go on. The type of parent that believes in S'hill is poor middle class, and although every new pupil is paying well, I have many old ones who pay nothing at all or a few shillings weekly, and I can't chuck them out. So that this trip to U.S.A. has an anxious side that I don't like. In winter I could have tried to arrange a few lectures there to raise our passage money, but lectures don't happen in summer. Things are to be worse, for it seems we are importing millions of pounds more than we are exporting, and prices here are phantastic . . .

Forest Hills, New York

February 3, 1947

My dear Neill:

I just received your letter of January 25th. In regard to Barakan, I think I already wrote you once that during the past 10 years I had to learn to distinguish between rational and irrational criticism. The difference between the two ways of human reaction consists in that rational criticism intends to help the task in the proper way and nothing but that; whereas in the case of irrational criticism the motive to criticize has nothing to do with the task in question, and the criticism is brought forth solely to satisfy some neurotic tendency in the one who criticizes. Finally, it not only does not help the work, but on the contrary, it is intended to disrupt and to besmirch human relations. I have also learned that if I wish to do my job well, my student has first to learn how to learn well and to listen, as we say in German *unvoreingenommen* [without bias], that means just listen and take in. Only after having grown himself practically and skillfully into the task at hand, his opinion, which may differ from mine, is valuable. When a man like Barakan comes over from England, enters my cabin at Orgonon, demonstrates clearly a definite uneasy feeling about his own person and on account of that begins instantly to tell me that Neill's school is no good, that Hamilton understands nothing of education, and that I made a mistake in book so-and-so on page so-and-so, without first having acquainted himself with the bulk of the task and the matter at hand, then, of course, I admit I get furious. On the other hand, I like a student when he does not believe me immediately, when I see that he tries out for himself whether I am right or not. I hate the student and the co-worker who is a believer and nothing but that, because he cannot do his job well. I love clever and good objections which lead further or which make me turn my attention to things I have overlooked. I am even greatly thankful for such "criticism." It is just that I do not permit people with such nuisance reactions any more to dance around on my shoulders and to hamper the serious work as I did many years ago. But I believe that this is an advance.

I would like to extend the scope of what I just said: I think that it would be one of the most crucial tasks of education and of leadership of human relations on the whole, to show the people in general to what extent loose talk, malicious motives in just criticizing and doing nothing, etc., is destroying their own lives. To show them further, how important it would be to train themselves in rationally putting their shoulders practically to the task at hand. As long as neurotic motives and neurotic behavior will pour into rational human relations, authority will have reason to justify its existence and social reaction will have reason to claim that it is right. I think finally, that the little man, who is just at the point to climb to power in the world, should look at himself first, what he never does and what he even hates to be reminded of. It is no use pitying him. He must know what he is doing, just as any teacher or engineer must know what he is doing or what he is doing wrong.

An accumulator has been shipped to you and is supposed to leave with the next sailing of the Queen Elizabeth. And a small tube box will leave by parcel post this week too. I am quite sure that you will not only enjoy it, but that you will feel objectively much better and healthier if you use the accumulator regularly.

I am looking forward to your coming. I think you need the rest and we both need this meeting. I want you to accept my hearty offer to be my guests during your stay in the U.S. We have a nice cabin for you and it will be only a pleasure to make your stay as enjoyable as possible.

———◆◆———

Forest Hills, New York

February 6, 1947

My dear Neill:

I feel the need to add a few lines to my letter of yesterday. My attitude in the matter of the right to criticize, expounded in my previous letter, may sound to you like an old disappointed man's attitude. Why not, you may ask, let people gossip and chatter, it does not harm anyone, and it means an outlet for their pent-up discontentments. I could agree with you, and I once even did agree with this attitude, hadn't two facts evolved to tremendous proportions in the meantime.

The first fact is a subjective one: I have to confess that I feel emotionally rather worn out after a quarter of a century of an exhausting struggle to put through most simple and obvious facts. It became obvious that what is in the way of simple fact getting through to the public is just the same kind of behavior of people that looks so innocent and so harmless when you meet it here and there singly. I found out that after 25 years people are "enthusiastic" and "enchanted" by my personality and my science. But in the general situation of adolescents and their main misery, practically nothing has changed, because everybody, except a very few, is chattering and gossiping around and away from it. The same chattering and gossiping and "being critical" prevents my kind of atomic energy, the orgone, to save, as it easily could, hundred thousands and millions of lives in cancer and other diseases. Thus, I became a bit allergic to people's way of merely talking and doing very little practically.

The second fact, which is an objective one, and has nothing to do with me personally, is that when you listen to a UN meeting or when you read any newspaper whatever, or when you look back into history of 2000 years, you find the same kind of superficial chattering, being busy with many words and avoiding the main issue to the detriment of the whole human race. I could feel easygoing in the face of a gossiping person, would this person's behavior not remind me painfully of one of the main reasons for the decline of human society. If you compare the behavior of the single individual before you and that of the huge political, medical and other organizations which determine the fate of every single human being, you will find they are identical in motivation, mechanism and expression. No wonder, since those political bodies are composed of individuals with the same characterological structure.

I hope you understand, my dear Neill, why I felt that I had to write this addition to my previous letter. It is not Barakan who is important, but Barakan as a symbol.

———————◆◆◆———————

Summerhill School
Leiston, Suffolk

February 10, 1947

My dear Reich,

Yours yesterday. It suddenly strikes me with alarm that Barakan is your Little Man plus brains which are rendered almost useless by his emotions . . . his irrationalism, in your own phrase. All through the war I had a succession of teachers who turned out to be failures just because of their emotional attitude to life and to me. So that B. is no new phenomenon to me; I've had him by the dozen. Conspiracies to chuck me out (of my own school) and put a younger man in my place, fights about freedom . . . that I wasn't allowing freedom, this said by emotional fools who confused freedom with license, so that one woman teacher encouraged ten normal kids of 6 or 7 to smash up £30 worth of my furniture, on the theory that all children must live out their destruction impulses. Most of these people had had nasty fathers who never gave any praise, and they accused me of never patting them on the back and telling them how wonderful they were. I have at least half my staff today who have this neurotic attitude to me and therefore to their work here. And . . . I don't know how to solve the problem. If people who are interested in my work or yours, are incapable of helping that work because of emotional complexes (and we seem to attract that type) what the hell? With his head B. is all Reichian . . . greatest scientist of the age etc. With his heart he is a neurotic little boy with one motive . . . to rise by knocking the other fellow down. It is so damned pathetic and alarming. Are there no complexless people in the world? Einstein apparently dropped you on emotional grounds, and when over here the Bernals and Haldanes say that your methods are unscientific, are we to say that their attitude is emotional and not realistic? I think it is emotional to a large extent. Then where is your Little Man to come in? You say he is almost ready to take over. But who is he? Is he more complex-free than the Barakans and Haldanes? B. says that you told him that the present generation is doomed and that no one ought to try to help it. I said he must have got you wrong, for the coming generation is to be educated by the stiff-stomached present one, and if we can't do something to change even a tiny fraction of this generation, the new one will be moulded wrongly all the way. My old pupils won't forbid *Onanie* [masturbation] in their kids, won't beat them, will treat them as human beings with rights of their own. Some will go all the way about adolescent freedom. So that the Zoë generation will start off without many of the ordinary handicaps, but will the kids of the Little Man who must go to disciplined schools where sex is taboo and morals are ready-made "don'ts" and religion is compulsory, will his kids have much chance in life? So that I take it that B. got you completely wrong. Yes, we are damned. Granted. Damned and blasted to hell without any atomic bomb. Tomorrow is a totalitarian one whether communist or fascist, or probably the two in one. And the little man is to be the big bureaucrat, and he isn't ready to be that. I fear the increase of mechanisation, that the little man will see life in terms of five-year plans and tractors and electricity, and freedom as we think of it will cease to have even a name. The little man won't allow me to say what I like about education; he won't tolerate your sex-economy ideas. It isn't the parents of the new generation I fear so much; the Führers outside the home will do the damage this time, the Adolfs and Joes. With their radio and films they can destroy humanity, and have gone far to do so already. So that I want to know more of your little man. I want to know how to de-Barakanise him.

Great news about the Accumulator. Please give us a *warning* timetable telling us how long it is to be dangerous for Zoë, meaning what is the safe period at a time we can park her there?

We've had fourteen days of intense cold with no coke and no hot baths, with half-pressure gas and hardly a hot meal because of that. We have spent days sawing down our trees for firewood. Luckily we've had food enough. Owing to English plumbing—putting all pipes outside on the walls—we are frozen up, and have only one W.C. working for 90 people. Still, Berlin and Vienna must be a hundred times worse.

——————◆◆◆——————

Forest Hills, New York

February 26, 1947

My dear Neill:

I have your letter of February 10th. I was so glad that you finally added to your love of the little man the full evaluation of that characteristic of his which makes him the pain in the neck of the world. I believe that the old socialist custom of pitying the poor has obfuscated the clear vision in regard to the little man's own faults for his destiny. I myself am fighting quite a battle in this matter for years, to keep myself clean of reactionary sentiments without losing my sight of realities. When you will be here in the summer you will hear a story of the Hamilton School which fits excellently in what you indicated about your own school.

I never told Barakan that no one should try to help the present generation. What I said was that his idea of saving the world with 500,000 vegeto-therapists is a completely illusionary one. I think that for the coming 3 or 4 hundred years each new-born generation will be a certain stretch less neurotic than the previous one, that neurotic traditions and the healthy future will be overlapping to a lesser and lesser degree. But it is true that the presently living generation cannot be restructured. Only the misdeeds of the emotional pest can be limited and dammed in. There is so much that we will have to talk about in the summer. I am looking forward to it.

Did you receive the accumulator already? There are no timetables to go with it. You sit in it just as long as you are comfortable; when you feel that you are getting warm, or when you feel that "you had enough," then leave it. There are no dangers connected with using the accumulator at all. All of us are using it daily since 1940 and it did us only a lot of good. I would advise not to let Zoë stay alone in the accumulator, to park her there, as you say, but let her go in with Ena. She will feel then when the child gets restless, a sure sign for getting out.

Of course, we would like to urge you not to leave Ena and the child behind when you come. It should be possible to arrange it somehow.

———————————◆◆———————————

Summerhill School
Leiston, Suffolk

April 4, 1947

My dear Reich,

I delayed writing until I had news of the Accum. and the *Reise* [trip] over. After much delay at the docks I have got the Accu now and we are using it hopefully. But I find it difficult to heat up inside, whereas Ena heats easily in a room without a fire . . . we have had no coke for a month lately and no coal for a week or more. So far my only observation is that I feel a prickliness of the skin which is pleasant. The baby has its daily doses with Ena. I like very much the easy design of it, and had no idea how easy it is to make it in sections as compared with a solid thing. As an article of furniture it looks fine too. We are to try all sorts of experiments with it . . . kids with impetigo, sores, colds etc. But I wish it were possible to sit in it with *ETWAS KLEIDER AN* [some clothing on] for I am never a warm person in this climate. Also, somewhere you write that one shouldn't have an Accu in a bedroom. Why? Why bad to lie all night with orgones floating about the room?

In seven days the three of us cross to Copenhagen and then Stockholm. Propaganda *Reise* [trip] really; I want to get students over to help pay our losing battle with money. I lecture in both cities and almost cover our fares with the fees I get there. We will be away 15 days in all. I don't look forward to travelling *Dritte* [third] on the ship; at my time of life I feel I ought to have the best *Erste Klasse* [first class] for self and family. I guess the aftermath of war will give us worse austerities.

Say, Reich, if we can't get a passage this summer, would it be possible to delay visit until winter, when I might get a lecture tour? A few lectures might get me a public over there. I have just had five lectures in the north of England, speaking to about 2000 people in all. Their enthusiasm was tremendous. I don't see why I shouldn't come to a "less advanced" country and wake folks up a bit about schools and children.

By the way, Eastmond fears the growth of Fascism in U.S.A. "There," he says, "Reich's work will be in danger. Can't you (Neill) persuade Reich to send you sealed information about his latest discoveries so that you can park them safely in a bank in England?"

We both look forward much to meeting Ilse in May.

P.S. Ena and I have talked about what would happen to Zoë if we both were killed in an accident. She says that the only people she would trust to bring her up would be the Reichs. Can I make a will so? Leaving all I have to pay for her upbringing.

Ena says: "Tell Reich how much I appreciate the Accu, and how good it was of him to send it."

———◆•◆———

Forest Hills, New York

April 14, 1947

My dear Neill:

I was glad to have your letter of April 4th today. Ilse has departed on the 9th for England, and she will be with you in a few weeks. She will be able to inform you of everything you wish to know about the orgone.

It is *not necessary* to sit in the accumulator naked. We learned that you obtain the same results if you are dressed, but, if possible, don't wear a coat in it. To judge from your description, you seem rather undercharged—I judge from the lack of sensations. In a few weeks your organism will have charged up enough, and you will feel the heat.

I would like to advise you against relying too much on lecturing here. America is a tremendous country with tremendous competition among lecturers, and the lecture-tour would have to be thoroughly prepared long in advance. I feel that coming this summer would be much more important seen from any angle.

Your request in regard to Zoë meant much to me, since you, the best educator of today, have so much confidence in me, but I am afraid that I personally am not a suitable person to give safety to the child, though children around me grow up in a good way. I mean my social position, which is dangerous and uncertain and open to any pestilent attack at any time in any country with any consequence. Discuss the matter with Ilse. I think she would be the one to take the responsibility, and I would help her as long as circumstances permit.

———◆•◆———

Forest Hills, New York

April 19, 1947

My dear Neill:

I spoke to Hamilton about a possible lecture tour. He will do what he can to bring one about.

The idea of Eastmond to deposit new discoveries in a bank in England is exaggerating the dangers in the United States. Sometimes I wonder where Fascism is growing, in the socialistic or bourgeois governments, since everything is topsy-turvy and upside down. I feel we can do nothing but wait and see, but I am preparing Orgonon for safety.

———◆•◆———

Summerhill School
Leiston, Suffolk

May 6, 1947

My dear Reich,

I had a wonderful time in Denmark and Sweden. Crowded lectures, in Stockholm hundreds couldn't get in so they asked the parson of a big church opposite if they could use the church. He consented on condition that I didn't attack religion or say too much about sex. Put me in a difficult dilemma, but I couldn't disappoint so many people and spoke for an hour from the pulpit. Later a smaller party at supper got all I couldn't say in church.

We stayed with the Leunbachs in Copenhagen. Met the psychology gang. Philipson very amiable. His ideal is to have no transferences, but from what I saw every patient of his had a very strong one, half positive, half negative. His technique is primarily a talking one . . . like Jung and Stekel; sit opposite and talk. The L.'s are giving their babies self-regulation, having them shit and piss all over the place, and it seems good, for at two the girl can handle cups and glasses easily, and they automatically begin to use pots for shitting.

Sweden was paradise; shops with everything we haven't seen for years here. I drank too much *Schnapps* and ate far too much and enjoyed it all. In Copenhagen lecture I spoke about your work and pleased the sex-econ folks there. But on the orgone question I got nothing definite. A doctor whose name I didn't catch in C. said that it was all phantasy on your part, but as he had never seen nor tried anything orgonish his criticism meant nothing. Leunbachs say they can't get any effects from their Accum, but as it is lined with thin foil I guess it isn't right. Ena and I are back to ours. The small one came yesterday. So far I have only the skin tingling to report. One woman on the staff has anaemia badly and asks if it will help her. I said we'd try.

Was puzzled when a cable came to me in Stockholm asking me to be head of Hamilton School. Couldn't make out if it were a genuine offer, but replied with a no. I can't leave my 70 kids here to start in a new land under a Committee, nay, not for 5 million dollars per annum. But it was most pleasing to have the offer.

I begin to be sure that I won't get a passage over this year. Nor with a losing income can I bring Ena and Zoë over. I have a neurotic fear of flying, and Ena would be scared if I flew over the Atlantic. Indeed I have more fears than I should have . . . z.B. [for instance] the customs people, yet once I am in front of them all fear goes even if I have things I shouldn't have. Partly a fear of being afraid. A neurosis, Reich, but thank heaven it isn't the type of neurosis that makes me incapable of work and happiness and a good sex life.

———◆•◆———

Orgonon
Rangeley, Maine

May 14, 1947

My dear Neill:

I received your letter of May 6th yesterday. In the meantime, I assume, Ilse arrived and has already told you most of the things about our lives that may interest you. I also hope that she will persuade you to do the utmost to get a passage this year and not next year. Matters of utmost importance should be discussed and I know no one in Europe who could listen better and understand better what is at stake at the present time in the development of our work. There is especially one first-rank point, which has to be cleared up. For 15 years now my work has had nothing whatsoever to do with psychoanalysis and its different variations. For 15 years now a new branch of *natural science* and not psychology is in full development. 15 years ago the psychoanalysts wanted nothing of it. Today they want all of it, but I shall not agree to this usurpation of my own work. In this orgone biophysical work I owe nothing to anybody; on the contrary, I had to overcome false idealistic and mystical concepts in psychology and psychoanalysis and other sciences in order to find the road to the blistering biological energy which you can see in the dark.

Therefore, the issues which interest Philipson are far behind, decades behind the present work. It is one of the most unfortunate habitudes of human beings that they come along for a short while with pioneer work, pick up a piece of it and then settle down, thus losing all perspective and all possibilities to go along and understand the whole development. Philipson would not do talky-talk with his patients like Jung and Stekel if he could understand that I am not doing psychology but biology with the patients and that working biophysically involves undressing of the patient and seeing his body. I am fighting desperately against being looked upon as a branch of psychoanalysis. I wish I had enough money to stop doing psychiatry at all and devote myself fully to the investigation and elaboration of the cosmic orgone energy. Unfortunately, I dare not lose my financial independence which is provided by my psychiatric work. To discuss the implications of the discovery of the biological energy for the evaluation of psychology would be one of the main tasks of our meeting. So I hope you'll come.

Your coming here would also be of some importance because we feel that the Socialists in Europe have spread wrong notions on the educational mentality in the U.S. I find conservative Americans much more open-minded and progressive in matters of living than the most rabid European Socialist. There is no doubt that the *niveau* [level] of education in the U.S. is in general and in average much higher than in Europe; and it would be a matter of evening out wrong ideas if you would see with your own eyes. You could bring it back to Europe. No European understands, for instance, that Roosevelt has given the workers in the U.S. much more than any Socialist government in Europe. I even feel that most conservative Americans have a fairer attitude toward labor than the "Father of all proletarians of the world." There is something important in American liberalism which is inaccessible to the average European.

I knew you would not accept the offer of the Hamilton School to be their director, but the offer was seriously made.

I know you will enjoy the accumulator very much, but it must be used regularly for a long stretch of time to show its effects.

I hope very much to hear from you soon again and to see you at Orgonon in about 2 months.

———◆◆———

Summerhill School
Leiston, Suffolk

May 22, 1947
My dear Reich,

Ilse left this morning. We hated her going, for we all liked her very much. She will tell you all about S'hill when she returns to you.

Your last letter sounded most depressed. Pity you hadn't given yourself a break and come over too. Ilse has laughed a lot here, and I guess you would have laughed too.

I haven't much to write this time. We have been going to bed too late, and missing our *Abend Sitzung* [evening session] in the Accu. From now until end of July my life will be one long miserable interviewing of visitors, most of them dull teachers and problem parents. And they all ask the same damn-fool questions.

I am glad you at last threw overboard the word analysis. But we'll talk about it soon I hope.

———◆◆———

Summerhill School
Leiston, Suffolk

June 5, 1947
My dear Reich & Ilse,

I sail on the Queen Elizabeth 9th August, and return on Queen Mary 11th Sept. Sad that I have to come alone, but neither of us would have Zoë vaccinated.

It will be a great joy to meet you again, Reich.

———◆◆———

[1947]

Summerhill School
Leiston, Suffolk

June 17, 1947

My dear Reich,

Thanks for the magazines. They might have been worse, but I hope this publicity doesn't interfere with your work.*

Had a letter from Hamilton saying he is to take me to the farm first. I do hope he doesn't keep me there long, for I am coming to see you primarily. He wrote that he wants to take me to the top of the Empire Building to see the city. I have replied to him that I don't want that. My emotional pest at the moment has revived my old height phobia.

By the time I sail I hope that the Accumulator will have made me more balanced emotionally. But apart from this phobia of mine, which by the way operates on the top of a mountain with sloping sides, and would operate if the Empire Bg. had a wire cage at top, I hate being taken sight-seeing. In Stockholm when they thought they were entertaining me by showing me old castles etc. I was just bored to death. So I have told Hamilton that I merely want to go around seeing the things that take my fancy, and I guess that after 7 years of empty shops, the N.Y. shops will fascinate me . . . and the food.

Now, Reich, if you can do so without offending the Hamiltons, try to arrange that I see YOU as much as possible. I want a quiet time with you and Ilse and Peter, and when H. writes that Ranger has arranged a seminar of teachers "at the farm" . . . well, *es tut mir leid* [I am sorry]. Of course I may like them a lot, but I wouldn't have crossed the Atlantic for anyone but you.

———◆•◆———

---

* Reich had sent Neill two magazines, each containing an article about Reich's theories and his work: "The New Cult of Sex and Anarchy," *Harper's Magazine* (April 1947), and "The Strange Case of Wilhelm Reich," *The New Republic* (May 26, 1947), both by Mildred Edie Brady. Purporting to be objective descriptions, both articles, and particularly that in *The New Republic*, were virulently hostile.

Summerhill School
Leiston, Suffolk

June 20, 1947

My dear Reich,

I sent you a badly depressed letter two days ago. I am out of the depression now, but the mere fact that such a depression can happen is so tiresome.

I don't know what to say about the articles you sent me. I suppose that to be in *Harper's* and *New Republic* means a wide publicity, and however stupid or hateful the articles, folks will be led to find out for themselves what you teach. The longer I live the more I see that you have touched the base of life. Knowing your work makes it impossible to read books on psychology. But I see, in my own self, how hard it is to undo the past, and how useless it is to "cure" by any analysis. So that the only thing to concentrate on is the new generation—Peter and Zoë, but Zoë has the better chance, for Peter will get too much that is false from the damned schools you will have to send him to. The fact that he has had to be vaccinated, while Zoë wasn't, is as it were symbolic of the freedoms allowed them. If I live long enough Z. will have an environment that won't compel her to have silly ideas on behaviour. Yet your home will counteract any fool work done on Peter by teachers.

———————◆•◆———————

Orgonon
Rangeley, Maine

June 21, 1947

My dear Neill:

We are still wondering why you did not arrange your stay in the States so that you could have spent a longer period with us.

Mr. Hamilton will meet you at the boat and will bring you up to Orgonon by car. I am sure you will enjoy the beautiful trip through the New England landscape, and at Orgonon we shall make it as comfortable for you as possible (coffee for breakfast and plenty of whiskey and soda). Furthermore, I promise not to bother you too much with too many heavy problems.

———————◆•◆———————

Summerhill School
Leiston, Suffolk

June 26, 1947

My dear Reich,

I'll have 14 days with you at Orgonon, long enough for one who can't take any part in the work. I won't be allowed even to mend broken fuses, for Ilse said she does all that. You can't let me do nothing while you all work at microscopes all the day. Give me a sharp scythe and some grass to cut.

Well, I take it that Hamilton will meet me in N.Y., take me to the train and next morning I'll be met by you or Ilse at your station? Fine. But have you any shops near you? I ask because I have no light clothes, and am told that Maine in August is hot as hell.

It is going to be a great joy to meet you again.

———◆◆———

[*Neill arrived in the United States on August 14, and took a night train to Farmington, Maine, where he was met and driven to Orgonon, Reich's property in Rangeley. He spent two weeks with the Reichs and from there went to the Hamilton school and farm, in Sheffield, Massachusetts, where he was to conduct a week of seminars.*]

———◆◆———

Orgonon
Rangeley, Maine

September 1, 1947

My dear Neill:

We are missing you very much. It was not only good and pleasant to have you here, but it actually helped to clarify most distressing problems. I hope very much that we can keep up our discussions by mail and that we shall continue to clear up things at your next visit.

I am enclosing a check for $100 of the Orgone Research Fund for your traveling and living expenses, as agreed upon.

I am sure you will find some or most of the people you will meet at the seminar and in New York pleasant and understanding. Most of them have struggled with our problems.

———◆◆———

Hamilton farm
Sheffield, Mass.

Labour Day

Dear Both,

I am still homesick for Orgonon. The drive was tiresome but I am refreshed now. The gang hasn't arrived yet, and Ranger says they have paid for a whole week and will be concerned if I leave before next Tuesday, lecture day. Going to be a 2-hour session mornings and one evenings, and Ranger wants me to have a special hour for individuals who want to speak to me, so it looks as if by the end of the week I'll have $600 plus a ruined constitution. However, I'll survive it.

Nice place this, warm, sunny, but the scythe is rotten, blunt, set at wrong angle and there is no whetting stone. H. has lent me this nice typewriter and I'll go on with my book afternoons. *Aber, Kinder* [But, children], I wish I were back with your typewriter.

I'll have only one day to shop in N.Y., but Ranger says I may get the clothes for Zoë here nearby in Barrington. Now I just long to get home; my vacation ended when they drove me away from Orgonon.

I miss the voices of Isabel* and Peter in the early morning, but the H.'s two young dogs started to bark at my door at 6 a.m. and at 7 the heavy footsteps above awoke me again. Good training for returning to Zoë. Nothing more to report so far. How in hell I can have things to say in six days 4 hours a day, God knows. I'll encourage them to talk about their own jobs but not about their own selves. Love to the three of you, bless you.

P.S. Say goodbye to Tom† for me. I like him.

———— ◆•◆ ————

Hamilton farm
Sheffield, Mass.

Thursday, 4th Sept. 47

My dear Reich,

Many thanks for the cheque for $100. Easy money when I think of the work I am doing here to get the Hamilton $s. I speak 4

---

* Maid and nursemaid at Orgonon.
† Tom Ross, the caretaker at Orgonon.

hours a day, and feel that I've said all I know and think, and I have still 17 hours to talk. I can't understand the 5 or 6 ministers here; they don't explain how they can follow Christ and that devil Reich at the same time. One said when I asked him that they were conscious hypocrites.

Well, there goes the gong for the morning Seminar. God 'elp me. I keep thinking of you three and the quiet of Maine. I try to go on with my book but have had to give it up; no energy after so much talking.

———◆•◆———

Orgonon
Rangeley, Maine

September 4th, 1947

My dear Neill:

We have your letter of Labor Day. We are still missing you, and it turns out true what I wrote you before you arrived, that it would be much too short. Well, we shall have to wait I guess for our next meeting.

———◆•◆———

Orgonon
Rangeley, Maine

September 8th, 1947

My dear Neill:

It's Monday morning, and I guess you are just departing for New York. I am sure your lecture will be a great success. I shall await your telephone call on Wednesday evening in my little cabin.

Again I wish to tell you how much I enjoyed your visit here at Orgonon. It is always invigorating to be able to speak out, without reservations and façades.

The best of luck to you and yours in England.

———◆•◆———

[1947]

Summerhill School
Leiston, Suffolk

September 20, 1947

My dear Reich,

Home again with happy memories of a wonderful trip.

The poisonous article in *Time** has been printed in the *London Evening News,* and I shouldn't be surprised if I have a visit from our own FBI soon. Our greatest danger is the yellow press.

God, I feel good after that visit to you. Lost all my neurosis; looked down from high windows in N.Y. without any vertigo at all. But life is to be dull now; I simply can't be bothered talking to my staff for it seems such a waste of time after Orgonon and Sheffield.

What about another visit next year with Ena and Zoë? We think we could arrange to come out in early April and return end of June. That would give me a chance to make all expenses by lecturing before schools in U.S.A. went on vacation, and then we could recuperate in Orgonon . . . but I don't know when you go up there each year.

Zoë is a darling. Taking a few steps now, and, alas, waking us at 6.30 a.m.

When I finish my book† I'll start translating the *Little Man,* whose ms. I got safely.

Cheer up, old Reich. You and I will beat the press gang with their insidious propaganda. I am writing a letter to *The New Statesman* attacking the yellow press and asking them to leave me alone. I don't believe in taking attacks lying down.

Wish I could have seen you again to give my impressions of the Sheffield crowd.

Back to cigarettes at 85 cents for 20, and rumour says they are going up to a dollar for 20. Must stop smoking, damn it all. And no whiskey.

◆•◆

* *Time* magazine (August 25, 1947), reporting on Neill's trip to the United States, made derisive fun of him, his school, and his ideas.

† *The Problem Family: An Investigation of Human Relations* (London: Herbert Jenkins, 1949). Neill pleads for more openness and honesty within the family and describes the ways in which personal prejudices and social pressures can distort parents' attitudes to their children.

Summerhill School
Leiston, Suffolk

September 26, 1947

My dear Reich,

My book is nearly finished. I have more than once quoted you, giving the quotation from the Orgone Press. The name Orgone will be Greek to many a reader, and I thought it would be a good idea to make the final chapter a simple description of what the orgone is and how it links up with the sickness of humanity. What do you think? I wouldn't dare to write it myself, but if you could dictate to Ilse I could put it in my own literary style so that the book would be in unison. I'll send you galley proofs of the book, for I will not say a thing involving your name unless you approve of it.

The chapter could tell of the discovery of the Orgone, how it is seen in biological life, how it can cure in the Akku, how the sickness of man is against it . . . I do so want England to know you, to get some of the inspiration you have given me for years, and in great abundance in the two weeks in Maine. It is time that your message were known here. Damn you, man, time is short. You must get in with the O. before the atomic energy kills us all.

School begins today, and 70 noisy brats have returned. I can't get an English teacher and will have to teach maths and English all day long. How can I do much to clear the *onanie* [masturbation] guilt of 70 kids then? I wish I had a Saxe* here.

Cold, and your wooly coat is a blessing. I guess Maine is cold too now.

Lots of real love to both . . . to the three. I wish to God (Orgonotic one) I were nearer you.

———◆◆———

Forest Hills
New York

October 3, 1947

My dear Neill:

I appreciate very much your offer to include a chapter on orgone energy in your book. You will find many important data sum-

* Felicia Saxe. Worked with Reich for a time; devised exercises to loosen children's tensions.

marized in the last part of *The Function of the Orgasm*. I am adding a few basic characteristics of later date.

Orgone can be seen pulsating and moving West-Eastward on calm lake surfaces and on stars by means of the telescope at about $80\times$ magnification. Arrangements which accumulate orgone energy show a constant higher temperature as compared with the surrounding air. This constant temperature difference can best be obtained through burying an orgone accumulator in the soil, and measuring above the accumulator and in simple earth. Orgone energy in its concentrated form can be demonstrated by means of the Geiger–Müller counter [the Geiger counter], the highest speed so far obtained being around 25 to 100 impulses per second. Of course, without any artificial radiating substance in the neighborhood.

Orgone charges blood and tissues biologically, removes secondary anemias, causes expansion of the vascular nervous system, thus helping in cases of high blood pressure and angina pectoris. By improving the general condition of the organism, it counteracts to a greater or lesser extent, depending on the case, the process of deterioration in the cancer biopathy, which is not to be confused with the cancer tumor.

The fertility of the soil (humus), the expansive processes of growth and development are due to natural orgone energy in the soil and in the air. Orgone can be drawn from humus into water and by a process of freezing can be made to concentrate into flakes of a biological nature (Experiment XX). These flakes constitute true plasmatic matter.

Orgone can be seen in complete dark rooms as a bluish-gray shimmer and moving shining clouds.

The earth is surrounded by a rotating orgone energy atmosphere, west to east. This "Orgone Envelope" is physically the same as the corona of the sun. Orgone energy has been used in promoting the health of mother and child in pregnancy. It is capable of healing wounds quickly. It is being used by many physicians, physicists and biologists in many countries. It is present everywhere and penetrates everything, and is, most probably, that which was for many centuries sought for as the "ether."

The universe is not empty as assumed by classical physics, but it is filled with the pulsating cosmic energy, the orgone, out of which the matter of the heavenly bodies most probably developed.

Orgone energy is a true physical energy demonstrable by physical means, and, at the same time it is that energy which we feel in our organ sensations as pleasure or anxiety, depression or elation. Our emotions are nothing but subjective perceptions of objective changes in the state of body orgone.

Orgone energy is within us and outside of us.

The health-enhancing action of sun and fresh air is due to orgone energy. The same is true with the hitherto ununderstood action of vitamins and natural foods.

The biological orgasm corresponds to a discharge of biophysical orgone energy through a series of involuntary total body contractions.

Cosmic and natural feelings of the human animal are due to the physical link-up of his body orgone with the cosmic orgone around him, a relation which cannot be accounted for by mechanical physics or chemistry. Orgone energy is, in contradistinction to atomic energy, present independently of matter and before matter. Atomic energy is secondary energy, derived from matter. Orgone energy is primordial cosmic energy before matter.

Orgone energy was not discovered by mechanistic physico-chemistry because it does not function according to known mechanical or chemical laws, but according to hitherto unknown functional laws such as pulsation, lumination, attraction of the weaker body by the stronger body, etc. Natural phenomena such as the aurora borealis, or the function of the divining rod, are due to orgone energy.

It is to be emphasized that orgone energy is neither mystical nor mechanical, but a truly physical, functional energy in the universe.

I think that's enough.

———◆•◆———

Summerhill School
Leiston, Suffolk

October 8, 1947

My dear Reich,

Thanks a lot for your letter. I'll try to write that chapter in spite of my woeful ignorance of anything scientific.

Visit from Barakan. He is doing therapy but not under your name. Claims he has discovered a way to eliminate all *Widerstand* [resistance] and *Übertragung* [transference], and explained it at length to me. I didn't understand it.

Ena and I use the Accumulator daily, but often with difficulty to find the time, for life in a school is one long dealing with people. Everyone says we are both looking well, and Ena says I look years younger and happier since I came back from Maine.

But I am very anxious about the world.

This new Comintern means the political line-up before the military one, and I foresee a universal bloodbath. Communism will win in the end, and my work and yours will be negatived by hate . . . for the chained workers must react with hate when they get what they think is freedom. The outlook is black indeed. But, Reich, I can't flee from it to U.S.A. I can't leave 70 kids when there is no one I know who could carry on my work.

I am getting at last a maths teacher and will be free to work with the kids individually. My visit to you convinced me that I have to get back to contact with the individuals as I used to do, easing their *Onanie* guilt as much as I can.

Let me know of any developments re the FBI and that stupid article.* The *Time* article about me was poisonous too. At least there is this freedom here, that Scotland Yard never sends tecs [detectives] to see what I am doing.

Sad to think you have all left Orgonon. I wish to goodness you could get out of your therapy work.

My book just about finished, and then I start to translate the *Little Man*. It is a great book that . . . the only one of yours I fully understand.

Re-reading the *Function of the O.* while I sit in the box, but, *mein Gott*, how difficult it is for me when I meet a word like sympathetico-tonia. Still I do get the most of it. And after seeing you again I get much more out of your books.

I want to write a chapter on Why Does Man Hate Sex and Life? But I have not enough knowledge to answer the question. I can see what you mean when you say man changed from matriarchal to patr. society when he began to have private possessions. But that doesn't tell me why Brown beats his boy for *Onanie,* or why mysticism persists. I wish I were a scholar and knew things historically. I know the answer is in your books, but where I dunno. My cat Jeep has no mixture of *Lust–Angst* [pleasure–anxiety]. I knew that I'd think of a 100 questions

---

* Neill here appears to confuse the FBI and the FDA. The article he refers to is "The Strange Case of Wilhelm Reich," by Mildred Edie Brady. On the strength of that article, an agent of the Food and Drug Administration, acting on instructions from his superior in Washington, had visited Orgonon during September to find out all he could about the orgone accumulator.

later that I should have asked you in Maine. You think . . . and do things: I do things . . . and can't think. This isn't false modesty; it is a real pain at not being able to explain what I see to be truth in children and adults.

Guess I need a whiskey to cheer me up. I can't get one.

All the best to you. And Ilse and Peter who is likely to succeed you in the work. He is surely bright, but I didn't like his being so much alone without other kids in Maine. Apt to make him old before his time.

Summerhill School
Leiston, Suffolk

October 9, 1947

My dear Reich,

Posted a letter to you today. Then Eastmond came down to see me. Re publishing your books here. He is very keen. Says he will call his firm the Biotechnic Press. I think it might be best to let him, Eastmond, carry on ON CONDITION that you have no financial responsibility, and must be consulted before anything of yours is published. I think he is reliable, and certainly he is most keen on your work. He has a steady sale for the journals and your books. Odd how they get known; today a student from a teachers' training college came here and told me the lecturer in psychology talks about Reich. That in Stafford in mid-England.

Next time you write let me know if you want E. to go ahead, and if so with *Char. Analysis* and not the *Function* or *Sexual Revolution* or *Fascism.*

More work for you . . . sorry.

Forest Hills, New York

October 16, 1947

My dear Neill:

It was agreed with Wolfe that *Character Analysis* should be printed in England and that the American Orgone Institute Press would order and sell *Character Analysis* here. My private opinion is that we should build up our own press in many countries to be independent, even if the beginning is small. We should not be impressed by big names. Our own name is big enough by now. 10,000 is not too big an edition for *Character Analysis,* because our press has sold 3000 copies within one year without any propaganda.

What you wrote about Barakan's work without any resistances on the part of the patient points to charlatanism pure· and simple. Please help to exclude Barakan from our circles completely.

———— ◆•◆ ————

Summerhill School
Leiston, Suffolk

October 27, 1947

My dear Reich,

I think I'll have to give up the idea of coming out in spring to lecture. There is no one on my staff I can safely leave in charge for two or more months. But Ena, Zoë and I could come out in latish July and be back to reopen the school in late September. If I could get enough lecture fees to cover our expenses that's all I'd want. I feel that I need to see you again, for since seeing you I've felt much stronger and confident, and more able to face the opposition of all the anti-life people who are becoming more aggressive. A headmaster of a Grammar School, in a long article in *The Fortnightly,* mentions me and suggests that such men as I should not be allowed to teach children because children need religion.

I don't know if at that time of the year enough people would want lectures. We could have longer in Orgonon too. I wonder how the fire in Maine affected Orgonon. I think you were well away from the trees but not possibly from the dry grass. Let me know; I am anxious about it.

Letter from Mrs. Sharaf saying how much the kids enjoyed the seminar, but they were much upset about my pornography. One of the ministers suggested we discuss what is por-y at a session. I told a few stories, saying which I thought por-ic and which not. My point was that por-y is simply sex repression of filth, but that I could laugh at a joke when it had wit or a ludicrous situation whether about sex, religion, schoolmasters, anything. The interesting thing was that the older generation laughed at my witty or ludicrous sex stories while the young one saw no humour in them at all. Today I do not think hardly any sex story funny, and find that I am bored by people who tell them.

I mention this pornography because you will have heard of it in your *Stunden* [treatment hours] probably.

I use the Box daily and read your books in it. Since I met you again the books are very clear to me. You have no idea how much meeting you again meant to me. You are a better tonic than your whiskey—how I long for a glass again, but it can't be got; most of it is exported. I see it in London shops at £10 a bottle (40 dollars). But *um Gottes Willen* [for God's sake] don't try to send me any or any cigarettes; the duty on both is prohibitive.

Seeing Eastmond this weekend. I have become a director of the Biotechnic Press and will see that your interests are fulfilled. Re Barakan. Don't call him a charlatan; he is only a poor devil seeking to solve his inner problem in his work. A charlatan is a man who consciously knows he is swindling. B. believes in his own theories.

Am still worried about humanity. I see C-ism growing in Europe and feel sure that the whole world will become C-istic in our time and then our work is finished. Three ex-members of my staff, C.P. members, told me that S'hill was of comparatively little importance, for there can be no educational reform until the economic factor is settled. *Mein Gott,* what fools!

Your wool coat you gave me is a great boon now that winter winds blow. And Ena is delighted with her green leather coat.

I lecture to the Sex Society (President Norman Haire) in February on "Sex and the Adolescent," in London.

Love to the family. And I long to show you Zoë, who under self-regulation is fine, but we have to go against her when she wakes at 2 a.m. sometimes and yells because we won't take her up to play games with her. She has a tremendous will, but is 95% quiet and happy. No signs of her wanting to play with faeces and urine.

———— ◆•◆ ————

Forest Hills, New York

November 9, 1947

My dear Neill:

I have your letter of October 27th. The fire did not affect Orgonon, it was about 100 miles away, but it could have happened. Your idea to come over to get some money and to rest is an excellent one. You did not tell me whether you would accept my offer to live in the cabin on the big lake, where you would have all the comfort you need, instead of being cramped in one room in the lower building at Orgonon. Please, give me your idea about this point.

Don't worry about the pornographic business. I know you are not pornographic.

In regard to Barakan, I feel that the man succeeded in making us make him important. He is not important. We judge a man according to what he does, and not to what he talks. Please, understand that we have to be strict about unqualified people doing the responsible job of psychiatric treatment. It always hits back at me, and our responsible physicians, if something happens.

Whether or not the C.P. will ever devastate the world depends on people like you and me. It depends on how clearly we shall be able to out-democratize and out-freedomize these little fellows who went berserk at the smell of political power.

Did you get some American children or prospects for Summerhill?

———————◆•◆———————

Summerhill School
Leiston, Suffolk

November 17, 1947

My dear Reich,

I have two of your letters to answer, the first offering us the lake hut, the 2nd asking why I haven't replied to the offer. Of course it would be delightful, but I'd need to hire a car, for I couldn't ask you or Ilse to fetch us each time. Your other question about how the little man is progressing . . . I haven't started to it yet, for my book* isn't off to the printers yet and I have more to write to make it the correct number of words. I have begun to translate it (little man) aloud to Ena.

I have moods about coming back to U.S.A. I half hoped that my visit would bring me letters from colleges, schools etc. asking me to come and lecture. None came. So I sometimes think: "Neill, you are cheating yourself. U.S.A. doesn't really care a damn if you come or stay at home." Hence I sometimes say to Ena: "I don't think I'll try to go back next year. I over-rated my reception there."

It just shows you how easy it is to get depressed again. I know it is

———————

* *The Problem Family.*

largely the state of the world that gets me down. [Oswald] Mosley and his fascism is again to the fore here, and I think Britain will soon be in two camps, fascism vs. communism, with the right-wing labour joining fascism. I fear c-ism is walking through Europe and when you say in your letter that it is up to men like you and me to stop it, I ask how can we? Who will listen to us?

My book can't appear for a year owing to shortage of paper, and that depresses me, for by that time what I write now will be out of date at least to me.

The editor of the *Times Educational Supplement* has written a book about how to be a teacher. He calls me a genius on a pinnacle that other teachers can't reach, which isn't very true, but nice to hear from one of the conventional leaders of education.

Haven't any more to say tonight. Life is very full, but I have at last got a maths teacher and after this term won't have to teach maths 5 hours a day. I'll get back to dealing with the individual kids.

Zoë flourishes, walks about everywhere and is no trouble at all, a fine example of self-reg'n. I wonder how my friend Peter progresses. So far I have no desire to have my hut outside the school. Tonight I have played games in the lounge with the small ones, played like a kid myself. How is the G–M counter doing now?

Forest Hills, New York

December 1, 1947

My dear Neill:

This is only a short letter. We are engulfed in work to save the work from the emotional pest. The Food and Drug Administration is investigating the accumulator on the suspicion of a vice ring.* We are taking action against this. Just like a cow can say nothing but moo, so a state official who deals mostly with swindle drugs against sexual ailments, cannot go beyond his pornographic mind.

It will be necessary to publish the *Little Man*. Would you kindly inform me whether you will be able to make the translation as you

* This is the first mention of the FDA harassment, brought on by the Brady articles, which lasted for the rest of Reich's life.

intended? Also, let us know whether you think that the *Little Man*
should go out only to influential centers or to the general public.

━━━━━━━━━◆•◆━━━━━━━━

Summerhill School
Leiston, Suffolk

December 13, 1947

My dear Reich,

Can't think why it is necessary to publish L.M. now. If in
connection with the enquiry into the Orgone Chamber I can't see how
it will help. *Meiner Meinung nach* [In my opinion] it would do harm,
for it will enrage many people, and such a book should be given to the
public ONLY when you are accepted as an authority. Otherwise you
would meet the attitude "Who the hell is this Reich guy who tells us
off, cheeky devil." If your name were as widely accepted as that of
Einstein, Shaw, Freud, even Chaplin, then folks would say: "This L.M.
is strong meat to swallow, but the great Reich says it, and there must
be something in it." If it is to be published I am all for its being for
your own circle . . . at first. That book would give your enemies the best
weapon against you possible . . . "Crucify this blasphemer" would be
the cry.

I wired you that I hadn't begun to translate. In school time I can't
even write my own book unless in snatches, and to translate the L.M.
would be a job for a long summer vacation. I fear that you'll have to
get someone in U.S.A. to do it, much as I'd have liked to do it myself.

I tried to write a chapter on your work and after a page of writing
decided that I couldn't. I do not know enough to present your views,
and it struck me that if anyone were to have a chapter in a book called
Neill and his work, I'd tremble with fear, and would be sure to find it
faulty.

I am worried about you, am completely in the dark. Has the State
to investigate every damn thing in U.S.A.? If in England, you could hire
out your Accu's without anyone investigating, especially since you are
not making a profit.

Longing to hear the latest about the G–M counter. Just thought of
this. It must be impossible to measure atomic energy in a bomb, so if
orgone energy is stronger than atomic it must be that in the pile [atomic
pile, i.e., a nuclear reactor] not the bomb, *nicht*?

Ena and I are both very tired after a term. She badly needs a rest and treatment, the snag being that we don't want to call in the local doctor who will simply prescribe pills. She is so conscientious about kids that often she leaves the Box to attend to them, but in this vacation I'll see that no one is there to interrupt her.

If you need me in a hurry phone me at my expense.

————— ◆•◆ —————

Forest Hills, New York

December 18, 1947

My dear Neill:

We are in the middle of a court action against the Food and Drug Administration. I shall need the *Little Man* as well as all other material pertaining to orgone energy. From the communications you receive you will get a picture of what it is all about.

I just read your letter of November 17th again, having had no time for a thorough answer because we are drowning in work necessary to keep the Food and Drug Adm. at bay. We are all under a terrible strain.

Things are coming to a head and are burning around us. It is a question of either high up or deep down. But we are fighting bravely.

I obtained 3000 impulses per minute, or 50 per second, or as much as a strong atomic pile would give, already with the third Geiger–Müller device, and that's good news.

We would like to know about your plans for the summer. Please write.

1948

Forest Hills, New York

January 12, 1948

My dear Neill:

I agree with you that you should not include any chapter on orgone energy in your book if you feel that you cannot do it.

We had a Christmas full of strain and worries, full of conferences with lawyers, doctors, etc. because of the pestilential attacks on us. The investigation is still going on, and our lawyer will take court action against the administration.

Thank you very heartily for the picture of Zoë. She is a lively child and a new promise. Peter is growing into a smart little fellow. We are very good friends.

Summerhill School
Leiston, Suffolk

January 16, 1948

My dear Reich,

I have been to Scotland seeing my folks. I don't understand how you can take action against the Administration, for it is seldom if ever done over here.

I am feeling lonely again; no one to talk to here, and I have staff trouble again, with a man criticising me to visitors and never saying a word to me. But S'hill has always attracted neurotics who want to take my place, the fools.

. . . Most depressed at international news, and can see no *Ausweg*

211

[way out] other than war, since all the men in power are stiff-stomached and anti-life. But on the other hand, Ena and I get great joy out of Zoë, although here again I often look at her and wonder sadly what life has in store for her. We had a Danish girl as housemother, an admirer of Philipson. Zoë was sleepy and Ena lifted her to take her to bed. The Dane said: "You talk of self-regulation, but you do not practise it; you should let her fall asleep on the floor and then put her to bed." Ena said: "She wouldn't fall asleep; she would cry for an hour with tiredness; what would you do then?" The Dane didn't know.

I STOPPED SMOKING at the end of the year. My throat was getting worse every day with the strong English cigarettes. I feel much better. But after tea I feel the want of a smoke.

School opens today and I am back to work, this term to do orgone therapy with a few problem kids if they will have it. Love to the family from this family.

—————◆•◆—————

Summerhill School
Leiston, Suffolk

February 12, 1948

My dear Reich,

Many thanks for the *Cancer By.** which I devoured, every page, even when the lab work was beyond my comprehension. Do you want to have it reviewed over here? It was so good to have it, for when one keeps hearing "scientists" say that you don't know the elements of physics, etc. one feels so alone, so hopeless of science.

I've written to various folks who have contacted me in the past. [But] I don't want to keep hopping about U.S.A. at all; my dream is the lake cottage with trips to Orgonon with of course whiskey and possibly by that time cigarettes; at the moment I am still non-smoking and have no throat at all.

Constance will give you all our news. I am glad she has gone to see you and the work, for she is loyalty spelled with a large L.

Zoë is fine, a lovely advertisement for self-regulation, compared with others around here who are reared in the old vile way. But Ena needs

* *The Cancer Biopathy* (published as Volume Two of *The Discovery of the Orgone*, 1948; reissued in a new translation, 1973). Defines and discusses cancer as "a systemic disease due to chronic thwarting of natural sexual functions."

looking after and I am strict with her about the Akku. I have it in my little office and wonder if it would be good to have it in the bedroom so that Ena would get an O.-laden atmosphere. You said once not to have it in the bedroom. *Warum nicht* [why not]? What is the objection to having a bedroom full of orgones?

So Peter grows? It will be fun to see him again. IF I get lectures, IF we get a passage, IF the British Govt. allows us to travel.

——◆◆◆——

Forest Hills, New York

February 20, 1948

My dear Neill:

Many thanks for your letter of February 12th. I saw Constance on Wednesday. She has changed quite a bit.

The Press will send you some *Cancer Biopathy*s. But please, do not try to make any propaganda for it. If the book is good, then it will make its way, and if it is not, then let it die. I am afraid you are still underestimating the recognition I enjoy in this world. But I have to confess that it is a quite different type of recognition, a noiseless one, so to say.

We shall be very glad to have you at Orgonon again this summer with Ena and the child. But I have to sell the cabin on the lake, because I need the money to put up a building on the Hill. We shall find a nice place for you to live in at Orgonon itself if it can be arranged. By the way, I stopped drinking whiskey.

The *Little Man* will be printed and distributed, after all. If I had listened to what people told me about the *Sexual Revolution* and *Character Analysis* in 1928, these books would never have been published. It took them 20 years, it is true, to break through, but they did break through. The same is true for the *Little Man*. I had a well-known artist* make some drawings for it. They are very good and you will enjoy them. When is your book coming?

——◆◆◆——

---

* William Steig.

Summerhill School
Leiston, Suffolk

February 24, 1948

My dear Reich,

I wish I could grasp what your attitude to publicity really is. I see that you don't want me to try to interest any scientist in the work. Good. I got that. But in my book I've given a list of your books and where they can be got in London. Is that allowed or isn't it? Let me know so that I can cut it out of the proofs if you want me to. You say: Let them come to us, not the other way round, but still you do send your books out to be reviewed by scientific journals.

Re our trip to U.S.A. nothing is settled yet. I'm sure we can fix up about living when we come, but I am alarmed about your no longer drinking whiskey, for with my non-smoking and your non-drinking that talk in your cabin from 4 p.m. onwards is going to be a bit dull.

The *Little Man*. I can't make up my mind about it . . . I advised waiting publication because I thought that if the State was against you owing to the Brady article, the *Little Man* might play into their hands, for they might cry: "See, this man is mad; he thinks we are little men and implies that he is a big man. The Brady woman was right, so let us crush this man."

You say I still underestimate your recognition. I possibly do because you are always alarming me about all the enemies and their work, giving me the impression that the chief ones who "recognize" you are the FBI, the Food & Drug Dept, etc. You tell me more about your enemies than your friends, and in summer actually gave me concern that the Ku Klux Klan or hired gangsters might invade your Orgonon.

My book* is being printed but it may take a year to get it published. Already I want to change what I wrote, and in a year's time it will be painful to me to look at it.

Had a good lecture on "Sex and the Adolescent" last week. Over 200 people were turned away. Haire in conversation at his house said that you haven't given proof that cancer has any connection with sex repression.

Ena and I find that the chief result of the Akku in cases of grippe is

---

* Neill sent Reich a copy of *The Problem Family* in manuscript. In his diary, Reich comments: "A very good book written by a child 64 years old; honest; playful; frank; full of love for children."

the curing of the head pains, and it seems to stop the nasal cold from going down to the chest.

Worried about my school staff. It seems that work is impossible without having trouble with staff . . . unless one is a disciplinarian who will chuck them out at the first sign of trouble.

———◆•◆———

[*Reich never sent the following.*]

Forest Hills, New York

February 28th, 1948

My dear Neill:

I just received your letter of February 24th. I think it will be important that I clear up a few points:

Of course, I want you to announce my books wherever and whenever you can. But that has nothing to do with trying to *convince* people and to beg them to accept my theories. You only become saddened and disillusioned if you do this. But I never meant to say that our friends and co-workers should not do all they can to make our work known.

I do not think that our discussions would be dull if you don't smoke and I don't drink, because I do not believe that our discussions depended in their subjects and luminosity on smoking and drinking alone.

The most complicated matter I have to deal with in my relation to you is the question of my recognition. When I said in my letter that you underestimate the actual recognition which I enjoy, I meant the following: To my mind, a man is recognized in the strict sense of the word, when he made a very great discovery—as a matter of fact, one of the greatest in the history of science—and when, accordingly, he is talked about everywhere in scientific, educational as well as political circles. Your idea of recognition seems to be that a man should be adored, or receive prizes. I don't think this is true recognition. They are meting out prizes and recognition today to men who did not accomplish anything, except complying with the rules. I would not like to be in their shoes, and I would not like to be mistaken for one of them. To have so many enemies as I have, alone proves that the world knows what I am doing, namely overturning a heap of stale and wrong self-damaging beliefs about nature and man.

The "State" is not against me. There are a few pestilent officials, who are a disgrace to the American administration, who are against me. If the State were against me, it would not, after so many thorough investigations of my activities have admitted me to the country and given me citizenship as well as recognition of my research activities, exemplified by the charter from New York State.

I feel most humble when I compare myself with the discovery I have made. Then I don't feel a big man, but a curious child which wonders and ponders. I feel humble and utterly simple at any simple honest question my child asks me. But when a pestilent, little fellow who shouts "Heil" or "*Rot* [Red] Front" all his life, accomplishing nothing, steps on my toes in order to annoy me, then I know how big I am compared with the rat.

Of course, I am telling you more about my enemies than about my friends. My friends don't endanger or impede my work, only the enemies do and, therefore, they are more important. And to count representatives of the Russian red fascism among one's enemies is quite an honor. Why should I go around bragging that at my 40th birthday I was hailed at a dinner as another Karl Marx, Sigmund Freud, Darwin and Galileo taken together? I don't find much joy in such comparisons, since I am only Wilhelm Reich and that is sufficient for me. And people always try to find out about me by comparing me with this or that great one, in order to feel safe, instead of really grasping what I accomplished. Why should I brag about Freud telling already in 1925 that I was the best head in the Vienna Psychoanalytic Society? Or should I go around telling people that about 300 universities and libraries are using my books to teach people to think straight? Or should I go around bragging that a recent bibliography, compiled from our archives, comprises some 40 tightly typed pages of books and magazines who wrote about me and my work? Or shall I go around telling all people that in France a medical journal called me the continuator of Freud? Or shall I publish the fact that there is scarcely a scientific or intellectual circle that does not talk about me and my work, in America and abroad?

The true recognition I enjoy is the fact that I am master over a vast field of natural functions, that millions of human lives depend on my knowledge and on the way how I apply this knowledge in the present and in the future. Is not your great concern about my being recognized partly due to true friendship, but partly also due to a wrong perspective in truly important human relations? When you asked that professor of psychology whom you met at my lab last summer, how she came to hear about me, I know that she felt most peculiar about it. And I think that you too felt peculiar when your audience in New York broke out in cheers when you mentioned my name. I am writing all this to help you change your ideas about my status in this world. It is not lack of recognition, but too much and a too responsible situation which prevent me from making full use of my great social influence.

A great recognition lies in the fact that I find myself together with men whom the world hails today as their true sages and who have been persecuted, burned and slandered all through their lives. *This* is the recognition I enjoy. I would not give one iota of it for recognition which a Norman Haire could bestow on me. Don't you see that people like Norman Haire, who claim that I have not given proof that cancer has any connection with sex repression, belong to a dying world, to an old, worn-out group of people who did not dare to touch the natural sources of life, and instead brought phalluses, condoms, perverted homo-sexuality, and bananas and cucumbers before the world as the true issue of human love life. Do you want me to beg or to ask for their recognition? Is not the fact that my orgone can stop a nasal cold from going down to the chest more important than all the brass-heads and the academic fools of the world taken together?

I hope you don't mind, Neill, when I spoke out this time about my true feelings. The cosmic orgone energy will be enjoyed, handled and studied by the human generations of the next few thousand years, when no trace will have remained of any one of present people whose recognition today is demanded. And, therefore, my *Little Man* will be published, come what may, state or not state, GPU [Russian Secret Police] or FBI, this or that pestilent gossiper. The orgone will exist and function, discovered by man and put to use for the human race when it will govern itself. And the mention and the memory of a dictatorial state official will be a painful and shameful one.

———— ◆•◆ ————

Forest Hills, New York

March 3, 1948

My dear Neill:

I had written a long letter to you concerning the question of the recognition I am enjoying. But I decided not to send it off, and to keep it for a personal discussion this summer.

I want you, of course, to announce my books whenever and wherever you can, but that has nothing to do with trying to convince people who are ignorant or inimical, and to beg them to accept my theories. While the first helps, the second harms the work.

The orgone work is progressing fruitfully and spreading steadily day by day.

Please, keep me informed on your plans, in order to enable us to provide quarters for your stay in Maine.

———————◆·◆———————

Summerhill School
Leiston, Suffolk

March 7, 1948

My dear Reich,

    I feel pessimistic and depressed about the world, and can't avoid the conclusion that atomic war is near. The dilemma is this . . . to die atomically, or to live in a Communist police state. We adults might say: better dead than that, but Peter and Zoë might say: nay, we want to live even if in a bad police state, for we can try to change it for something better. My point is that we may be ready to die for a principle but have we the right to drag our kids into the death we choose? Rather like the familiar case of the bankrupt man who shoots his children and then himself. I hate the idea of Zoë growing up in Communism, but I hate more the idea of her not growing up at all. It sure is a difficult dilemma. I think that Communism is coming all over the world, logically following your argument of a castrated society. Its anti-life discipline will make it conquer, and politically it is a sternly disciplined force, whereas against it is only a loose union of U.S.A. capitalism and British social democracy. Two elements that are opposed to each other. What a dilemma for us who don't believe in either camp.

    Well, we'll have much to talk about when we meet again.

———————◆·◆———————

Forest Hills, New York

March 12, 1948

My dear Neill:

    I do not agree with you that the Communists will conquer the world. The forces of life are much stronger than the forces of darkness and dictatorship. Red Fascism will go down just as the black fascism went down. It is only a question of how many innocent human lives they will take with them. You underestimate America in its youthfulness, ability to change and to adjust to new situations.

◆•◆

Summerhill School
Leiston, Suffolk

March 19, 1948

My dear Reich,

Please send me a formal invitation to come and lecture under the auspices of the O. Institute. I need written evidence before I apply for a visa. It isn't at all certain that we can come, for the Cunard Line says that all berths are booked all summer.

As to communism, maybe I am more pessimistic than you because I have it on my doorstep now, and if war does come it means that this country will be a chaos of death, for it will be U.S.A.'s aircraft carrier No. 1.

Ena is so keen on helping me with the small children that she thinks she might stay on for a few months to get O. therapy in N.Y. after I go home.

God I am longing to see you again, even *ohne* [without] whiskey!

I'll telegraph when I get dates of landing . . . if I do get 'em.

P.S. Most wonderful is self-regulation with Zoë; she shows no sign of hate or destructiveness. It is a joy to watch her grow. One of the staff has a girl of two and the difference between the bodies is great. Zoë is as loose as a kitten; Deborah as tight as a drum.

◆•◆

Forest Hills, New York

March 25, 1948

My dear Neill:

I am in a turmoil, since during the past two weeks I succeeded in demonstrating the orgone energy in a complete vacuum (evacuated tubes). I obtained blue colored lumination and up to 25,000 impulses per minute on the Geiger–Müller counter. (Please, don't ask Bernal what he thinks of it. He doesn't know anything about it.)

If Ena wants to study orgone therapy, she should make arrangements already now with one of our doctors. Their time is filled to the utmost.

I am sending you by separate mail the invitation you want for your visa application. But this invitation is going out for an important conference, and not for a lecture. May I ask you, if you are interrogated by the press on your arrival, not to forget to mention the Orgone Institute, as happened last year. I know you don't mind my saying this. The omission of the Orgone Institute from the press conferences has puzzled many people, including me. I would rather be frank about it.

The conference at Orgonon is meant factually, and not merely formally. There are great responsibilities and difficult questions involved. Most probably, Hoppe from Palestine will be there too, and so will a few medical orgone therapists from the U.S.A.

We have beaten off so far the attack of the Emotional Plague, but we are not sure whether it will continue or not. The work is in a very critical and promising development right now. With the exception of a few impertinent psychoanalytic business men who feel threatened by my theory of orgastic potency in their commerce with human misery, and, therefore, fight it, the public has become aware of this problem to a great extent. Here Kinsey's book,* which was sold in 600,000 copies and deals with the orgastic function in the human male, has helped quite a bit to break through the Chinese wall which had been erected and is being kept up by psychoanalytic merchants and red fascist politicians in unison.

What you write about Zoë only proves the correctness of my statements during the past 30 years. This is the only hope left to us, and it is wonderful to have something so important to fight for. Including, and not excluding, the core of the matter, that is, the sexual development of the child and adolescent.

———— ◆•◆ ————

Summerhill School
Leiston, Suffolk

March 30, 1948

My dear Reich,

Both letters from you today. Thanks for the official invitation. And we want to come very much, for we are depressed. We fear that atomic war may be very near . . . Tito has only to march into Trieste

---

* *Sexual Behavior in the Human Male,* by Alfred C. Kinsey and others (Philadelphia: W. B. Saunders, 1948).

and you have it. The fools in parliament are talking of defence dug-outs etc. U.S.A. may get off lightly but this island as an air base for U.S.A. would be wiped out with death rays. Zoë's delightful happiness and cleverness and beauty make the picture terrifying for us.

I don't get you about the Institute not appearing in press notices. Can you imagine my sitting for the first time in U.S.A. and NOT telling them the main object of my visit . . . to see you? I think you are being a bit unfair to me here, for I never fail to acknowledge my debt to you and your work. If you came here to lecture under the auspices of Summerhill, not one paper would mention S'hill; all would simply write about what you were here for and what your message was. Also consider that the Orgone Institute may be on the black list of papers. Here the *Times* would never allow my name to be mentioned; they refuse to publish any letter I write. I wish to God I knew what your attitude to publicity is. If I mention your work to a Bernal you get angry, but if you think I don't mention it to some journalists you get annoyed. In the New School where I lectured last summer, I said that your work wiped out the old psychoanalysis, but if I lecture again I won't know what to say about you. I'll give you a fatherly lecture about this when I come over, my lad.

Your new news of the G–M counter is fascinating. But I won't tell Bernal!

As for Ena and treatment, I fear it is impossible. I won't earn enough. I have put our names down for passages on a slowish ship, the Britannic, for the Q. Elizabeth and Q. Mary are fully booked already. And I am anxious in case we can't go (the Cunard can demand full payment if we don't go).

Am having staff difficulties, a most tiresome thing. Some new ones sit with sneering faces when I talk of children, and one of them thinks I am an old out-of-date fool . . . and I can't do a thing, for teachers can't be got.

I want very much to be at that conference and meet the doctors you mention, especially Hoppe.

Ena and I often say we should start a home for mothers and children of a week old. The more I see of stiff stomachs the more I feel that the start should be made with infants. Ena has been an ideal mother for Zoë, and the result is just excellent.

Forest Hills, New York

April 5, 1948

My dear Neill:

I just received your letter of March 30th. I understand your depression very well. The difference between you and me seems to be that you seem to lose hope whereas I, relying on the untouchable life principle in children and on the discovery of the cosmic energy, am full of hope and pep for a future, better society, whether I am going to live through the holocaust or not.

Please, don't worry about the publicity business. I only mentioned it to you because it happens so often that people love the Orgone Institute but are afraid of mentioning it in public. It has to do with the orgasm function, you know. I may confess that I have to grit my teeth very often when I see how the fear of natural love and life distorts people's reactions.

My attitude towards publicity is clearly this: We want all publicity possible, but not in the wrong way and not with the wrong people. And, first of all, we are not begging for recognition.

I understand your situation with your teachers. You have entered the age of the "Little Man," this time in the form of teachers.

I am completely in agreement with your last sentence and Ena's idea of starting a home for mothers and children right after birth. It is to my mind the only real way of doing something lasting in education: prevention of armoring. Whether you can still do it, I don't know.

The Orgone Institute is not only not on the black-list, but on the contrary, its publications are ordered and read by most of the American universities and college libraries, a total of about 300 or so. You have still a wrong view on my standing in this world, due to the lack of publicity noise.

◆•◆

Summerhill School
Leiston, Suffolk

April 4, 1948

My dear Reich,

I note what you say about my pessimism and your own hope for humanity. But I am taking a narrow view . . . I want Zoë to live and flourish, and it doesn't console me to think that in the year 3000 A.D. life will be grand. But we'll leave all this for our talks . . .

although I won't enjoy sitting in your cabin drinking Canadian rye while you drink orange juice!

You always complain that I underrate your popularity in U.S.A. *Aber mein Freund* [But, my friend], I seldom ever get from you any literature that acknowledges you; but I get much that shows what the pest is saying. I have read Wolfe's booklet* and think it very well done, but, oh, the idea that he and you have to waste time and energy with the Bradys of life is so appalling.

I fear that it is going to be impossible for Ena to go back to U.S.A. for therapy. One joy is that without therapy, she hasn't made a single mistake in Zoë's case. The result is pure delight to me. She is talking quite a lot at 16 months. So Peter is reading! Both cases make me think there is nothing in heredity!

Forest Hills, New York

April 28, 1948

My dear Neill:

I have your letter of April 12th. Again, in regard to my popularity: To my mind it is much more important to emphasize the obstacles than to rest on one's laurels. I could fill about 200 pages in print with positive acknowledgments, but that would not bring any true friends. On the other hand, to put forth the attacks of the emotional plague makes for fighters, and keeps out the chatterers. That is not conscious policy, but just my way of living. May I also add that booklets like Wolfe's are not a waste of time, but, on the contrary, they reflect our task as physicians against the emotional plague of the 20th century in an unequivocal manner.

We shall most probably have the 6–10 day conference at Orgonon during the last part of August.

---

* *Emotional Plague versus Orgone Biophysics: The 1947 Campaign* (1948), written in response to the Brady articles.

Summerhill School
Leiston, Suffolk

May 1, 1948

My dear Reich,

I am not pleased with the way our relationship is going. Our letters seem to get more aggressive and argumentative each time, chiefly over this publicity-recognition business. We'll have to agree to differ about it. I say that Wolfe's booklet is a waste of time in that it is diverting creative work to defensive war. You say it isn't. Our methods differ. I've lost thousands of pounds in bad debts and could not take any case to law, because the lawyers would simply read out passages from my books (out of context, of course), and any judge or jury would conclude I had an immoral school and that sort of publicity would kill my work. BUT, Reich, against that negative aspect is the fact that my books appear in Japanese, Scandinavian, and now they are to be published in India in native languages. That is what matters to me, although I grant that your situation is different to mine.

Spending all my time gardening, trying to grow as much food as I can in these hard times. The kids return from vacation in three days.

I look forward to long talks with you. Just have a vague feeling that you are critical of me for some reason . . . it began to arise from what you said about the press conference and the O. Institute not being mentioned. But speaking is better than writing.

———◆◆◆———

Orgonon
Rangeley, Maine

May 25, 1948

My dear Neill:

I received yesterday the copies of your correspondence with Marika Hellstrom.* I had a feeling before the matter started that it would not be easy to arrange lectures during vacation time. But somehow it must be accomplished that you come over with Ena and the child to visit Orgonon again . . .

It will interest you to know that I have worked with Constance for about two months. She was a bit astonished to find that over the past ten

---

* Hellstrom was trying to arrange lectures in the United States for Neill.

or twelve years my work had developed quite a bit, with a score of important medical practitioners around and being talked about all over the U.S. and abroad. It was clear that difficulties which would have taken years of work to eliminate, could be cleared up in a few sessions.

Please let me know by return mail what you are deciding to do. I would love to see Zoë and Ena, and have you for talks *with* and not without whiskey.

———◆◆◆———

Summerhill School
Leiston, Suffolk

May 25, 1948

My dear Reich,

Yours today. I guess we'll come even if we don't make our expenses. Meanwhile I won't cancel the passages. But if our stay means that you or Hamilton or anyone else have to give us dollars to travel etc. I can't come on these terms.

Regarding Constance and others, I should think that O. therapy *ohne* [without] the opportunity to have a love life is not successful.

I look forward much to meeting you again. I get depressed with all my troubles with staff etc., and a visit to you bucks me up a great deal.

———◆◆◆———

Orgonon
Rangeley, Maine

June 5, 1948

My dear Neill:

I agree fully with you about your statement that orgone therapy without concrete establishment of a satisfactory love life can only be a partial success.

I want you to accept my offer to be my guest together with your family. Thus, the danger of not earning your expenses will be greatly diminished. The funds of the Orgone Research Fund are exhausted, and extremely strained by the construction of the observatory building* which we are putting up at present. But I don't doubt that you

---

* This was the second major building to be put up on the Orgonon property.

will have enough seminars and lectures to cover expenses in connection with your travelling.

———————◆◆————————

Summerhill School
Leiston, Suffolk

June 29, 1948

My dear Ilse,

Yours today with the great news of the motor turning.* Wonderful. Longing to see it. We sail August 3rd and it takes 8 days. We both look forward a lot to seeing you both, and my only anxiety is the international situation which looks as black as hell today. We are both very tired out with the constant flow of visitors, mostly dull Scandinavians. They muck up our lives . . . for instance, four times last week I had to come out of the Akku to deal with some new arrivals. Most of my staff are too hopeless to do even that.

Love to you both.

P.S. I can't get over the big news of the motor. I'll flourish it before all the idiots who say that Reich is a charlatan.

———————◆◆————————

Summerhill School
Leiston, Suffolk

July 9, 1948

Dear Both,

We've all had a war scare again over the Berlin affair,† and I hear that schools in London are seeking castles in Scotland to evacuate to. I don't think it will come just yet, but in case some Russian or American idiot starts shooting in Berlin I am posting on to you the page proofs of

---

* Reich recorded this event in an affidavit which he had notarized on June 30, 1948: "On June 26, 1948, at 1 p.m., I succeeded in setting a motor into motion by means of the Orgone Energy Motor Force which I had discovered by way of the Geiger–Muller counter on August 8, 1947." As witnesses he lists his wife, the caretaker, and three of his associates.

† The Soviets had blockaded the city, hoping to force the Allies to abandon the Western sector.

my new book . . . so that if the worst does happen, it won't be lost to humanity! But I'm not quite so pessimistic as I sound. We are nearer to the danger here and our anxiety is naturally greater, for if war does come our island will be wiped out this time.

Delighted to hear that the wheels are still turning.

Summerhill School
Leiston, Suffolk

July 17, 1948

Dear Both,

We got our visas easily and all is set to sail on the 3rd Aug. Only bother is that the Bank of England wouldn't grant me any money, so that all we are allowed to take is £5 each so that we can pay our rail journey when we return. So that we shall arrive without any dollars at all.

The war cloud comes and goes here, so that we can't forget it for long. Oh boy, it is to be good to see you again. Good to taste Canadian rye and ice cream sodas and smoke cheaply . . . damnation, I gave it up and began again. Weak guy am I.

Love to you all. And I hope to see your cheerful faces one day at Farmington,* but if that fool man Reich starts to brag about his new car it will surely break down.

Summerhill School
Leiston, Suffolk

July 27, 1948

My dear Reich,

I can't wait till I see you to say how much I enjoyed the *Little Man*. It is brave, true, a shattering indictment, and, tell Wolfe, excellently translated. I was against its publication, you will recall, but I think you were right and I was wrong. It forestalls the plague folks,

---

* The town with a railroad station closest to Orgonon.

hits them before they hit you, so to say. I wish it could have a wide circulation in England. Good woick, wise guy!

The only thing I hate is the voyage of 8 days. I hate the sea because I have nothing to do but read and eat, and I hate train journeys for the same reason. I can drive a car 400 miles with much pleasure because I am doing something, not being static.

It will be a great joy to meet you again. This time I may again beg for the use of a typewriter, for Ena and I want to write a joint book on bringing up babies. And for a time I'll try to forget the war-makers and the Little Men who let them make wars. God, what a hell of a lot of truth you have packed into that book.

Love to you and Ilse and Peter. It will be wonderful to see him and Zoë together.

◆ ◆ ◆

[*Neill, Ena, and Zoë arrived in the United States August 10. After spending several days at the Hamilton School in Sheffield, Massachusetts, they went to stay with the Reichs at Orgonon in Maine, where Neill took part in a Conference on Prevention of Biopathies. In the middle of September, Ena and Zoë returned home for the beginning of the school term. Neill stayed on at Orgonon till the end of September. He spent October in New York, part of the time with the Reichs in Forest Hills, and gave a number of lectures and seminars before returning to England in early November.*]

◆ ◆ ◆

New York

Sunday [October 3, 1948]

Dear Both,

I hated to leave you and the loveliness of Maine . . . and Peter's milk & the whiskey & of course the arguments about Stalin, but I think I was right to leave you, for there is so much to do here. Yesterday in my jeans and no collar I signed a contract with the Hermitage Press and got 500$ advance royalties. Now I sit down to write an article on discipline for the *N.Y. Times* Mag. and lunch with the editors on Tues. Guess that means a suit and tie though . . . damn 'em.

My love to the observatory. Send me a picture of the finished building, that is if friend Collins* isn't too old by the time the roof is put on.

It was a great treat to be so long with you.

———◆◆◆———

Orgonon
Rangeley, Maine

October 5, 1948

My dear Neill:

When you left, there was quite a gap at Orgonon. There was no emperor figure, walking slowly and meditatingly up the road towards the lab, there was no one playing around with the lathe and envying me for having it; there was no one I could tease with Stalin and no one to pour drinks into. Well, we shall have it again.

We shall be back in New York some time at the end of next week, and shall call you as soon as we are settled.

———◆◆◆———

Orgonon
Rangeley, Maine

October 7, 1948

My dear Neill:

I hope that your plans are proceeding well in New York.

It will interest you to hear what happened with Peter after you left: These facts corroborate fully my statement as to the core of his troubles. First, he developed a great love for his doll Erica. He takes her to his bed every evening, caresses and hugs her and shows clearly that he is longing for a girl. Second, he told Ilse last night the following: "I have a dream about being grown-up and married with a woman. We undress and go to bed and I hug her breasts." Well, you cannot have it more clearly than that. All the other aspects of the problem are secondary to this core. I am ready to take all responsibility in public for the overall important and crucial point in the education of small children. Peter is very fine, lovely and healthy again. But the problem is not solved. It is not solved for millions of children. The evasion of the words orgasm,

---

* Rangeley contractor who built Reich's observatory; he was just out of college.

orgone energy and orgone institute, is closely connected with the general human evasiveness in these questions.

We are slowly preparing for home-coming (and hate it).

We shall call you at the Haymes'* soon after our return. Your place at the table looks still empty, and so do all the whiskey bottles.

———— ◆•◆ ————

Summerhill School
Leiston, Suffolk

November 14, 1948

Dear Both and Peter Thumper,†

I had a great welcome; whole school at station shouting and cheering. Thanks to Haymes's pal in the Cunard I was transferred to A deck with pursers etc. bowing to me and giving me fruit in the cabin, and I had an official come to take me off the ship before all the others. Bloody king I felt. I liked it of course.

Found the *Stimmung* [mood] of S'hill lovely. But, fine as it is to be back, I have still part of my heart in Forest Hills. You were far too good to me. I suppose I carried off the door key because I wanted to open your door again many times.

Reich, a Nature Cure Chiropractitioner said at the British Naturo-pathic Conference, 1948, that healers must go to Reich for their funda-mentals. That is good to read. It would be odd if the unqualified practitioners saw your light before orthodox medicine did.

Well, my very dear friends, now I must go down and tell the assembled school all about my trip. Blessings to you all.

———— ◆•◆ ————

Summerhill School
Leiston, Suffolk

December 1, '48

My dear Reich,

I am sending on a copy of the *Sex Journal* with a review of the *Sexual Revolution*, a good review too. It will be read by many people.

---

* American friends, Duncan and Angelica (Geli) Haymes, with whom Neill stayed until the Reichs returned from Maine.
† Neill's pet name for Peter Reich.

I am also sending you a watercolour picture I made specially for you. It isn't art, for I am no artist, but it splashes color about, and I enjoy doing that. Lots of Orgone blue in it too!

Have been working hard since I returned, finding satisfaction in discovering the tensions of kids. Worst case a boy of 4 who can't speak. He screams when frustrated by a closed door. Parents beat him for shitting etc. A bad case that may be beyond my skill, but I am attacking his steel tensions with some success I believe.

I am using the box for a girl of eleven who is anaemic, and one of my staff (a Communist woman!) sits in it daily for she is also anaemic! Another staff woman with chilblains used the funnel* twice and all pain went.

I've forgotten Bourbon and Chesterfields, but my resolution to stop smoking broke down even at the awful price fags are here. Part of me is still over there with you both, in dear old Orgonon and pleasant 99–06.†

Haven't heard a word from U.S.A. since I came home. Yes, a few letters sent to *Times* about my article,‡ all of them favourable.

I took the liberty of sending a *Little Man* to Sir Stanley Unwin of Allen & Unwin, one of the best publishers in London. If he wants to publish it I advise you to agree.

I keep damning the ugly fact that we are 3000 miles apart.

———◆•◆———

Summerhill School
Leiston, Suffolk

December 5, 1948

My dear Ilse,

Tut, tut; the moment I leave you you get into trouble again. I am worried about Reich having to devote all his energy to pest people,§ while I wait here impatiently for my orgone motor to make my light. Damn 'em all.

---

* The small, hand-held accumulator that Reich sent to Neill.
† Reich's home in Forest Hills: 99–06 69th Avenue.
‡ "Love-Discipline, Yes—Hate-Discipline, No," *The New York Times Magazine*, November 7, 1948.
§ That is, the enemies of Reich's work; in this case primarily the agents of the Food and Drug Administration.

Times Mag. tells me they had a lot of letters about my article. One schoolboy wrote asking for 50 copies "so that I can send a copy to each of my teachers."

Ena very tired; has had too much to do owing to my absence.

You say that Peter isn't quite all right again. I guess we shall all find that our self-reg. kids are problems to some extent owing to the environment. Pity S'hill isn't near Peter, for he'd find all his love life here easily enough.

Young doctor here this weekend, a psychiatrist, has read all the literature and is very keen, says that the Freudians in London are alarmed about Reich. One said to him: "I want to believe in Reich's work but if I did I'd have to admit that all I have learned already is wrong."

Our love to you, Ilse. And tell that Reich guy that he is no good standing alone. The moment I leave him his enemies begin to attack. I long to know who the enemy is this time.

———— ◆•◆ ————

Forest Hills, New York

December 6, 1948

My dear Neill:

I did not write for so long because I was rather taken up with difficult stuff, and also suffered from a very reasonable depression. I had the feeling that I am working in a desert, and that if anything big were to turn up, either a big task in mental hygiene or some horrible attack by the plague, no one would be there to help me to fight it. I am recovering slowly from this not too subjective feeling.

I think you will find great satisfaction in learning to diagnose armorings and blocks in kids and in removing them at least superficially.

I still think back with great pleasure to the many evenings we had chatting about everything from Heaven to Hell.

———— ◆•◆ ————

Forest Hills, New York

December 9, 1948

My dear Neill:

We just received your letter. Yes, my work has burst open everywhere and it is now rather much to handle, since I feel quite like in a desert with no real active, eager fighting helpers around. There is some basic hesitancy or reluctance to stand up clearly and faithfully for our work and to defend it in public just as eagerly as the enemies of this work are attacking it by defamation.

The latest news is that some psychoanalysts apparently ran to the District Attorney to stop my work. They pulled out some law from the books which said that whoever directs mental hygiene work must be licensed to do so, or something similar. This is, of course, nonsense, since I am the one who licenses doctors and educators to practice what I found and teach. I would appreciate it highly if you would make it widely known that the psychoanalysts and some psychiatrists who have no answer to my work are cowardly enough to use defamation, distortion and denunciation.

There is no doubt about it, as we have found out lately through many witnesses who have sworn to their written statements, that there is a concerted effort to smash my work by denunciation. For instance, the rumor was circulated about 2 weeks ago in many places that a woman patient had been masturbated at the Orgone Institute and thereupon had a breakdown. The woman, whose name was mentioned in this connection, had never been here. We went after this story immediately with the help of our lawyer and the man who spread the rumor took it back immediately. Well, that is what I call plague. The greatest riddle is what blocks us ourselves from standing up for the truth and decency just as vigorously and determinedly as Ivan the Horrible stands up for the lie and defamation. This is the big headache.

When I shall have answered this question practically, then I shall proceed to finish my orgone motor and to install a very large one in your school. Only, watch out that the nationalized electric industry of England does not come down on you as a cheater of "public interest."

----◆•◆----

Summerhill School
Leiston, Suffolk

December 12, 1948

Dear Both,

Re Peter. Have you considered the sleep angle? Recently our kids have been breaking all bedtime laws. A meeting was strict about them, and for a week they have gone to bed early. Result: most of the bad tempers, destructiveness etc. have lessened greatly. Zoë, if too late up, owing to the exciting life here, is a problem next day, whining, ill-tempered . . . and in her case there is no question of anything genital at all. Peter goes to bed far too late. Here in the Cottage he'd be bedded by 6 or 6:30 . . . and in Orgonon he was often up until ten. I'd play the heavy parents about sleep if I were you. Self-regulation be damned sometimes . . . today is very cold; Zoë wanted to go out in her thin frock. Ena said no; must wear overalls. Anger, tears, but Ena insisted and put on the warm things.

I don't like to challenge the greatest authority on human nature in the world, but I think that no behaviour is "nothing but." I think that if Pete could have his real Erika in bed with him AND still sat up late, he'd still show signs of problemicity. It is nice and easy to write that, knowing that the great man isn't going to lay down his glass of Bourbon and argue the head off me.

Using the small Akku a lot with kids' sores with marvellous results. Still puzzled about having an Akku in a room. Do the orgones, concentrated in the box, stray out into the room? A most important point to me, for mine is here by my desk all day.

Our love to you all. I got both your letters. Come off it, Reich. I won't have this depression. Of course you are in a desert, but a desert has some protection; enemies suffer from heat and thirst.

———◆•◆———

Forest Hills, New York

December 14, 1948

My dear Neill:

I have yours of December 12th. I am glad you discovered the healing effects of orgone energy. I only ask myself why it was not discovered by you some 3 years ago?

In regard to Peter's situation, I must continue to argue with you. Of course, lack of sleep will make a child nervous, but we know perfectly well that the child will hesitate to go to sleep, will even develop a sleeplessness if his biosystem is frustrated, that is, excited sexually without being satisfied. In Peter's case it was quite obvious and clear that he began to stay up late when his genital excitation began to disturb him. Old Ferenczi* said that *Schlaflosigkeit* [sleeplessness] is *Beischlaf-*

---

* Sandor Ferenczi, psychoanalyst, and member of Freud's inner circle.

losigkeit [lack of intercourse] and that is very true. No, Neill, I am afraid there is no escape from the one conclusion that the core of all these difficulties of children and adolescents, whatever their variations might be, is the genital frustration as far as their energy metabolism is concerned. Everything else depends on this energy metabolism—from sleeplessness to infantile paralysis. And I would not be too sure that in Zoë there is not some kind of frustration, genital or otherwise, which is responsible for her being ill-tempered. And by the way, how do you get children to sleep if they don't want to?? No command will achieve that.

As far as the plague is concerned, I am not depressed, I am only disquieted because I don't know how to make our friends fight it.

All the best to all of you, and a very good Christmas.

———— ◆•◆ ————

Forest Hills, New York

December 17, 1948

My dear Neill:

I had qualms about my argumentative letters of late to you. You know I am not a fussy person deep down, but in matters of infantile genitality I somehow feel easily challenged. I am sending you a color photo from Orgonon to cheer you up.

I received the review of the *Sexual Revolution*. I also read the nasty poisonous review about your *Hearts Not Heads*. What fools they are!

———— ◆•◆ ————

Summerhill School
Leiston, Suffolk

December 20, 1948

My dear Reich,

But why shouldn't we argue? It isn't argument anyway. You kept saying to me in Orgonon that no one knows what a normal child is. I agree. I agree that genitality is the central point, but I argue that making sex right will not be a success unless the other factors are right too. Take Zoë. I am convinced that her bad temper after too little sleep has nothing to do with any thwarting of genitality. I say that lack of sleep will cause unhappiness in her case, and I made the suggestion that it might also apply to Peter.

I say again that our gangster group of boys, 8 to 12 or so, is hateful and destructive if late to bed. I must watch to see if their periodical times of love-making coincide with their feeling rested bodily. Fancy me trying to be scientific!

Pomerans.* My present impression is that he is one of the young men who take up your work for neurotic motives, but let me give a report when I talk to him. I've impressed on Eastmond that no one is allowed to practise therapy using your name. Dunno how you can protect yourself.

My adolescents after 5 weeks' treatment are all brightening up a lot, but there is a snag about adolescents . . . one of them biffed me hard on the jaw and a girl gave me considerable scratches. I've moved my chair back a foot or two now.

Still thinking of America with warm feelings . . . even tho today's paper says there are 20 inches of snow in N.Y. None here so far, but bitter east winds.

We had a lovely end of term party. I acted in a Scots play I had written. And our kids act wonderfully well.

I hope you have a merry Xmas with lots of rye . . . An old boy [former pupil] brought me a bottle of Scotch last night, so that mine won't be a dry Xmas after all.

P.S. Ilse, *Peter Pan* is a most demoralising story. Barrie, the author, fled from life, was impotent, but had a great childish phantasy. Here the play is produced every Xmas (in London) and the stalls are full of bald heads who never grew up, like Peter Pan, and children who go for the Indians and the Pirates.

Next morning. Pomerans went off last night with the neurotic girl who is promiscuous, so I haven't heard his tales of orgone work in S. Africa. No, I don't feel he is the type we want in the movement, but then I am always prejudiced against men who visit us and take no interest in the kids or work, and only use S'hill as a place to have their promiscuous free love in. However, don't take my opinion as yet; I may be misjudging the fellow . . . he is just over 20 and wears a beard, and the established Jesus in S'hill doesn't want any rivals.

---

* A young man from South Africa who called himself a psychoanalyst and claimed to be much interested in orgone biophysics.

1949

Summerhill School
Leiston, Suffolk

January 1, 1949

Dear Ilse,

Zoë tiresome at bedtime, keeps getting up. Ena suggests owing to her genitality not breaking through. Since there has been absolutely no repression and her genital interest hasn't awakened, I wonder if it is due to the fact that Ena's milk gave out after three weeks, so that she missed the oral orgastic phase. There is no boy her age or a little older for her to make play with. I am so ignorant about babies that I simply don't know when a girl reaches genital interest. A boy earlier surely, for his apparatus is so outstanding.

I hope you will all enjoy a Happy New Year. Personally I feel a bit dull. After the great stimulus of talk in U.S.A. I feel so lonesome with a staff and visitors who have nothing to say . . . Ena says I miss the applause of audiences. Very likely. Love to you all.

Forest Hills, New York

January 5, 1949

My dear Neill:

I was so occupied with big and petty things during the past two weeks that I could not answer your letter sooner. I could easily prove to you that the question of children's genitality is a basic question of the theory of human disease. With it everything that pertains to the main body of knowledge that I have created stands or falls. The genital

237

disturbances in children as the cause of trouble are to the incidental lack of sleep as all the water in all the oceans of the earth is to the incidental break in a water-main. Of course lack of sleep will make for trouble. But that is nothing compared with the tremendous background of the horrible genital frustration of children during first puberty. Genitality is a *total* bodily function with special qualities of energy discharge.

I am glad that you are working with children again therapeutically. They need it.

Things are moving fast in a slow way, if I may say so. The talk about my work does not stop, but increases considerably. The other day we had a message from the West Coast that the Director of the Veterans Administration there and a score of physicians have ordered *Character Analysis* and are eager to get our literature. We have also started to fight the gossiping psychoanalysts. Some of our physicians are hitting hard. Great interest is popping up everywhere.

Peter tells now nearly every day about the children in school not breathing. He shows exactly how they keep their mouths closed and their chests up.

Yesterday we had a report from Sim Tropp* that an X-ray taken on Bill Steig's mother, who had developed a cancerous tumor in her chest, has shown a great reduction in the size of the tumor. This *will* get around. I hope so in the name of the thousands of cancerous people.

Write as often as you like, Neill; this year will be one of hard fighting and pushing through to the top.

———— ◆•◆ ————

Summerhill School
Leiston, Suffolk

January 21, 1949

My dear Reich,

I went to see Eastmond. He says he knows of no one attempting therapy in connection with his end of things, barring Barakan of course who isn't considered a Reich man anyway. Eastmond now counts only as a book distributor.

---

* Simeon Tropp, M.D., for a number of years a student and practitioner of Reich's medical orgonomy.

I am much worried about money. I have my own private account in the bank and the school has its own. Lately there has been a loss every year and I have been paying out of my savings into the school's account, and I have hardly anything left for sickness, unemployment, Zoë's career. Fees do not cover expenses. If I go on losing I'll have to close the school. We must think of ways and means.

All private schools have to be inspected by the govt. authorities within the next 18 months. With me it is no compromise; take Summerhill as it is or shut it down.

Oh dear, you run away from me again; I can't follow you. You say that genitality is a total bodily function with special qualities of energy discharge. I try to think in terms of Zoë.

All her interest seems to be in things, in making toys work, in seeing how and why everything is there. Her play with little boys and girls is all out-going. Now that the kids have come back after the vacation she is so excited that she can't wait to eat a meal, and wakens at night unusually often. Watching her makes me convinced that I don't know a thing about kids or human nature. She seems to me to behave almost exactly like the kittens we have . . . just delighted to be alive to chase a bit of string. So that the more I think of the word genitality the more confused I get. All I see in Zoë is Life-ality.

That is wonderful news about Steig's mother. But I take it you still hold that no box will cure cancer so long as the psychosomatic condition is a tied-up one of tension.

I gave up smoking three weeks ago because the English cigarettes were making my throat very bad, and also were costing me about 7 dollars a week. When I return to you in summer 1950 I wonder if a carton of Chesterfields will tempt me to smoke again. Anyway I've already saved 21 dollars . . . said he mournfully.

Love to you all, and write again soon by *air* this time.

Forest Hills, New York

January 31, 1949
My dear Neill:

I agree fully with you now since you realized that Zoë and Peter behave exactly like kittens. And this is exactly what all the quarrel is about. Human beings are born healthy because they are born as little animals and nothing else. Now, the only difference between the later grown-up human being and the newborn little baby—I repeat, the only and sole difference—is that the little kitten and the newborn baby has its genital function in proper coordination with the organism and the later human being has not. In other words, the exclusion of the genital and its function from the rest of biological functioning distinguishes man in a disastrous manner from the rest of living nature. It is specifically this exclusion of genitality which causes the later armoring and all the other differences which justify the claim of *homo normalis* that he is "different from the animals." Genitality, therefore, involves not only the local function, but its whole impact on the whole organism, and in this sense genitality equals life-ality.

I wish that people would have more trust in some of my statements. I have tried to make clear on several occasions that the war of classes is over and that a new war is on, on an international scale: that between life and work on the one side and politics and emotional plague on the other side. Seen from this angle, you will understand better why your school is in danger of being closed by a socialist government. Your school represents life and work and those socialist state governments represent politics and plague far worse than anything we knew before. That is not exaggerated.

Please write more often, since you are one of the very few to whom I can talk.

———◆•◆———

Summerhill School
Leiston, Suffolk

February 5, 1949

My dear Reich,

Yours today. See your point about genitality/life-ality. Will use it in two days when I lecture to Sex Education Society in London. My subject is "Sex and Self-Regulation." Am rereading *Function of the Orgasm*, getting confused as usual in distinctions between real neurosis and psycho-neurosis, etc. just as I never can distinguish between conversion hysteria and, well, all the terms used. Seems to me the whole literature of psychoanalysis and psychiatry got lost in words just as ordinary medicine did. So in psychology. David here aged 4 who can't talk and is just beginning to notice people after being here 3 months was sent to a clinic which gave a long verdict of "spiritually rather than mentally defective" which doesn't mean a thing to me. To

241 [1949]

me the only question is: Can this blocked kid ever catch up with life? And that is what has resulted from your work—that I can't read books that define in sections under specific headings. You really say: "All diseases are the same disease fundamentally, and cure depends on how and when the anti-life blockage took place." In other words, this paragraph simply means: To hell with disease; let's think only of health. That's what your books are doing as opposed to a new book by Melanie Klein* full of castration and anal characteristics and mother's penis and what not. To read her is like being in a graveyard with open putrefying bodies; to turn to your *Function* is like going out into a meadow in spring. Question . . . Is there after all a Death Instinct which is confined to psychoanalysts?

My Cambridge meeting was good. Full hall. Came out all the way on sex. Now Oxford wants me to lecture there. On the other side, the law that makes the govt. inspect private schools has come into force and S'hill can be inspected any day now. I am not worrying too much. I know I shall refuse to compromise with their standards of education, but I can't fight them if they say I haven't enough bathrooms or W.C.'s or that too many kids sleep in a room. I haven't the money to make the place perfect from a medical officer point of view. However, they may be kind to me because of my long experience and grey hairs. The socialist govt. has put the little man in the saddle, the official, and remember that in England the private school has always been for the upper and middle classes only, and all the politicians who were once manual workers must hate the private school's guts. The typical Communist criticism of S'hill is that it is a class school not for the *workers*. I wish that my visit were not so far away . . . 1950.

————◆•◆————

Forest Hills, New York

February 11, 1949

My dear Neill:

You met Bill Steig, the famous cartoonist. He met the editors Breit and Schwarz of the *New York Times Magazine*, after he had sent in an article about me. Here is what Steig wrote to me:

"I've just had lunch with Breit and Schwarz. They say: The subject is

---

* *Contributions to Psychoanalysis, 1921–1945* (London: Hogarth Press, 1948).

'controversial' and not 'timely.' Schwarz admitted that they have to be wary of the subject of sex. They've just had to edit an article of Neill's 'though a good deal of the sex remained.' Breit made the point that the magazine section does not announce discoveries but deals with more familiar and accepted things. When I told him about my mother, he asked me what the orthodox doctors said. I told him they dropped the subject after being surprised at the X-rays. Both seem friendly to you and are enthusiastically fond of Neill. Breit quoted a statement of Neill's that you are one of the world's really great men.

"Breit has sent Neill's *Problem Family* for review to, I think, John Dewey."

Steig's mother had a malignant cancer tumor in her chest and was freed from it by orgone treatment by Simeon Tropp.

Things are moving fast here. The other day, the Orgone Press received an astonishing letter from the famous Mayo Clinic. They wrote that the Mayo Clinic is establishing a Reich Clinic in their psychiatric department.

Please keep me informed on the socialist state measures against your school. I wonder when these little fellows will start thinking in terms of the human soul. They are horrible. I have still the opportunity to utter such an opinion freely, without being arrested for lèse majesté. What a holy crowd! thriving on the utter characterological helplessness of the average citizen.

———————◆•◆———————

Summerhill School
Leiston, Suffolk

February 20, 1949

My dear Reich,

Writing is so confusing. I can't remember if I wrote you before or after my Cambridge lecture; can't remember what news I gave you, for I never keep copies of letters I send. All I am certain of is that I got yours the other day. The news of Steig's mother is staggering, as also that of an organized body actually taking up your work officially. Fine. The movement grows. At my Sex Society lecture last Monday in London the hall was packed full. It was a good meeting, marred only by a few communists. One said: "What good have you done talking to us tonight? You haven't told us what to do." I asked: "What do you want me to do?" "Organise, organise in a political party like ours." I got a lot of cheering from the audience when I answered that the C.P. was no nearer freedom than any party, and spoke of Russia 1917 as compared with Russia 1949.

My book came out a week ago* and already I've had a few reviews, which I'll send on to you. Most you send sit on the fence; they are afraid to come out, just as here my reviews don't say a thing about the sex in the book. It seems that a journalist must always be on the safe side if he or she is going to keep the job.

Life rather worrying at present. I can't bring myself to sack one of the teachers who has managed to get many kids attached to him emotionally by flattery, football etc. There would be a revolution in the school. But the moment I can get someone better to take his place I shall try to be brave. Also my own orgone therapy isn't satisfying me. Only in one or two do I get any reaction. I may be at fault owing to a poor technique or it may be that I can't be Neill the headmaster and Neill the doctor at the same time. A big worry too is *Geld* [money] and I don't see how income is to overtake expenses.

Don't like the idea of John Dewey reviewing my book. He is 90, and very unlikely to have any truck with self-regulation.

No news of state inspection yet. I'm not worrying about it, but realise that when it comes life won't be worth living; it will be full of blue forms stating how many cups of tea have been served per month to age group 9 to 12, and similar important items.

It will soon be time for you to go north again. I hate to think it will be another year before we see you and Dodge Pond and the Observatory.† And the rye. Ah, I stopped smoking seven weeks ago . . . I feel fresher in the morning, also I feel more aggressive. I don't think you should stop, Herr Doktor, for you might be dangerous to builders & baracans & bradys.

◆◆◆

Forest Hills, New York

March 7, 1949

My dear Neill:

I am in a great hurry, and tired at that, so my letter will be short only.

---

* *The Problem Family.*
† Now the Wilhelm Reich Museum.

All the work in biopathies, including cancer, has been delegated to the physicians. I practically do not do any medicine any more, except training medical doctors. Somehow this coincided with a great fatigue which overcame me, as if the whole strenuous effort of two decades had broken out at once. Ilse tries hard to get me off for a longer vacation which I have not had for nearly 10 years. But I can find nobody to take over the agenda of the Orgone Institute. I shall write you again very soon and shall be happy to see you back here in the summer of 1950. I enjoy the success you had in the U.S.A.

I read through your new book again, and was happy to find the sex-economic problems so very well presented in it. They have sold 1000 *Character Analysis,* even before the announcements went out.

Please give my regards to Ena. I hope she will be able to make the trip with you to the U.S. next year. And I, on my part, hope to be able to show you the finished observatory by then.

———◆·◆———

Summerhill School
Leiston, Suffolk

March 12, 1949

My dear Reich,

Yours this morning. I don't like it. The great fatigue you mention is obviously nature's way of crying: Reich, you fool, stop burning yourself up all the time. You say you can't take a vacation because you can "find nobody to take over the agenda of the Institute." *Um Gottes Willen* [For God's sake], man, if you consume yourself so violently and drop down dead, what does the agenda of the Institute matter? Is it too late for you to take three weeks' skiing? I tell you I don't like it, Reich. I very much doubt if you use the Box either. To put it neatly and bluntly I refuse to allow you to kill yourself with work and worry, and you damn well will kill yourself if you can't relax . . . yes, I know you can relax in body, kick your own nose etc. That isn't enough. You have got to live till you are at least 90 for there is no one to carry on your work, and speaking selfishly, how could I ever come back to U.S.A. if there was no dear warm friend Reich to greet me?

Sorry to act the part of the heavy father, but someone has to bully you into taking some care of yourself.

Just returned from lecturing to a Teachers Training College in Birmingham with 350 students. Awful *Stimmung* [atmosphere] there; staff all religious and they attacked me for two hours on religion. I came away depressed, for they mean EDUCATION and power over millions of kids. And all I got for talking for three hours was £5 . . . 20$ plus train travel of 14 hours.

No sign yet of govt. inspection of S'hill. Since inspectors will have the mentality of the Training College staff I feel very uncomfortable about it.

Zoë always a delight, but we both worry about her having no chance of good sex play. In the train I read part of a book on Oedipus, giving a synopsis of Freud's ideas. It struck me that much of Freud's theories about babies are just wrong, for instance, a baby's attitude to father's penis and mother's envy of boys' penes seems to me to be based solely on a family with authority. Indeed all Freud's *Realitäts Prinzip* [reality principle] seems to be based on the family as it is now. Castration seems to Freud to be a normal fear in every boy, but will it be in Peter? Will Zoë fantasy that someone has cut her penis off? Oh, I wish I could talk instead of write to you.

I have slowly come to feel that if your world ever comes, people will read about castration and incest and anal eroticism as we read about witchcraft. I have forgotten much of my Freud but this book seems to make him consider sadism a normal part of sex, which is absurd.

———◆◆———

Forest Hills, New York

April 12, 1949

My dear Neill:

The problem of how to go about organizing and training teachers in our field becomes more urgent with every passing day. It is of life-importance that the self-regulatory principles of education should become teachable, so that they can be transmitted from generation to generation. I am planning to hold a preliminary conference of American educators to clear the rubble off the field of survey. Would you be willing to hold a similar preliminary conference in England concerning the development of the healthy child? I would like to stress the necessity of shifting the emphasis from the handling of sick children to the handling of healthy children in our environment. We could then proceed to the arrangement of a thorough discussion of all pertinent questions at our convention in 1950.

Please inform me about what you think of this.

———————◆•◆———————

Summerhill School
Leiston, Suffolk

April 12, 1949

My dear Reich,

This cutting* may mean the beginning of a witch hunt. The fool of a man has started something that may end badly for others. He got much publicity recently by inviting a cane merchant to visit the school, and then at a signal from him, the big boys took the cane from the man and beat him. We all wonder if S'hill will be next to be enquired into. I at least have 28 years of work to show, and have a lot of supporters, but if you get into the hands of the law, some little judge has the power to kill your work.

I have just been to a conference of co-ed head teachers. The conference depressed me; they are all tied to religion and their morality.

The kids are all home for a month but we have much to do in this place. And this threat of government inspection tends to make us depressed too. To go against the stream of education requires much courage and anxiety.

Since I stopped smoking I seem to eat more and am getting so fat that I am worried about it. Your Rangeley belts will hardly meet round my waist now.

Questions are being asked in the House of Commons about private schools, and I expect to be enquired into very soon. My fear is that I MAY BE TEMPTED to compromise so that Zoë can stay in a school of my making. If I have to shut down I don't know how to live. You'll say Come to U.S.A. but if my school were closed by authority here, U.S. authority wouldn't likely give me a visa. And even if I came, with no capital, how could I set up a school? I may sound pessimistic, but I am sure that bad times are soon coming. Financially we cannot make S'hill pay, but that is a minor matter. One question about adoles-

---

* A newspaper report of an event in a self-styled "free" school.

cent sex in Parliament and any Minister will at once make urgent enquiry and of course take the side of reaction and anti-youth.

I enjoyed the *Bulletin* very much. It makes such a difference now, knowing people who were only names before. Only Mickey's* report of the Conference doesn't convey the vitality and life of it, not Mickey's fault; simply the necessity to condense.

How about that vacation you are to take? Sad that I won't be there to boss you around this summer.

P.S. If S'hill IS closed what could I earn as Tom Ross's assistant plus Honorary Compost Expert for the Frau Doktor? Reaction grows daily here and I am sure I shall soon be on the carpet before stupid officialdom.

———— ◆◆ ————

Forest Hills, New York

April 18, 1949

My dear Neill:

I just received your letter of April 12th. I do not feel that it will be easy for the reactionary government in England to take your school. It is much too well-known and it would raise quite an upheaval if they did try it. But I admit that the situation for progressive thought and action is rather bad in the face of advancing statism. It does not matter that this statism is carried mainly by socialists and communists, since statism is statism, no matter who advocates. Furthermore, it has by now become quite obvious that the masses, comprised of Little Men, are basically reactionary.

I believe that the only way to stave off danger coming from reactionary officialdom against free education of children is to get the whole sex question quite into the open, to stand up for it and to fight it through, but of course not by beating up the sadist.

———— ◆◆ ————

* Myron Sharaf, a young adherent of Reich, who for a time was employed by the Wilhelm Reich Foundation.

Summerhill School
Leiston, Suffolk

April 21, 1949

My dear Reich,

Your letter brings up the old conflict we had in Oslo. You say to get the whole sex question into the open. How? One parent wrote that the police in C.'s case* hinted to parents that if they sent their children back to his school, they might get their children taken away from them as unfit parents to have children.

The dilemma is so. To say in a law court: "Yes, my adolescents can have a love life together," would mean the closing of the school, and if they were under 16 (the age of consent in law) the teacher would go to prison. After the nine days' wonder the teacher and school would be forgotten, and also many Zoës and Peters would have to go to more or less anti-life schools. If questioned I'd want to say: "I have said and written publicly that love should be free to children all the way from the beginning. The pupils in my school know my attitude and they do not consider sex sinful or smutty. They fall in love with each other in a natural, tender way, and I never spy on them nor do I make any supervision at all."

The dilemma was voiced last night by an old boy who is sending his son next term, aged 4. He said: "All very well, Neill, to fight for adolescent love life, but I want my kid to have ten years of S'hill, and it doesn't seem fair to risk being closed when the babies risk having no S'hill freedom to go to."

Give me your opinion on the great dilemma . . . complete bravery and honesty plus martyrdom and loss of work, OR conscious hypocrisy, plus the chance to help a hundred or two Zoës. The dilemma would be less urgent if I didn't think that martyrdom here would likely mean no visa to try freedom in any other land. Put it this way: in war to be taken prisoner means that you are out of the battle. If S'hill were ended, on what front could I fight?

Do give me your answers.

---

* Copping, the headmaster who had had his schoolboys beat the cane merchant with his own canes.

Forest Hills, New York

April 25, 1949

My dear Neill:
Yours of 21.4. at hand. The problem of how to handle adolescent genitality is, of course, a trying one. Seen from the standpoint of an educator or a physician, neither keeping quiet nor running the gauntlet will help. It is a basic question of human society, and basic questions have never yet been solved without great danger and anguish. It is not a question only of whether one wants to submit to such dangers. If one does not, the only thing for an honest worker to do is, I believe, simply to state the facts in public. We can state the problem as it stands today and add that we are not capable or not willing or not strong enough to do anything about it. This, at least, will save us from *impeding* a future solution of the problem, i.e., of adding to the confusion and delaying the final answer. It is most unfortunate that these problems of living, tough as they are in themselves, are made so much more complicated by the fact that educators or physicians who are supposed to handle them are themselves structurally not able to do so.

I would suggest again, as I did in my last letter, that we prepare a thorough discussion and, if possible, arrive at a final solution through discussion by the summer of 1950, when we shall devote a whole day of the proposed conference to this problem of adolescence. Would you be willing to help in that?

———◆•◆———

Summerhill School
Leiston, Suffolk

May 10, 1949

My dear Reich,
Ena and I like the idea you suggest of a conference here on self-reg. The snag is how to exclude the element one might call the Barakan–Copping–Eastmond element, or the enemies who would come to argue not to construct. I am trying a letter in the journals as a kite to see if anyone would come.

How sad I feel that you are in Maine without us, sorry also for poor Collins and Son, for I am sure they are still as bad as ever. But give 'em hell anyway.

Yes, you are right about the *N.Y. Times.* They paid me 200$ for the second article and never used it. So far my book is being killed by silence. I mean in U.S.A.

Say, Ilse, if we are coming in 1950 who is to arrange lectures for me this time? I must earn 1000$ if I am to cover all expenses—and this time I insist on paying for my food in Orgonon. And no presents . . . limited to one belt.

I have written Eastmond saying he can't sell Orgone Institute books and practise any therapy at the same time. I lecture again tomorrow in Wrexham. As in Oxford, there will again be enquiries about how to get your books.

Thanks for the reviews you sent me of *Little Man, Fascism* book, etc. Do I detect an increasing change of attitude, one that can be expressed as: We'd better be careful what we say about this Reich man, for apparently he isn't the madman we wanted him to be.

Zoë running all over the place. *Daily Herald* woman coming today to see her and to ask about self-reg. *Picture Post* wants a woman photographer to spend 8 days here photoing Zoë, saying: "Nowhere in England has any baby the environment and chance to be self-regulated and we ought to make a record of it." But I fear that all this worship will be bad for Zoë, for up to now she has shown no narcissism or self-consciousness. Our unself-reg boys are too sadistic and rough.

Buddha Leunbach talked rot when she said a baby self-regulated itself in cold weather re clothes. Zoë would die of all the acute diseases in the world if Ena didn't insist on her wearing warm things.

Many thanks for the Orgone Inst. leaflet re my book, and for the kind things you say there, Reich.

————◆◆————

Orgonon
Rangeley, Maine

May 18th, 1949
My dear Neill:

I just received your letter of May 10th. We have been at Orgonon since May 3rd.

There are no doubts whatsoever to my mind that the psychoanalysts have mobilized all their forces to counteract our influence in the public in America. Due to this, they apparently did not print your article in the *Times*.

The problems as presented by Copping are quite tremendous. They are not bad fellows, basically, and yet it is so hard to keep apart the natural from the slightly neurotically pornographic. But how to keep out the neurotics from our movement is surely a hard nut to crack.

———— ◆•◆ ————

Summerhill School
Leiston, Suffolk

June 3, 1949

My dear Both,

At last we are to be inspected by an H.M.I. [His Majesty's Inspector] on June 13th. The H.M.I. is called Pemberton and he was chief inspector for Suffolk in 1939. He came to see me officially then and we got on so well together that I wrote asking him to come again. A week later we had to flee to Wales. Now he is retired and has been dug out to inspect the private schools. I would rather have him than anyone else. I have also contacted the Ministry of Education through two friends who write that they find the Ministry friendly to S'hill. So that it looks as if things won't be so bad as I thought. I'm not hallooing until I am out of the wood, though.

Usual summer trek of visitors. And dreadful cold and wet weather. No sun or sea bathing yet . . . a lousy climate compared with yours.

Norman Haire wanted me to have an open debate with a man, Wildman, who sells canes for teachers and parents. I said I refused to debate with a pervert and lend him publicity. The man publishes a sheet called *Corpun*, typewritten, the most utter sadistic rubbish imaginable. Copping got cheap publicity by inviting Wildman to his school and then getting his big boys to beat him with his own canes. In a case like this I never THINK; I just feel that I don't want to do it.

I keep picturing you at Orgonon . . . the trips up to the Observatory, the rows with Collins, the compost heap . . . say, Ilse, I find now that I left the gaps between the boards too wide. Get Tom Ross to move them with only a ¼ inch gap between boards. I did that this year and the heaps heat up strongly without any animal manure. I'm scything long grass daily and have four heaps. But without anyone to cut grass and gather it I don't see how you will make a good heap. Cover it up; a night's rain soaking it completely stops all chemical reaction.

Eastmond is very concerned in case you drop him altogether. I think that his promise not to do any therapy should be enough. He will then only sell the books. Barakan I never hear of or from, and I begin to think I'll never see any money from him. Constance seems happier. Don't know if she is going to work or at what.

I am wondering if I should continue treating adolescents here. There are snags. As a layman I daren't treat naked boys or bathing-costumed girls, at least it might lead to bad gossip, and treating them with layers of clothes on isn't satisfactory. A bigger snag is my ignorance of anatomy. I could easily mistake a swollen gland in the neck for a muscle rigidity. Perhaps I should stick to my job—teaching. On the other hand, some of them do get a lot of relief from my treatment.

A bit early to make plans for next summer trip over. With my book more or less a flop in U.S.A., with training colleges paying poor fees (some of them anyway), it may be that my name won't get me enough income to pay our travel expenses. Ena says if not I should go alone, but if I can't bring her and Zoë I ain't coming.

———————◆•◆———————

Orgonon
Rangeley, Maine

June 10th, 1949

My dear Neill:

I have yours of June 3rd, and I am glad that you refused to appear together with this sadistic pervert. Somewhere, the action of Copping, though it was irrational from the standpoint of success, appears very rational in a deeper sense, if you understand what I mean. Such fellows who produce and sell canes for teachers and parents to beat up their children, deserve to be punished severely by society. But since society not only does not punish them, but gives them all honors, even that of appearing in public supported by organizations, I can understand the action of an idealist like Copping. The law and public opinion unfortunately will for a long time be on the side of the pervert and against the one who rebels against it. This does not mean that I defend Copping's action, but I understand it.

In the question of your treatment of adolescents, it is hard to give advice. To my conviction, only medical men, well-trained in orgone biophysics, should do medical orgone therapy. But I don't see, on the other hand, how educators like you or Hamilton can avoid treating adolescents.

I am postponing the decision on the Eastmond affair until further discussions will have taken place.

I agree with you that when you come over in 1950 you should not give any lectures beyond the minimum necessary to refund the travel expenses. You and Ena and Zoë will be welcome guests at Orgonon, and we shall not accept any pay for your stay.

Your book *Problem Family* is no flop whatsoever in the U.S.A. It is being sold steadily, according to the rules of biophysical organic development which characterise my work: No flare-ups and no comets which come and vanish, but slow, steady, patient conviction of people. Your book is going very well, seen from this angle.

The roof on the observatory will go up next week, and thus a very exhausting process will approach its end.

I hope all is well with you and that you survived the Ministry of Education.

———◆·◆———

Summerhill School
Leiston, Suffolk

June 23, 1949

My dear Reich,

Our inspection is over. Two oldish men were here for two days. Both very friendly but obviously puzzled how to inspect. As I had expected they bypassed the big question of character, balance, sincerity etc. and concentrated on French, maths etc. finding, as I expected, that in these we were inferior to State schools, not so much because lessons are optional as because of the difficulty of getting the best teachers at the small salaries I can pay. They said they would not give an adverse report, and that I had nothing to fear. In two days they never mentioned sex or anything emotional. I think we were lucky to get them, for we might have had nasty men. Interesting to note that they had no real interest in kids. When Zoë entered the room for the first time they hardly noticed her. We can at least breathe freely now.

The conference on self-regulation you suggested we think would be best at Xmas or Easter. Summer is hopeless, for people book up their holiday months ahead. Ena and I and Zoë are to go to a seaside village in Scotland for 14 days. The rest of the 8 weeks vacation we spend painting S'hill etc. We keep looking forward to next summer in Maine, bless you both.

I lectured to 60 students last week in London University Education Dept. Later over tea the staff asked me questions about your work. One

Mrs, a practising Freudian, said she disagreed about sex for youth (she has two adolescent daughters). Youth not ready for it and all that bunk. And my old friend Thomson the Naturopath in Edinburgh told one of my old pupils that her miscarriage was due to her starting sex intercourse too early . . . the damn fool.

I long to see you send a description of the motor working without any electric current at all. That would be the most convincing evidence possible.

No more now. Too many visitors etc., so that I can't concentrate on writing.

———————◆·◆———————

Orgonon
Rangeley, Maine

June 29, 1949

My dear Neill:

I am glad that the inspection which you dreaded so much is over and that no damage has been done.

Now I want to tell you a story. Storytelling, I hope, is still permitted in the face of this righteous world of ours! The editor of an American political journal made inquiries about my work among American people. Among them he asked the head of the American Cancer Society about my cancer work. This gentleman referred him to the latest authority on natural scientific matters in the 20th century, Mildred Edie Brady, who did not like my work and hated the fact that it was commended in so many places.

The phantastic thing about it is that in this 20th century it has become a habit of so-called scientists, instead of looking into a microscope and seeing the blue in the bions and the blood corpuscles, instead of putting cancer patients into orgone accumulators and seeing whether it works or not, they run to biopaths in order to listen to opinions about this work, as if natural functions could be judged by opinions.

I think I shall concentrate, as soon as the observatory is finished, on attacking these gentlemen in public and exposing their sabotage. Most of American pathology and biology is under the influence of the geneticists who are utterly hopeless in their scientific outlook. They are the heirs of the old mechanistic and mystical hereditarians. These people are the worst enemies of anything that is moving or changeable, be it social, biological or otherwise. Now, the Russian dictators picked up this issue and had Lysenko* fight against the American geneticists on the basis that acquired characteristics can be transmitted to the next generation. This, in itself, is true. However, the motives are decisive in this case. It is a purely political issue and has nothing to do with deciding any scientific matters.

It is quite clear that, had the Americans represented the idea of the inheritance of acquired characteristics, the Russians would have defended mystical geneticism.

Would you be kind enough to gather all the material and opinions you can find in England on the healthy child, and bring them over here next year?

———— ◆•◆ ————

Summerhill School
Leiston, Suffolk

July 18, 1949

My dear Reich,

Thanks for the *Bulletin* and *Character Analysis*. Owing to end of term and countless tiresome visitors I haven't had time to read both thoroughly, but your schizophrenia case I had to read to the end. Reich, it is the most fascinating case I have ever read. It is a classic of the future. There is only one big snag: is there another man who could have treated it so? There isn't, and that brings up the question of how much a man's work can get across to others. Incidentally, the case demonstrates finally your point that orgone therapy can be done by doctors only, and one good (or bad) effect of that case is that a man called Neill has decided to give up trying o. therapy.

Ena and I have both that exhausted feeling we get after a heavy term giving out to the kids all the time. And I begin to feel age now, find it difficult to get up when Zoë makes me lie with her on the floor. Yet I can dance all night.

---

* Trofim Lysenko, Russian agronomist and biologist. Leader of Soviet school of genetics which declared that characteristics acquired through environmental influences are inherited.

We used the small Akku on a girl of 15 with a boil on her leg. It cleared up in 3 days, and we are to have her in the big box next term too.

Congratulations on your English in this your first book published in English. It flows freely and no one would ever guess it wasn't your native language.

We are concerned about Zoë getting fears and complexes from badly reared kids in the Cottage which houses the smallest children. A trying problem to you and us and all the other believers. It makes me furious to hear a kid say to Zoë: "Let's shit here but don't tell your Mummy."

No official report from the Educn. Dept. yet. I am not safe yet. One inspector was worried about the opportunities for sex life here, in view of my published views on child sex, also about the absence of religious instruction. In the report (I saw a rough copy before they sent it to headquarters . . . very decent of them to show it to me privately) I saw a sentence about sex opportunity and then this: "The headmaster however says that in 28 years no girl pupil has been pregnant." When he asked in conversation I added to that statement: "I'm not proud of the fact," and they both smiled. I can see they are trying to be fair to me, and I don't fear being closed: No, but I do fear interference—more W.C.'s, more baths, too many in one room etc.

Nay, Reich, liberty is fast disappearing from Britain, and to anticipate your answering: "Socialism, Neill," I hasten to say that the Educn. Bill inspecting private schools was made by the Tories and handed on to the Labour Govt.

We are both sad at not coming over this year. It seems so long to wait till next summer.

Our love to you all. Send me a picture of the completed Observatory with, I take it, Collins hanging from the top balcony. We all must have some outlet for our murderous wishes.

———◆◆———

Orgonon
Rangeley, Maine

September 9, 1949

My dear Neill:

It's a very long time since I have written. The summer was a very hectic one. There were many physicians in two cancer courses. A lot of visitors, nuisance and good ones.

Washington* did not turn up for work as scheduled, the motors disappeared together with Washington in a most mysterious fashion—a much too long and complicated story to be told in a letter. The observatory has been completed with the last few touches still to be done. (A beauty ...)

A nurse from the New York Memorial hospital for cancer turned up at Simeon Tropp's office with a lump in her breast scheduled for operation and was freed of the tumor within a few days.

Peter went to public school here in Rangeley on Sept. 6th for the first time and loved it.

Preparations are being made for the convention in 1950.

Dr. Raphael† has fallen in love with this region and with Orgonon and has conceived the plan of a hospital at Orgonon (I had made the plans for it in 1943 already). Several doctors want to transfer their lives here.

A new worry of where to get 200,000 dollars arose. Selling of Christmas trees and bringing to market of accumulators is contemplated. I wrote my first paper on orgonometric equations.

We hate to go back to N.Y. and would like to stay here. But Tropp and Willie‡ told me that I must go back to N.Y. because I am still needed badly since I am "so handy."

This is not all. Now, how have you been and Zoë and Ena? Why did you not write lately? You are not cross for some reason, are you?

Would you like to review Anna Freud's new papers in the book on education? Thanks for your nice little article. It will be published in the *Bulletin*.

———◆◆———

Summerhill School
Leiston, Suffolk

September 15, 1949

My dear Reich,

Your letter today. I wrote you weeks ago and wondered why I wasn't hearing from you. Your news of Bill surprises me. Am I

---

* Bill Washington, a mathematician who was working for Reich.
† Chester M. Raphael, M.D., student of Reich's and medical orgonomist.
‡ James W. Willie, psychiatrist and student of Reich's.

to believe that the mild Bill simply walked out with the two motors? *Unglaublich* [Unbelievable]. So glad to hear of the Observatory. I long for next summer to see it.

Bulletin 3 is very good. One thing astonishes me in the Institute policy . . . page 114: "Wherever a local tumour can be removed by radium we advise to do so." I don't see the point when you claim that the tumour is only a symptom.

Speaking of diet, I still think diet or absence of it might help to solve that problem (also page 114) of the clogging of the excretory pathways, but here the layman talks. I know that food is subsidiary, that sex-economy is the first vital thing, but I am sure that if a man eats stodge, takes no exercise, drinks too much liquid, sitting in the Box won't have the effect it should have. Yet in my native village a woman died at 104 last month, and she ate stodge all her life!

The N.Y. publishers sent me a book *Love and Death*, a study in censorship.* It gives a grim picture of sadistic comics, and makes much of the fact that sex is suppressed in U.S.A. while murder is approved by the state (in literature). The author, Legman, mentions you on the last page. If you haven't seen it, shall I send you a copy?

Xmas trees versus sales of Box. I doubt if the former would bring in much, owing to cost of transport. And to sell the Box would mean guarding against all the devils who would cry: "Quackery!"

Barakan paid me another £20. I haven't seen him nor Eastmond. I reread your *Character Analysis* with great pleasure. I wish it could be read by millions.

Our love to you all. Hope the compost heap is a success.

Yes, send on Anna F.'s papers if you have them.

———◆•◆———

Orgonon
Rangeley, Maine

October 6, 1949

My dear Neill:

The book on *Love and Death* by Legman has stolen the sugar from my *Function* and used it in a very bad way to put something over

---

* *Love and Death: A Study in Censorship,* by Gershon Legman (New York: Breaking Point, 1949).

on the "U.S.," not mentioning the fact that it is single irresponsible individuals who misuse freedom of expression to put out the murder stuff and that, furthermore, there is a heavy fight going on in the U.S. against this misuse. It is a typical red fascist manner of smearing. Legman is the man who called up our Institute some 2 years ago and started to insult us on the telephone about "this obvious quackery of the orgone accumulator." This means, summed up, he is a thief, a red fascist and a nuisance in addition to that. (After having dictated the above, we received a letter containing the following passage: You may be interested to know that G. Legman, author of *Love & Death,* wrote to —— that he has just read *Mass Psychology of Fascism* and found that Dr. Reich had already said everything he wrote in *Love & Death* and had said it much better than he.)

I am preparing a special number of the *Orgone Energy Bulletin,* "Towards the Healthy Child." In this context your nice little paper will find its proper place.

I shall send you Anna Freud's book for severe criticism.

Everything points in the direction of my remaining at Orgonon. The pros and cons are too entangled to be set down in a letter. The plan has shaped up to build up an Orgone Energy Hospital at Orgonon and there is great enthusiasm among the doctors of the New York area to pitch in, economically and otherwise, and to have the hospital functioning by 1952. My staying in Orgonon would be the first serious step in the direction of building up at Orgonon the University of Orgonomy. If things go wrong I might break my economic neck. But it is tempting to jump once more over a wide abyss, as I did so often before, but this time at the age of 52. Ilse is all for staying here, and Peter loves the public school at Rangeley. However, we must wait and see.

As you know, I have reserved a whole day for the discussion of the Healthy Child Problem next summer. Would you be willing to prepare a lecture of about 45 minutes or 1 hour duration for this occasion? The whole emphasis should be on the problems of health in children as they arise in an environment of armored parents and teachers.

Write again soon.

Orgonon
Rangeley, Maine

October 21, 1949

My dear Neill:

        I received the number of the *Journal of Sex Education** which contains the slander, together with your reply. I wondered why you did not say point blank that you are using an orgone accumulator for yourself and your family with some benefit.

        Would you kindly try to find out the name, profession and background of competence of this fellow who is, to all appearances, either a pervert or a delegate of the C.P.

———————◆◆◆———————

Summerhill School
Leiston, Suffolk

October 28, 1949

My dear Reich,

        You ask why I didn't mention our own use of the Accu in my reply to that interview. Simply because such a reply would cut no ice, and would be attributed to blind faith. Whereas your doctors can give definite seeable results . . . tumours lessening or disappearing. But I wouldn't have done so for myself [i.e., written a reply to the bad review], for, as you know, we differ about fighting back, and I have seldom if ever replied to a bad review of my books. I regret that you do so much of this—to me—negative fighting; it takes you away from genuine work, and the papers and journals have always the last word. I've always ignored my enemies, and I don't think they ever did me any real harm. But this will take up an evening in O[rgonon] next summer, this argument. The J.H.H.'s† are *unbedeutend* [insignificant]. Flies annoy a cow but they don't seem to hamper her milk supply.

        Sure, put me down for a talk on education next conference. I am hoping that education will come more forward than it did last summer and that the medical and scientific men will share the talks with the self-reguln. guys.

        Life goes on here as strenuously as usual. We sit in the Accu daily,

_____

* Edited by Norman Haire.
† The author whose review had so angered Reich.

but Zoë won't *mitmachen* [join in] . . . she is too energetic to sit still for long. Ena and I both feel the result of the sittings, and we find we sleep more deeply than before, maybe also due to the Accu being in our bedroom. By the way, the *Bulletin* says keep the room well ventilated, but if O[rgone] is everywhere can a draught of air drive it from a room? I have so many questions I want to ask you. About disease for one. I've never discovered in orthodox medicine any philosophy of disease. Has the disease a function? Is it an attempt at self-cure? I can see your cancer idea and feel that it is right, but why does Jones take [get] cancer while Brown takes [gets] diabetes? I am not asking you to answer all this, but I warn you that I'll bore you with questions when we meet. Meanwhile my ignorance troubles me about the Akku. It gives health but what gives unhealth?

I long to see the Observatory but with the anxious thought: "If I can't grasp orgone physics in the lab how the hell can I have a hope when Reich takes it to the stars?"

The latest *Bulletin* is grand. Your own article was understandable even by me.

Good that Pete likes his school, but don't ask my advice about staying all the year in O., for I have none to give.

P.S. Your letter to Haire [protesting the bad review] is almost certainly wrong about the man being a communist. Few doctors here are, and I am pretty certain that none of them ever heard of your work.

———— ◆•◆ ————

Orgonon
Rangeley, Maine

November 4, 1949

My dear Neill:

I have yours of Oct. 28; you are quite right saying that flies annoy a cow but do not hamper her milk supply. But any normal cow will try to get rid of the annoying fly by wagging her tail. This seems quite natural. I have never answered any pestilent attack, not even during the long-drawn-out Norwegian campaign. However, I do not intend to keep our hardworking people from protesting the action of rats.

Would you be kind enough to let us know the exact title of your lecture at the 1950 conference. The educational problem will be quite in the foreground next summer. Our medical men are keenly aware of the urgency of the educational task.

I am still at Orgonon, but shall go back to N.Y. in about 10 days. There are too many obligations in N.Y. to be attended to. During October every weekend 4–5 doctors came up for courses. Also the plans for a hospital are taking shape.

We are looking forward to seeing you, Ena and Zoë here next summer. We shall discuss whatever you like. However, mentioning Haire and similar types will be taboo. We are looking toward the future and not toward an ugly past.

You know more about Orgone physics than you are ready to admit if you could follow my latest article on orgone and ether.

I become more and more fascinated by the Christ story. Am reading every book on it that I can reach. It becomes quite clear that the world-wide interest in Christ is due to the clearcut disaster due to emotional plague; though not a single writer so far seems to have grasped the true secret of this horrible story. The murder of Christ goes on unperturbed through the millennia. To reveal the secret will mean *more* killing, and not less.

———◆•◆———

Summerhill School
Leiston, Suffolk

November 8, 1949

My dear Reich,

Yours tonight. Our names are down with the Cunard for the first Queen to sail after end of July. I'll have to do what I did last year, wait till colleges etc. reopen in October and lecture then.

Re a lecture tour. One snag is that I am not well known in U.S.A. I wonder if an ad or two in the best educational journals would bring forth offers, but I don't even know their names.

I don't know what title to give you for my talk at the Conference. Why not simply "The Pioneer School & Its Problems"? The title of course doesn't matter much.

Re the Christ story. I once read it to a group of children who had had no religion at all. Their opinion was that J.C. was a fine guy, but that Judas had had a dirty deal in some way. The interesting point was that they thought Judas was a fall guy for someone else, and one of them, without knowing that [George Bernard] Shaw had said it before, said it was odd that Judas had to betray his master with a kiss when every cop must have known who Jesus was anyway. Interesting from your angle that Judas must have represented the pest. Possibly the kids saw that the man who carries out the dirty work of the pest is generally more of a weakling than a villain. I guess your study will go much deeper than Stekel's theory that Judas was a homosexual jealous of the beloved disciple John. The difference (or one of them) between Reich and Stekel . . . S. could think only in terms of the personal (jealousy) while R. thinks in terms of life itself.

I was 66 the other day and hate the idea that time runs so short.

I am hoping to have a local conference on self-regn. at Easter. Parents and teachers but no doctors . . . not that I exclude them, only that I don't know any to ask.

Oh, have you seen the news that Poland and Czechoslovakia have stated that they will not give divorce on personal grounds; it will be left to the judges to decide if a divorce is beneficial to the State. Brave new world indeed.

P.S. Re age . . . I find my love powers diminishing too fast for my liking, but I am fairly philosophical about it.

———— ◆•◆ ————

Summerhill School
Leiston, Suffolk

November 23, 1949

My dear Reich,

But I don't want to come to U.S.A. and do nothing for three months. I don't want to take any salary or money from the Institute. And I want to reach as many students as I can without over-exerting myself with travelling long distances.

Lectured to 300 people in Watford outside London last night. Lot of young psychiatrists, doctors there, all interested in Reich. All grumbling about the difficulty in getting your books in England. One said: "Freudianism has gone barren and Reich is the new discovered land." Your influence is growing among these young fellows.

I'll send you the government report on S'hill. On the whole it is favourable and there is no chance of our being closed down.

I am much troubled with a riddle . . . A child frightens Zoë by saying cows will eat her. We tell her that is nonsense but she doesn't believe us . . . the word of the badly reared child of 5 has more weight than anything we can say. Why? In spite of her fearless life of 3 years she is prone to accept fear even though it does not stiffen her stomach. What structural feature in a baby reacts to fear? Tell me the answer, but even if I know it I can't eliminate that fear. I took her to the zoo yesterday with a girl of just 6. A lion roared. Amarilla fled in fear. Zoë who hadn't minded the roar saw the other's alarm, and she also showed fear. I wish I knew even the elements of child nature. Puzzled too when Zoë sometimes says at bedtime: "Go away, Daddy, I don't LIKE you." Maybe I am not a good father, distributing my love to 70 children, but that would apply to Ena too, even more so. Ena asked her who said that about not liking Daddy and she answered "Debby" . . . the "trained" stiff-stomach girl of 5 who makes Z. taste her shit and threatens to beat her if she doesn't. Again apparently the self regn. child accepts what the spoiled brat says even about Daddy. Makes me long for an island with only Zoë, Peter, Pussy* etc. on it, but even then I guess fears would appear. Prophylaxis has its snags I see.

I fear that Haire will have the last word to your letter, for he will revive the story of the Sex Reform League where you wanted (according to him) the Communist line, while he and others wanted the League to remain middle class. Never argue with a guy who owns a journal in which he has the last word. IGNORE 'EM ALL, man.

———— ◆•◆ ————

Forest Hills, New York

December 1, 1949

My dear Neill:

The convention will be held from August 20th to the end of August, and we want you to be there. I suggest coming to Orgonon directly, and lecturing after the convention.

The understanding of and enthusiasm for orgonomy is growing everywhere by leaps and bounds, not only in England. It sometimes seems frightening to what dimensions the responsibilities have grown. One of these responsibilities is exactly the problem which you pose regarding children who accept pestilent thoughts and attitudes so much more easily than rational ones. When I said in 1947 that the Brady attack came from

---

* Dr. Wolfe's young daughter.

communist sources, nobody wanted to believe it, in spite of the fact that I was the one who knew the communists best. When I say, out of good experience, expose and fight the emotional plague wherever you can, lest you be smothered by its evil doings, I am told not to worry about it. But if we are ever to save the life and health of new generations from the claws of the emotional plague, we must start finally to shed our fears and wrong considerations and start fighting the evil-doers. I am still advocating fiercely what I did 15 and 20 years ago in matters of sex-economy. The red fascists fought me then on this issue as they fight me now, because everybody who has some knowledge of history in natural science knows well that I was right in my predictions which came true.

I never wanted the communist line in the Sex Reform League. There was no communist line in sex reform. Always, the red fascists, the Norman Haires and the Catholic Church embraced each other when it came to fighting sex-economic insights into the necessities of a rational sex education of children and adolescents. And please, don't let the vicious Norman Haire blur your clear vision. He will not succeed, defamer that he is or tries to be, to discredit the revolutionary insights of sex-economy by stamping them communist. They never were and never will be. The only mistake I really made around the early thirties was to believe that the communists, on the basis of their proclamations, would be the ones to establish a rational sex-economy in Russia. We all know what happened there.

I am afraid, Neill, we are in a bitter, desperate fight for the rescue of childhood and young adulthood. The sex-economic movement was the first in the history of sexology and natural science which put the severe problems of natural genitality to the foreground and into the consciousness of the world; and the representatives of condoms and pervert homosexuals never could swallow or condone this great advance. That is why they spit. And the last word will be ours and not theirs.

I am trying very hard to convince one of our good medical orgone therapists to go over to England and to start a serious job there in medicine. We have requests also from the Middle West, the West Coast, South America and other regions of the globe. Things are moving very fast and well.

My best to all of you.

1950

Summerhill School
Leiston, Suffolk

January 4, 1950

My dear Reich,

Your New Year telegram of good will gave Ena and me a very warm glow. We reciprocate the wishes sincerely.

I haven't written for some time. We both had breakdowns, a sort of grippe I think, and in spite of orgones and rest we have taken a long time to get back to normal. The Nemesis of our work mostly, for we have to give out all the time, and since we left you in U.S.A. over a year ago, we have met no one to give out anything to us. Add to that the terribly exhausting fact that we are losing money every day. Some parents cannot or won't pay and if they did we could make ends meet. It is so tiresome to think in terms of money when intrinsically money doesn't mean much to us. I long for the first of August when we'll rest on the Q. Elizabeth I hope.

I'll possibly not hold that Easter Self-Regulation conference at Summerhill after all. To have an exhausted Ena finish a busy term of school and then switch over to be a hotel keeper isn't my idea of fairness, AND there is no one else who could or would take over the domestic side of the conference. This finding people who can be trusted to do work is a nightmare. As you know, S'hill attracts neurotics and you have said many times that neurotics can't work. My experience proves you are right all the way.

Today I have no worry about State interference. The only worries are money and health . . . and here Ena and I are up against a difficulty: we both hate all drugs and have no faith in them, so that we don't call

267

in a doctor because all doctors here automatically stuff you up with M & B (Sulfa) or Penicillin whatever the trouble. And as for the Accu, there is always the nasty thought: Is it effective enough in damp England as opposed to dry Maine?

Just had a letter from a woman who has a son here. She is one of Raknes's patients. Criticism in *Aftenposten* [the Oslo afternoon newspaper] was aimed at him and the Reich method. Dr. Raknes then came out with a reply in which he defended Reich. He was booked to give lectures to students but the authorities have cancelled his lectures. A bad blow for he may be forbidden ever again to speak to students and he may lose his licence. It looks as if he alone is to fight in Norway.

I have nothing much to say in this letter. I am dull and feel dull and rather kidneyish. But Zoë is bright as hell and too clever for my taste.

P.S. Just got the appeal for money for the hospital in Orgonon. I wish I could help, but while you think in thousands of dollars I have to struggle to raise the 2000$ that would pay up our adverse bank balance. My own opinion is that you should have begun with a school for self-regn. in Orgonon instead of a doctors' therapy building. The design seems very good.

———————◆◆———————

Forest Hills, New York

January 10, 1950

My dear Neill:

I just had your letter of January 4th, after having received word yesterday of your coming in August. I am looking forward very much to seeing you, Ena and the child.

I can imagine how very much exhausted you and Ena are. Therefore, the rest at Orgonon will be all the more beneficial.

You are quite right in saying that we should put up a self-regulation institution for infants instead of a hospital at Orgonon. This was my plan all along, but a hospital for research in biopathies is needed too, of course.

I escaped a great danger, Neill. In November, I nearly fell prey to the mystical expectation that I should stay in Maine, on a high mountain, gazing at the stars, as the overall genius, far removed from petty human events. Maybe I should have. But as I pondered over the problem whether to stay in Maine or to return to New York, I felt that I would not be able to produce a single orgonometric thought if I were to discontinue my work on the human structure. And I returned to New York at the end of November, and swiftly chose from a list of about 120 physicians, educators, nurses, social workers, psychologists, etc. etc. about 40 of the best-suited people, and began to establish an Orgonomic Infants' Research Center for the STUDY OF HEALTH and not of sickness. We must finally get away from pathology and start our work with the healthy child. We have already had two meetings and the first child demonstrated was Peter. I shall report on the project at the conference at Orgonon to some extent. We shall have with us several actually practising child nurses and social workers. One whole day will be devoted to this problem.

The Raknes situation in Norway is known to me. He is a very courageous and honest man. I don't think that he can really be touched. The work is too far along.

The doctors should, of course, not have asked money for Orgonon from you. It was probably a routine mailing.

Albert Einstein performed here quite an amazing somersault in publicity articles, with a formula on gravitation which nobody understands and which has no experimental basis. It sounded a bit frantic. The gravitation problem cannot be solved without careful study of the cosmic orgone energy.

***

Summerhill School
Leiston, Suffolk

February 2, 1950

My dear Reich,

I fear that this letter is to be a big grumble, but you are the only friend I have to whom I can let off steam, and you will have to be the victim.

I'm filled with worry. The school lost £860 last year because fees do not cover expenses. In three years I have used £2250 of my own to keep the ship afloat, money I got from the military as compensation for damage and that should have been spent on repairing the property. The parents simply cannot pay bigger fees, and I have had the sad task of telling the worst payers that they must leave. I think the school will have to be cut down to half the present number of pupils, and then I can do away with a few teachers and housemothers. Then the snag will be that pupils won't stay on until 17 because of lack of specialist exam teachers, and without a good few adolescents self-government is impossible. With all the worry about the school it may be that we can't come out to the conference this year.

I have thought a lot of the chances of settling in U.S.A. The advantages would be that Zoë would have a better chance of continuing to live if this new H-bomb is to be used in the next few years. It would wipe Britain out. On the other hand, how could I earn a living in U.S.A. At 66 I can't open a new school. I'm not well enough known to make a living by lecturing nor by writing. Again I begin to feel my age, not only sexually but in general; have less drive and enthusiasm in me. I should have been able to slack off at my age and have a peaceful old age, but with a baby to work for I have to go on struggling till I die.

With all this worry I find myself contributing not a single idea to the work. I dream at nights of bills for gas and coal etc. All I have in the world are houses whose rent brings me in £120 a year and my book royalties which are not many.

Oh, well, I've got all that grouse off my chest. Unfair to worry you with my miseries.

Ena and I sit in the Box every night for half an hour each. Ena says that she sleeps far more deeply and longer when she has sat in it.

———— ◆ ◆ ————

Forest Hills, New York

February 7, 1950

My dear Neill:

Yesterday I received your letter of February 2nd. I want you to feel at ease about your "big grumble." I don't mind it at all, and if I can help in any way, I shall be only too glad to do so.

I realize fully the precarious situation your school finds itself in, in present-day England. Understanding the awful misconception of socialism as practiced by socialist state governments will not help. The question is: What could be done to save your work?

The following is only an idea, not even a well-considered plan as yet. It is an idea which I nourished for a long time but did not know how to realize. During the past few years my work in bio-energetics and prevention of armoring has, naturally, more and more been centered on newborn infants. The idea of organizing and building a home for infants and small children at Orgonon, where plenty of space is available and where the population is friendly, grew by leaps and bounds. Two months ago, this idea came closer to realization with the establishment of an Orgonomic Infant Research Center. Its task is mainly to study *healthy* children and the prevention of armoring from birth onward. I chose about 40 persons, gathered them into a work group and began with demonstrating beginning biopathology in fairly healthy small children. Now the plan slowly emerged, to build a children's home with a small hospital attached to it at Orgonon, instead of the planned Orgone Energy Research Hospital which would require some $300,000 which at present are not easily available. What has all this to do with you?

You remember that I urged you to come to the U.S., in order to escape the ravaging effects of the welfare state. We believe that burdening the working population with responsibility, and not state welfare, is the future development of society. To this end, the safeguarding of the natural self-regulatory principles in newborn babies is of paramount importance. Now, of all people, you and Ena of course would be the choice to be entrusted with the directorship of such a children's home which would be devoted to the natural scientific, orderly study of the natural principles of self-regulation from birth onward.

My question now is this: *Would you and Ena be willing and feel ready to take over the directorship of a children's home at Orgonon, Maine?* We could pick the appropriate staff from among the many dozens of well-trained and restructuralized nursery school teachers, nurses and educators. These people know you and like you. We do not have to solve all the details and problems now. We can choose to go ahead when this plan will have matured into a proposition actually capable of realization, say in a year or two.

It would of course be best if you could carry out your original plan to come over this summer with Ena and Zoë, to talk over this plan, to look over the sites personally. There is nothing binding in it yet on either part. It is important to stress the point that the plan was not conceived in order to help you, but was considered independently of your situation.

Please, let me know as soon as possible how you feel about it in principle.

My love to all of you.

Summerhill School
Leiston, Suffolk

February 10, 1950

My dear Reich,

Thanks for your most cheering letter which I hope we can discuss in person in August. The idea is of course fine, and the details can be left until later. At the moment the question that occurs to me is: When our self-regulated infants are nine or ten, where do they go then? My chief difficulty would be to keep [from] shooting all the therapists who wanted to come and therapise the children. It is fascinating to dream of the possibilities of our being in charge of an Orgonon kindergarten.

Apart from financial worries I see clearly that my interest in Summerhill is less than it was when we were building it up, when every new child was an interesting "case." Now that it is obvious that every problem child is the same problem child in essentials, there is no fun in dealing with children whose reactions to freedom one knows beforehand. The more we have to raise the fees to make ends meet, the more we get the children of the dull petty bourgeoisie who have no idea of how to use freedom.

Just had a cable from Copenhagen from an ex-parent. CONFIDENTIALLY I ASK YOU POSSIBILITY OF MOVING WHOLE SUMMERHILL SCHOOL INCLUDING YOURSELF TO DENMARK AS AN INTERNATIONAL SCANDINAVIAN SCHOOL GUARANTEED ABSOLUTE FREEDOM AND ECONOMY?

I replied no. A charming offer to be sure, *aber* [but] . . .

New *Bulletin* to hand. I grasped at least something of your own article, but can never follow you and never will be able to follow you into the depths of orgone-energy-philosophy.

To go back to your Orgonon idea, I don't quite understand it. Would it mean that the Wolfes would park Pussy at O[rgonon] with a dozen other self-regulated infants? That would be wrong; up to the age of at least 5, the infants would need to be with their mothers for love and warmth. And even if they began at 5, I think mothers and fathers in N.Y. would hesitate to send their kids to a home 500 miles away. But all this will be discussed in Maine I hope.

Zoë grows big in every way. Demanding reading lessons every day and far too bright for my taste, for she never lets up, simply goes on energetically all day till she gets tired, which I suppose is the normal thing to do in life. No interest in having a sweetheart yet. I wonder if

Peter will have any interest in her this summer. Maybe too young for him.

————◆◆◆————

Forest Hills, New York

February 20, 1950

My dear Neill:

At a meeting of the Board of Trustees of the Wilhelm Reich Foundation last night, I told them about the plan of your coming to the U.S. Everyone was enthusiastic. We cannot of course discuss details now. However, a few questions would have to be answered already within the next few weeks.

In case you immigrate to the U.S., would it at all be possible for you to get some money over from your buildings if you liquidate them, and if so, how?

We plan to start building the children's home already this summer. Would you leave the arrangement of the children's home to us, or would you care to give us your ideas and sketches of how it should be arranged?

The school is planned as model and training school for the Orgonomic Infant Research Center, for nursery and kindergarten teachers, etc.

The Infant Research Center is a part of the non-profit Wilhelm Reich Foundation and the school could, therefore, not run as a private enterprise, to fulfill the requirements of tax exemption. But you would be, of course, your own master in the school as far as the self-regulation and administrative processes are concerned. I do not think that we disagree basically on these issues.

I would appreciate having your answer to these questions as soon as possible, since we are going ahead with the plans. Otherwise, we would have to wait with the building for next summer.

The Infant Research Center course turns out to be a very great success. We are pulling all pertinent and hot questions unhesitatingly into the open, grouped around two basic issues:

a) the natural laws of self-regulation in newborn babies before armoring sets in;

b) the hate of armored living beings against the natural-given living principles in the baby.

All my best to all of you.

————◆◆◆————

Summerhill School
Leiston, Suffolk

February 27, 1950

My dear Reich,

Your letter gives me a bad conscience for it came at a time when a special meeting of my parents was setting about raising a fund to save S'hill, and naturally I couldn't tell them that I might—say, next year—go to U.S.A. for good, and I say might, for there are so many factors involved that only long talks with you in August–September will make the final decision. It isn't going to be easy to decide, and in a letter I can only suggest a few pros and cons.

Pros. I am learning and doing nothing new dealing with un-self-reg. kids.

U.S.A. has more self-reg. kids than England has.

To work with and near you would be a great delight and tonic.

Cons. I'd feel bad leaving so many kids here with no one I know capable of carrying on S'hill as I'd like it carried on. And all old pupils would feel I had left them in the lurch, for they assemble here thrice yearly at end of terms.

Here I am known, a man of some importance, acknowledged to be the leading pioneer in Britain. In U.S.A. I'd begin as a nobody.

I dunno the snags I'd meet in the way of opposition from church or state.

I kick myself for giving you the impression in my last letter that I had finally decided to come over for good . . . I was overwhelmed at the time by the financial mess the school is in. On the other hand I'd hate to say: Leave us out completely, and I do think my suggestion of talks in Maine should be left to settle all problems. Note my cowardice in the matter, for I was really trying to let finance decide the future . . . "I can't make ends meet in S'hill, therefore, it must close and then I start again in America." Then the parents' meeting and plans took away from me this cowardly solution.

That is briefly my side, but it leaves you with the unsolved question: Shall we build the school this summer or wait? It will have to be built, whoever runs it, so why not start building? But here again questions arise. Is a school in Orgonon the best place? I think of the comparison between Leiston and Festiniog. In Wales we were in the mountains, isolated, away from towns, films, libraries etc. The kids didn't mind much but the staff got disgruntled at the isolation. And the parents groused because they couldn't come a ten-hours rail journey to see their brats. On the other hand I can see that you want all concentrated in Orgonon. I'd have two houses, summer in Maine, winter (seeing the babes can't ski) in a place near to New York.

Ena has strong ideas of the way the building should be planned, and is to send you them soon, and whether we eventually come or not, her experience may help you.

Re your query about being able to bring out money if we emigrated, I don't know the latest law on the subject, but up till now one could take very little per annum, and in any case it would break my Scots heart to change £100 at $2.80 to the pound.

I am reading your *Ether, God and Devil** book to the staff at staff meetings. It is really a delight to read it; possibly the clearest book of yours I have read.

Sending out invitations now for our self-regn. conference week after Easter. Last invitation brought exactly three replies.

No seminar this summer at Sheffield but Mrs. Haymes, if still there, promises a seminar at her house with all fees to me. *Nicht so staubig . . .* a phrase you possibly don't know! We say "not so dusty" in England when a thing is good, e.g. a film.

Forest Hills, New York

March 13, 1950

My dear Neill:

I have yours of February 27th. I can understand why you withdrew your first suggestion. I hope you will be at Orgonon in August so that we can talk over everything.

---

* *Ether, God and Devil* (published as Volume Two of *The Annals of the Orgone Institute*, 1949; reissued in a new translation, 1973, in conjunction with Reich's *Cosmic Superimposition*). Reich here describes the process of functional thinking, using it to illuminate the traditional view of God and Devil, and recounts how the inner logic of this thought-technique brought him to the discovery of cosmic orgone energy.

Summerhill School
Leiston, Suffolk

March 18, 1950

My dear Reich,

Ena and I are in a mesh of care. Finance gets worse each day and I am in the horrid position of being the rat that left the sinking ship. The cry is: Neill and S'hill must be kept going, but no one seems to know how. We can't get new teachers because they won't come for the miserable pay we give. All private schools here are in the same boat; taxation of parents and high prices are killing all those that are not endowed with trust funds. Part of me longs to run away to you and U.S.A.; part of me is bound by the many parents and old pupils who implore me not to give S'hill up unless it fails completely. *Ja*, Reich, I am in a hole and lie awake worrying, a thing I have never done in my life before—worrying about money and the future.

A committee of parents wanted me to allow them to ask for money in a letter to the *New Statesman & Nation*. I refused to beg. But in this week's issue is a letter begging for another "progressive" school which they call a pioneer school. The comic side is that in the winter this school asked me to come and tell the staff and parents what pioneering was, which I did, telling them that they were not real pioneers, only moralists playing with a kind of freedom.

We have looked forward gladly to a break—our visit to you this summer but even that may not come off. Marika wrote that she would not do the lectures and suggested that my publisher get a lecture agency to handle them. My fear there is that they would get me the wrong audiences and wear me out with travel and hotels (which I hate). So that the prospect there isn't so rosy either. I don't want to come alone, for Ena needs the change more than I do. Also I'd love to bring Zoë over. She is the bright star in a rather cloudy sky at this time.

We have put our Easter Self-Regn. Conference off. Only a few wanted to come, and Ena has had such a heavy term and I also am so tired that we didn't think we could do justice to it.

Sorry to write you such pessimistic letters these days.

Forest Hills, New York

March 23, 1950

My dear Neill:

I have your letter of March 18. It sounded sad again, but I know the next one will be more cheerful, and I know that you will turn up at Orgonon together with Ena and Zoë sometime in July.

May I repeat my suggestion that you do not waste time and effort with lecturing unless the occasion is an important and satisfying one.

Don't let the depression overtake you. The world has not come to an end with Attlee and Bevin or even with Stalin. On the contrary, I have the feeling that we are just beginning to see new light against the background of the ghastly ignorant liberators, but I admit that at times things look quite bleak. Please let me know how things develop with you.

Summerhill School
Leiston, Suffolk

March 27, 1950

My dear Reich,

Just got your letter by air mail. All very well, friend, to say don't lecture, but unless the Haymes seminar comes off with a good fee in dollars, I can never pay our expenses. Come we must though by hook or by crook. So much I want to talk over with you . . . especially about the devil. Your explanation of him* is new and penetrating, but I am still troubled about his dual personality, for just as God is the creator of the universe and the old man who forbids sex life, so the devil seems to me to be two guys, the one who approves of joy in life, dancing, card playing, theatres, ungloomy Sundays, and the guy who makes people cut throats or torture Jews. "The Devil has all the best Tunes," is a very old phrase, possibly dating back to a much less armored civilisation.

End of term is in a week and then we'll get some rest. I don't know how long Ena can go on being sucked dry for 8 months of the year. I feel likewise but not so much as she does, for to be a mother to about 90 people who demand all day long is most exhausting. And we never get anyone who will take on responsibility.

---

* In *Ether, God and Devil*.

In ten days I lecture to a large conference of teachers in Swansea, Wales, invited by the City Educational Director. That I get only £6 for it shows how difficult it is to make money in England these days. More and more this country gets reactionary. Much juvenile crime and the usual demand for flogging which so far the govt. refuses to allow.

Leunbachs are coming over for a week or two in June with the whole family. It will be interesting to see what they have made of self-regn. (We must call it simply S.R. in letters.)

We have put up all fees and, alas, some who have been here for years have to go because they can't pay the new rate. I think it might be a good idea for the Institute to join a press-cutting agency in England for all mention of it and your work. In U.S.A. it is expensive I found, but here I pay £2 10 a year and get almost everything that mentions my name. Useful to me, for if—say—a comparatively unknown paper in Scotland mentions me wrongly, it gives me a chance to do a little propaganda in correcting the statement. We can discuss it in August.

———◆·◆———

Forest Hills, New York

April 5, 1950

My dear Neill:

I just had your letter of March 27th. I am glad that you decided to come. I believe that you will make enough money so that you will at least have your travel expenses paid.

About the "Devil," more in Maine. The British Society of Dowsers has become very much interested in the orgone energy, since it seems to put their empirical practical profession on a scientific basis. I know that water dowsing is, in the main, a decent profession based on facts and used all over the planet by governments etc. They wrote a very good review on the orgone work.

Let me know in time when I can expect you at Orgonon. I am leaving for Maine at the end of this week.

———◆·◆———

Summerhill School
Leiston, Suffolk

April 27, 1950

My dear Reich,

Above copy of my reply to Katz* adds to my conviction that U.S.A. is no place for me. It doesn't want me.

I get more and more pessimistic about coming over this August. Earning our passages is essential, and there isn't a sign that I can earn a dollar. If there is no sign of lectures or seminars by the end of May I'll have to cancel our passage. If I try to cancel them later I may have to forfeit the passage money.

Eastmond's Biotechnic Press is bankrupt, owing a lot of money. I can't get an answer to my letters from him and therefore have resigned my directorship.

I hear that Barakan is working full time with patients. I've written him telling him he is dishonest not to pay me back my money. Snag is I am not sure of the amount now.

———◆◆———

Orgonon
Rangeley, Maine

May 10, 1950

My dear Neill:

I received your letter with the copy of your correspondence with Mr. Katz yesterday. I agree with you fully, but I disagree very sharply with your statement that the U.S.A. is no place for you, because there are such intellectuals in the U.S.A. Mr. Katz is not the U.S.A. They are psychoanalytically spellbound intellectuals who enjoy words more than depth. Briefly, they are hopeless.

I insist that you come over without having to lecture. Would you kindly let me know by return mail what the expenses for the passage are. You won't need any money here at Orgonon, but you will need a good rest together with Ena and Zoë, and we need you at the conference.

---

* Sander Katz, editor of *Complex*, an American journal of "psychoanalysis and society," had asked Neill to write an article, which he then rejected on the grounds that "it was not up to the level of our readers." To this, Neill responded bitingly, writing among other things: "To me the journal is in the past tense," and "Reich has killed psychoanalysis . . . the new era is a biopsychological one."

This matter will be settled by the end of May. I advise against lecturing by you, first because of the great heat in the U.S. during the summer months, and, second, because you should not bother about it.

———— ◆•◆ ————

Summerhill School
Leiston, Suffolk

May 16, 1950

My dear Reich,

Thanks for your most generous offer to see that our fares are paid. As they come to £300 for sea fares alone, I refuse to allow you to pay out anything, knowing well the struggle you have to get the money you need for your own work. Also, Reich, forgetting for the moment our warm friendship, I want to feel independent, and that is why a letter last week saying no lecture agent was interested, made me pessimistic and feel unwanted. However, today a letter comes from Liz Badgeley,* cheerfully saying that she thinks a seminar can be arranged in New York when I arrive, one that will bring in at least 400 dollars, and is sure she can get lectures in N.Y. State for me. I don't want to encroach in any way on Orgone Institute funds. And of course I want to preach to as many students and teachers as I can, want to feel I am doing something, working not just holidaying all the time. Anyway the three of us are coming, and we are delighted at the prospect. We have so much to discuss with you.

———— ◆•◆ ————

Orgonon
Rangeley, Maine

May 22, 1950

My dear Neill:

It is cheerful to know that you are coming and that arrangements for taking care of your fare expenses are being made. Please, let me know exactly when you arrive.

Looking forward to seeing you again.

———— ◆•◆ ————

---

* A nursery-school teacher, formerly connected with the Hamilton School.

Summerhill School
Leiston, Suffolk

May 26, 1950

My dear Reich,

Your friendly advice not to lecture in August touches me, but, alas, I shall be completely under the dollar compulsion.

Ena and Zoë will have to return in late Sept to open the school, but I don't want to stay as long as last time, for Summerhill affairs, staff and finances, are so difficult that I can't leave Ena to have all the responsibility alone. I'd like to sail in October not November. We'll have long talks about the future, a most worrying business.

I think I spoiled my Accumulator by adding layers of steel wool and asbestos wool. I ordered rock wool and the manufacturers wrote they were sending asbestos wool which was called rock wool in England. But I have a nasty feeling that asbestos wool absorbs moisture. Ena says she doesn't feel anything in the Box now. And she doesn't look well. I hope the trip will restore her a lot.

———◆◆◆———

Orgonon
Rangeley, Maine

June 5, 1950

My dear Neill:

I rejoice in your having found out that the accumulator is not just a simple box, but a scientific instrument. You are quite right, material that absorbs humidity will spoil the functioning of the accumulator.

We shall see about Ena's troubles here at Orgonon.

———◆◆◆———

Forest Hills, New York

June 29, 1950

My dear Neill:

I just had a letter from *Complex* and from Paul Goodman to you. I suggest you forget Goodman. He is one of those intellectuals who does everything only in the form of words. What he suggests in his letter, for example, the derivation of social requirements from the needs, like separate rooms for young couples, has been done repeatedly by me some 20 years ago. It was the psychoanalytic movement, which he so arduously defends, which choked those demands off wherever it could—Freud among them. He did not understand a thing, and he is fresh to boot. Such a man has no idea whatsoever what it means to build up a school practically to keep it going as you did. I would not bother about them. The forming of the "New Era" will surely not be the work of fellows of this type.

I hope to see you soon no matter what will happen in the world.

———— ◆ ◆ ————

Summerhill School
Leiston, Suffolk

July 15, 1950

My dear Reich,

I thought it best to Roneograph [mimeograph] the story, for to write it over and over again would be too much.

U.S. Consul refuses visa for A. S. Neill and Family.

On Friday July 14th at 9 a.m. we went to the London Embassy to ask for visas. For two hours we saw others being served, then we were handed back our passports and told to return at 2 p.m. We then saw the Consul. He of course knew that I had been twice in U.S.A. lecturing, and he asked if I were going again under the sponsorship of the Orgone Institute. I said yes, but also that of a group of New York teachers led by Mrs. Elizabeth Badgeley, and showed him letters from the Institute telling me about my lecture there, and from Mrs. Badgeley telling of the two seminars arranged for me in New York. I also showed a letter from my banker saying that I had funds to pay expenses. The Consul then said that we could not have visas. I asked why but was not told. He said we could apply again but that it might take up to six weeks to get an answer. I said that was impossible, for then I could not hold the seminars nor attend the Conference in Orgonon, Maine; also that we would have to cancel our passages on the Q. Elizabeth sailing first August, and could not possibly get other passages. Moreover we have to re-open our school end of September.

We are left to guess underlying motives. A political one is improbable, for I have never been a member of any political party, and in my books have strongly criticised the later developments in Russian education, which to me are reactionary. There remains the question of Dr.

Wilhelm Reich and the Orgone Institute. Is the Institute on the black list, and if so, why? My passport showed that I had been in U.S.A. lecturing, and therefore that I was not on any black list then.

Naturally our disappointment is keen, for if we had had any suspicion of a refusal we should have applied months ago. We'll have to cancel our passages at once, and this means that, even if visas were granted later, we could not possibly get berths. Something, call it pride of work perhaps, makes us dislike begging for a reconsideration of what should be right . . . the right of educationists and psychologists to meet and discuss the most vital subject in the world.

This is the story in brief. It is indeed a strange situation in which thousands of Americans visit Britain this summer, sight-seeing, while we, who have something to offer students and teachers and doctors, are excluded from the U.S.A. And under democracy, as opposed to totalitarianism, one would expect to be told explicitly why a visit to a friendly country is forbidden.

[*Neill added the following paragraph to the copy of the mimeographed letter he sent to Reich.*]

I don't know what is behind it all, Reich. If Raknes and Hoppe get visas then it can't be the Institute that is taboo. Why the long morning wait? Enquiry of course, but from whom? London Home Office dossier or maybe telephone to New York. The consul was a cold fish without any humanity at all. Ena and I both sensed we were to be rejected. He was obviously under higher orders. It may be that all Left Wing people are being now classed as Communists, by left wing meaning against the majority in education etc.

What grieves us is having to cancel our passages. Damned annoying we are so far apart and can't react without expensive cables. My own opinion is that there is nothing to be done, that the embassy would feel it was losing face if it climbed down.

I am telling all who matter in New York.

Summerhill School
Leiston, Suffolk

Sunday, July 16th, 1950

My dear Reich,

I have written to the Ambassador himself stating the facts and asking for a reason, saying that in a communist country no reason would be given and to ask one would be fatal, but since U.S.A. and Britain are friendly democracies it is a rightful demand to know reasons why. I can't do a thing until I get the reply.

We'll have to cancel our passages now or be compelled to pay the fares. Unless you have managed to get powerful influence on your side, there isn't a chance of our coming over.

I keep wondering why, why, why? Are your enemies now so strong that they can get the State to consider you a danger to national safety? I should have thought that your strong anti-communist writings of the past few years would have shown how safe you were. If I was refused because of myself, why? True, although I never was a communist I did at one time approve of much that Russia was doing and wrote about it. But in recent years, partly through your teaching, I saw where the creed had led, to hate and repression and power and loss of all personal freedom. No, I don't think I was refused because I was suspect. I don't suppose we shall ever know. One sad factor is that if ever we wanted to emigrate to U.S.A. we'd never get visas.

This has been a miserable weekend for both of us; we feel just washed out and dull and in a way frightened, for State power is always frightening. However we had one cheering letter from a rich young man who came to see us some weeks ago. He has sent a lawyer's letter saying that for seven years he will give £1000 p[er] a[nnum] to S'hill as a fund to help poor parents to pay full fees. That is very pleasing even though one has the horrible fear that long before 7 years are over, hell will be let loose and S'hill gone with the atomic wind, for it is apparent that the war has begun now and must extend until either communism wins (and the damn creed has millions behind it now) or democracy wins, or more likely until both lose.

An odd factor has come in now . . . Ena and I have lost our desire to come over. If we came we'd fail to get rid of the feeling that we were unwelcome guests. As S'hill isn't England, so Orgonon isn't U.S.A. I think of your praise of American freedom and democracy when we talked two years ago. You must have forgotten aspects of U.S.A. that are not free.

Well, Reich, I feel ten years older than I was last week, depressed about not seeing you, depressed about the future of us all, especially our wonder child Zoë. But also angry, furious that petty officialdom can step in to hinder our meeting and working together.

———— ◆•◆ ————

Orgonon
Rangeley, Maine

July 21, 23 p.m., 1950

My dear Neill:

We are still waiting for answer from Washington. Your depressed letter of July 16 arrived only yesterday; I wrote handwritten and wired right away. This is briefly the story of our endeavors:

[*Here Reich sets out in some detail the numerous steps he had undertaken on Neill's behalf. The State Department had been alerted, and the senator from Maine, Margaret Chase Smith, had promised to intervene.*]

We have the strong impression that it is a Catholic action against you. Is the American Consul a Catholic? Can you find out? This would explain it. It is also possible that he stumbled over your innocent "I am basically a communist" in your English *Problem Family*, which I had already criticized. You are *not*. However this may be, there is something wrong and personal in the London action. Could you see and talk to the consul to convince him? You will get the visum but you must do something there to get it in time to sail.

Should you miss your boat you could still sell your tickets in the last moment and get a plane to come over. It is of utmost importance that you come with Ena and Zoë, for your and our sake. The Convention will suffer from depression if you do not come. And we need you at the Infant Research Center meetings.

Do not yield to false pride or depression. Send some important English friend of yours to the American Consul.

So, Neill, do not yield. Fight it through, with no regard to costs.

———— ◆•◆ ————

Summerhill School
Leiston, Suffolk

July 21, 1950

My dear Reich,

I went to apply again yesterday and discovered what was behind it all . . . "Mr. Neill, have you ever at any time written anything in favor of Communism?" I answered: "Yes, years ago when communism was love and progress I wrote in favour of it, but on the other hand, since it hardened into hate and dictatorship I have written strongly against it." Grim silence on Consul's part. He said my second application would be considered but might take some time. I have had to cancel the passages, and if a visa does come, heaven only knows how we'll get over if at all.

All this strain and uncertainty has already spoiled the trip for me, even if it comes off. And with the cancelling of sailing my New York seminar is off and 500 dollars lost.

I'll cable you if the visa comes and a passage can be got. Thanks for all you have done. I couldn't have better friends.

———— ◆•◆ ————

Summerhill School
Leiston, Suffolk

Morning, 25 July, '50

My dear Reich,

Your long letter this morning. I also wondered if the vice consul (McIntosh, a Scottish name) were Catholic, and said so to Ena after our first interview. He was hostile from the first. He may have read a book of mine long ago for all I know. You say get someone to approach him on this side, but I know no one of any importance in political circles, and I am sure that nothing anyone could say would influence him. He simply didn't approve of me and showed it in his cold, indifferent attitude . . . a shrug of the shoulders when I said we'd miss the boat . . . "That's a matter between you and the shipping company."

At my second interview I almost came to jumping up and saying: "Keep your damned visa," and was only restrained by the thought that saying so would cut me off from you for a long time, maybe for ever.

What maddens me is the idea that I am being stopped for something that I don't believe in. There must be hundreds who liked early communism and then hated what it became, e.g. most Labour M.P.'s, but

I guess a visa wouldn't be refused to one of them. Would they refuse Shaw who still says he is a communist? Of course they wouldn't. That's why I suspect it was something personal to the consul.

If the visa comes and there is no other way we'll fly . . .

I'll cable you if I get a verdict either way.

Re the question if he is a R[oman] C[atholic], when he asked me if I were a C-ist, I said: "Politically no and never was, but in life I practised the c-ism of Jesus, sharing all with children and staff." At the mention of Jesus he gave a nasty exclamation of annoyance. I have no way of discovering if he is R.C.

Well, nothing more to say at the moment. Only I do feel so warmly about all you and yours are doing to help me. At the Embassy Ena said: "Don't give way; he is the little man, not you." I know it, but to be cross-examined by an official who obviously has no idea of your work and worth is most upsetting and degrading.

———◆•◆———

Orgonon
Rangeley, Maine

July 28, 1950

My dear Neill:

I just received your letter of July 25. Whatever the matter with the Vice-Consul McIntosh may have been, the *official* standpoint is this: Your visa was never denied, only its issuance was delayed. If you had applied 4 or 8 weeks earlier, you would not have had any trouble whatsoever. I received an answer from the American Consul General in London. The letter assured me that your visa was not denied and that the London Consulate "would have been happy" to accept your application but that you refused to apply. It seems now that your visum will surely be granted. The delay is due to the effect of the red fascist underground and underhanded maneuvers and spying. I do not believe there is the slightest reason to assume that either the American State Department or the Consulate in London had anything against you personally.

Also, our impression here is that you were hypersensitive in regard to the whole thing in London.

Well, Neill, see you soon, and until then all the best to you, Ena, and Zoë.

———◆•◆———

[1950]

Summerhill School
Leiston, Suffolk

August 1, 1950

My dear Reich,

I have heard nothing from the consul. I have done nothing because there was nothing to do. A visa has just been refused to Stephen Spender the poet who was one of the disillusioned writers of *The God That Failed,** so that it seems that however much a man is now against communism, he is suspect because of his earlier beliefs. It is alarming, for if universal war comes every C-ist in Britain will be imprisoned as dangerous, quite rightly, but people like me will probably have to share their fate because once we thought C-ism was going the right way. I can think of nothing more dreadful than to be a martyr for a cause you don't believe in. If the policy is to exclude everyone who has ever had any suspicion of being left wing, I guess that nothing I've done or said will alter things.

We have got the children off for the vacation today, and this last week has been very hard, for we had to deal with many parents and visitors while all the time we were worrying about our cancelled trip.

All this trouble has helped to make me more pessimistic than usual, but the risk of a general war looks so great that it would require a lot to make anyone an optimist. I want Zoë to live and keep thinking of what to do if and when war comes. And I want my work to live and grow, which it can't if hate and hell breaks out again.

One horrid feature of not going to U.S.A. is that the feeling of standing alone becomes greater. In Orgonon the fact of being one of a crowd of people who are life-positive is enough to inspire, but here I never meet anyone with anything to give; they all want me to give to them. The result is that I dry up, exhausted.

It seems certain that everything is left to the decision of McIntosh here. Sure, they did not *refuse* me a visa (I said to McIntosh): "Sure, you said apply again and it might take up to six weeks, but you refused me in effect, because I have to cancel my seminars and am likely to miss the Conference and in any case won't likely get a passage."

A Danish student here put it neatly . . . "Neill, this comes of patting

---

* Essays by Arthur Koestler et al., edited by Richard Crossman (New York: Harper, 1949).

the red dog when it was a puppy." But I didn't know the puppy would grow up into a wolf.

Summerhill School
Leiston, Suffolk

August 2, 1950

My dear Reich,

Yours today (dated July 28th). O.K., I guess I was too sensitive and in consequence have put you in an awkward position with the State Dept. But what would anyone have done when told that a visa might take 6 weeks to come through? Meaning that the conference might be missed, and certainly the chance to earn seminar dollars would be gone. I grant that I felt it was my right to have a visa straight away, especially when apparently there are a few thousand U.S.A. tourists here now without any visas.

I have no idea if I'll get a visa or not. So long as we can arrive for the 20th, all is well. But will I get a visa? Up to the war at least half my staff were party members, and I had to sack one man because he was preaching communism in the school. Also the fact that in my writings there was enthusiasm earlier on, and a lack of force in my later attacks, a lack due to fear on my part, cowardice encouraged by reading books like [Arthur Koestler's] *Darkness at Noon* and Kravchenko['s *I Chose Freedom*]. And I am no fighter; for children yes, for my ideas of education, yes, but for creeds and religions outside my sphere, no. I could never be a member of any party and wave a flag.

Ena and I aren't as optimistic about our getting a visa as you are. The vice consul's cold manner chilled us both. Ena says: "If it lies in his power only, we won't get 'em."

Latest *Bulletin* just arrived. I feel warmly about your friendly words on myself, warmly and proud . . . and homesick for Orgonon.

Orgonon
Rangeley, Maine

August 4, 1950

My dear Neill and Ena:

I just received your letter of August 1. Let me first of all ask you not to yield to depression because of the delay of the visum.

If you had lived in the U.S. and had enjoyed the freedom of movement for everybody, until a short while ago including the red fascists, if you had furthermore experienced the totally different character of the whole atmosphere as compared with the senile and authoritarian Europe, you would understand as I do that the American is determined not to permit any pestilent little man disguised as a vicious "liberator" of mankind to destroy America's possibilities for freedom. Many of us here find that the American Government is much too lenient with these prototypes of slander, defamation, underhandedness, and politically organized emotional plague.

I am sure you will get your visum. It was never refused according to two informations, from the Consulate and the State Department. You made your application too late. I suggest most sincerely that you come over in any case whenever the visum is issued. It will strengthen your spirits and pour hope into your hearts to be here where, in spite of all, a better future is fought for in decency. What is absolutely necessary in present times is to take a clear-cut stand against red fascism.

The State Department has given its recommendation to the Consul in London on July 31. And forget about McIntosh!

―――――――◆•◆―――――――

Orgonon
Rangeley, Maine

Saturday, August 5, 1950

My dear Neill and Ena Neill:

I just received your letter of August second. I guess your opinion in regard to the reason for the delay is correct. Not so much the fact that you had C.P. people employed but that you did not clearly and sharply write *against* them in accordance with your true conviction so often expressed in private for many years. It will greatly help to alleviate your depression if you only could readily understand the necessity of the precautions taken by the U.S.A. The C.P. gangsters are still running around free in the U.S.A. causing much trouble. While holding on desperately to the first amendment which guarantees free speech to every citizen, it is desperately hard to find an answer to these fellows who reduced the whole Marxian sociology of 100 years ago to mere spying, disturbing, undermining of everything, but everything that is not under their hideous control, no matter whether good or bad. There is just no clear answer to these murderers of freedom, the Little

Men in power for power's sake only. Neither war nor crossing out of the liberties will do. They misuse them wherever they can. We suffered in our educational institutions quite frightfully from their underhandedness. And they thrive on the sickness of the masses of Little Men— a horrifying problem for humanity to be solved.

We here believe that your visum will come soon. I believe that a visit now would be most important for you to gather strength for the coming years. Thus, I suggest to fly if necessary, no matter when, if the visum comes through.

The people here were very helpful. Senators and famous lawyers intervened. The State Department was friendly and cooperative in its procedures. You must try to understand that the screening *is* necessary and takes time. If you had only applied a few weeks earlier all would have been all right. The American Consul in London wrote to us that he would have "been happy to receive your application." It might well be that the vice consul interfered and caused the delay for religious reasons. But if we accept the C.P. slander murderers' talk even at this late hour then we cannot possibly forbid a catholically minded vice consul to object to your visum.

I believe that these considerations will help to dispel your depression somewhat. It would be depressing here too if you failed to join the convention, since it will be mostly devoted to the problem "Children of the Future" to which you have contributed so much—also indirectly against the pestilence of red fascism which has no regard and only despise for human life and happiness.

Should you miss the convention, then I would still advise you to come over, if for no other reason than to get rid of this feeling of "not being wanted in the U.S.A."

Keep in touch, Neill. We have done here what we could and I think successfully.

———◆◆———

Orgonon
Rangeley, Maine

August 10, 1950

My dear Neill:

There is still a chance that the visum will come in time for you to fly over. However, should the visum fail to come through, I want you to take it calmly and without depression. This incident has a very deep meaning. It may sound strange to you who do not know America that the U.S. Government is a highly differentiated organism, with many contradictory tendencies within. There are radicals, progressives, Catholics, reactionaries in it. It is quite possible that your case was chosen as a test case in a struggle between Catholics and progressives in the State Department. The Government is investigating your case very thoroughly so we heard. This would only be to the good in the long run. I do not believe that the Catholics in America have the power to impede the broad stream of enlightenment which has developed during the past few years in regard to an entirely different type of early infant education.

If you look at the whole thing from this angle, the situation is much less gloomy than it appears to be. We shall keep in touch and decide further steps as things happen.

------◆•◆------

Summerhill School
Leiston, Suffolk

August 11, 1950

My dear Reich,

Yours of August 5th today. No word of a visa yet.

I can't get over the feeling that if I get one it will be too late. If too late for the conference then I'd want to postpone the visit until perhaps next summer. I've gone through so much misery and depression these last weeks that I feel the trip would be only half a delight now.

Yes, yes, I of course see the U.S.A. viewpoint, but if I'd come out in writing with attacks on Communism I doubt if it would have helped. And it isn't my way to attack. I think our Public School system of segregated education appalling with its Eton and Harrow, etc. but I've never spent pages attacking that system, preferring to give the positive criticism by showing the other way. And remember that it is only comparatively recently that British Socialism broke away from communism, so that if past sympathies are the criterion of visa suspect, hardly a member of our government would be allowed to enter U.S.A.

I am so angry at being held up *for the wrong reason*. My line is children not politics and if I were shut out from U.S.A. because of my views on children and their love life and their freedom, I'd have at least the satisfaction of knowing I was being martyred for something I believed in. To be martyred for an alien creed that I know would shut my school at once if it succeeded, is too much to bear. I think that consular experts should be better oriented about who is dangerous and who isn't.

The only pleasing feature of the whole sad story is our warm feeling for you for all you have tried to do for us. Pleasing but, alas, making us sad about not seeing you.

An American woman has just told me that she thinks the visas are issued by the State Dept. but the Immigration authorities act independently. The American woman didn't have a British visa, a fact that annoys me, for we, who are much nearer the red peril, don't seem to be afraid of red agents entering the country. Like U.S.A. we also have freedom of speech but of course when the shooting starts, that will naturally be taken away as it was last war. But if I write anything more about the shooting war I'll end the letter with too much depression.

Our love to you both and to Peter who must be a big lad now.

———◆•◆———

Orgonon
Rangeley, Maine

August 15, 1950

My dear Neill:

There cannot be any doubt that you will receive the visa although it may be late. I have put the most essential child subjects to the last day of the convention, Friday, August 25, so that there is still a chance for you to speak personally that day.

I expect your manuscript any day now. It will be essential to have it here and to read it at the convention. Keep in touch with us. *The New York Times* has brought a brief note that "passport has been refused to you." We shall bring a correction—your visum was not refused. Keep your chin up. I understand your depression very well. Everything will be all right and the reason for the delay of your visum has to do with your life work problem. Love to all of you.

———◆•◆———

[1950]

Summerhill School
Leiston, Suffolk

[undated]

My dear Reich,

    This is all I can do in the time given,* for I must post it today. It is only a skeleton and without my presence the flesh can't be added to the bare bones.

    The Embassy remains silent. Maybe your last letter was right about the various elements in U.S.A. government offices. This is a fear among many here that the MacArthur policy on Formosa may bring the world war very soon. The insoluble question seems to be: How to combat communism without having to ally oneself with corrupt governments as in China and Korea, governments that the native populations won't accept. That seems to me the greatest weakness in the fight against Stalinism, and one exploited by the other side cleverly.

———————◆•◆———————

Orgonon
Rangeley, Maine

August 19, 1950

My dear Neill:

    There is still hope that you will be able to read your paper personally. It is scheduled for Friday, August 25; however, there are a few points which I would like to have corrected and on file:

    1. It is utterly incomprehensible to me how it is possible that you still believe that it is "the working class which took over half the world." Why can't you see, Neill, (it is high time), that it's a bunch of political crooks who took over the working class of half the world? What in heaven's name has Stalinism to do with the working class?

    2. You know me well enough to permit me to say and be understood plainly when I say that as the situation in the world is today, with the given emotional plague all around us, any king, any conservative, any Christian Catholic is much preferable and less dangerous to mankind than these abominable and despicable lot of gangsters who have ruined not only a great system of thought but have surpassed in cruelty,

---

* Neill had enclosed the manuscript of the paper he was to have given at the conference in Orgonon.

cunning underhandedness, political gangsterism, murderous hate of all decent and straight living, anything that has ever plagued the human race.

In the discussion of your paper at the Convention I shall criticise your statement that the working class have taken over half of the world. Unless you prefer to have it either left out or changed. I am bound to do so not only because it is confusing to our workers if a man of your standing and influence says that it is the working class which took over, which is obviously not true, but also because we are the ones who want work to take over against the Stalinite band of bums and louts. Please let me know by wire whether I can take out this sentence. I hope to have you here by the end of next week.

* * *

Summerhill School
Leiston, Suffolk

Sunday, August 20, 1950

My dear Reich,

At last I have given up hope. The embassy remains silent, and in two days every plane seat is booked.

Give me your opinion of my publishing the story here, not in a nasty way, but simply making the point that a well known educationist has been prevented from taking part in a vital conference on children. *Mein Gott*, Reich, the publication here the other day of a book by one of the Scottsboro Negroes* will do more harm to U.S.A. than any visitor could do.

I feel so lonely, so isolated with all my best friends and supporters in U.S.A. And the affair has made me timid, as you will see from my short lecture for the conference, where I was afraid to say much of moment about sex relationships etc., afraid lest letters should be opened. Irrational no doubt, but a rebuff like the one I have had awakens all sorts of fears and suspicions. In short, it arouses the little man in me.

I picture you all meeting today in Orgonon. A memory comes to me of when I was 12 and my mother wouldn't allow me to go to a picnic, and I spent the day wandering in misery and wondering what the picnickers were doing.

---

* *Scottsboro Boy*, by Haywood Patterson (Garden City, New York: Doubleday, 1950).

I feel I may have dwelt too much on the war danger. My excuse is that while your children over there will have a good chance of survival, ours will not. We are near the danger, and everyone we know here has a similar feeling to the one we have, a terror of what may happen to the young in atomic warfare. It may not come, but something must come, and it is not pleasant to think that half a dozen men in the world can decide whether our children will live or die.

What of the future? If I am to be banned from U.S.A. I am banned from you. Letters are not enough. The idea crossed my mind that we might meet in Canada, but of course that would be impossible, for we can only meet in your lab and house and with your co-workers around. We were to discuss, *inter alia*, the chances of our coming to work in U.S.A., but if a visitor's visa creates so much fuss, what chance would we have of immigrants' visas?

I spent the days painting wooden buildings, and find that occupation as soothing as any other could be at a time like this.

Do tell me what your attitude is to my putting a letter in the *New Statesman* about my visa.

Our love to you, and give my best greetings to all my friends in the Conference.

———◆◆———

Summerhill School
Leiston, Suffolk

Thursday, August 24, 1950

My dear Reich,

I have wired you today saying that there is no news from the Embassy. I gave up hope a few days ago.

I feel a bit hurt at your attack on my working class phrase. Granted that they are led by gangsters who use working class power to get power and then become dictators. The point I implied, but didn't make is that the workers will accept the hate gang way but not the Summerhill love way. This is clearly seen in, say, Czechoslovakia where the children of the middle class are refused places in universities etc. It is seen outside communism in our British socialism, where the working class as represented by the Labour Leaders want schools that are the opposite of S'hill, and gradually will make private enterprise in schooling impossible. I have wired you to cut the phrase simply because I can't be there to explain what I mean by it.

The situation here is that the communist teachers and parents (I mean in Britain) demand for the working class what they consider the privileges of the upper classes, meaning that they accept Eton and the Grammar School standard, as they are doing in Hungary, Poland, etc. In a communist Britain Zoë would be kept down while children of manual workers would get a higher education, and, gangster led or not, the workers with their big numbers would take the hate way, and swamp the other classes.

This is all outside my province I admit. I only give facts, and these are that at least half the domestics we've had, some of them for ten years, are cynical or even hostile when they leave.

You keep writing that I shouldn't get depressed. I don't feel so much depressed as dead, numb, frustrated, puzzled, afraid. I can't be positive and do what I long to do . . . publish the story as a warning that that isn't the way to fight communism. I can't do it and thus assure my being blacklisted for ever from U.S.A. But things seem to move so fast to a world war that no one will be interested in whether an individual gets a visa or not. Our daily papers get more disturbing every day.

Depressed? My dear Reich, I can't see the silver lining of the clouds, and I don't mean war clouds; I mean the working together in the interest of babies, the personal contact that inspires. If a visa is refused then you and I are parted for a long long time.

Back to my phrase! I say the workers of this generation GIVE power if they don't HAVE power: I think that Stalin and Co. could not exist a day if they did not know the working class are still thinking of the class war, jealous of the middle and upper classes, but wanting to copy them at the same time. In short, the previously exploited millions are easy to exploit in their turn, changing their masters only. But this is an argument for a long evening over a bottle.

To think of practical things, what do I do IF a visa is granted? I might come alone if only for a few weeks. I do so much want to hear what happened at the conference.

And don't let us quarrel about phrases, my friend.

———◆•◆———

Summerhill School
Leiston, Suffolk

September 5, 1950

My dear Reich,

We are just setting off for Amsterdam for a change. We'll spend a couple of weeks on the sand near Haarlem, a poor *Ersatz* [substitute] for Dodge Pond* indeed, but . . .

The sad feature of the whole miserable history is that now when I think of America, I don't think first of all of you and the people round you, I think of the reactionary U.S.A., the narrow tough officials with their lack of vision and their fear, those who think they can fight communism with bombs instead of by showing the world a better plan of living. My exclusion from U.S.A. isn't exactly an advertisement for a democracy that fights the lack of freedom in communism.

From now on I won't write to you about visas or communism or fascism of any colour.

When we return from Holland I guess we'll just have to start a new term without having had any mental refreshment. I have taken on a few lectures to teachers this autumn and these will help me to get away from the rather narrow life in the school, narrow because there is no one to talk to on a higher level than gossip and cinema.

———◆•◆———

Orgonon
Rangeley, Maine

September 7, 1950

My dear Neill:

It is only today after the cessation of the great turmoil at Orgonon that I find time and leisure to answer your letter of August 24th. We shall be staying here all winter and eight workers of the Institute are settling down in Rangeley.

There is no doubt that you will obtain the visum. We have corrected the note in the *New York Times Magazine* to the effect that your visum has been refused. I had to send them the letter I had received from the Consul General in London which said clearly that he would have been glad to receive your application.

---

* The small lake in Maine which Orgonon overlooks.

It is not my fault or responsibility that your visum has become a matter of public magnitude and importance. I fully agree with the American government that it is necessary to screen every single person very carefully. We simply do not want Stalinists around here. We are still breathing the air of freedom which grants citizens the right to bear arms by constitutional stipulation. And our fight against any type of dictatorship and totalitarianism is seriously meant and goes to the bottom of our existence. We here still maintain that government is an administration and responsible to the people, and this we live practically.

America is not a capitalist land. These old terms do not fit any longer, and it is quite obvious that it is socialism and not capitalism in America which provided the homestead for authoritarianism and dictatorial social procedures.

May I say, Neill, that it is of the utmost importance for your lifework as well as for the yet unborn babies of the future that you revise your basic attitude in this struggle for freedom in our times.

Once your visum question is settled, we shall be the ones here to publish an account and a criticism of the whole procedure. Don't worry about that; and our influence here is now quite great.

The Convention was a very great success, so was the cancer course. The work is rolling full speed ahead. There was a lively discussion after your paper was read. Nearly all the papers and major discussions will be published in the *Bulletin*.

Please keep in touch with me. Everything will be all right. Let me know how you are.

———◆•◆———

Summerhill School
Leiston, Suffolk

September 15, 1950

My dear Reich,

You tell me that I must revise my basic attitude in the struggle for freedom in our times. I simply don't know what you mean by this. Of late you have appeared to me to be pretty close to the Americans who are witch hunting, and at least in part, on the side of the consul who so far hasn't had the good manners to tell me if I've got a visa or not. You have written as if I were rightly suspected, instead of seeing that Mr. McIntosh was a fool and a hater. In fact you sound as if you think communism can be halted by keeping reds out of U.S.A. or by fighting them with bombs: you sound as if you believed that the anti-communists of the MacArthur type have the same basis as you have. They don't, of course, and that is the tragedy of the whole fight, that people like you are forced to be allies of all the reactionaries who are putting the whole native peoples of Asia and Africa straight into the hands of Stalin. You are fighting to keep freedom, but you have to be on the side of the guys who want to keep oil wells and rubber and what not. It isn't a clean-cut war.

What do you want me to do? To start slanging communism in newspapers? Don't you realise that the Soviet School Laws given at the end of *I want to be like Stalin* are laws that 99% of the parents of Britain would approve of as against the S'hill way? You have preached for years that a patriarchal society has so castrated humanity that it must seek hate and death, and now you seem to have turned completely round and expect this society to fight the hate and death in Stalinism. And, really, Reich, when you talk about the socialism of U.S.A. being the basis of authoritarianism, what do you mean by the word socialism? Every country has socialism if the word means public ownership of roads, post offices, etc. A matter of degree. Here we have more than U.S.A. has, yet here I can refuse to have Zoë vaccinated while you have to vaccinate Peter when he goes to school. If Hamilton visited England no one would ask if he were communist or fascist, and communism is much nearer England than America geographically, and just as much feared.

What a pity we can't talk all this out.

We have just returned from nine days in Holland. I saw the celebrated "free" school of Kees Boeke where the Dutch princesses attend and do exactly as the others do. It is far from freedom; ordered freedom describes it.

Fellow called P. writes from N.Y. saying some of the subscribers to my seminar want to give me the fees as a gift to S'hill. Very kind of them.

I look forward to reading about the conference. Mrs. Haymes writes saying the members came back full of enthusiasm about it. Undiplomatic of her to tell the frustrated me that.

Our love to you all . . . and, friend Reich, do stop lecturing me on my basic principles. Damn you, man, they are in my work not in what I say.

P.S. The photo of the Observatory is intriguing. I take it that it will finally have a dome for the telescope. Do you live in it? And if your 8 workers are to be there all winter how are they to earn any money to

live on? Without your New York practice how are you to make a living?
And are you selling 99–06?*

——————◆•◆——————

Orgonon
Rangeley, Maine

September 20, 1950

My dear Neill:

I have your letter of September 15th. I suggest that we discontinue our discussion on political matters. It leads nowhere. Instead,
I propose that we stick to our work-democratic line which, applied to
this special case, would mean the following:

We are standing outside politics, working at the problem of the
children of the future, and we do not drag in any political questions.
There would be only one request and that is to acknowledge the existence of this or that killer of freedom, development of thought, self-
regulation in childhood, genitality, functional thinking, etc.; whether it
be an American, Russian, Hottentot or some other kind of killer. Please
let me know whether you can proceed on this basis. I never believed that
political discussions could help along in actual work.

In regard to Orgonon, it is interesting that after the cancer course
and the convention, 8 workers in our field have decided to stay up here
in the Rangeley region to help build up the university. During the
winter, Ilse and Peter live with me in the Observatory. Among the 8
workers there are six who are paid by the research fund, and can live
on their income. I have given up my New York practice completely. I
had finally to break away from the old ways and devote myself entirely
to orgonomy, physical and astrophysical research. This meant a sacrifice
of a yearly income of around $40,000. So I did not go capitalist and
reactionary completely yet, Neill. I am not earning any money at
present. Neither did I sell the Forest Hills house. I put it at the disposal
of some of our physicians who have established clinics for treatment
and diagnosis in the various rooms. I do not derive any income from
Forest Hills.

Another question: Would you object if I use some of the material
which came up in the course of the disagreement between us in political

---

* Reich's house in Forest Hills, at 99–06 69th Ave.

matters in the book I am writing now on *Children of the Future,** as a
master example of what politics and political discussions can do harm-
fully to life-important work? Let me know how you feel about it.

Keep writing, Neill, and try, if you can, to see that the old distinctions between a capitalist class and a working class, etc., have in the
old economic sense completely disappeared, and that entirely new social
conflicts have appeared on the horizon. We shall have ample occasion
to discuss these things next year when you are here; but solely from the
standpoint of the newborn infant and not any more whether Truman or
Stalin, or whether Marshall or some Russian general are right or wrong.

———— ◆•◆ ————

Orgonon
Rangeley, Maine

September 22, 1950

My dear Neill:
Dr. Baker† called last night telling me among other things that
according to a personal message he received from a Senator, the U.S.
State Department has, after thorough investigation, consented that your
visum be granted. You will soon hear from the London Consul.

Thus it is quite clear that no visum has ever been refused but only
delayed. May I suggest that to comply with the truth you send out
another letter to all people who received your first message on the visum
telling them that the visum was not refused but only delayed.

———— ◆•◆ ————

Summerhill School
Leiston, Suffolk

September 23, 1950

My dear Reich,
Good. Fine. I agree with you. We'll cut all political argument.
But I must say that we have proved that politics are corrupting, for
they made us quarrel over what really wasn't *bedeutend* [important] to
either of us; they side-tracked us in a dead end. I suppose the real

---

* This manuscript was never completed.
† Elsworth F. Baker, psychiatrist and student of Reich's.

reason is that politics belong essentially to the little men, the haters, the power merchants. Damn the lot. *Fertig* [Finished].

Yes, use the material as you like.

A most pleasant surprise to know you are on a book on children. The demand for your books grows apace, alas, mainly among poor students who can't afford to buy them and implore me to tell them where they can be read in public libraries.

I think that your vital decision to stay in Maine will have a big influence on you personally. I take it that Peter will go daily to Rangeley school.

September 27

Your letter with its news from Baker and his senator came and I waited to hear from McIntosh before writing you. His reply came today . . .

"I regret to have to inform you that it is now determined that you are inadmissible under the Immigration Laws and regulations, and a visa may not, therefore, be issued to you." Signature Clarence J. McIntosh, Vice Consul. *Mein Gott*, there must be no connection between the London office and the State Dept if Baker can get such optimistic news from a senator.

P.S. I'd like to publish the story because it may be McIntosh was in touch with our own Home Office, and if I am on their undesirable list there, I'll be interned if a war comes. I want publicly to declare my position.

------◆◆◆------

Orgonon
Rangeley, Maine

October 3, 1950

My dear Neill:

I must leave the decision as to whether to publish the story of the refusal of the visum or not to you, since I am not too thoroughly aware of your situation in England. I myself shall write up on this story among others, using it as an example, in *Children of the Future*. To my mind, this was a Catholic action and has nothing to do with the constitution of the U.S.A. I suggest that you correct your first statement of two months ago that your visum was refused then, if you want to get the point through according to facts.

More next time.

———◆•◆———

Summerhill School
Leiston, Suffolk

October 14, 1950

My dear Reich,

Today's news of the U.S.A. ban on travel visas makes me very downhearted, for it can mean that you and I cannot meet again. Either world war will make it impossible, or years of American fear of communism will make U.S.A. a forbidden land for even the most mildly liberal of guests. So that our contact will have to be the very unsatisfactory one of letter writing, and if the scare continues, letters also may become censored.

I had a visit the other day of James Telfer, a Scots osteopath. He and another enthusiast friend of his are much alarmed that some commercial firm will begin to sell accus here, and they want to know if it is protected by patent in Britain, and if not, can they do something about it? I think they are right there. Interestingly enough, the osteopaths in general are more interested in the work than the *echt* [genuine] physicians. It is the tension part that attracts them of course. The two men have carried out several of the experiments from your books and are delighted with the results. When Lucy [Francis] had a new lump on her face under the operation scar, she applied the small accu and it went in a fortnight. When she told the surgeon about what she had used he sniffed and said: "Oh, it won't do you any harm anyway."

I don't know how you will view an unqualified man experimenting, but if the medical profession won't take it up, someone has to do it.

You will recall the many talks we had in Oslo and N.Y. about being on the side of the adolescents in their love life. I don't think it is wise unless they have had freedom from a young age. For instance: couple came late to S'hill. I approved of their love. In the vacation they get together and she becomes *schwanger* [pregnant] . . . and turns on me as responsible. First case of two pupils in 30 years. I am going back to the old way, simply refusing to back up untrustworthy adolescents, and so risking my life's work through scandal and hate and fear. No, one can only "be on the side of" children who have had freedom from the

[1950]

beginning. The others simply *ausnutzen* [exploit] one. And at my age I
can't stand the strain of taking responsibility for those who don't think
it worth defending. Yes, this age question is a real one now . . . 67
next week.

My potency has gone. And my work is mainly repetitive now. I fancy
my high day is over, Reich. The stimulation I had looked forward to at
Orgonon and its loss has affected me more deeply than I yet realise.
More than ever I feel ALONE. I haven't your optimism about humanity,
and today when I read that the people of East Berlin have been warned
that if they don't vote in the elections a cross will be put against their
names as U.S.A. military sympathisers, I wonder how many poor devils
will have the courage to not vote and face a concentration camp.
Perhaps if I sit down to write a new book I'll feel better, but again I
feel that I have nothing new to say.

Well, I end this not very cheerful letter.

P.S. I wish I knew if it is safe to use the small box and funnel on my
nose and throat. It seems to be a chronic catarrh, which so far sitting in
the accu doesn't touch.

Orgonon
Rangeley, Maine

October 19, 1950

My dear Neill:

I have yours of October 14th. I hope you realize now that the
difficulties in entering the U.S. are not concerning you personally at all,
but are entailed in the rational and justified fear of the innumerable spies
that used to enter the U.S. from everywhere without any control. I had
fear of communism already in Europe for the same reasons that the fear
besets you in regard to your school, and besets every single free man
over here. I am sure it will pass over soon and that I shall see you sometime during 1951.

We cannot possibly keep a monopoly on the orgone energy. It belongs
to everyone. It is not true that the medical profession rejects us. We
have numerous friends among American and European physicians and
medical men, also those who use the accumulator in their medical
offices.

I agree with you fully that it is not possible to take responsibility for adolescents' love life unless these adolescents grew up our way.

Your catarrh will only yield if you use the accumulator regularly and faithfully daily over months and years.

I received the English publication of my *Character Analysis* which looks very good and I hear it is selling very well.

Keep in touch and write frequently.

———◆•◆———

Summerhill School
Leiston, Suffolk

November 5, 1950

My dear Reich,

Firstly my warmest thanks to you both for your birthday telegram. Your letter [unavailable] repeats our previous controversy when you say: "I deeply regret that neither you nor the Hamiltons . . . are entirely aware of what red fascism means." But we said we wouldn't argue about politics, and all I say here is that I think you attach the words red fascism to people who are plagues if you like but not communist sympathisers, e.g. Haire who is attacked by all the reds in London as a reactionary.

What troubles me more than fascism of any colour is the fact that some big curtain has fallen between you and me, a curtain that only long talks could raise, and these are not even on the horizon (for my ban will be permanent I fear), I look on the future relations with anxiety. Not the personal ones but the ones connected with our ideas and priorities and above all, work.

———◆•◆———

Orgonon
Rangeley, Maine

November 11, 1950

My dear Neill:

I have your letter of November 5th.

I have the firm impression that the arguments between us of the past 2 or 3 months have done a lot of good to me and to you. To me in learning that there is a way out of politicking, i.e., through sticking to positive work problems. To you in that I believe your formerly some-what confused attitude toward Russian imperialism and fascism has clarified to a great extent. Basically, I don't think there is any disagree-ment between us. I only feel that I am a decisive stretch farther removed from my socialist past than you are. I would not call it a curtain that has fallen between us, but only a thin veil which a breeze of a clean talk will easily remove again. I am also sure that sooner or later the con-fusion brought about by the international conspiracy will clear up and that you will surely get your visum to reach Orgonon.

I did not shift from being a seeker of truth to being an authoritarian general. It is true, however, that I learned to pursue the truth with much greater determination, vigor and decision to fight the obstacles in the way, than I ever have before.

Summerhill School
Leiston, Suffolk

November 16, 1950

My dear Reich,

Thanks for letter received 3 days after posting. I also had Sharaf's Report [of a Symposium held at Orgonon in the latter part of October]. It has raised thoughts like these: If all your doctors have something that is a danger to a new-born babe, what chance has any infant with doctors and others who never heard of O. Therapy? Ilse and Ena must be character-structured in some ways and a danger to infants, yet they have both raised a more or less self-regulated child. I, with all the neck stiffness and the Calvinist background you know of, although I haven't had infants to deal with, have allowed a few hundred children to grow freely when compared with other children. Maybe I am prejudiced by the thought that if an Ena, who never had any therapy, can do so good a job with Zoë, why is it that you have to tell your own trainees that some of them aren't fit to deal with the young? True, they are your disciples, and most disciples remain so . . . and as such are in-ferior and possibly not teachable. The teachable ones don't remain as disciples; you left Freud when you felt you had to go on alone; I left Homer Lane and the Freudians and Stekelians. I make the guess that you often feel you want to shake the lot of them and make them big men.

Re the doctor who confessed he grudges paying money: let me be his advocate for the defense for the moment . . . "Gentlemen of the jury, my client Dr. X is not actuated by malignancy or greed; his main fault is ignorance. Look at his position. A disciple of a great man whom he can't possibly understand. I happened to watch his face when Bill Washington was demonstrating the motor; it was that of a wondering baby who didn't understand a word that was said. He doesn't believe in Orgones; he merely believes that the great man has got something else he can't understand. And because his position of ignorance makes him feel so small a worm his personal devil whispers to him: 'Why the hell should you support financially a thing that is far beyond your grasp?' And maybe your great man Reich isn't so great after all; maybe he is getting a rake-off from the money collected. That thought would at least bring R. down to my low level." Frankly, Reich, in 1948 I had the impression that hardly one of the assembled workers had the faintest idea of what you were talking about . . . myself included. Are you asking too much from them? Loyalty, yes, you can demand, but invention, originality, inner freedom? No.

Maybe I am too old to grasp it all, but it seems to me that you have around you a crowd who are waiting for you to tell 'em what to do. Reich, you are one of the great men of our time; I say it as a simple fact without any meaning of flattery or worship. Your message to the world is a tremendous one that will only be realised later, i.e. if we remain a free world. One result is that you are like the captain of a ship, lonely apart, protected by an unwritten code . . . you are Doctor Reich not Reich. Jesus did not have a Jesus among the twelve, unless Judas was a rival one at bottom. You have no Jesuses among your more than twelve disciples, and, it seems to me, you are grousing at the fact that there aren't any.

Gott sei Dank [Thank God] here is a letter that doesn't mention politics!

Oh, can you give me any news about Bill Washington and the motor? Was he disloyal? Why did that motor rotate in summer 1948 and since then I haven't heard a word about motor energy?

Did I tell you that I got 325 dollars from 20 people who had subscribed to the seminar and refused to take their money back? A most touching gift.

P.S. A most arresting idea that of yours, that humanity rejects the Christ, Lenin and seeks the hateful lesser Paul and Stalin. In a minor way Adler, by cutting out sex, got many followers who otherwise might have gone to Freud, but Adler isn't big enough to be Freud's St Paul, nor hateful enough.

Just had a fine example of smear. I told you how brilliantly our boys had done in their exam. Some local beasts rumour that I opened the exam papers the night before and worked out the answers with them. Makes you despair of humanity, yet one consolation is that one evil person isn't Leiston.

———————◆•◆———————

Orgonon
Rangeley, Maine

November 23, 1950

My dear Neill:
    You are right, I am in the deep sense of knowledge quite alone with only a very few people, scattered across the world, who really know what I am doing. I am continuously hard at it to clarify and to bridge the gap that exists between me and my closer co-workers. I am deeply entangled in basic problems of natural science and natural philosophy, in orgonometry and, especially, in infant research. The first child of 3 years with a diagnosed infantile paralysis was brought to me a few days ago from New York. A thorough examination convinced me that infantile paralysis, as I always thought it to be, was a result of emotional mistreatment in early infanthood, with as the consequence retrograde damage to the nerves in the spinal cord. This will have to be corroborated. I always feel awe when I see these two things together: the tremendous nuisance torture of infants on the part of parents, educators and physicians, and the utter ignorance of what is going on.

I am fully prepared not to let happen to me what happened to Freud and people in similar position. The attempt to escape the braking effect of the social pressure against the core of my work presses me forward more than I like and widens the gap between me and my immediate fellow-workers. This is very distressing.

We just had a meeting of the Board of Trustees of the Foundation in which we all agreed that what is needed is an organisation like that of a medical clinic with the responsible head and a few well-skilled and devoted assistants. This has nothing to do with dictatorship. It is work-democratic necessity.

I am still at my book *Children of the Future*, the writing of which is thrilling.

How are Ena and Zoë?

◆◆◆

Summerhill School
Leiston, Suffolk

December 14, 1950

My dear Reich,

I haven't written you lately simply because I had nothing special to say. And I haven't anything much to say now. I've lost heart, Reich. I don't see the tomorrow. I fear that I'll never get to U.S.A. again, whether because of war or the *Verbot* [prohibition] by visas. I suppose age has much to do with it. I think that when the O. Reflex dies much creative ability must die with it. I find myself wanting to do unimportant things like making wine of fruit juices, tinkering with radio, playing golf, avoiding if I can all conversation. And there maybe is the trouble. For two years I had looked forward to great talks with you in Maine, and when that anticipation was shattered, I had no one to talk to, no one who could give me anything new. And the fear of never being allowed to see you again keeps depressing me. Then there is the horrible thought: "If Communism wins all over, my work is all in vain. My books will be burnt and S'hill methods will be abolished."

Possibly it is better not to write you at all rather than give you so depressing a letter.

The joyful side of life is Zoë, who has at last reached the Daddy stage and makes me play with her for hours. I'd rather she played with other children, but only one or two had self-regulation and she finds the others unwelcome. They are so prone to frighten her with stories of wild animals and bloody deaths. Death of mice and rats etc. doesn't seem to affect her; she accepts the fact that they are dead, but in phantasy stories she asks me to kill some animal or person and then bring them alive again.

Going back to this business of inability to work, apart from any neurotic element in it, it seems to me that a prospect of peace is essential to work. Especially work with children where the tomorrow matters so much. My reason says: Go on working and damn the future, but my fear says: Go on working for what? I haven't your faith that Communism will lose; it has so many millions now that I fear it may not lose.

And, I've said it to you before, war would not stop your work in Maine, but it would stop mine in East England.

I wish I could see a silver cloud in the black sky of today.

I sent the *New Statesman* a letter about the visa situation, but the editor says that even anyone who took an active part in helping the Left in the Spanish Civil War is unlikely to get a visa. I didn't do anything other than having a few Spanish children here free of charge. The nasty parallel to that would seem to be that if I'd fought for Franco I'd have been acceptable to U.S.A.

Our love to you all, and our hopes that Peter will have a happy Christmas in the snow.

Orgonon
Rangeley, Maine

December 22, 1950

My dear Neill:

I know exactly how you feel, Neill. Things look dark, indeed, discouraging also for all of us here. It is too much to be discussed in a letter. Keep on writing. Never mind whether it is cheering or saddening news. It always helps.

May I tell you frankly what I think about the basic reason for your depression? It is not your "aging"; you are younger than many an adolescent. Neither is it that you cannot reach U.S.A. for the moment; you know that things will change again, once the answer to the sneaking of plaguey scoundrels has been found. It is something else entirely:

You have spent your life so far getting along with people well, spending your time, effort and soul to help children. Then, after thirty years of effort, you find that they still ask the same questions as in the early twenties, that they still talk and act as they have acted 300, even 3000 years ago, in spite of all socialism, all revolutions and evolutions. You find that nothing whatsoever comes out of them, paying back in part for what they have swallowed through the years. Nothing but nothingness, emptiness, babbling, gossiping, sniping, cheating, politicking and the rest. Somehow you found yourself facing NOTHINGNESS in the human animal. And you feel that making wine is more rewarding. Let me tell you that this realisation brings you closer to the truth than all the books you have ever read, all the speeches you have ever heard or given. What stares you in the face is the perfect human desert, the ultimate result of thousands of years of devastating upbringing of new generations. The more millions follow the little great man, the worse it gets. This is an unsurpassable lesson. It is also the great beginning of an entirely new age. It has to precede the new ages that are coming. Things have to go down before a new education will win out. And it is winning out, slowly, painfully, regardless of our lives or our happiness. It is on its way, doubtless and firm. The realisation of a whole emotionally dead humanity will never again vanish from the hearts of men. And since life cannot be extinguished, since it always goes on, a new kind of life is coming. I am very hopeful. The future does away with the past. Nothing remains of old ways. No socialism, no communism, no liberalism, nothing, just change, that is all. And every newborn child brings it with it. What you are going through is the breakdown of all old illusions about man, the little man who began to take over. I followed this process with awe for many years, trying to hold on to some illusions; in vain. We are facing point blank the greatest revolution in human existence.

I do not believe that the dictators can win out. There is still too much thinking and searching in the world. There is too much longing, and there are some hard facts about infants and life. Did you ever see a seedling germinate and push through big, hard pebbles of stone and earth? This is what I mean. Look at Zoë as I look at Peter and see the new life. I see Peter already succumb here and there to the plague, but the new life is there unmistakably. And this is what I am working for. It should keep you cheerful and hopeful. Your life's work is a part of this new life, since you have helped in shaping it, in bringing it forth, in delivering it. Why don't you describe Zoë, Neill, in detail, every move, every battle she fights with the old, spoiled life? Why don't you use your gifts as a writer to convey what it is like to grow up without armour and to have to fight hard to keep free of it? Lately Peter hates me, hits me with glee, because I keep him going MY way and the world pulls him THEIR way. Does not matter, he loves me and not them. He comes to ME and not to them to get help and advice. We are the witnesses of the first true blossoming of life among men, Neill. No plaguey dictator can take this away . . .

Forget the present and think in terms of 1000 years hence. It is very hard but possible.

We are preparing for Christmas, looking forward to it.

My love to all of you. A good New Year . . .

1951

Summerhill School
Leiston, Suffolk

January 7, 1951

Dear Reich,

Your cheering letter arrived when I was in bed with a flu epidemic that has caught us all. Your diagnosis is absolutely correct so far as outer things are concerned. At present all sorts of educational bodies meet to discuss things, but not one asks me to lecture at the meetings; they get prominent teachers who say only the dead things about life and education.

I shall not try this spring to get a U.S. visa, for there is no hope at all. Sad, but there it is. I am realistic enough to know when I am beaten.

I have decided to write another book, mainly about Zoë, but not giving her name; it is embarrassing for adolescents to find that as infants they were "cases." Your own daughter said at my Hamilton Seminar: "I'm tired of being called the Result of the Function of the Orgasm," said it with humour, but enough suggestion of truth to make me hesitate to use Zoë's name. Apart from embarrassment, if we say too much about Zoë and Peter and their like, the poor things will feel it difficult to live up to what we say of them.

I wish I knew more about the contest between the world and you for Peter's soul. Here our trouble is the world of un-self-regulated children who infect Z. with their fears and hates and sadisms, but so far, not making her sex conscious in a wrong way. She still doesn't want much of me; I am only the man who can tell her stories of animals. Her identification of self with animals persists all the time; she wears out all her stocking knees and shoe points crawling on the floor as a zebra or a

313

horse or a Bambi. One thing I have learned, that the Freudians are wrong when they say that fantasy is a flight from reality, for Z. is at home in both. Still her identification with animals may be a flight from the wrongly reared human animals around her. No, for now during vacation she plays animals more than ever, so that I have to scrabble about the floor as a "friendly lion what doesn't eat people" twice daily. Again, *pax* old Freud, she has never shown any desire to be a boy, and in play all her animals must be female. I do wish we could meet to compare notes on our brats.

———— ◆•◆ ————

Summerhill School
Leiston, Suffolk

January 22, 1951

My dear Reich,

In the absence of a skilled therapist, orgone therapy in Britain will be poor; worse still, get into the hands of cranks and neurotics. But I see that a doctor coming over would have to make a sacrifice of a good dollar income for a relatively poor pound one. And of course he might be prevented from practising by the orthodox B.M.A. [British Medical Association]. Do keep me informed about the latest news of the lab.

———— ◆•◆ ————

Orgonon
Rangeley, Maine

February 8, 1951

My dear Neill:

I wonder whether I answered your letter of January 7th. I also have your letter of January 22nd. We know that a skilled medical orgonomist should as soon as possible be sent to England. The pound-dollar relationship would be a minor issue. The true difficulty is that all our physicians are tremendously busy over here.

We had a very exciting and also dangerous experience here at Orgonon with anti-nuclear experimentation. You will soon be able to read about it in the report which will go out.

In spite of sometimes severe cold, it is beautiful at Orgonon in winter. There are about 12 people working at present here, and the work is spreading rapidly far and wide.

Peter has emerged fully from the troubles which he had during the passage through the first puberty, and is flowering in a most beautiful manner. He is one of the very few living humans with whom I have a simple and immediate contact of understanding and of love. He learned how to shoot well, and I am happy to be able to teach him to do so, since, as the little men in this world continue to improve their lot the wrong way, there will surely be war when he will be 19 and I feel that in such a case it is better to know how to shoot well.

———— ◆•◆ ————

Edinburgh, Scotland

March 6, 1951

My dear Reich,

I am in Edinburgh doing a "cure." I got fatter and fatter and had no energy. I don't believe in drugs and injections, and there is no Orgone therapist in England. I returned to Thomson the nature cure man. I am playing golf much of the time and the unusual exercise must be helping to reduce the weight. I hope that when I go home next week my sitting in the Akku will be, as it were, under less of a handicap. I still think that the Akku should not be asked to contend against too much intake of food and drink, and I guess that in—say—diabetes the Akku would be used plus a sugarless diet.

You'll see the *New Statesman* review of *Char. Analysis,* a nasty bit of work by a name I never heard of. It is a cheap review written in prejudice not knowledge.

An M.P. friend is trying to get an interview with the U.S. ambassador about my case. I fear he has a 100 to one chance against, but if the one chance came, I'd come out this summer and trust to get enough lectures to pay our passages. But if the Paris conference* breaks down there is no hope of much other than war.

Will write when I get home.

———————————

* A conference called by the Western powers to establish a treaty organization to contain the spread of Soviet power; the organization was to include a partially rearmed West Germany.

P.S. Telfer [the osteopath] is a bit pessimistic about Akkus in England owing to the long winter damp. I have the same doubts.

———————◆•◆———————

Orgonon
Rangeley, Maine

March 22, 1951

My dear Neill:

Please let me know whether your M.P. friend had any success. Could you find out who the crackpot was who wrote the slander in the *New Statesman*?

It has been known to us for a long time that accumulators work much better in dry than in humid climates. The only way to get around it is to build more layers.

How are you? Write often, please. We here went through a hell of three months with the Oranur experiment.* It's too complicated to describe in a letter.

———————◆•◆———————

Summerhill School
Leiston, Suffolk

March 23, 1951

My dear Reich,

The M.P. who took up my case with the U.S. Embassy has got so far as to get the consulate to send the case to headquarters in U.S.A. But I have but little hope of success. Much depends on the Paris conference. If it means peace maybe the U.S.A. will stop being fanatical about visas, and if it means war, then, visas are a very minor consideration.

My two weeks of nature cure made me lose ten lbs. weight. Now I can sit in the O[rgone] A[ccumulator] with the feeling that I am not asking it to do what it can't do. I see a danger that folks will use the O.A. as a lazy way to get well without doing anything but sitting in it, making no effort to help get themselves well. In short, use it as a

———————————————

* A series of experiments designed to determine the effects of orgone energy (OR) on nuclear energy (NR).

doctor's drug . . . "I can live as I like so long as I swallow the pills the doctor ordered."

I am not continuing with the Oranur project.* I wrote to an old acquaintance I met in Vienna in 1923. He is now professor of physics in Bristol Univ'y and is called the most brilliant physicist in Britain. He replied that he was not in the atomic movement and had nothing to do with civil defence, but ended with the words: "I wouldn't attach too much importance to orgone energy if I were you." You see how hopeless it is to approach anyone.

I long to hear what happened in the lab and how Peter got ill through rays. I do hope he has recovered entirely.

Ena and Zoë are well. Zoë grows daily and is so delightful.

My *Dreadful School*† has been banned by a library in Sidney, Australia, and one or two Australian papers have given the incident publicity . . . which I hope will sell the book.

If I can't get a visa this summer and have no hope of seeing you again, I'll be very much depressed.

———◆◆———

Orgonon
Rangeley, Maine

March 29, 1951

Dear Neill:

I hope very much that your M.P. will be successful. The State Department here, to my knowledge, has not objected to your coming.

I am hard at work to find somebody well trained and reliable, a physician, to go to England for 2 to 3 years to introduce medical orgonomy. As yet nobody wants to go, since they are doing very well over here.

Re Oranur: We stopped the whole experiment a few weeks ago, and are recuperating from very severe blows we suffered in this experimentation in regard to personal health as well as to shaking scientific insights.

---

* Neill had been asked to distribute the descriptive pamphlet, *Orgone Energy Emergency Bulletin*, and had planned to give it to civil-defense people.

† *That Dreadful School* (London: Herbert Jenkins, 1937). Tells of the experiences and aims that have guided Neill in running Summerhill, so often felt to be a "dreadful" school by those who disapprove of freedom and self-government for children.

There is no physicist in this world who is trained or competent to judge the Oranur Experiment. I cannot understand why you continuously try to convince those brilliant people if they are thoroughly incompetent. I am sure you would strongly object if I were to send your *Problem Family* to the head of the Board of Education in New York for scrutiny and approval. Is it not quite obvious that those whose total base of operation and intellectual existence is being slowly overturned with each single step we are making forward into the realm of the cosmic orgone ocean, cannot but be inimical and full of hate toward us. Please, may I ask you to avoid further embarrassing and humiliating situations of such a kind.

There is very much in educational matters I would love to talk over with you.

Summerhill School
Leiston, Suffolk

April 3, 1951

My dear Reich,

I gave up approaching orthodox scientists long ago. Then Mickey S. sent me the Oranur pamphlet, asking me to try to contact defence authorities on this side. Newspaper reports had given me the impression that Prof. Powell was one of the big men in atom research. I thought it would be Powell or a man of his position who would be consulted by any defence group, and naturally, having known him, I thought I'd get at him before officialdom got there. I was wrong, but still I can't understand what was expected of me when Sharaf asked me to distribute the pamphlets.

Rumours go around about Oranur . . . that Eva nearly died. We long to get the inside story, which we hope will come in the *Bulletin*. I fear there is hardly a chance of a visa for me. If your Oranur trial were known to the State Dept. I haven't a hope, for, to them, I might be suspect as an enemy who will come to Maine to steal the results to give to the U.S.S.R. or some nonsense of the sort.

I have moved the Accu into a room with a gas (that is a dry) fire, and I am sure the reaction is much stronger. The small Accu has been wonderful with scaldings on a boy's foot.

Just looked at [L. Ron Hubbard's] book on Dianetics which sounds to me utter bunk without a sign of any philosophy or science or education behind it. I hear it is selling all over U.S.A.

---◆◆---

Orgonon
Rangeley, Maine

April 22, 1951

My dear Neill:

This is late to be answering your letter of April 3, however we have been living here over the past four months like drunks on a powder keg. Oranur has overthrown everything, but everything, plans, the research laboratory, made the summer dwelling probably unusable, has thrown many workers down with their special illnesses etc. It was a terrible and at the same time exhilarating experience, as if I had touched the bottom of the universe. It is still rather confused, but never in my 30 years of research career have I experienced such an upheaval. It is true that Eva nearly passed away one day, and Ilse fell ill; she went to New York for a major operation. Peter had scarlet fever which lasted exactly four hours and was gone, brought forth by Oranur and killed at the same time. Oranur has attacked every single person at his or her weakest spot, driving the disease to the surface and killing it. I was the only one who did not suffer except in the beginning from severe malaise. I have written a report which cannot be published without further consideration. The results were tremendous.

Our policy has not changed. However, we are widely read, discussed, talked about, "controversial," universities are giving courses. We have come of age. The few quacks in physics and medicine, though, still in power, have little to say. They are finished, theoretically, and the good ones know it.

Did you hear from the American Consul? The State Department and the President's Office are fully informed on Oranur, so are all Governors, Defense authorities, etc. There is no secret about it. You seem still to be under the influence of a finished socialist ideology.

A report on Oranur will most likely appear sometime during the summer.

Our infant research center is doing well. Several babies have been born and are taken care of with *amazing* results. It is incredible what the release of early chest blocking or removal of routine mistakes on the part of the mother can do. There is very great hope for the future. But one must stick to sex-economy and orgonomy. One must [not] stray away from it if one wants these results.

Write again soon, Neill. Hope to see you this summer, but where do I put you up if the summer dwelling is unusable? We'll see . . .

———◆•◆———

Summerhill School
Leiston, Suffolk

May 7, 1951

My dear Reich,

So eine Geschichte [What a story]! I can only guess that if it hadn't been for the curative reaction of O. energy you'd all be dead in Orgonon. But, friend, I fear that you won't have to worry about whether the cottage will be safe for us to live in in August, for my chances of getting a visa are I should think nil. I am trying to get reconciled to the thought that I may never visit you again. The war situation grows rapidly now, and I can't see any reconciliation between East & West taking place.

I lectured twice last week. New Education Fellowship of Leicester, about 100 teachers, and University College, Leicester, about 200 students. There I had a roar of hostility when I mentioned religion suppressing sex. Maybe in these days of uncertainty the young are seeking religion as a faith more than they did.

We may be going to spend the vacation in Norway. Elsa Backer has invited us to her mountain hut. I'd have a chance to meet Raknes in Oslo, but it will be difficult to pick up old threads. I've accepted the invitation on the condition that no U.S. visa appears. Oh, I have discovered that my theory of the Consul was right; he is a Catholic.

A New Zealand teacher visiting us is trying to persuade me to migrate there. I'm rather old to emigrate, and N.Z. would feel very narrow after England. The temptation of course is to get Zoë away from atomic war, but possibly N.Z. would get it too.

Isn't it interesting to think that stuff like Dianetics immediately gets a big public and sale while your work and mine has to fight for years to get a place?

You say the result of releasing very young babies is astounding. But why is it so necessary? Kittens don't need it, and, I presume, Trobriand mothers do not have stiffened babies. My concern about such methods of treating babies is that it can only touch a very few. But I grant that

I can see no other way but dealing with the few . . . as we have to do in S'hill.

The *Bulletin* isn't enough. I want to see an Orgone Child Study Magazine. If the visa question didn't stand in the way I'd think of coming over to edit such a magazine. Standing out in my ignorance from the scientific side of the work, I am handicapped. I can only write and talk about actual children. The job for my old age is obviously to be employed by some advanced Government to go round all the schools telling teachers what *not* to do; the positive side would then come of itself.

Ena sends her love to you all, and both of us often say: "If only Zoë had Peter to play with."

Summerhill School
Leiston, Suffolk

May 30, 1951

My dear Reich,

We have been waiting to hear good news of Ilse. It was after I wrote you that I reread your letter and saw that you told us of a major operation . . . Do tell us about it.

No word from U.S.A. re my M.P.'s application. We have booked our trip to Norway, realising what a poor *Ersatz* [substitute] it is compared with a trip to Maine.

Lectured to Birkbeck College, London, last week. Very enthusiastic audience which accepted the Reich–Neill plea for the rights of youth to love. I *übernachtet* [spent the night] with Flugel, friendly as usual, but when I talked about Zoë and the fears other kids give her I could see that the language was Greek to them. Mrs. F. said: "But it is necessary, for she has to face all sorts of things in life." The good old Freudian Reality Principle.

The summer stream of visitors has commenced. I get lots of New Zealanders and Australians and Indians. Nearly all the Indians are moral and fear the sex issue.

I still feel bitter and wretched about being cut off from you. If the war situation were less threatening, I'd hopefully say: "Maybe in 1952 I can go over." But the plethora of world hate makes planning impossible. I can't see an end, can you?

I often think of your motor in Orgonon with Bill Washington in attendance. It is a mystery to me. Why did Bill leave? What became of the attempt to use orgone energy as power?

I sit in the Accumulator every night reading, holding the funnel to my catarrhy ears. It feels stronger now that warmer dry weather has arrived.

I told you I'd decided to begin a book on Self-Regulation, but so far I have not been able to concentrate on it. I may write it on the Norway mountain for, miles from anywhere, I shall have lots of time on my hands. I may stay on in September and lecture in Oslo, Stockholm and Copenhagen. But maybe the university attitude to Raknes will prevent my being asked to lecture in the Oslo University.

Do write and tell us about Ilse and about Peter.

----◆◆◆----

Orgonon
Rangeley, Maine

June 7, 1951

My dear Neill:
          I have your two letters of May 7th and 30th. Ilse was one of the victims of the Oranur experiment and had to undergo a major operation. Oranur had brought out the specific disease in every single person. It was a great horror. If art is a disease, Oranur has brought out the artist in me. I have painted some two dozen pictures in oil over the past three months, and people, who claim they know, say that they are first rate; that nobody has painted that way as yet. I cannot tell, I just enjoy painting tremendously. It teaches me a lot about our miserable failure to see nature correctly. It is incredible to detect that you do not know how sunlight hits a tree, and that there is no color to render in true fashion the color of sun and daylight. I came to call this special color which is not white, "*orgonite*," only to distinguish it from other colors. I am also playing and enjoying the organ, and have begun to write down my melodies of which I am quite full. I do not know where I am going. I gave up a 50,000 dollar a year practice in New York in the spring of 1950, when I moved to Maine permanently, in order to stop outfitting nuisance doctors and psychologists with the great authority they obtain gratis simply for having studied with me. Also I cannot stand pathological expressions very well since I shifted my main biopsychiatric work to the problem of the *healthy* child. Peter is a wonder to all of us here. Here something entirely new is growing up,

something that seems to fulfill all the requirement of sociality, goodness and natural morality for which mankind has for ever clamored. It is a very great thing and we follow it with respect, even awe and humility.

Oberleitner* has behaved badly recently, and we are disconnecting him. Little Man stuff, on account, most probably, of the animosity to orgonomy of his wife.

Also in other respects I am going through a terrific breakover in my life. The work is now spreading rapidly all over the world in a very good way, and I seem to be quite high up. My work is being taught in many colleges and many references and papers appear at an increasing rate. The world of pathology slowly vanishes beneath the horizon. I am facing the task of giving up entirely all my old type of writing and of finding a new way of expression in words, as I did find one in colors. With the Oranur experiment, in which Cosmic Orgone Energy licks the malignant atomic energy, I seemed to have reached the limits of my natural scientific possibilities. I do not quite know where I am going. Many human relationships suffer from this tremendous change in my development. I am glad I am moving, while so many remain sitting and stuck.

Summerhill School
Leiston, Suffolk

June 11, 1951

My dear Reich,

Yours this morning. You say you don't know where you are going, you lucky man. "Tis better to travel hopefully than to arrive." (Stevenson) However there is a doubt in my mind . . . Is Reich painting and musicking because he has despaired of humanity (barring Peter)?

It has been obvious for the last years that you were finished with the pathological in life, from Peter's birth onwards. It seems to me that the new art life is an expression of the back-to-health movement, perhaps an attempt to get back to Peter's stage and find out what you

---

* Toni Oberleitner, a former teacher at Summerhill. He later spent some time studying with Reich at the Orgone Institute in New York.

missed then.* Our art teacher is away and I have been in charge of the art room, painting with the children, but realising that I couldn't do anything so good as they did; my painting was sophisticated, more or less conscious and stylised, while theirs was straight from the soul and of course brilliant. I am—say—a Royal Academy formal painter, while each child is a van Gogh. Your description of your painting makes me think you have "regressed" to the Gogh stage.

Correspondence is so difficult. You write of OIRC [Orgonomic Infant Research Center] and its work but I have no details and can't imagine what is done with newborn infants. Dammit, man, you didn't do anything with Peter newborn, did you? And he seems wonderful. So is Zoë. However, I keep hoping the method will come out in a *Bulletin*.

How to meet you again worries me. I'll apply again for a visa when I return from Norway. Then I'll try to get a visa to visit you either at Christmas or in the spring. I'd hoped to be able to show the visa people two published articles showing that S'hill was the antithesis of communist moulding of youth. The trouble is that although progressive papers are anti-communism, they aren't pro self-regulation or pro sex. Indeed I often wonder why there is so much antagonism between the West and East, for fundamentally they seem to share so many factors in common, e.g. the moulding of infants, the sex taboo, the Oedipus family. Stalin's rules for school children would have the complete approval of 90% of British teachers. Possibly that is why I can't get articles published. As for a visa, my hopes of this are very dim indeed. It is so frustrating. I need you and I know you need me in some ways, and we are separated by a futile suspicion.

Love from us all, and we hope that Ilse's operation was a success.

———◆◆———

Orgonon
Rangeley, Maine

June 22nd, 1951

My dear Neill:

I have your letter of June 11th. The revolution in my life and work is very deep going. I am not despairing of humanity, and I am not running away into painting and music making. I am just begin-

---

* At this point, there is a fierce underlining of Reich's and, in the margin, the comment "I had it."

ning to get going at "humanity." After having written several thousand pages on the subject, I find myself in the position of having to rewrite the whole thing, this time to nail it down for good. I began writing the *Murder of Christ,** and it runs very well. It is a better *Little Man* book, further removed emotionally from my own sufferings due to the Little Man. It is incredible to realize that a whole world of statesmen, philosophers, psychologists and the rest of them have so thoroughly avoided heretofore touching the main subject of mass-psychology and sociology, the detailed routine behaviour of the so-called man in the street. There is no hope at all if we don't start getting at that. I keep hitting right and left around myself at every single worker in my neighborhood, when I see them patting people on the back instead of telling people the truth about themselves. What a hideous, cowardly evasion of the issue.

I wish I could talk these things over with you, and I am quite sure that very soon the opportunity will offer itself here at Orgonon. The complete and frank revelation of the catholic action in the U.S. Embassy in London would be entirely in agreement with the American way of procedure and would help to get you the visum. Americans don't like Catholics very much.

———— ◆◆ ————

[*On June 28, 1951, the American Consul in London wrote to Neill's M.P. friend, Mr. Moeran, informing him that the State Department, "after careful consideration," had decided that it would be "prejudicial to the interests of the United States" to grant entry to Neill. Neill forwarded a copy of this letter to Reich.*]

Summerhill School
Leiston, Suffolk

July 3, 1951

My dear Reich,

Well, well, looks as if I'll never see you again. I wish I could get some magazine to print a letter of protest, but the dollar dependence on U.S.A. precludes even that.

No, I don't hold that art is an escape, in part possibly, for I find

———

* *The Murder of Christ*, first published in 1953, explores the meaning of Christ's life and attributes his death to man's conditioned hatred of everything that is truly and fully alive—whenever and in whatever shape it may appear.

that if I am interrupted in a sketch by visitors my annoyance is greater than when reading a book or even writing one.

Hal M. Wells who bought the magazine *Complex* asks me for a long article on communistic education, saying they would add a paragraph saying I had been refused a visa. I am going to do it.

I don't agree with you about my American boy pupil not fitting in because England is different from U.S.A. To me it is much simpler than that . . . the kid is parked here without ever having a home and his lack of home love is enough to make him unhappy.

The new *Bulletin* is fascinating. I see now what you meant about new-born babes, and your explanation of dowsing seems to be final and true. I must have a shot at it. But your pages about not approaching orthodox scientists do not seem to me to be the whole story. There is an element of *Schadenfreude* [malicious gloating] in it. "See here, Bernal, I want to show you that a better man than you has got more of the truth." I don't think it means an attempt to say: "You are a prof of biology, do tell me if Reich is right or wrong." However, I'll never try to approach any orthodox scientists on behalf of Orgone science. By the way the leading name is now [Jacob] Bronowski in scientific circles.

———————◆•◆———————

Orgonon
Rangeley, Maine

July 23, 1951

My dear Neill:

In the meantime you have replied to Wells and though it may cost you some dollars it will certainly be most helpful to your reputation not to have published in Wells' journal.*

I am enclosing a copy of the laws of immigration. I still want you to know that your trouble is not due to the basic structure of the United States but to the fact that the arbitrary conduct of a single Catholic consul can remain unchanged because people keep silent. I still think it will be possible to counteract the situation in London and to get you a visa next summer.

We have had some most crucial experiences with Peter and a girl

---

* Reich had wired Neill to have nothing to do with Hal Wells, the new editor of *Complex*, who, he said, was an enemy of the Orgone Institute.

lately, and we have learned how little we know about children, especially their genitality. The depths and scope of this realm are endless and I look forward to the day when the educators of the world will start digging up these sources of living life, as they are only burying them in a lot of verbiage today. I am just about finishing my book on the murder of Christ after about twelve years preparation and two months emotional agony just before I began to write it.

The Foundation has just sent over $500 for Korean children's relief and is going to send more. The trend in the Foundation is to become a grant-giving Foundation with the center of attention on the misery of infants and adolescents.

Write soon again and amply so. All my best to all of you.

Summerhill School
Leiston, Suffolk

July 30, 1951

My dear Reich,

I don't know if my visa letter reached the U.S.A. press. The press here took it up and gave it a lot of publicity.

We are off in a few days to Norway. Elsa Backer has invited us to her mountain hut, 9 hours by rail from Oslo. It will be peace. I have the first [lecture] in Oslo on 5th Sept, and am dining with Raknes. Then I come home after lectures in Stockholm and Copenhagen.

I'm worried about Ena. She has a constant pain across the back. Admittedly the school work exhausts her, but work shouldn't exhaust a healthy person. We've both had an additional worry put on to us. Girl of 13½ missed her periods. Nice kid, clever, charming but she will go to bed with anyone. I can cope with a genuine love affair but with promiscuity I am lost. The parents know all about it and are pro-sex. It isn't any joke having the responsibility of other people's kids. A boy of 7 fell from a high tree recently and fractured his skull. Luckily he has just come out of hospital. All such worries pile up, and we sure need a break in peace.

I am longing to read your Christ book.

Is there anything in Orgone study to destroy a guy's sense of humour? Paul Ritter wrote saying his wife was to have another baby, and I wrote saying that it was all very well, but a pity that the man didn't have more to do with birth. He replied as if scandalised at any suggestion of levity about such a sacred thing as life's functioning. I had to reply that behind my fun was the serious question that nature hadn't given the sexes a fair deal, that the tom cat has his orgasm and nothing more, while the mother has the pains of birth and the joys of motherhood. Also that to some extent humans have it ill-divided also. After I posted the letter Zoë said to me: "I wonder why I like Ena much more than I do you." Which hints that behind my desire for equal sharing in pain and joy was the feeling that the mother has the best of it really.

In the peace and remoteness of the Norwegian mountain I hope to sit down and write another book.

Let me know if my visa letter got publicity in U.S.A.

Wells hasn't replied to my refusal. I didn't mind, only I sighed to think that my dream of making a few dollars had to go.

I am looking forward to a good chat with Raknes, but don't fancy meeting Philipson again in C'hagen. I don't like clever guys with no guts. Hoppe wants me to have a lecture tour of Israel, and I've said okay, I'm all for it.

Still in the dark about the atom experiment. Sounds very brave, seeing that all the other men dealing with atoms go about encased in lead or whatnot. Heard the other day of an atomic workman who took home a screwdriver, and they had to clear out of the house in a hurry, but that is maybe a fable.

Love to you all from us all. We hope Ilse is completely recovered and Eva too.

Orgonon
Rangeley, Maine

August 13, 1951

My dear Neill:

Send me all details you may know about the American consul in London who acted not as an official of the United States where the church is strictly divorced from the state, but who acted as an envoy of the Vatican under the disguise of an American representative. It apparently had nothing to do with communism but with the anti-genital attitude of the catholic church. Here in the U.S. such things are not taken lying down, and the catholic church is not too much liked.

Stockholm, Sweden

September 13, 1951

My dear Reich,

I thought I'd wait to write after I'd met the Oslo folks. I am on my way to Copenhagen after lecturing to crowded houses in Oslo, Stockholm, Gävle and getting well paid for it too. Raknes had invited two young couples (patients) to dinner, so that the heart to heart talk with him did not come off. I can only give you what is more or less gossip. Judith [Bogen] has a theory, expressed something like this . . . "When we were all *per du* [the familiar form of address] and called Reich Willy it was wonderful, but when he left us we all felt lost, and some tried to stand on their own feet by trying all sorts of methods. We weren't disloyal and are not still, for you can't love Willy and later be disloyal to him. If some broke away it was through weakness not desire to. Philipson to this day worships Reich."

When I mentioned you in Oslo to 600 in the Univ'y *Gamle Saal* [Old Hall] I got no reaction at all. None of the papers spoke about my mentioning you, pity, for I told Oslo that you are the only man who has contributed anything of value to the science of humans since Freud.

We stayed with Elsa Backer in her hut in the mountains for over 3 weeks. Ena and Zoë got bored after a time but I took the chance to begin writing a book about babies. They went home end of August and I stayed to earn money. But at my age lecturing is very tiresome, not the actual lectures but the meeting people, especially the press. Queer that I can get a much bigger audience here than anywhere in England.

You want me to give you proofs about the R.C. man in Visa office, but I can't. And in any case that letter replying to my M.P. friend, from State Dept. refusing the visa again, that had nothing to do with Mr. Clarence McIntosh of the London visa section. Nay, Reich, *nichts zu machen da* [nothing to be done there].

Going to stay with Leunbachs whom I saw on my way up. I expect to meet Philipson again. But my next letter will I hope give the Danish *Lage* [situation].

I heard a Swedish doctor say: "Reich was all right up to *Character Analysis* but after that, of course, he went astray." It is the typical Freudian viewpoint in London also, as you can guess.

Orgonon
Rangeley, Maine

September 26, 1951

My dear Neill:

It was a great nice surprise to me to hear that I was wonderful and that "you cannot love Willi and later be disloyal to him." But the worst haters came from the ranks of my early students who loved me dearly and that was not my fault.

The fact that you did not obtain any reaction in Oslo at the University lecture only confirms the fact that we are through and accepted everywhere, and are no longer to the same extent the "red cloth" I used to be. My old enemies are wise enough to keep silent at present.

I still believe that you will attend the 1952 conference if you only try hard enough. But it becomes clearer now that the refusal of your visum is due rather to a mechanical application of the McCarran Act* than to any special consideration of your person. As long as these ghastly spies and sneakers will crawl around among decent people, snooping and sniping and slandering and stealing secrets, there will be many decent people who will suffer from it, and I am waiting for the day when one of them will speak up against the hideous rats of *Sowjet* [Soviet] design, and not against the American public who is in full agreement with the measures taken to keep out thieves and murderers. Why don't you speak up against the sneakers and snipers? We here at Orgonon feel that such diversion of attention can only protect the emotional plague.

Let me know what impression you had of Philipson. I still feel that with some good effort he could be made going again and become a member of our organisation.

———— ◆•◆ ————

* The McCarran–Walter Act, which, among other provisions, barred from admission to the United States anyone who advocated doctrines or was affiliated with organizations held to be subversive.

331

[1951]

Summerhill School
Leiston, Suffolk

October 2, 1951

My dear Reich,

Yours today. I can't share your optimism about being at the 1952 conference, indeed I am reconciled to the sad fact that I won't be there. Your suggestion that I ought to "speak up against the sneakers and snipers" does not appeal to me. I don't think there are many of them, and if there are I have no evidence that there are. And objectively ALL nations use spies and snoopers against other nations. You say: "We here at Orgonon feel that such diversion of attention only protects the emotional plague." What you mean I simply don't know. I am not fundamentally interested in either U.S.A. or Russia; I am only interested in you and a few others in U.S.A. The visa situation separates me from you and if you lived in Brazil and I couldn't get a visa to go there I'd feel strongly against the Brazilian laws. I speak when it is necessary; in every lecture in Scandinavia I attacked the anti-life policies of Communism, and never mentioned my U.S. visa refusal. By the way, the tour was a great success; crowded halls everywhere, and much enthusiasm and, I am afraid, hero worship. There I am a Big Man, but at home a very little guy.

I specially asked Philipson to meet me and had a long talk with him. I asked him how he differed from you and he replied that he didn't think your vegeto-therapy was necessary, that character analysis alone loosens up the somatic rigidity. He spoke of you warmly and regretted that you didn't open your publications to any criticism, meaning, I took it, that he'd like to give his argument for character analysis in the *Bulletin*. For myself I ask "Why not?" It would be one answer to the people who say that you have become a Stalin, a central authority allowing no one to have any independent opinions of his own, demanding All or Nothing from all workers. The latest news I have is that Oberleitner has been chucked out of the movement. I don't know why, but such a happening adds to the talk about dictatorship. This talk isn't in Scandinavia, indeed I found that few knew anything about your more recent work. But it worries me, Reich, especially when I can't talk it out with you. I hate to hear the words Orgonon and Orthodoxy linked together. Maybe it is that I don't fully understand your term emotional plague. Is it plague when old Raknes lectures about the scientific part that is not in his training line? What I fear is that some genuine students and enquirers will be put off. Your remark about Philipson, that maybe he could become a member of your organisation, made me think about and write down thoughts about the so-called dictatorship. If P. firmly believes that he can get there by character analysis alone, is he thus hostile to the work? I am sure you will say no, he isn't necessarily hostile; he is a co-worker trying in his own way to think for himself. I wish we could talk this out. Barakanism, the arrogance of ignorance, would be a danger to any new work, but the others?

My visit to Norway made one big impression on me, viz that none of your old pupils and co-workers became really emotionally plaguey; that they drifted because they did not know, feel enough to stand alone. They retained their personal love for you, and felt to some extent that your new life had left them out of everything, beginning with the enforced segregation made by war. They are all good honest folks trying hard to understand and to work. I feel that they should all be in the fold, but independent too. In your article last summer you spoke of my unique position, being in the orgone fold but at the same time being independent, an excellent position to be in. But why can't it apply to all the others?

Get angry with me, swear at me, call me a victim of the plague, but also do tell me what standard of loyalty to an idea you expect and demand. I can't just fathom it. Hal Wells may be the nasty guy you say he is, but if he had printed my article and reached a few thousand readers self-regulation would have made more contacts and converts. I consider Kingsley Martin, editor of the *New Statesman,* to be a most reactionary man about education, but he prints my letters and no one thinks of him when they read them. It would take more than one bottle of rye to talk this out together.

Ena and Zoë send their love. Ena complains that she never gets any news of PEOPLE . . . of Ilse, Peter, Wolfe (his wife writes Ena that he is off work).

———— ◆•◆ ————

Orgonon
Rangeley, Maine

October 7, 1951

My dear Neill:
        I think two glasses of good whiskey soda would suffice to clear up our disagreement regarding my relationship to people who call

me a dictator. Suffice it to say that I have to carry on a hell of a battle, in addition to my main work, to keep out people who try to get to fame and riches on MY broad, powerful shoulders with their own cock-eyed ideas about what they think orgonomy should be. I let everyone do what he pleases. But this is not sufficient to them. They want me to confirm and support with my authority what I cannot possibly consider as a part of or as in agreement with my work. You ask why my basic attitude of loving people being in the field and yet being completely independent applies to you but not to others. This is so because you, when you realize that you cannot make a decent go of orgone therapy with children, will say so and stop doing it, while the [others] will not realize that they harm patients and work by doing what they call therapy. Because when I stop supporting them or warn them against the consequences they slander me.

Neill, this work of mine is the most devilish task a man has ever encountered in the history of human knowledge. I had to destroy one organisation after another which grew the wrong way and with the wrong objectives. I had to restrict what you call the organisation to a very few well-trained, responsible men and women who are my assistants and help me to carry on the terribly dangerous and emaciating tasks. You yourself warned me against organisations with pupils and you were right. I had to give up the pleasure of public acclaim, of empty friendships, of what is called "recognition," in order to keep clear of the pitfalls of human interrelations, and this against my basically social nature which thirsts for human contacts.

Philipson wanted me to open my publishing organ for him to proclaim nonsense. I asked him several times to write down what he has to say. He never did. I am still ready to publish his viewpoint if he restricts himself to factual argument and withholds personal attack. What the Scandinavians don't understand is that I have moved ahead over these 12 years at a fast rate and that I am far out in space and no longer in the realm of a restricted psychology of technique. It was they who failed to keep contact and to move on. Should I too have remained sitting in order to retain a few doubtful friendships? I still like them and think of them much, maybe more than they do of me. There is no reason for animosity, as long as they do not try to make me bad because THEY did not develop with me.

I am afraid Neill that we all, including myself, are afraid to touch upon the true nature of human nature, the sitting on the spot, the reluctance to risk friendships, to fight the plague of mankind. By the way, "emotional plague" is a strictly scientific term to denote evil social action from irrational motives with irrational evil results, in contra-distinction to simple neurosis which just suffers but does not kill life in newborn infants because it has lost life within itself.

Beyond this I feel that my work has taken a very dangerous turn since the insight has become so very practical that it is the suppressed man himself who carries all the responsibility; not Stalin, not Hitler, not anyone but he himself. This is a most unpopular insight and will, I fear, cost me much. Be assured, Neill, that I did not change away from my line of 20 years ago, I only pursued it further. It is the friend, the pupil out of touch, the admirer, the hero worshipper of two decades ago who changed by remaining sitting on the spot.

I also fear that those who were closest do not quite realise the great progress the work has made in the world today. It is rooted and taught in universities all over the world. The literature is streaming steadily at a rate of about five hundred copies a month OVER YEARS all over the planet. The effects are clearly there in the basic change of attitude in infant upbringing, in handling of human problems, in a growing aversion against mechanistic philosophies, including the Russian. My success is very great and far more than I dared dream of only 10 years ago. And it is acknowledged. Of this the old friends know little because some newspapers are still silent, which does not matter a bit. The aware-ness of the discovery of the Life Energy is here growing by leaps and bounds. And this alone is what matters to me who has sacrificed so heavily to bring it about. And I could with a clean conscience put on the scales of human history my love for man in what I DID to im-prove his lot against what those have accomplished who call me a dictator because I keep them strictly out of my way in order to prevent their spoiling my clean, honest job.

I SHALL see you again here at Orgonon, no doubt!!

Write again, Neill. I like it. I have written three books this year: *The Oranur Experiment,** 2. *Cosmic Superimposition,*† 3. *The Murder*

---

* A brief description of the experiments was first published in the *Orgone Energy Emergency Bulletin*, in December 1950; the full report then came out in booklet form, *The Oranur Experiment: First Report, 1947–1951*, 1951.

† *Cosmic Superimposition*, first published in 1951. Discusses man's position in nature. Reich, citing the genital embrace as an example, sees the superimposition of two orgone systems as a common functioning principle throughout nature.

of Christ. The first two are to appear within a few weeks. You will like them.

---------◆•◆---------

Orgonon
Rangeley, Maine

October 8, 1951

My dear Neill:

I read your letter again since I sent my answer yesterday, and I find that I did not answer your inquiry with my usual exactness. Your question about my alleged dictatorship rests within and upon a much wider and deeper foundation, though you may not be aware of it, than my answer encompassed. The problem involved is a general human problem, more, a problem which is at the root of all dictatorships. It is exactly the sickness in human character structures which, through irresponsibility and helplessness, forces the rise of dictators. I feel the pull toward dictatorship quite clearly, though I never yield to it. *It comes from the people,* in many ways. If you have to keep a scientific theory clear and clean, based on facts and observations, if you have to keep an industrial process going, if you have to keep trains running and a whole society from starving, and at the same time the Barakans enter the scene by the million, the pull toward dictatorship is tremendous. The difference between Stalin and myself is that he does not see the problem, that he likes house-sized pictures carried in parades, and that he has no answer nor does he ask for one. I, on the other hand, suffer from this sickness of humanity gravely, to an extent that amounts to dying. I know the problem in its full impact upon human existence and I try desperately to find the answer and to make it work. My answer at present is: There is no way of basically changing people once they have developed the wrong character structure. You cannot make a crooked tree straight again. Therefore let's concentrate on the newborn ones, and let's divert human attention from evil politics toward the child. This is the new social movement. I alone carry the responsibility for the elaboration of the necessary scientific tools to cope with this problem in a practically efficient manner. If you hit upon this in public lectures, please let the responsibility be mine. It is heretofore in its very practical aspects nobody else's but mine. I am willing and able to carry it.

Now the freedom peddlers like Barakan and the rest are in the way with their fake, do-nothing "love for mankind." They mess up clear thoughts and spoil a clear-cut road to answers to the problem. The red fascist movement rests fully on the evil doings of the freedom peddler. It hurts badly to see that you are unaware of the true nature of the red fascist regime, telling that *all* governments use spies. Of course they do. But the Canadian or English or American government still lets me work successfully on the problem of the Children of the Future, and Stalin does not. This, and this alone, is where my interest in existing governments comes in. I judge them by the amount of freedom we have to DO THINGS FOR CHILDREN. I regret that you do not see clear in this respect.

And to DO THINGS means to keep human thought and practice in the pioneering plants of science, medicine and education clear of crackpots and bandwagon riders. It is not enough to lecture to armored people who get easily enthused but do not move a finger practically. It is necessary to penetrate the wall of human indolence. Then the Stalins will fall of themselves.

Raknes came over here several times and studied in the laboratory. He knows what he is talking about and he is willing to learn more. He is in touch with the greatest force at the disposal of mankind in this mess. Philipson is NOT. He wants to sit on the spot I was on 25 years ago, in order *not* to have to *learn* and *do* ORGONE ENERGY PHYSICS AND BIOPHYSICS. And this I cannot let pass.

We refuse to let quacks of my science grow up and spoil the work. I confess to being adamant in this respect. Call it dictatorship if you will. But there are matters in human affairs, such as knowledge, which cannot be decided by votes, nor be done by pats on the back and "love of the Neighbor." Once you realize fully that the Little Man, characterologically speaking, has ruined every single bit of knowledge that could have helped him over the ages, you are in the right perspective of things. It is of course much easier and less dangerous to have "sympathetic understanding" than to do basic scientific work which has to stand up against a mountain of false beliefs, human evasion of truth, gossip, murder in the lands of heirs of Karl Marx, and against the tendency in one's own friends to support the distractor from painful work and duties. I do not mind when Philipson does Ch.A. of 1928, but I do not permit him to use my publication organ to "CRITICISE" me for having proceeded toward demonstrating at the microscope what is at work practically in the character and in the human emotion. This will not change, cannot change, and if it will cost me dear friendships, I shall not be able to help it. The fault is not mine. Orgonomy is ONE piece of labor, and not many things. One cannot really at present understand emotions unless one has learned what orgone energy really is like, looks like, and how it functions. Let them be on their own, but do not permit them to hate me because I moved on and work on the *whole* of human misery.

All the best with love.

––––––◆•◆––––––

Summerhill School
Leiston, Suffolk

October 14, 1951

My dear Reich,

Your letter [of Oct. 7] makes it all clear; the only unclear thing to me is the question: Are the cast-out ones malignant or merely *dumm* [stupid] or ambitious? The subject of hatred has intrigued me for some time now. *Character A[nalysis]*, page 169: "The [genital character] is capable of intense love but also of intense hatred." Putting aside for the moment your statement in Oslo days that I was repressing my hatred all the time, and trying to be objective, I feel like querying the hate angle. Just as the Freudians found much aggression in every child they concluded that aggression was the norm, but I find in Zoë little or no hatred. She wants to give out love, to ask for love, and because in her environment she satisfies both wishes she is no hate person. Later when she finds her love attitude met by hate she will react in hate, but would this be necessary if all kids were free and loved? Why no real fights among S'hill children?

I grant that my Scandinavian tour influenced me. I kept wondering why I had so many listeners and so friendly listeners. Why, I asked friends, do the Swedes etc. show so much interest in freedom yet don't practise it in their schools? The answer I got was: "It isn't only freedom, Neill, it is your personality. An audience feels a warmth and sincerity coming from you and it reacts accordingly. Even people who don't agree with you at all about freedom and children, feel friendly to you and that accounts for the lack of criticism and nasty questions after you lecture." This looks as if I am patting myself on the back saying: Good old Neill! Wonderful guy! But I am trying to see what is behind it all. I am sure that it is this part of myself that has made S'hill a success for 30 years . . . the absence of expressed hatred on my part.

Then when I heard and knew the love that is still given to you I had to face the question: Why do I give out love and get much love in return while Reich gives out so much love and gets so many Barakans in return? Is it that people feel that I am a simple guy, not very clever, not very original, a guy that most ordinary folks can understand, while you are so far ahead of the ordinary man, so creative that you are always a step ahead or a few miles ahead, a man to whom to attach awe and wonder . . . and envy? I am ignoring unconscious drives etc. purposely, for they don't mean much here. We can guess that St Paul spent much of his time trying not to think of fornication, but we can't even guess if Jesus had any interest in Mary's figure. Motives be damned, I say; we must look at hard facts. I can't even guess the truth. Here you have two pioneer affairs: Summerhill, disapproved of by the Blimps, of course, but if hated I don't see the evidence. We get staff who stay for years or who have to be sacked for neurosis or incompetency, but none of them become enemies and work against the school. On the other side Orgonon with helpers wanting to rival you and improve on your work. (I've had that too, but mainly from obvious climbers and incompetents, and seldom with anything like hate or fear.) Do I tolerate more than you do? Do you demand wholly allegiance? I have never accepted your judgment of the world's opposition to your work, and the sales of your books would show that the world isn't so hidebound as you think. We are both apt to think everyone is *gegen uns* [against us]. When I lectured last week in Birmingham a teacher said afterwards: "You don't seem to know that things have moved in State schools during the last years; there is much more freedom in them than you think."

In writing all this seems bald, leaving so much out that a couple of ryes would make clear. But, alas, I can't see that meeting. It is useless for me to apply for a visa again, and unless someone or some body can apply to London on my behalf I haven't the chance of a snowflake in hell.

You say that Wolfe has been out of the work for 5 years . . . but he was in it when we were over.

————◆•◆————

Summerhill School
Leiston, Suffolk

October 16, 1951

My dear Reich,

    I wrote the accompanying air mail letter before your second letter came. Let me state that I take no sides re Philipson and Raknes; I simply told you what I heard said. And my suggestion that you let P. write his viewpoint meant simply that you'd answer it and make a lot clear to humanity that might never come out . . .

    Because I don't feel passionately the same things that you do, you always conclude that I am lacking in grasp or *so etwas* [something of the sort]. This communism business, which you say hurts you that I can't see its dangerous vileness. I see it as an extension of existing conditions, the same thing as anti-semitism, negro race hatred, South African Apartheid, caning in English schools, beating children and animals . . . in a word hate. I hold it is because we have not put our own houses in order that we have allowed communism to win so much. In 1936 [on a lecture tour in South Africa] I saw Boer policemen chase natives out of a public park with whips at closing time; these natives, given the chance, will become communists, indeed the ones I spoke to then said they were communists and they had no idea what the word meant or that Marx had lived. When you write about *doing something* I ask what one can do so long as the factors that make for hate are not attacked at the same time? We both preach love and freedom for babies and reach some folks, a small number indeed, a growing number but far too small to arrest the hate in life and politics *in time*. The Stalins will be top dogs for many years before Peter and Zoë grow up to try to take over the world. Partly of course because Barakanism breaks up the united front of freedom. Now my dilemma is this: If you have to, and it is clear that you must, shoo off the band-waggoners, they become enemies in a world that has too many enemies. You may say What the hell! Let em be enemies! Better open enemies than false friends. True, but is there any other way? That is the fundamental question, how to keep a united front against hate. These letters of yours show that in two old friends and to some extent fellow workers there is not enough unity. It isn't enough for you to say that I am unaware of the "true nature of the red fascist regime," seeing that my whole life has been for child freedom and absence of moulding. It seems to me that you see ONLY the red fascism and not the other coloured ones that are in Catholicism, Moral Rearmament, Ku Klux Klan, etc. Bertrand Russell in a letter to me recently said: "It is a terrible world today when I am asked to fight either for Stalin or Syngman Rhee when I hate them both."

But when we argue about politics you and I get nowhere. I prefer to go back to the love emotion as seen in the 2500 people who listened to me in Scandia the other day. You write: "It is not enough to lecture to armored people who get easily enthused but do not move a finger practically." That is a very important statement indeed, and in the main it is true . . . *sie machen gar nichts* [they do absolutely nothing]. You see, Reich, if we are to divide humanity into the free and the armored, we are likely to get pessimistic; if a division is to be made it should be . . . those who warp babies and those who don't, and there are a lot of still armored people who are *not* warping and destroying babies. I say that all who are against baby life are red or black or blue fascists and that politics don't make fascists; they only organise them.

This crowd emotion (again) would seem to show that humanity is biased *toward* life and love; of course, for the vast majority of people are good citizens and peaceful and simple-minded. You say fascism of any hue gets hold of them easily and I admit it, man; it sure does. When in 1934 or so I stood in the Tempelhof [workers' district] in Berlin and listened to Hitler, the million there gave him what seemed the same emotion Oslo or Stockholm gave to me . . . enthusiasms, joy, approval. I suppose the answer is in your *Psy of Fascism* book, but I cannot remember it. Better for me to grope without books.

I think that my confusion is due in some measure to the two aspects of your work . . . the self-regulation for babies (accepted in full by me) and the biological microscopic work that is beyond me. Query: Who is this Reich guy? Chap who is all for free babies, but also the chap who studies blueness in the sky. Is it because I don't see the deep connection that I can't always get your point of view? My simple mind says that when babies are free there won't be any use in studying cancer cells in the microscope. In short, I get confused between the therapeutic and the prophylactic aspects of Orgone work.

I shall be 68 tomorrow, friend, too old a dog to learn new tricks. It is wonderfully good of you to argue so patiently with me.

————◆•◆————

341

[1951]

[The following letter was not sent.]

Orgonon
Rangeley, Maine

October 26th, 1951

My dear Neill:

After long and strenuous thinking about you, I found out, painfully enough, that you have not the slightest awareness of the fact that I have discovered the life energy as a function of the cosmic energy within man, some 12 years ago. This means opening a way for a complete re-evaluation of all human judgments and values acquired over the past 8000 years.

———◆◆———

[*Telegram*]

OCTOBER 20, 1951

ALEXANDER NEILL

MANY HAPPY RETURNS. PLEASE UNDERSTAND LIFE ENERGY DISCOVERED BY ME WILL KEEP YOU GOING FOR A LONG TIME TO COME ALSO CAUSING MISUNDERSTANDINGS ABOUT INFANTS BASICALLY BEING HEAPS OF COSMIC ENERGY.

———◆◆———

Summerhill School
Leiston, Suffolk

October 22, 1951

My dear Reich,

Many many thanks for your thoughtfulness in sending me a birthday telegram. Yes, I hope that Orgone Energy will give me many more birthdays. I feel it will now that the Box is well made. I don't feel old most of the time. But I can't run after a bus as I used to do, yet can dance a whole evening without tiring. On the other hand, friend, I do nothing new, discover nothing new, introduce nothing new in my school. S'hill will be 30 years old at Xmas, and I guess I should be content to sit down and look back and say: I did some good work in the past, but it is good to live even if the main work is past.

I don't think I'll apply for a visa for 1952. I'd only get another rebuff.

Zoë will be 5 next month. Our headache is a girl of 6, "trained" to be clean at nine months, whom Zoë follows all day. She tells Z. that witches are in her toy cupboard and keeps talking with guilty giggles about shit and piss. We feel like telling the parents to take their trained brat away, but can't face the row that would follow our "sacrificing" their brat for our own. Get me a visa and an island out in the lake at Rangeley . . . and then my worry would be Zoë falling into the lake. In other platitudinous words . . . there is always a bloody snag somewhere.

Teaching maths all morning to save money on a math man's salary.

I do feel so impatient to read about the atom experience. Seeing that the official atom men go about in thick lead or asbestos suits, I keep wondering how the hell you dared try the experiment.

Love and blessings, friend.

Summerhill School
Leiston, Suffolk

November 5, 1951

My dear Reich,

ORANUR.* Just arrived. Sat down to read it at once and read it to the end. You have told the story so clearly and so modestly with hardly a sign of impatience *gegen* [against] the little men and the haters. In the big Oranur job you are neither the big nor the little man; you are the selfless observer, humble, astonished, fearful. The whole report just shines with sincerity. And it sounds *true*.

But the report ended by making me afraid. Your claim that OR gingered up by a little NR should be a great curative factor in the hands of physicians . . . that is what scares me. I know you are completely pro prophylaxis yourself, and no doubt see the same danger that obsesses me. I can see a hundred thousand doctors using OR/NR Boxes all over the world without seeing the fundamental necessity of self-regulation. In short, the danger of your work being taken up and castrated by the mechanistic medical science is urgent and fearsome.

I was disappointed not to find at the end that the State Dept. had

---

* *The Oranur Experiment.*

shown interest. This raises the nasty question: Would the orthodox scientists allow humanity to die of atom ray poisoning rather than admit that another view of science was the right one? You say rightly: Don't try to convert the mechanistic professors. True, yet these profs stand as the bodyguard of society, and you, Reich, can't get your drama across the footlights because of these men. How to get behind the little men of power to the people?

I can't understand why the AEC [Atomic Energy Commission] did not demand the presence of one of its men to see that you weren't going to explode a bomb.

These doubts and fears always come when I hear from you of a new discovery. This one sounds so overwhelmingly important and true, that I want the world to grasp it and USE it *sofort* [immediately]. I must feel that more than you do, for your great moment is the discovery and not its reception. In ordinary times you would wait for the more or less slow reaction; in these anxious days, to sit and wait is too alarming. Hence my impatience.

Congratulations on a brave adventure. *Gott*, if only you could have had the whole tale filmed! And congratulations to your helpers who seem to have been a splendid team.

P.S. Ena is getting wonderful results using the new-made 5 ply Shooter for children's cuts and scalds. Healing in half the time usually taken, she says.

———◆◆———

Summerhill School
Leiston, Suffolk

November 9, 1951

My dear Reich:

A short and hasty and urgent note to ask a question. One of our mothers, a dentist's wife in her early forties, has got thyroid badly; Graves' Disease I fancy by her prominent eyes. Is Thyroid a disease that has benefited from the Box? Or rather, is it SAFE to use it without a genuine Orgonon expert within visiting range? It seems to me that it is her only chance, for I don't know of any successful orthodox medical treatment of the disease.

I find myself that I have to lessen the period of sitting in my five-folder. After fifteen minutes or so I get so very hot that I take it as a warning to get out.

———◆•◆———

Orgonon
Rangeley, Maine

November 14, 1951

Dear Neill:

It is always quite impossible to answer medical inquiries without having seen the patient. I have no experience with orgone therapy in Basedow's Disease, which is the name for what you describe. The only thing that could be done eventually is to use the orgone accumulator under medical supervision carefully in small doses, and to see how the patient reacts. If she reacts with improvement, then it could be continued. Should severe anxiety attacks of any kind increase badly with the use of the accumulator, then it should not be used, except under highly skilled supervision. Of course, no cure can be promised in any case.

I am in bed with a heart trouble which broke out after I put an oranur funnel on my heart. I am in bed the 4th week, and was nearly passing away twice. It seems as if Oranur has not left untouched a single latent reason to die. We are still collecting the medical experiences which came up with the tremendous upheaval in Oranur. Thank you for your kind remarks on it. I had 2 Oranur books sent to you without charge as a Christmas present.

———◆•◆———

Summerhill School
Leiston, Suffolk

November 19, 1951

My dear Reich,

Tut, tut, we can't have the ship's captain trying to navigate when he needs a rest. I told you in a letter months ago that you are the sort of man who drives the somatic car all out, and I make the layman's guess that the heart engine will recover when you slow up a bit. You always strike me as working against time, trying to do the work of centuries in a lifetime. Naturally when you have discovered so much.

H. G. Wells said: "You are just beginning to understand a little about life when Death the nurse comes and says Put away your toys, child, for it's time to go to bed." Maybe a man dies when he wants to die, when he feels he can't do more. But in your case this phase will happen when you are 90 plus, and even then I can picture you on your 92nd birthday hopping about on one rheumatic leg in great excitement at discovering something new about the moon. All of which means that old Reich is to defy hearts and bodies and go on and on. Mind you I think you neglect yourself a lot. As an old man I can lecture you about this, you being a mere youngster. Note that I am hitting a man when he is down. Yet who knows the secret of life anyway? I knew two Scots farmers who ate all the wrong food, drank a bottle of whiskey daily, and smoked strong tobacco all day long. They died within a week of each other at the age of 93.

Oh, Reich, good old friend, I feel like coming out now to boss you around and bully you into slacking off, and I'd do it if they gave me a visa, and damn the expense. You've GOT TO GO ON LIVING. Living until you can die knowing that the world has acknowledged how greatly you have added to its knowledge.

Sit up in bed and paint, Reich. I rejoiced recently when you told me you were painting and composing music. Two excellent antidotes to eternal thinking.

Let us know soon how you both are. As a layman again I don't get pessimistic about hearts. Twenty years ago a S'hill parent was forbidden to play golf because of his very bad heart. He is still winning medals at his golf course.

Ena joins in sending you both our love, but Zoë really doesn't remember you. She can talk about daddy catching frogs for her at the lake and about Hamilton's calfies, but I am sure they are memories of things we have said only.

Orgonon
Rangeley, Maine

November 27, 1951

My dear Neill:

I have been up again for the past 10 days, and I am slowly regaining my old self. This heart trouble was a clear-cut Oranur effect.

Oranur elicited it to the surface and . . . what? I don't know, maybe cured in advance. This is my hope.

It is hard to imagine how I could ever do my job at a reduced rate of effort. Only very few know how much effort went into this discovery of the life energy. I came to think in all earnest that almost all heart diseases are originally heart break diseases.

———— ◆•◆ ————

Summerhill School
Leiston, Suffolk

December 4, 1951

My dear Reich,

Good to hear you are now up and about. I hope your guess is right, that Oranur made the heart do its worst and fail to kill you. But do take care of yourself from now on. Make the other guys do the heavy work and walk round with your hands in your pockets and see they are doing the job . . . but I can't ever see you standing aside patiently watching another man make a mess of things.

I feel sure now, and have gradually reconciled myself to the fact, that I won't ever see U.S.A. again, and apart from losing touch with the Reich family and a few others, I don't care now. Also I fear that world affairs will settle the matter for me, for I can't see any hope in the clash of ideologies. When I read that N.Y. had a practice air-raid warning, I felt that there is little hope of peace now. Here if one talks of peace one is branded as a supporter of Stalin . . . "playing Russia's Game."

We are both feeling fit. We stick to our Box daily. I feel fine, full of energy, but so far my ear, nose, throat catarrh has not been helped. Have an idea that breathing is the best for it.

———— ◆•◆ ————

Summerhill School
Leiston, Suffolk

December 14, 1951

My dear Reich,

Cosmic S[uperimposition] I read at a sitting, understanding, *mirabile dictu* most of it, not the trigonometry part though. It is brilliant. You make Freud a parochial fellow, confined to his Vienna and his neurotic patients, but not touching the great fundamentals of existence. I wonder when you wrote *C.S.* Dates may discount my theory that, after you got rid of so much hate in *Little Man*, you took a great stride forward into realms beyond good and evil. Your absence of dogmatism is fine; indeed the whole theory of Superimposition just sounds TRUTH, great truth never thought of before. The book makes me sadder than ever that I won't see you this coming August. I shall not apply again for a Visa. Another man, a Dr. Head who was one of the penicillin pioneers, has been refused one seemingly on the grounds that he went to Prague to meet other penicillin experts. He isn't in sympathy with Communism either.

I am pessimistic about the future. I can't see how the drive to war can be stopped. If the West thinks to stop communism by war or if communism thinks it is its mission to overrun the world, war must come, and we in England will be killed. And if war comes I and other liberals will be shut up in prisons and my Zoë will have no one to help her. It is deeper than West versus East; forces unknown to us are working for hate and chaos.

So that, when I read your words of hope for humanity, I keep thinking of the awful world you are speaking to.

Met a man Mackenzie, a garage owner, who reads all your books. "Reich is 200 years ahead of his time," he said. I asked him how he discovered you and he said through my books. I make a good John the Baptist!

Many thanks for the presentation copies of *Oranur Experiment*.

1952

Summerhill School
Leiston, Suffolk

February 1, 1952

My dear Reich and Ilse,

Many thanks for the delightful parcel of sweets. They are indeed a wonderful luxury to us with our sweet rationing.

I want to make a sad proposal . . . that I stop corresponding with you. I have just been reading an American novel about the witch hunt, showing that the least small association with a person who is suspected of being semi-communist or pacifist is enough to get the haters of life busy hunting out the witches. The novel convinces me that I need not again bother to try to get a visa. I don't want to endanger you dear people in any way. The mere fact that you correspond with a man who is considered dangerous to the U.S.A. might, if known by letter opening or any other way, be enough to make you suspect too. I hate communism and am coming to hate and fear the methods used in fighting the damned creed, for they are not love nor charitable methods. They are arising in this country too.

I have just had a week up north in England, the first time in my life that a university (Durham and Newcastle) has ever asked me officially to talk to them in this country. I held a seminar of profs and lecturers and I think made them think. They had never heard of your work and I told them they must have your books in the university library.

I have been asked again to lecture in south Sweden and Denmark at Easter, taking in the smaller towns like Malmö, Göteborg, etc.

How are you both in health? How is that heart, Mister Reich? Are you taking things more easily? I make the guess that you damn well are not.

I have no special news. Just the old daily round. I am teaching maths all day and hating to do so, but I simply can't get teachers these days; the salary is too small.

Zoë is well and growing and learning fast.

Our love to you all and our misery at not ever being able to see you again.

--------◆◆◆--------

Orgonon
Rangeley, Maine

February 12, 1952

My dear Neill:

I have set out to write to you several times, but again and again I failed to get you properly. What in heaven's name do you mean that you are endangering us if you write to us? The fact that books which attack the government can be published in the U.S. is alone proof enough that you are on the wrong track. Will you permit me to be frank: I have the impression that you are spell-bound by fear of the red fascists' possible victory in England to such an extent that you run right into their arms. You speak at times, against your will, like a communist stooge, but you are certainly an anti-communist liberal rebel individualist. Why do you do this? I am certain that this is what has cost you your visa to the U.S. It is unnecessary, untrue and harmful. Already, the anarchist politicians in England have depicted you as a fellow-traveller. Did you see it? It would help if you would learn to distinguish between the democratically-minded communist and the clear type of red fascist. They have nothing to do with each other, except the common origin.

We here are fully busy with research and some public affairs. The Orgone Energy Accumulator slowly penetrates the American scene. But Oranur is a very dangerous venture. The outcome is quite uncertain.

Write again, Neill, and stop fearing the red fascists. We are doing all we can over here to cut them off.

--------◆◆◆--------

Summerhill School
Leiston, Suffolk

February 16, 1952

My dear Reich,

Too often do we get at cross purposes. I simply read *The Troubled Air*, by Irwin Shaw, of whom I had never heard. The novel read as if founded on facts, and in my innocence and ignorance I said to myself: "Even if it is only partly true, Reich has so many enemies among doctors, scientists, etc. that friendship with a suspect like myself just MIGHT happen to harm him." Dammit, man, it was quite an altruistic motive. You call me a liberal: true. Right, but these days liberalism is classed with communism, and not only today. In 1920 before I had ever thought about communism I became sponsor for a German girl who wanted to be naturalised. Months delay till she got it; the police inspector said: "The delay was because you got that Bolshy man Neill to sponsor you." In 1920! Simply because in one line, education, I was a rebel I was on the Home Office records as a Bolshy.

Maybe geography makes a difference between us about events. S'hill is surrounded by U.S.A. bomber bases, and U.S. planes manoeuvre over our heads daily. We know that if the necessary rearmament is to be the only factor we shall all have a most dreadful death. And I have never known how you stand to all this. I don't know if you think that the West can stop communism in Asia by war instead of by making people happy and free and well fed so that communism won't have any attractions.

You say I fear red Fascism in England. I don't now; the people are almost unanimously against communism of any kind. What I fear is a war that will probably end in chaos, a good breeding ground for the worst type of communism. I fear the death of free liberalism in the name of safety of the State. But the position of a pink person like me is a poor one, for I don't want red fascism or communism, and I don't want to see any other fascism grow up to counteract the red kind.

But all this dispute between us never gets anywhere. It just tires us and saddens us. It isn't our line . . .

Yes, it saddens, the more so because I sometimes fear we shall never meet again. I am not going to try again for a visa, and I see no signs that things will quieten down in my life time. I get so depressed to think that all my work for children will be lost for ever in a changed hateful world. But one sort of consolation at being banned from U.S.A. is that

U.S.A. has no use for me and my ideas. My book has sold very very badly over there.

You don't mention your health, and I take it you are back to normal again. Good.

Don't let us continue arguing about politics and policies. Let us write about important things. Why won't you tell me the sequel to the moving motor and Bill W[ashington]? Why did the experiment stop there? You were so optimistic then about using Orgone for power. What was the snag?

———◆•◆———

Summerhill School
Leiston, Suffolk

July 17, 1952

My dear Reich,

I know it was I who suggested we cease corresponding. I gave you my reasons, reasons you thought wrong ones, and they possibly were, for from this side one can't get a true picture of anything. But in the past silent months I have often felt very sad, asking myself questions . . . Is this the miserable end of our warm friendship? Should two men who matter so much to children be separated by the political plague? Am I cut off for ever from news of the Orgonon work? Worst question of all . . . Am I now in the class of Hal Wells, Saxe, Barakan?* But such a thought comes only in more pessimistic moments.

My only source of information now comes from *U.S. News and World Report* which you so generously send me, but it is a poor substitute for the word and the world of Reich, so far from that new world we dream about for our Peters and Zoës, the world of love in its widest sense.

Life and work go on as usual. And in early September I hope to have another lecture tour of Scandinavia. Since Raknes will be at your Conference I may not see him this time.

Zoë will soon be six. We seldom see her all day, for she is so busy with her own gang. I wish you could see her now, and that we could see Peter. Unfortunately we have no boys her age who were self-regulated. Ena has lost weight, is slim and like a young girl, but is very well and full of energy. She works all day long.

---

* Onetime admirers, all of whom had, in Reich's view, become "pestilent."

Marika Hellstrom is sending her daughter here as a pupil next term. No news of the Haymes's since they went to Uruguay. Difficult to keep in touch when people can't meet.

————◆◆◆————

Orgonon
Rangeley, Maine

July 24, 1952

My dear Neill:

It was nice to have your letter of July 17th. It had slipped my mind entirely that you had ever suggested to cease correspondence. On my part, there was no resentment or grudge against you whatsoever. To be blunt, I just believed that you are somewhat stuck in socialist ideas of the 1920's and refused to see that the world, apart from all politics and economics, has drawn forward, and that Marxism as well as Freudism are dead cats, even if they may still succeed in causing nuisance for a few centuries to come. Still, they are dead cats. The world most likely will be oriented in the future around an entirely new kind of human thinking, functional thinking, and the discovery of the cosmic energy which will have no likeness to what we knew in our early life.

I hope somebody will write to you about what happened here during the past year. I can only tell you that our buildings were knocked out of use in early spring, that for many months I did not sleep in one place for 2 nights in a row, that Ilse and Peter had to evacuate Orgonon and live in town, that all normal activities have been cancelled and that we are trying desperately to keep our boat on an even keel. All this will be extensively dealt with in future *Bulletin* publications. Somehow the universe has knocked us on the head for our daring impertinence in challenging its secrets.

Write again, Neill, it's nice to hear from you, though, due to my development during the past 5–6 years, the gap between us with regard to the view of man's existence has widened considerably. This, however, should in no way impede continuation of our old friendship. I still respect your zest and zeal, although I came to disagree very sharply with the premises for a happy human life in the future as they are set by old-time liberalism. The problem is the human plague.

There will be no convention this year, and probably none next year. My work has carried me onward to the problem of weather functions and rain making over deserts. I am planning a small expedition to the Southwestern parts of this continent.

———◆·◆———

[The following letter is from Ilse Ollendorff Reich]

Orgonon
Rangeley, Maine

July 26th, 1952

Dear Neill:

Reich said in his letter that he hopes somebody will write to you and tell you about what happened here, especially since the end of March. So I shall try to give you some idea of what is going on here. Around March 22nd, the Oranur at Orgonon became so strong that it not only made it impossible to stay in the Observatory and the Students' Laboratory and the Lower Cabin for any length of time (10 to 15 minutes maximum), but it reacted on all of us in a very deep way, bringing all the hidden fears and hatreds so much to the surface that they either had to explode and give way, at least partially, or made it impossible for some to continue working in this atmosphere. I myself was most strongly hit, and it is only during the past month that I am slowly emerging and that I have started functioning again and begun to realize the extent of what happened. The purely physical conditions of living are absolutely impossible, especially for Reich who has been living partly in a tent, partly in hotels in Farmington [some 40 miles away] and Rangeley and who, every once in a while, insists on going back to the Observatory and tries to live there again, with quite disastrous results once or twice, when he nearly died. He still hopes to regain the Observatory and the Lower Cabin, but the Students' Laboratory is still absolutely unusable for longer than ½ hour at a time. Reich is planning for the winter or late fall an expedition to the desert parts in the U.S. Southwest to study atmospheric conditions and the possibilities of cloud formation and rain making on the spot. Eva came back to Rangeley this spring and is working part-time assisting in Reich's experimental work. Tom Ross, too, is helping with the experimental

355   [1952]

work, besides continuing his care-taking of the property. In him, Oranur developed hidden scientific qualities, and he has become a keen observer of the phenomena. I think he and Peter are about the only ones who have not reacted at one time or another plaguey against Reich, blaming him for things that we had only ourselves to blame for. I can only hope that those of us who have come through so far will be able to continue to help Reich rather than to hamper him in his terrific task.

I have a vague plan of coming to England some time next year, but with things as they are, no definite plans for anything can be made at present. We do not even know where we shall live this fall and winter. I would very much like to see you and Ena, and especially Zoë again, and hope that the plan will materialize. My best to the three of you.

———◆•◆———

Summerhill School
Leiston, Suffolk

July 31, 1952
Dear Ilse,

Reich's letter made me very sad, and yours just makes me sadder and much puzzled. It looks as if all the doubts and fears and hates of humanity boil down, not to glandular action in the body, but to rays in the universe. A terrible idea, for the release of atomic rays in a war would apparently mean a clash between them and orgone rays and a reaction of all humanity similar to that among your small number at Orgonon. I try in vain to see the connection between the Orgonon reaction of emotion and the easy brutalising of humanity, in—say—the Gestapo, Franco Spain, Communistic hate, Negro lynching. There were no gamma or other rays in Hitlerland.

I hate to think of you all with your miseries and frustrations in tents and hotels. Reich may have left me behind in what he calls 1920 liberalism, but he hasn't left me behind as a sincere friend, one of the few, I fancy, who can speak to him frankly and be spoken to frankly by him, and if that damned McCarran visa *Verbot* [prohibition] did not stand in the way, I'd come over and slap him on the back and cry: "Buck up, Reich. Let's talk it all out over a rye and a packet of Chesterfields."

IS THERE going to be a final report on Oranur? Does it mean that in the end O. energy cannot protect against the death rays of an atomic bomb? Is Reich a Moses who never reaches the promised land, only points the way? I think of the motor that worked . . . and then went out of the picture. I think of the Oranur experiment with only Reich left and apparently no help or support or belief from the official atomic energy people. And the desert-rain project without official backing is to me just a wonder how it can be done.

I get more and more uncertain about that word plague. I see it in politics, in diplomacy but, maybe because of a blind spot, I can't see it prominent in Summerhill. Cattiness, bitchyness, especially in girls and women, but gradually mellowing in S'hill.

Reich says the future is in functional thinking . . . and I don't know what that means. I can only think concretely and never abstractly, hence any book on—say—philosophy with its absolutes etc. is always beyond my grasp.

I worry at the idea that Reich is standing alone, not having his family with him.

A play is running in London for ten days only. *Blue Armour*. An Accu on the stage, and a drama between the orthodox doctor cancer researcher and the Reich practitioner, who does not claim a cancer cure, only the right to try the unorthodox way. It is good drama, tense, not dangerous to Reich. The newspaper reviews have not been good; they mostly assume that the Accu and Reich were names invented by the dramatist. I talked to two press women after the show and both were most eager to hear about the "box."

[*The following letter is from Ilse Ollendorff Reich*]

Rangeley, Maine

September 22nd, 1952

Dear Neill:

I know that we owe you a letter for some time, but things are still rather hectic around, for both Oranur and Plague reasons, and we just did not get around to keeping up with the correspondence. Reich is still unable to stay for longer than 4–5 hours at the observatory, and every time he tries to sleep there, he comes near death. He has to go away from the Orgonon region, as far as 60 or 100 miles, before the body symptoms ease up. Peter and I finally moved to Rangeley, where I have rented a small, very nice house for the next 6–8 months and we may take it permanently. It is big enough for all three of us to sleep and for me to work there, but it is too small to house both Peter and his cronies and Reich and his work. So this leaves another problem to be solved, as long as the observatory is not back in its function.

I still hope to come over next year and to see all of you again. My love to you, Ena and Zoë.

◆◆◆

Summerhill School
Leiston, Suffolk

December 23, 1952
My dear Reich,

It was a joy to get your Xmas letter. From my side, I too wish you a prosperous New Year, the three of you.

And to hell with political disagreements! I haven't given politics a thought for months, but it is so difficult to stand alone.

For instance, they want me to add my name to a petition to the President to reprieve the Rosenbergs.* I want to ask them why they did not petition against the Prague executions† also. I don't like it; humanitarianism says, yes, save the R.s from death; self-interest says . . . And get my name associated with Communism again? I do want to stay clear of the whole damned lot.

I have written a new book,‡ lots about Zoë and self-regulation, but it won't be out till the fall, for my publishers say that the coronation [of Queen Elizabeth II] will swamp all papers and any book appearing in spring will go unnoticed. Much of the book damns Soviet education.

Lectured in Sweden and Denmark again last September, but didn't go to Norway.

Got a new book on Cancer, thinking to send it on to you as an Xmas present. His [the author's] point is that wrong feeding is the whole story added to artificial manures and poison sprays for plants and trees. So I didn't send it to you. Reminds me of a question some visitors put to me . . . "If Reich is right about cancer and sex, why has cancer in-

---

* Julius and Ethel Rosenberg, Americans convicted of espionage in 1951 and, after much controversy, executed in June 1953.

† Eleven old-guard Communists were hanged in a purge of those opposed to tightened Stalinist controls over Czechoslovakia.

‡ *The Free Child* (London; Herbert Jenkins, 1953). Neill sums up what he has learned in a lifetime of work with children and makes a strong plea for full freedom and self-regulation.

creased enormously since Victorian days when sex was much more repressed than it is today?" Luckily I was not called upon to answer.

With all this screening of air crews and ship crews the odds are against my visiting you until 1984. I have been invited to lecture in Japan but can't make up my mind. At 69 I find a lecture tour tiring, not the lecturing but meeting new people all the time. I have £800 book royalties in a Tokyo bank, frozen, but could use it to pay my fares. I'd have to fly for the voyage is 6 weeks.

Ena and Zoë fine. Z. is now 6 and nice to look at and clever and easy to live with. She now lives in the school while we are in the cottage. She brings the usual plague remarks from other kids . . . "Daddy, it is rude to say cock, isn't it?" Damned annoying all the same to find how strong a hold the other side gets on a kid. Ena and I counteract all the time of course.

I often wonder what is happening in Orgonon, picturing it in snow and in summer.

Well, again, old friend, the best of everything to you all. And our love to you all.

P.S. Xmas card from an old pupil in New York says: "Orgone therapy is getting very popular in New York."

1953

Summerhill School
Leiston, Suffolk

June 29, 1953

My dear Reich,

The Murder of Christ is easily the most important book I have ever read. I appreciate very much your gift to me, and if I have to "look a gift horse in the mouth" I must; you would hate me to do otherwise. Firstly however let me congratulate you on your English style. Short, sharp, clear sentences . . . they make me feel how much was lost by translation in the other books. You have tricks of style, good ones such as repetition, which makes the argument mount with great force. I couldn't tell, no one could tell that you were writing English as a foreign tongue . . . a considerable achievement.

So much for the frame. But the picture itself? I grasp it with my head, my eyes, my ears, but not with my guts. It shows me so clearly the gulf between the man of talent (me) and the man of universal insight (you). Do you recall our discussing the idea of my coming out to run a school in Orgonon? Your idea in 1948. I knew it could not be, knew that the danger would be that I became your disciple. Your Garden of Gethsemane, Oranur, was simply a *Wiederholung* [repetition] of the evils of discipleship. It troubles me. The seer, whether a Jesus, a Gandhi, a Reich, cannot contact even his nearest ones; he must stand alone in essence. Hence, I take it, your scorn of liberalism, a scorn I think rather unfair. The pioneers, even the minor ones . . . folks like myself, liberals in outlook, at least we do something that never would be done by the Churchills, Ikes, Trumans, McCarthys, Stalins etc. We are John the Baptist preparing the way for future messiahs. Doubting often where salvation is coming from.

I simply cannot give you an opinion on Jesus as a genital character. Your argument for sounds just truth, but I shall have to read the Gospels again to see if I can see the context.

I shall have to reread your book more than once; it is too vast to grasp in one reading. I kept looking for the answer to the question . . . Why, why, why? Why the hate of genital life? The origin doesn't matter much, but the perpetuation does. Theories of father jealousies, patriarchal states, suppression of sons simply don't click, and if they did one would still have to go behind them and ask why, why? Five minutes ago Zoë was undressing to go to bed. Our history master came in; she told him to shut his eyes till she had her nighty on. She didn't get that from us, but from other adults (domestics) and kids, but why the devil does she seek Barabbas? Why is anti-life so easy to be captured by a child? You end the book on a note of hope. Things are moving, you say, towards real freedom, towards Life. But so slowly, so prone to back-sliding. A hundred or two parents in Britain approve of auto-genital play; less in number of adolescent love. 40 millions spank and repress . . . and the 100 or two are liberals!

You have said that I have one foot in the past. True, stuck fast in the structural mud of Calvinism. I expect it is this that makes me fail to accept in full your so sharply drawn distinction between embracing and fucking. You accept no middle way, yet when I see our adolescents have sweet love affairs for years, tender, giving and taking, I hold that it does not matter what words are used. (By the way, they use neither embrace nor fuck; they "sleep together.") A rustic here never heard the word embrace, and if fuck is his only means of expression, his marital life can be orgastic. I sometimes wonder if you have too easily judged all mankind by the standards of all the neurotics you as therapist had to meet. No, Reich, I think you overvalue mere words.

Do you recall when I said that one day people would be bottling holy Orgone water if you didn't look out? Your book suggests to me that that danger may not be far off. Because you refuse to be a Führer you are alone in Rangeley; because you refuse to raise their Lazaruses and make the halt and blind sound, your multitudes will seek to touch the hem of your garment . . . modern version—sitting in the Box.

In reading your final chapters about the new leader I kept asking myself where the anti-life Paul was to come in, the guy who is to oust the leader. In my own little work I see the Pauls. They open schools and advertise "ordered freedom"; they have co-education with boys in one barracks and girls over the way and a housemother with a flaming sword on guard. They take your idea and suitably castrate it . . . and incidentally get big fees and prosper, while S'hill struggles to make ends meet. I can't do a thing about it, and if a little Jesus cannot, what can a big one do?

Recognition. How you hate that word. "Let them come to me: I won't go to them." You and I have fought about this since 1938. You always seem to take it that I want you to be recognised by the Einsteins, Bernals, Haldanes, wanting them to assure me that you really are right. But I think of recognition in another way; I think of reaching as many as possible. I'd publish your *Christ* at 20 cents and broadcast its message to the world. I say that the only way to preserve your message in its original form is to broadcast it to the four winds. S'hill has had influence over half the globe simply because I wrote about it.

Jesus and women. The criticism will be: What is your evidence? I am here taking the post of Devil's Advocate deliberately. The critic will say: Sure, he had women who adored him, but so did Rudolph Valentino, so does James Mason; any man who can hold an audience will have women who adore him. The religionists will of course argue that Martha's annoyance with him and Mary was due to the fact that they were talking while she had to wash up. Personally I think the best proof of his lovelife lies in the open anti-sex of all the other "saviours." Paul, Calvin, John Knox, the Popes, the bishops. None have associated with publicans and sinners. But proof there can never be.

Why did you leave out his disciples, his best-loved John, his stupid Peter? Because of your disgust at your own disciples? And I think you might have made more of the anti-life, hateful Paul, the man who seemed to go about trying to keep down the wrong kind of erection. Had his tirade against women anything to do with his views on Jesus and his women?

I can see that this great book of yours will make the enemy nod his little swelled head and say: "Now we have proof at last. We knew he was mad, but this is the final proof . . . he thinks he is Christ; he is a genital character and so he makes his Jesus one too." And of course you are a Jesus. A Jesus is a man who feels completely distressed at the misery of mankind. We others are common clay; we do our crosswords, play our bridge, our golf; we talk about nothings. I don't run my school because I think of the misery of millions of moulded and beaten children; I simply do it because I think it right and fascinating. I am too little to think of humanity by and large. Or rather to feel for humanity by and large. I will not risk my school life so that a couple can have a love life that is disapproved of by their parents, parents who would kill my school if they knew.

Query: why did Jesus lose his temper with the money-changers and the fig tree and yet mildly ask that his crucifiers be pardoned as men who knew not what they did?

But back to the book. It is too stunning to be grasped at once, in its way too simple. It makes me wonder if Communism will conquer the world and in the process kill religion with its mysticism. Then a new anti-life force without the sky mysticism will be easier to be conquered by a desperate humanity to whom Life will not be complicated as a mixture of earth and heaven. Meaning that I can't see universal salvation until utter misery has forced man to look at Life and Christ as you have seen them.

But again and again . . . Why the hell? Why anti-lifism? Don't laugh at a man of nearly 70's theory, for it is honest. Gluttony is not a sin, drinking is always pardonable, slander and gossip are tolerated evils but are not suppressed. Only love is. My new theory arising out of my almost sexless time of life: Sex is the only instinct that decays. We eat till we are 90 or more, we laugh, we gossip, like Sir Winston we have our brandy. Age does not touch any pleasure except the genital one, so that the old men, few of whom have had a full love life, feel bitter and frustrated, and they hate the young savagely for their ability to have genital pleasure, and hence the Oedipus suppressions. (I hasten to say that I have no conscious jealousy of the young myself.) How to tackle the something in us that compels us to murder Christ? In one reading I haven't got the answer from your book, and until we know that answer I can't see how we can love Life. True, our Peters and Zoës will have less murder lust and their children less still, at least we hope so.

Well, Reich, I have written too much. I had to because your book has stirred me up so much. It also troubled me. It is also the story of your tragedy, of a prophet who in essence feels as lonely as Jesus must have felt. You grew away from us all. Jesus was tempted to become a Führer, to save mankind. You were tempted to save mankind from atomic disaster. You both went off the rails. Poor old Jesus was not permitted to try again, but you are luckier, for you have tried again and tried in a better way than Oranur. This Christ book is of much more value than all your Oranur experiments, your equations, your *Bione*.*

You may reply that you came to Christ via *Bione* etc. True, my point is that if all your other works were lost this new book would contain them all in a way that the reading man would understand with his guts.

Take care of yourself. Ilse says you stopped smoking two years ago. I am always stopping and regressing to it in a very weak way. Bless you.

P.S. Oh, what is the secret of anti-life? Why are the animals the only ones to be tensionless, to be natural about their sex and excretal functions? Why are we the lower animals? Rats don't make bombs; cats don't wage war; cows do not moo plague murmurs. The secret has worried me for many years. If man had had a dog's periodical sex would he have been anti-life? Was there a woman rutting season a million years ago, and was man at peace then? The devil you say is the perverted god. That is true, undoubtedly true. But Adam and Eve must have been embracing long before the serpent entered the garden. The one optimistic feature seems to be that the secret of source can be by-passed. Peter the First and Zoë the First will not be completely free from that serpent fellow, but Peter and Zoë the Twentieth may be because freedom will wax with their generations. They will conquer the serpent in time, long long time, but will he die a natural death? Will he still walk the earth with cloven feet? I can't kill him in myself because I am fixed (*und fertig* [and finished] at 70). Can you kill him in yourself? Is he your Little Man all the time?

You have killed the gentle Jesus meek and mild . . . or have you? If today he were in East Berlin would he meet the Russian troops with a sword? No. His answer to Brady would have been: "Woman, go and sin no more." He could hate evil but not the men who did the evil . . . a vital difference. Indeed I suspect that he was more of a liberal than you allow!

And all this letter merely goes to show how much you have stirred me up. You've given me an indigestion, a bad one, for how can I digest your astounding Jesus when the Christian Jesus has been in my bowels since birth? And this genital character worries me a lot. You write as if the teeming millions have mostly been ungenital characters, that

---

* Reich underlined the passage and wrote one word, NO.

Christ was the only man in the regiment in step. But surely that isn't true. Have all the great men and women been handicapped by the plague? Goethe, Shakespeare, Rembrandt, Milton, Beethoven, Charlie Chaplin? Have a million carpenters since Christ only fucked?*

I hasten to say that all these questions are rhetorical; it would take a new book if you tried to answer them. They are simply the bubbles arising from the cauldron you made boil by your book. Letting off steam. Sorry.

———————————

Orgonon
Rangeley, Maine

July 8, 1953

My dear Neill:

I was deeply touched by the manner in which you responded to *The Murder of Christ*. It not only revealed the fact that you remained my good old friend, but it also showed me that any suspicion of disruption of a good relationship has been false. And this is as it should be, since factual medical and educational ties are incomparably more solid than any that political views have to offer.

The answer why natural genitality is being fought in such a murderous way is clearly given in all my clinical investigations, including *The Murder of Christ*. What remains unsolved is the problem how the armor came about thousands of years ago in one animal species only. I would like to assert my point of view that the emotional plague did not arise from any political necessity or from any economic compulsion. It is clear that the economic miseries are results rather than causes of the political plague. This means that Marxism as well as Freudism are dealing with merely secondary symptomatic appearances of social ills.

I wish I could have you here for a discussion. It may soothe your own feelings to know that the American government was hesitant last year to issue a passport to me. This, to most of my friends, was a sign of concern about my safety abroad, and not an expression of animosity. In the meantime, what I would call a false liberalism has suffered its greatest defeat in the uprisings of the people of Eastern Germany and the satellites against political horsethieves and petty crooks in power. [It] would be a sign of utter misjudgment, no matter what attitude any-

———

* Reich scrawled his answer in the margin: YES.

one is taking for or against Western politicians, to weigh two lynchings per year in the U.S.A., fought severely by the government, against the murderers who have slaughtered millions of people and who shut all doors of access to liberty. The Western statesmen have at least retained a sufficient amount of decency in handling human affairs which the little horsethieves in Russia never possessed. However you may feel about this attitude of mine, it cannot possibly ever shake our friendship.

Did you receive the 2nd volume, *People in Trouble*?* I personally am looking forward with excitement to settling down to the writing of the final volume *The Silent Observer*.†

Ilse has told me much about you, and I wish you all the best of luck and happiness.

———— ◆·◆ ————

Summerhill School
Leiston, Suffolk

July 11, 1953

My dear Reich,

Troubled People? You've said it, brother. You have made me one of them. My first reaction was entirely subjective. My new book *The Free Child* is in the press. After reading you I felt like withdrawing it. Your brilliant analysis, your manifold experience, your power of deep thinking made me feel that my book isn't worth a dime, feel that it is shallow and ignorant and full of wrong thinking. Then I went on to think that that is the real reason why you are a very lonely man, alone in Maine, not understood by all the Neills and Hamiltons. When I finished the book I laid it down and said to Ena: "And this is the man they call paranoic!"

You know me well enough to realise that I am no flatterer, and you will take it at its deep value when I say that I know of no one in the world who has seen so deeply as you have, no one who is so modestly

---

* *People in Trouble* (published in 1953 as Volume Two of *The Emotional Plague of Mankind, The Murder of Christ* being the first; reissued in a new translation in 1976). Reich's autobiographical account of the development of his sociological thinking (1927–37) and of his growing awareness of the essential part played by character structure in the social process.

† This was never completed.

sincere. There are thought-provoking sentences on every page. And I wonder why these two books you sent me have taught me more than all your other books; I think one explanation is that you are writing direct and not through translators, but another may be that you have increased your own clarity with the years.

The sadness of the book is that you apparently hardly ever found one person who was loyal and brave; too many denied when the cock crew . . . and I don't mean denied you, I mean the cause, the idea, the battle. I understand at last why you see in Communism the anti-life par excellence, but I think you were wrong in not realising that Hamilton and I could not possibly see the truth if only because we never went through your experiences with the Party. Leaving out your genius for the moment, you lived a most strenuous life in your work in Vienna and Berlin, a life that hammered you into a steel weapon against life aggression, while we . . . I can only speak for myself, I led a sheltered existence without external hate and aggression and betrayal. Life itself compelled you to wrench from it its secret, and I wonder now how you could have all your Neills and Wolfes around you without their boring you stiff . . . it must be because of your naivety which you so often mention in the book.

But, damn you, man, you spoil a chap's reading! I simply can't read any book on psychology or politics or what not after reading you. *Gott sei Dank* you haven't yet tackled fiction, so that I can still sit in the Box at night and read stories.

Thanks, Reich, for giving me two great stimulants to thought and realisation. My morning paper had an article last week . . . "Can Science Produce Life?" It quoted Bernal and dwelt on all the chemical trials to produce life. The writer was a man born in my native town, a "science correspondent." I longed to shove your books into his hands and say: Fool, leave the dead and learn from a man who deals with life and not chemicals. At the same time I knew it would be of no use. With children my virtue is patience but with Reich I am impatient . . . I want to see life accepted before I die, but of course I won't.

———— ◆•◆ ————

Orgonon
Rangeley, Maine

July 17, 1953

My dear Neill:

I just received your good letter of July 11th, reflecting on *People in Trouble*. It was a very good letter, thank you. However, you overlooked the fact that the second volume was not written by me in English personally, but was a translation done by several non-professional student translators. All the best.

———◆◆◆———

Summerhill School
Leiston, Suffolk

August 10, 1953

My dear Reich,

Rainmaking article good. *Aber* [But] it will be a comedy if you attain "public" fame as a getter of rain instead of a getter of public health (pro-life). I can imagine a National Biography (published 1984) saying: Reich, Wilhelm, famous scientist, discoverer of rain-making process. It is a pity that this great man wasted his time and energy in advocating views on sex that were of no importance.

Just been to Oxford University lecturing to a Teachers Conference. How dull they were, how divorced from all that matters.

———◆◆◆———

Orgonon
Rangeley, Maine

August 21, 1953

My dear Neill:

Just got your good letter of August 10th. Don't worry: I won't go down in history as the rain-maker, since I'm careful to maintain my already famous status as the discoverer of the cosmic Orgone Energy, the Life Energy. It is really the Oranur Experiment which puts the foundation under my whole scientific and personal existence.

Why don't you forget the Freudians for a while? They did their job, and they were an important link in the chain of great events which lead from the past into the future.

I hope you are well. Hoppe and Raknes are here, and we are conducting important discussions. I shall send you soon a copy of the Bibliography which will prove to you, who plays such a great role as my public conscience, that the discovery of the Life Energy is turning over human thinking in all branches of living and can therefore not be "recognized" by anyone in the usual way. It just simply bulldozes its way through.

———— ◆•◆ ————

Summerhill School
Leiston, Suffolk

October 5, 1953

My dear Reich,

If enclosed review of *Flying Saucers* is of a book that you don't know, I'll send a copy to you. Hoppe says he thinks you will be interested to see it. He has been here this weekend and it was a joy to have him. For three days we talked nothing but Oranur, so much so that it made me very sad to think that all this wonderful experiment is being made and I can never be allowed to come and see it . . . and you. The rain-making sounds fantastic, like a Wellsian phantasy story of the First Men in the Moon type; it brings conjectures of a new world with food growing in the Sahara. I never heard of DOR [Deadly ORgone] until Hoppe used the term, the T bacillus of the cosmos. But won't it take a lot of proving to show it is caused by the atomic explosions? I read they had 8 inches of snow in Cape Colony, an unknown event. If it is due to DOR how can one prove it?

I am second-reading the *Christ*. It is too full of ideas even for a second reading to satisfy. It isn't a matter of being for or against the book; the argument just feels true, unanswerable, final. And yet I am still bewildered about first causes . . . why my dog shows its genitals and I cannot show mine, why the human parent moulds and the animal doesn't. I simply can't *see* the something that has to turn God into the Devil. Hoppe says I should reread your *Superimposition* book, but it has been "borrowed" like the Oranur booklet and all my copies of my own books.

I feel much out of touch with you. I haven't seen a *Bulletin* for, oh, two years.

You seem to admire Eisenhower with his mild look. I don't have any opinion of him, only that he might have spared the Rosenbergs from death after three years of suspense. I was asked to sign a petition on their behalf by a Communist-inspired body. I replied: "I shall gladly sign the petition if you will at the same time ask me to sign a letter of protest against the Prague executions. Humanitarianism is indivisible." I got no reply. Must all sides kill?

I shall be 70 on the 17th of this month. My old pupils are having a party for me in London, but I'd rather be 30 and miss any party.

P.S. *Mein Gott*, Reich, how I miss seeing you. Meeting people who do see you, like Hoppe, brings back so many memories of great times in Orgonon. Damn the McCarthys and Malenkovs of life.

———◆◆———

Orgonon
Rangeley, Maine

October 16, 1953

My dear Neill:

I sent you a telegram today to congratulate you on your 70th birthday. I truly hope that you enjoyed your anniversary. Many happy returns. I also sent you some bound volumes of the *Bulletin* for your personal use and nobody else's.

Your letter of October 5th was a great pleasure. You are quite right: There are serious prospects of making deserts fruitful again. However, there is also the opposite process of fruitful land being turned into deserts because of evil men.

The problem about the first causes of man's degeneration has been tackled both in the *Einbruch der Sexualmoral** and *Cosmic Superimposition*. The problem is not fully solved.

I liked very much your answer to the Red Fascists.

Write again soon. All the best to you and yours.

———◆◆———

---

* *The Invasion of Compulsory Sex-Morality.*

Summerhill School
Leiston, Suffolk

November 13, 1953

My dear Reich,

Many thanks for your valuable birthday gift of 4 volumes. It is a delight to sit and read all the latest about your work. *Aber* [But] those equations are far beyond me, and will always be.

At last the plague has reached me. A few weeks ago an Australian journalist came to interview me. He seemed to me to be a scholar and a gentleman, talked as any modern progressive would talk. Like a fool I talked freely to him off the record. Now a poisonous article appears in a Sydney *Sunday Telegraph*, headline: "School where children have a full sex life," a smear all the way. My lawyers have written demanding withdrawal on the ground that it can make me lose pupils. What I fear is that one of our own Sunday papers will print it and then the fat is in the fire. If I take it to court a clever counsel will ruin my work, for any judge would be against love for youth, any jury too. If an M.P. were to ask a question in the House my school would be closed. I am indeed in a hole. If I stand up as I should do and proclaim bravely that adolescents have had a love life in S'hill, I lose my work with all the small children. If I pretend that nothing has taken place I am a coward and a swindler.

In any case I can't afford to issue a writ against a rich newspaper; I have not enough money to run my school, and as the paper would almost certainly win I'd be left with an enormous debt. I am taking the blackest view in case the article is published here too. And how I wish my good friend Reich were here to advise me and support me.

My book is going well. Good reviews so far, and the radio book review in Woman's Hour told all mothers to read it, but of the few millions who listened I doubt if many will read it.

I go to Scandinavia in January on a lecture tour, mainly to make some money, for our numbers have dropped from 60 to 42; people simply haven't the money for private schools today.

Yours, rather frightened and depressed.

1954

Summerhill School
Leiston, Suffolk

January 9, 1954
My dear Reich,

Thanks for your New Year wishes which I gladly reciprocate. I am just off to Norway and Sweden to lecture again. In Sweden I have five lectures on consecutive nights . . . too much for an old man like me, but I must earn money somehow. I return via Copenhagen.

Zoë has had whooping cough; Peter I hear has had appendicitis. Why should they? I make the guess that Trobrianders of their age wouldn't. We know so little. How much is in heredity? How much in our canned feeding and doubtful candies? I am ruling out for the moment genital frustration, for I see no sign of it in Zoë and don't suppose there is much in Peter, although Ilse did tell me that his girl friend wouldn't let him have genital play. Even so why the appendix and not the bladder or penis or what not? Or is the appendix the aftermath of Oranur?

A man called Masserman has an article on P.A. [psychoanalysis] & Biodynamics. His up-to-dateness is shown, or rather his lack of it, by this sentence: ". . . the success of a course of p.a. therapy is the re-establishment of a capacity for sexual orgasm. Short of the *reductio ad absurdum* to which, for instance, Reich has carried this concept, there is of course a measure of truth in it . . ." They won't accept you but they have a compulsion to bring you in even if only to slay you.

What do you think of Ritter's journal?* I have no special opinion

---

* *Orgonomic Functionalism*, published in England.

371

about it yet, only that I didn't see anything dangerous or misleading in it. If he sticks to concrete stories of self-regulation okay, but will he?

———————◆•◆———————

Orgonon
Rangeley, Maine

February 1, 1954

My dear Neill:

I wish to acknowledge briefly your letter of January 9th. Are you still worried about my acceptance by the good world?

I would like to grant every healthy child of the future the right to have a fit, whooping cough, an occasional accident and similar innocent neurotic happenings. By all means, don't have them perfect! What counts is the foundation and not the surface.

I am preparing beautiful material for a book which will be called "Babies' Peace Offensive U.S.A."* Could not do it in Moscow.

I was very happy to have had news from you, please write again.

———————◆•◆———————

Summerhill School
Leiston, Suffolk

February 10, 1954

My dear Reich,

Just back after four weeks lecturing, once in Oslo, 7 times in Sweden, twice in Denmark. Big audiences and good money . . . brought home £150 after paying fares etc. Helps to keep the school off the red in the bank.

Judith gave a party and to my delight, Sigurd Hoel came and was, as he always was, charming. Nic was there and got aggressive after some drinks (as she always does, although she is a very nice person). Raknes and Frau were there and next night he gave a birthday party with Nic and Henrik Sorenson, an old acquaintance of mine to whom I can't speak, for he knows only French and I don't. Judith was in bed with something wrong in her back, but managed to get up for her party. Lovely person Judith.

---

* This project was never completed.

No one in Sweden seems to know much about you, but in Copenhagen several said to me: "If you mention Reich in your lectures some folks will be wild." I did mention you a few times but couldn't see any visible reaction.

No one in Oslo had any news of Elsa Lindenberg. Ola Raknes is a tower of strength, appreciated by everyone, a slow man but a sure one.

Met a lot of Communists in Denmark among the intelligentsia, but they are not so narrow as the British ones; most of them will agree to bad things in Russia, but of course they all think the economic solution the main one. I asked them why Margaret Mead found the Arapesh tribe in New Guinea loving children and growing up peaceful, while 100 miles away another tribe hates kids and their sex act means blood and tearing? I told them both tribes had the same economic basis . . . living on yams and fish. No answer. Some had been to see Russian schools and they rhapsodised about what they did for children. I asked: Do they allow adolescents to have a sex life? They didn't know but thought it was very unlikely.

Several people here keep asking me to go to see Russian schools for myself, saying that the U.S.S.R. would gladly give me all expenses. Without knowing the language I could not get a thing firsthand from teachers or kids, and of course if I went it would mean that I could never again come to U.S.A. . . . not a likely event in any case. I'd go only if the U.S.S.R. govt. invited me to come and talk to their teachers about free children, and they are not likely to do that.

What do you think of Ritter's magazine? Raknes doesn't think much of it. I must read it carefully myself.

----◆•◆----

[*Neill's letter of April 17, to which the following is an answer, is missing. An injunction which included prohibition of the rental or sale of accumulators had been issued on March 19, 1954.*]

Orgonon
Rangeley, Maine

April 22, 1954

My dear Neill:

     Your letter of April 17th arrived yesterday morning. I share your worries about me, but in a certain way I am glad it happened the way it did. It freed me, with one stroke, of a lot of unpaid administrative work which I have done for years for the Foundation. But it also has cut off an income of about $3,000 per month, an amount badly needed to keep the work going at Orgonon.

I assume you have understood why I did not go to court. In this manner, I at least maintained my honor and intellectual independence. I am not standing convicted. I did not concede any authority to anyone who had nothing to do with the primordial Orgone Energy. You are, of course, free to write whatever and wherever you please. You would not damage me.

The injunction is being contested as unconstitutional and on many other grounds. I do not think it will stand. If it stands, it has only killed a little branch of the total body of my work. I am proceeding with cosmic engineering, desert work and the cloudbuster which has been televised both in Maine and in Arizona. I am not going under yet. One does not do such big things as I do without the risk of breaking one's neck, and should I ever break my neck, it would make quite a bit of noise.

I am sorry not to be able to write too much about things, mainly because I hate touching this stuff. The physicians in New York are going to fight in court, and there are also powerful friends around who are fighting the evil in chemistry and medicine on my side, though I scarcely know who they are.

———— ◆•◆ ————

Summerhill School
Leiston, Suffolk

July 13, 1954

My dear Reich:

Glad to hear from you again. We are all waiting for news of your work and its future, but it seems to be a case of our waiting all the time, waiting to see if Indo China is to be the starting point of our universal extermination, waiting to see if Ike will show himself a strong man, if Malenkov is any real improvement on Stalin, if McCarthy is finished or not. The world sure is a melting pot at the moment. The only big question is: Will we destroy ourselves with H- and Cobalt bombs BEFORE Reich's peaceful orgones are accepted? You ask what has happened to Churchill? I don't know. His position must be most difficult, for he knows that in a war Britain would be wiped out while parts of U.S.A. and Russia and much of China would survive. I think that the differences between us and U.S.A. arise from the fact that we are much more vulnerable.

Ritter is making headway with his journal which has got an unexpected push forward owing to the legal verdict against you over there. He says that W. Steig has written him about getting subscribers to his O.F. in U.S.A., but if your own work is forbidden there, can he import matter dealing with O. energy.

I wish I could share your optimism about the way one can fight bad government. On this side of the Atlantic I think freedom is more free; no judge can kill a book unless it is obscene. But I still don't know what is behind your case, why it suddenly came to a point. I recall your sitting with a Food & Drug guy for two hours in the lab in 1948 but nothing happened then. It is all so mysterious. I keep wondering what you are doing, how you can work, if your personal life is free.

Ena isn't well. She is difficult to advise, hates all medicines and of course works far too hard. I try to get her to use the Box regularly but she uses it one day and then says she hasn't time the next. I fear for Zoë, for I can't live much more than ten years and I want Ena to live and care for her after I go on. Zoë is still a darling. I begin to feel my age; have to force myself to do what I used to do easily . . . tell kids a story, rehearse a play, dig a plot of ground, meet new people. I have nothing new to give the school and the world. Genius and energy go together; I have proved clearly that I'm no genius. A lazy devil.

I can't overcome an unscientific doubt I had long had. A G[eiger] Counter reacts to death rays from atoms or radium; it reacts to O. energy, hence my doubt which can be expressed as a question: Is there any other known good energy that reacts to a G[eiger]–M[üller] Counter also? I don't want your answer; too much to do without dealing with my ignorance. But I'd like to know how all the orthodox scientists explain the fact that the box does have a Geiger reaction; I mean how does it fit into their scornful dismissal of OR as phantasy and bunk? One bright young scientist when he read of your G–M reaction said: "Obviously the G. Counter was a faulty one." Good old science!

Send us latest photos of yourselves and Peter. We do feel so much out of touch these days.

———————— ◆•◆ ————————

Orgonon
Rangeley, Maine

July 17, 1954

My dear Neill:

Your letter just came—a great pleasure, indeed . . . You ask, will the Orgone come through before the mechanists and chemists—thus I understood it—will blast the world asunder . . . I do not know. But I *do* know that this mechano-mystical world is dead already, having tortured itself and billions of children and men and women to death at an accelerated pace. I am still standing outside this holocaust . . . quite an accomplishment you will admit. Nobody has succeeded in confusing me yet. It's hard, I admit, to keep up one's natural standing in this mire of blood and stupidity perpetrated upon a gullible world by the liberators. I was glad you wrote [asking] whether Eisenhower has taken control. He seemed quite dazed for a while, a few months ago, because of the newness to him of the political hoodlumism rampant here, but he caught on quickly. He is much firmer now. Your question regarding the present moment of the eruption of the plague against me is good . . . I found myself suddenly in the middle of the American fight for truth and justice against a great heap of political and other crooks. It is dangerous but most thrilling. I cannot tell more at present, only so much: My Orgone is fighting bravely, in many places, in the hands of people unknown to me. The FDA did not come through till now. The judge had signed the injunction unread. We are expecting the result of the interference* any day now. But no matter what the outcome may be. Also my own world of yesterday is dead. And I know it. Nothing remains standing except my good, valid facts and my theory based on these facts, i.e., the true nature of the living. Whether it will govern the public in a few months or in one hundred years I do not know. The sea of emotional plague is deep indeed. And I remain rather detached. I am having my first vacation in ten years. I am just enjoying Orgonon and Peter and Eva and looking into the sky with the new knowledge in my head.

They have cleared out 114 political hoodlums from the very department of government from which emerged the conspiracy against my discovery. The fight is on everywhere, hard and relentless. No quarter

---

* Some fifteen physicians trained by Reich tried to intervene in the case, in the hopes of overturning the injunction.

is given or expected. It is a new world against an old and dead world. Eisenhower spoke publicly of the American revolution. I called it, months ago, the second American Revolution.

Write again Neill. Now I have more leisure and heart to read and write letters.

———◆•◆———

Summerhill School
Leiston, Suffolk

August 9, 1954

My dear Reich,

Poor old Wolfe.* I think of him as a happy schoolboy out with his motor boat, then in the evening a miserable fellow drinking to escape life. I have often thought of him in connection of your saying that no therapy in the world can alter fundamentally early character formation. Orgone could not fight Swiss Calvinism because it started later. But still it had much success, for he did fine work. Ena and I liked the guy a lot; my own Scots Calvinism was perhaps a help in my understanding him. I don't suppose Gladys helped but no woman can help a sick man.

Ritter. I can't do a thing, can't even hint that you are critical of him. He of course is cashing in on the U.S.A. ban . . . "I can now publish all Reich's articles, etc." I don't know what you can do about it unless you simply tell him harshly that you don't want to be interpreted by anyone. But you and I are always handicapped by seeing the other guy's point of view; it would be a little cruel to stop his evident enthusiasm. But I fancy anything he writes about your deeper work will be inadequate. I know how I'd feel if some young fellow started to explain my Summerhill. I have also to think of the plague angle, have to ask myself: Neill, aren't you envious of Ritter? Half my age, understands more about Orgone science than I do, is rather patronising to me, half sneering at my last book as saying nothing new. You say his stuff is "on the verge to drown in Little Man Socialism." I see the Little Man part, but not the socialism, but then I confess I haven't read his journal so thoroughly as I might have done.

Communism. Ex S'hill teacher on deputation to Rumania, party

---

* Neill had just heard of Wolfe's death.

member of course. Said: "I tried to sell S'hill to teachers there, but they knew your books and said: Neill's methods are all right for delinquents but not for normal children." So now we know, eh? I see U.S.S.R. has reintroduced co-education, but it means only attending same classes; it is only a HEAD co-education.

Off to lecture to Cambridge University. Did Oxford last summer. Query: Am I out of date or have the universities progressed? The Conference programme is called "Freedom in School and Society," but I don't see sex freedom in the syllabus.

Tell me how you are, how the work is going—or stopped—how you can live without an income. Not curiosity on my part; concern rather. Is the appeal going through? If so, what chances of success? And what progress in rain-making? Did the authorities *probieren* [try] it? I wish Raknes had stopped here on his way home to tell me the latest.

Oh, I wish I could talk with you. A hundred questions strike me . . . what is the observatory doing? When will Orgonon be clear of danger rays? Damn all political things that prevent our meeting again. East and West both show the same futility. New Zealand has just built her biggest school, costing £200,000. Over the front door are the words: The Motto of this School is Silence. And a magistrate here has ordered a book seller to burn *The Decameron* as obscene . . . Not bad after a run of 500 years.

———◆◆◆———

Orgonon
Rangeley, Maine

August 29, 1954

My dear Neill:

     I am late in answering your letter of August 9th. Here is a brief summary of our situation:

We have won the case against the FDA factually.* There is still the legal angle of lifting the injunction. No books will be burned. We have strong support from government quarters in matters of drought combat. An expedition of 4 men, including myself, is preparing to go to the S.W. Arizona and California to do serious desert work. We have

---

* Reich believed that he had blocked the FDA by not appearing in court.

broken the drought in the East on several occasions. Moise,* our operator, and Dr. Silvert† did it with my advice. I shall have the "conspiracy" material, the background of the FDA–EP [Emotional Plague] case—which is dead—sent to you.

Ilse is gone for good. She was too afraid of Oranur for years. Since she permitted herself to *know* it also, things went much better with us, and our separation was felt as the proper and rational solution. I am alone. Peter is with Eva and Bill Moise in Hancock, Maine.

The Ritter case has developed unpleasantly lately. He claims now to establish the TRUE Functionalism. I am a kind of precursor. He is ending in utter confusion. If there is any kernel of science in him, he will get out of the tangle. Otherwise he will submerge in obscurity or insanity. He has no right to publish any of my works without my permission.

Wolfe's death has left questions open which require answers. He died from his basic decency which objected to his inability to work continually. Though I had no contact with him for several years, I was deeply saddened.

Neill, I am far out in space as it were. Are you oriented about the new menace from outer space? If not I shall send you some authentical literature.

My ship is flying high and fast. Most people have gone, looking on from the platform of their respective stations in life. This keeps me strong though not too happy. My work is very productive, and I hope to get some opportunity to talk things over with you.

It is always a great thing to have a letter from you, therefore, keep writing please.

In spite of the world being on fire, we are moving . . .

———— ◆•◆ ————

---

* William Moise, Reich's son-in-law.
† Michael Silvert, M.D., a young associate and student of Reich's.

Summerhill School
Leiston, Suffolk

September 15, 1954

My dear Reich,

Someone sent me the *N.Y. Post* [article].* What interested me is the FDA "tests." Is there any proof of their attempts? Any written details of what they tried? Any guarantee that they constructed their Box in the right way? The answer of course to all these questions is no. I was surprised that you gave the guy an interview at all, but I see it was better so, for he might have written much damaging stuff in revenge. He reads as if he were trying to be fair, an unusual thing in journalism.

That article in the *Post* fails to see why Freud was accepted comparatively soon while you weren't. Freud didn't go deep enough to touch humanity on the raw. No, Reich, you'll be universally acknowledged when all kids have soft stomachs . . . and by that time you and I will be a long time dead. Sad thought though.

Your last letter was joyful for me to read.

What of Peter? When Ilse asked about a job in S'hill I asked her if it were good to be 3000 miles from her son. I told her that the saddest cases of children of separated parents in S'hill are those who don't see both father and mother in vacations. Do you agree? Eva may be a *Mutterersatz aber* [mother substitute but] any *Ersatz* [substitute] isn't good enough.

Letter after almost a year's silence from Mrs Haymes. She said she had been in U.S.A. and had seen you . . . and I was a bit jealous of her luck there.

That article talks as if the Observatory is now livable in. I hope so. Do send me any newspaper cuttings about any results with your rain-making. And can't you get McCarthy to investigate the FDA?

———————◆•◆———————

---

* "The Strange Case of Wilhelm Reich," September 5, 1954, by Irwin Ross.

Summerhill School
Leiston, Suffolk

October 16, 1954

My dear Reich,

For the past weeks I have been concerned with the vexed question of health, vexed because I cannot find any solution. My orthodox medical friends say I have caught a bug. But I can't believe the bug theory. What troubles me is that no one seems to know the root cause of disease. So many think they hold the secret of health. Naturopaths with their diet and cold compresses, doctors with their drugs and injections, all sorts of cranks who think that higher thought will give health. The young doctors here all talk of psychosomatic. Then a Churchill full of energy who has eaten unbalanced diets, smoked too much, drunk too much brandy is a fit man, while many a vegetarian crank is not.

I have slowly come to the conclusion that the Box isn't suited for this climate. Raknes's shooter in Oslo gave me hot waves; mine here, with more layers, does not. I say it is the dampness ever in our atmosphere. I can sit ¾ hour in mine and not get too hot. It doesn't help me to think that R. is more fully charged with orgone energy.

I am 71 tomorrow and I take it that from now to the end health and some illness will take more of my attention. I hear that Ilse is at the Hamiltons'. Only other news is that Dianetics is becoming a popular craze in London. The tenth rate always succeeds.

I fancy that the Democrats will get a majority next month and if they do there just *might* be an easing of the visa situation, but the hope is only one in a million. I wish I could think that east and west could live in peace; I can't and fear that next year the Chinese will attempt to take Formosa, U.S.A. will support Formosa and the 3rd war will begin.

Danish teacher back from visit to U.S.S.R. says to me: "The Kindergartens are all Pavlovised. A baby must never be alone because he would become an individual, so that teachers see that every child feels and thinks as the group."

Sorry to send so dull a letter.

P.S. Still no word of the federal verdict being annulled.

———◆◆———

Summerhill School
Leiston, Suffolk

December 7, 1954

My dear Reich,

I look every day in the papers to see a headline: REICH REIGNS IN ARIZONA DESERT . . . in vain. Reminds me that the government here has issued a booklet on rain-making; I'll get one and send it to you, but there won't be anything in it that you don't know already . . . and dismiss as useless.

Steig sent me a circular with extracts from a speech of yours. It gave me a great shock to find you believing in visits from other planets. No, I said, it can't be true; Reich is a scientist and unless he *sees* a flying saucer he won't accept it as a reality. I can't understand it. This CORE men idea.* Too deep for me. He mentions a new publication called *CORE*.† I haven't seen it.

I take it that Orgonon is closed up now. God, Reich, you have had a hell of a life of struggle and work and opposition. It looks as if every disaster was simply a reason for your going on to something else.

No special news from here. Zoë was 8 the other day; she is tall and bonny and quite clever. She has little interest in grown-ups (including me) but enters fully into the group life of her pals. She has just come to me reciting a very obscene rhyme a boy taught her, and last week said she liked hymns and would like to go to church. Just shows how far a journey it is to a self-regulation world.

You wrote me to worry less and live more. I don't worry much really, but at 71 I find it difficult to live more. No, Reich, I am just a getting-old man with simple interests now—chopping wood, golfing, listening to my super radiogram LP records (mostly Chopin and Wagner and Schumann). Lecturing sometimes to try to make a penny or two. Worst of all being lonely. My long separation from your dynamic personality has been a long sadness for me. I literally have no one to talk to about anything of value. Most visitors have nothing to offer me, just conventional gossip about cars or cinemas. Mrs. Haymes is coming over in May and she will bring a little of the inspiring breeze that blew around Sheffield and Rangeley.

---

* Cosmic orgone energy, Reich believed, was the power used by the spacemen in UFO's.

† Cosmic ORgone Engineering. The successor journal to the *Orgone Energy Bulletin*.

I begin to tire of the expression self-regulation; it is now getting to be an organised affair and will soon lose most of its life therefore.

School still always near bankruptcy, only 42 pupils instead of the 60 necessary to make it pay. I guess you also are feeling the financial strain after losing so much of your income from books and boxes . . . and a girl of 18 gave a party the other day in a London hotel. It cost £10,000. Her father made a fortune in Malaya. Nice advertisement for the communist papers of course.

Well, Reich, bless you, I think of you often, especially when I am in trouble and want to talk to someone who will listen. Damn the man, why must he always be thousands of miles away from me?

1955

Summerhill School
Leiston, Suffolk

January 15, 1955

My dear Reich,

Thanks for *CORE*. I said to myself: If I had never heard of Reich and had read *CORE* for the first time I would have concluded that the author was either *meschugge* [crazy] or the greatest discoverer in centuries. Since I know you aren't *meschugge* I have to accept the alternative. I can't follow you . . . is there anyone who can, barring Raknes and Hoppe? You see there are so many contradictions. You hold that the internal desert will prevent humanity from accepting a cure for the external desert. But is that true really? Suppose you are able to turn a chunk of Arizona desert into fertile land, will American farmers refuse to use that land because of their inside deserts? Were the two fruit farmers in Maine free from the internal desert when you got rain for them? I incline to think that the internal desert does keep scientists from accepting Orgones, the Bernals, Einsteins. They have too much to lose, but the ordinary business man thinks of gain not loss. The farmers who sow by the moon and Rudolf Steiner* are convinced that they get better products.

Emotionally I can't see any proof that space ships have come to this planet. Do they land and then go away at once? Otherwise there would be some witnesses who took photos or spoke with the guys or at least described them. I am not thinking of scientists; I am wondering why

---

* German occultist, philosopher; founder of anthroposophy.

our sensational press has not got hold of ordinary citizen witnesses and made a stunt out of their reports. The press could not resist so wonderful a chance of a scoop. The editor of a paper like *Sunday Pictorial* would publish a photo of potatoes growing on his mother's grave. You can't tell me that if you made it rain in the Sahara the whole world press (and people) would ignore it because of inner plague. It is a different matter in the case of health. The inner plague would make a thousand doctors reject an orgone cure for cancer; millions of parents reject self-regulation for the same reason. What I am trying to say is that if self-regulation paid in dividends and profits it would be advertised and exploited. I'm not being cynical, only realistic in a material age. If you can make Arizona sand into cultivated fields the Americans will bypass their inner deserts . . . and of course say: It wasn't Reich really; it was the H-bomb.

Incidentally, how you get the money to build rainmakers and publish *CORE* I can't guess. This is pure envy; I can't get pupils, I can't get staff and life is one long worry about the future. Added to that I see fascism growing and freedom for children being hated. Caning in our schools gets worse; lack of discipline is blamed by judges for the cosh [blackjack] boys who rob with violence. Makes me feel depressed, makes me feel that most of my work has been in vain. They have debates in press and radio here about education. No one ever asked me to take part. I haven't your pioneering patience, Reich. You are content to see your work triumph in a hundred years (Or are you?), while I want to see mine triumph in my lifetime. Only 40 pupils now out of a few million British kids.

However, there are compensations. Zoë is a delight and I am not ill in body.

Just heard from the N.Y. publishers who published my *Problem Family* in '48. They had to sell out 3500 as "remainder" stock because U.S.A. didn't buy the book. Odd though that the Japanese translation sold so well that I have £800 in a Tokyo bank as royalties, frozen, no chance of my ever touching it unless I go to Japan to spend it on wine, women and song . . . rather late at 71 for geisha girls I fear.

A depressing letter. Partly the awful weather. By the way I see no sign of blackening of stones or queer cloud formations here,* but then I wouldn't know one cloud from another. Piece in today's paper says the

---

* Manifestations of DOR (Deadly Orgone) in the atmosphere.

Coliseum in Rome is in danger of falling owing to crumbling of the upper stones. And Hoppe said Westminster Abbey stone was peeling off.

Finally . . . damn you, why are you so far away?

———◆·◆———

Summerhill School
Leiston, Suffolk

February 5, 1955

My dear Reich,

Ritter came to see me yesterday. He is much disturbed by your letter to him. I told him the difficulty in explaining an idea when the originator was alive and at work and advised him to change the name of the journal so that he did not appear to be interpreting you officially. He doesn't want to do that. If it rested with me I'd say to him carry on, hoping and thinking the good he does will much outweigh any wrong interpreting.

To me the matter seems *klein* [small] today when it looks as if the Formosa affair will end us all over here. Bertrand Russell said yesterday that if the Formosa issue is not settled humanity may be destroyed by the end of this year. I see no way out for China or U.S.A.; I see no way out at all for us if world war comes. The biggest U.S.A. atom bomb airbase is seven miles from Summerhill; we'd be the first target, but in any case radiation will destroy life on this island. I think that the fundamental ground is that U.S.A. especially will rather see humanity destroyed than have universal communism. I fear your plague is too strong on both sides to save the situation. Long ago you said that War III would come and I didn't want to believe you. I miserably think you prophesied rightly.

Sorry to write so cheerless a letter. Your spacemen may be benign but the blighters are too late to save a very unbenign world.

P.S. Do try to give Ritter a little hope for his enterprise.

———◆·◆———

[1955]

Summerhill School
Leiston, Suffolk

[undated]

My dear Reich,
Ritter is upset about your letter to him. I have tried to explain how it is, that he didn't go through therapy, that you must wonder how qualified he is to interpret OF [Orgonomic Functionalism]. I have advised him to change the name to Self-Regn. [Regulation] and not claim to be an interpreter of OF.

He is a well-meaning guy but how tactless! Latest number says Zoë won't put on warm clothes because she has met with authority or life-negative people. He must realise that to readers that means me and Ena. *Kann sein, aber so etwas sagt man nicht* [Perhaps so, but one doesn't say such things].

Much worried about Formosa and the danger of a world war. Nearest U.S.A. airbase is seven miles away, so that . . . well, I don't want my Zoë to die for Chiang Kai-shek or Malenkov or Ike or Churchill or anyone else. I sadly think that the fighting forces will destroy us all . . . Big question: Is conscious knowledge that atom war means total destruction enough to prevent war? To hell with nationalism of all kinds, say I.

[*Neill enclosed the following notes on a separate sheet.*]

Fragments of an Analysis with Freud, by Joseph Wortis, M.D.
[New York: Simon & Schuster, 1954]
Page 106, Freud said: "An analyst by the name of Wilheim Reich went to Russia and lectured there, and talked so much about promiscuity that they finally asked him to leave."*
Page 165: "Reich, a talented psychoanalyst, will probably have to leave the movement because he has turned Communist and altered his views. He believes, e.g., that the aggressive instinct and sex problems are products of the class struggle instead of inborn biological drives."

———◆•◆———

---

* Reich underlined this, and wrote in the margin: Liars—Scoundrels!!

Desert Research Area

February 17, 1955

My dear Neill:

I have received your several letters. We are so busy here with desert research that we have little time to keep up with correspondence that is not immediately urgent. Therefore the delay which I hope you will excuse.

I have sent you a "bibliography" in order to convince you that I am, even in England, not dependent on people like Ritter. Permit me to say: I feel you are so hurt by not being recognised by your enemies that you feel I am a failure since the London *Times* does not mention me. Why in heaven's name do you, who has given so much to education, yearn to be honored by nobodies like Bernal? Your name will stand in history as a great educator when the world will have long forgotten such petty stuff as [Bertrand] Russell's on the twentieth century of late. It is the lovely look in a child's eye that constitutes my compliment and not what you expect. I would feel something was wrong with me if I had to share a present-day Nobel Prize with a researcher in anti-biotics. Enough of this now.

If you have mercy for Ritter, please convince him it would be to his best advantage to stop using and further abusing the well-defined term Functionalism.* Also, he should stop printing our material without permission; and he should not dare to do therapy using my authority in any way. He is a most tactless, neurotic fellow. Even his outpouring on self-regulation is babble of the worst, cheap sort, which avoids the true issue in order not to make enemies. Would you try to get him off my neck please . . . I would hate to have to use moral force against him. The advice you gave him already may serve as a springboard for further moves to *disconnect him completely.* Otherwise, soon all crackpots and neurotics who failed to reach my bandwagon will be gathered in an awful cacophony around his lack of responsibility and tact.

With regard to Wortis: He is a well-used stooge of the American Red Fascist conspirators. I do not believe that Freud ever said such things to him. This stuff was put into his writings by Moskau hoodlums who

---

* Defined as the study of living, changeable, functioning processes (in contrast to repetitive mechanisms) through which Reich came to discover the presence of an energy ("orgone energy") which he saw as actuating such functioning. Thus, "orgonomic functionalism" became the conceptual framework for all his further research.

fear me. After I had left Moskau the Moskau Academie Kommunists printed my *Psychoanalyse und Dialektischer Materialismus** in both their Moskau and Berlin editions. Also, I have never turned Communist and I have never said that the neurosis is due to the class struggle. What I have done and what these psychopaths hate most is that I brought depth-psychology into Marxian and other sociology, including an understanding of such psychopaths as Stalin, Hitler and the like.

We are continuously drawing moisture into the desert, causing rain at times, and we keep the deadly DOR out in a realm of about 60 to 80 miles radius.

I hope you do well and are cheerful as much as matters permit. Keep writing.

———◆•◆———

Summerhill School
Leiston, Suffolk

February 21, 1955

My dear Reich,

Just got your letter. But how to convey to Ritter the verdict without being brutal? I can't quote him your words. All I can say is that R. wants you to cease interpreting him in Britain . . . and then of course he will raise a sheaf of whys?

I think you get me wrong about my wanting to be recognised by my enemies. Nay, where I get impatient is to see the other side making victories; here caning in schools increases, here the talk of religious moulding flourishes; on the radio you hear only the one side—the enemy one. It doesn't matter if I am recognised, but it matters much that children aren't recognised.

I am very pessimistic these days. I am almost sure the idiots on both sides will kill us all. The official line now seems to be atomic death to all rather than have communism. But what a choice! I don't have to choose, but I tremble to think that our fate depends on men who must have been made anti-life in their cradles . . . Will no great statesman arise and shout: War is universal suicide; no one can win; all must lose.

---

* *Dialektischer Materialismus und Psychoanalyse* (1934), and in English, "Dialectical Materialism and Psychoanalysis," in *Sex Pol Essays, 1924–1934* (New York: Vintage Press, 1972).

The only chance is to disarm all round, to divide the world and stick to the division. But I fear the plague would not let his voice be heard.

How there can be peace I can't imagine; too much hate and fear on both sides. Meanwhile we just wait; the common man has no say in his destiny either in East or West. But I wish we did not have to live on the edge of a volcano as we now do.

My dear friend, I don't care a damn if I see you acclaimed in the *Times* or not. I do want to see your name in all papers, not for your fame, but for your turning desert into fertile land. If a Bernal could do it I'd be pleased to see it broadcast also.

Last week I gave the Foundation Oration at a large gathering in London University Education Dept. Over 600 there including profs of psychology etc. They seemed to enjoy the lecture.

Now I must sit down and think out what I am to say to Ritter.

Mein Gott, the young are so difficult to handle.

——— ◆•◆ ———

Summerhill School
Leiston, Suffolk

February 23, 1955

My dear Reich,

I have written to Ritter telling him in very guarded words that you don't want him to carry on with OF [*Orgonomic Functionalism*]. I could not of course quote what you say about him. One result will most likely be that he will send you long letters of defence and explanation and you'll get fed up with him. So I am going to make the suggestion that you settle the matter by telling him plainly but kindly what you don't like in his magazine. I am getting tired of explaining to him that you won't tolerate any interpreters, especially any who have not undergone therapy with a qualified man.

Where I am troubled is his enthusiasm, his genuine belief that no one alive has anything to say of any value barring W.R. That makes it difficult . . . how to restrain him without dealing a mortal blow at his enthusiasm.

You are like me, you hate to be cruel to folks. In a fit of temper we can act but when one has to censure someone in cold blood it is an unhappy business.

Damn all this waste of time and paper and postage on Ritter's behalf. Go on, Reich; tell him his self-regn. is wrong, his functionalism abused, etc. I say this partly in self defence; I don't want to have him on *my* neck because he thinks that I am your sort of official deputy on this side of the ocean.

————◆•◆————

Summerhill School
Leiston, Suffolk

March 5, 1955

My dear Reich,

Yours today. But you don't say if you have written to Ritter yourself. I can do little with the guy because I simply must not quote to him what you have written to me.

Thanks for the [flying] saucers book which came a few days ago. It sure made me sit up. So much air force testimony can't be ignored. I then got hold of the other book.* Leslie almost gets near your Orgones, but I can't accept Adamski's account of his interview with a spaceman. How could he possibly get all the conversation without language? Why you write that the space problem is quite acute I don't guess. Inclined to accept your opinion that they are benign, the only acute problem I can imagine would be their arrival here to stop the inevitable atomic destruction of all life. Mutual fear won't stop war. Almost looks as if Freud was right in saying there is a death instinct when one sees the whole mass of people thinking of football and radio etc. at a time when the sinking of a U.S. aircraft carrier off Formosa or the enthusiasm of a U.S. pilot might set the light to the gunpowder barrel. Hence I say: let the spacemen come; they might save us and if they came as destroyers they could not be more dangerous than man himself. What do you mean when you say the problem is most acute?

I wish I could talk with you. I wrote to the Hamiltons after years and got a long reply from Tajar. It was good to hear from him again.

So you have been on TV again. Good. I wish I could have seen it. I am in so much of the dark about what you are doing and what results you are getting.

Things all right at this end. My only trouble is *Angst* about my child mostly. I simply can't see how East and West are to go on without war.

---

* *Flying Saucers Have Landed,* by Desmond Leslie and George Adamski (New York: British Book Centre, 1953).

If only they could meet openly and say: Let us see what things we do want in common . . . *aber* [but], what meeting could get down to fundamentals? Our Govt. published last week story of Chinese atrocities in N. Korea. Every C.P. member in the country sneers that it is all a bundle of lies. If the Chinese gave out a report that S. Koreans had tortured N. Koreans and Chinese with the aid of U.S.A. men, every communist in the world would believe the story. And, alas, such emotional determination is on both sides, on all sides. Everywhere. In other words the main and dangerous plague is the political one. But you said that years ago.

You write: We cannot be, must not be liberal to evil. *Aber, Freund* [but, friend], what is evil? Ritter, for instance, isn't evil so far as I can see; he is just suffering from the emotions and egocentricity of youth. How to see evil? To me the Chinese who want to take Formosa by force are evil, and for the same reason the Pentagon which thinks that force can settle anything important is evil. And what do you mean by the word liberal anyway? Latin: *liber*, free. To me the word means taking the unhateful way if possible, not killing the Rosenbergs, not shooting Beria,* not hanging criminals, not caning children, not exploiting workers. To me liberal means knowing at once what side you are on, Malan† or the Natives. Dislike of all tough guys. But what is the use going on. You seem nowadays to mix up liberalism with weakness. Maybe you are right. I don't know what you think these days. Do you think that the men who can decide Peter and Zoë's fate, the Molotovs, Edens, Dulleses are wiser than you and I are? Do you approve of this idea that fear of war will restrain anyone? Damn it all, how we could talk over a bottle of the best. We never will. It is a most depressing thought.

---

* Lavrenti Beria, for many years head of the Russian secret police; shot in December 1953.
† Then Prime Minister of South Africa.

Summerhill School
Leiston, Suffolk

May 4, 1955
My dear Reich,

Ich komme sehr selten zum Schreiben [I very seldom get around to writing]. I always lose energy in spring. The cottage in which we live has very little heating because we are mostly over in the main school building. So every winter the Box feels damp and useless. It is only now that the spring winds have come that it functions. I can now use it for at least six months. I think that in this country that difficulty of dampness will be everywhere; hardly a house has central heating.

Thanks for *CORE No 2.* Fascinating reading, but to me most irritating. You say I am too impatient for recognition, but when I read of your telegrams to State Heads and Ike etc. and know that they are given no attention I get wild. If you don't you must be super (or sub) human. I can understand officials and scientists saying: "Orgones are bunk. We can't see them," but if you bust a cloud and make rain that is visible to one and all, I can't see why someone doesn't take it up as something new or at least as news. Hoppe tells me you got grass to grow in Arizona and cactus etc. to die. It just beats me. Saucers and orgones come from too far off to be accepted by the masses. So I'm not quite sure why you bombard officialdom with telegrams about what you are doing about rain. Unless to force them to have a record that can be consulted in the year 2000.

Much worried about money. Constant fight to make ends meet and I don't know how long we can carry on. Numbers dropped from 60 to 42 and our fees just about half those of big schools, reason being that believers in freedom are nearly always poor folks.

Invited to an educational conference in Weilburg, near Coblenz, in August, free hospitality from the German teachers. Will meet people I haven't seen for over 34 years. I fear it will be a solemn conference, for pedagogues can't laugh.

Ena and Zoë both well.

———◆•◆———

[1955]

Summerhill School
Leiston, Suffolk

May 25, 1955

My dear Reich,

I am not sure which article you mean;* if the one read for me at the 1950 conference please cut out anything that might be dangerous to my school . . . *z.B.* [i.e.] if I mentioned *Beischlaf* [intercourse]. I can't find the copy I kept and fear that I might not agree with what I said five years ago.

Had a visit from a man I met some years ago, a curious card, teacher of motor driving. He has a Reich library but never lends out the books; his interested friends come to his house to read. He is a genuinely keen guy, and his library readers are all young folks who want to get as much as they can of your work.

I have been thinking of U.S.A. a lot recently. What puzzles me is that so large a nation does not seem able to produce leaders. Ike, for example, appears to some of us over here as weak, and like Dulles, open to influences, like the China Lobby which would risk a world war. Voting is tomorrow and looks as if the Tories are going in again. Most voters seem not to care about who rules them. The Saturday football match takes infinitely more emotion from the millions than does the thought of a DOR world. Our election now is a dirty business; men like Eden and Attlee saying things that children would say about each other. I know of no politician in the world I'd trust to give me advice on any damned thing. I share your contempt for the lot.

Anarchist paper *Freedom* has new editor who seems to be anti-Reich and anti-Neill. *The New Statesman & Nation* won't have either of us nowadays. Makes me begin to share your long view on liberals in general.

I'll strengthen my Box.

P.S. For weeks now I am in U.S.A. in my dreams almost nightly. I awaken feeling sad about their stupid visa rule, but an American professor tells me things are slackening now that McCarthy is a negative number. But I doubt if the time will ever come when I can get a visa.

———◆◆———

* Reich had asked about publishing the paper Neill gave in absentia at the Orgonon Conference of 1950.

Summerhill School
Leiston, Suffolk

June 8, 1955

My dear Reich,

Thanks for ms. Do you mind if I rewrite it? It could be called a 1950 Conference Speech re-edited five years later, *nicht* [no]? One difficulty is what to say about adolescent sex. The truth simply can't be published if my work is to go on. But how to write an honest article with this proviso I dunno. Two years ago a lovely Danish girl of 17 came. When she left her mother never paid the whole bill and never answered requests for payment. I got a lawyer in Copenhagen to write her mother. Now I have a nasty letter from the woman saying her daughter came home pregnant because there was no supervision of the sexes etc. The girl was all sex and spending-money, and had I been wise I'd have sent her home at once or have had *Vollmacht* [full authority] in writing from the mother. I tell you this to show that approving of adolescent sex may lead to disaster. I told the mother in a letter that if the girl was pregnant it was the first time a boy had made a girl pregnant in 35 years of S'hill.

I read your response* with enthusiasm, wondering all the time why you can publish it since the Clifford† judgment prohibited any mention of Orgones in print. I also wonder why you always find a red fascist setting the house on fire . . . why a fascist of any colour? If the drug factories see you as a danger to their wares where does the political colour come in? Why should the prosecution be Moscow directed? Must you find some external reason for every American act of hate and greed? What red has any power in the U.S.A. today? I don't try to defend Moscowism; it is evil, but I say that when you meet evil in U.S.A. why not see it as a home product? McCarthy isn't inspired by red fascism.‡ A review of one of my books from Rome says I ought to be shut up as a danger to all children, but the writer isn't a fascist of any colour, only a R.C. priest. I think you spoil your case by introducing the political factor . . . UNLESS you have secret evidence of the fire-raisers. Profit

---

* *History of the Discovery of the Life Energy*, Documentary Supplement No. 1 "Response to Ignorance" (Orgone Institute Press, 1955), in which Reich explains why he did not appear in court as a "defendant" to answer the complaint brought by the FDA.

† Judge John D. Clifford, Jr., who issued the default injunction against Reich to which Neill is here alluding.

‡ In the margin are two words, strongly underlined: HE IS.

and defense of profit has no political label; it is a *Tatsache* [fact] anywhere.

We are always having something to differ about, you and I! Why is everyone silent about space ships now? No reports of them anywhere.

I'm posting ordinary post copy of *Freedom* because it has an attack on Ritter. I send it sealed so that no one can accuse you of receiving an anarchist paper.

Summerhill School
Leiston, Suffolk

August 22, 1955

My dear Reich,

My Weilburg Conference was what I expected, almost completely divorced from reality. I took up sex only to be left almost unanswered. I told them they were all theory and mysticism. So far as I could see the German educationist is where he was in 1921, concerned with forming character by setting an example. But I did drink a lot of my favourite drink *Helles* [light beer] and ate a lot of my pet *Leberwurst* [liver sausage].

Had a visit from Ritter the other day. He tells me that Barakan is now a leading Dianetics man, which doesn't surprise me one bit. The book by Hubbard just seemed utter bosh to me when I read it a few years ago.

I feel sad about the death of Flugel. He really was a nice chap. I owe my friendship with you mainly to him indirectly, for when my chairman at my Oslo meeting said after the lecture: "You had a very distinguished man in your audience tonight . . . Dr Wilhelm Reich," I was excited because Flugel had lent me your *Fascism* book to read (in German) and was so interested in it that I at once phoned you and you invited me to dinner. Yes, he was a good guy, Jack Flugel, the only *echt* [genuine] Freudian who was human and genial. True he stuck like so many at your *Character Analysis.* "Up to that point Reich was brilliant and great, but . . ." but you know the story told so often.

To return to Ritter . . . he can't see my point when I say to him: "My dear fellow, if you started a magazine called *Summerhill News* I should object strongly, for as long as a man is alive and working no other man can possibly interpret his work." I think he is genuine in his desire to spread the gospel according to St Wilhelm. That is why he worries me;

I don't like to see his enemies crow: "So the great Reich has given you the big push!" I think Ritter is, as I say, genuine even with all his faults of youth. I have a sneaking admiration for his decision to carry on in spite of your opposition, even if I think he is misguided.

I wonder if after Geneva [summit conference] U.S.A. will relax her visa policy. It would be a great joy to be able to come over to see you again.

———— ◆•◆ ————

Summerhill School
Leiston, Suffolk

September 8, 1955

My dear Reich,

Here is the copy [the edited version of Neill's 1950 paper]. I simply can't say more about sex; safety first must continue to be my motto as long as I have Summerhill.

Your new booklet about Red Fascism* makes sad reading for me. I think: "It is appalling to think that a creative man like R. should have to waste his time and energy on fighting enemies who fundamentally don't mean much . . . who will know Brady's name in 1974? I wish I could see you ignore the whole bloody mob of nobodies."

True I have never been persecuted, never been attacked by the law, so that I can't think personally about it all. But, my dear friend, I feel you overstretch the red fascist element; innovators were persecuted before either communism or fascism were invented. Would you say that Galileo was the victim of red fascism? Unless you mean that the colour today of yesterday's Pharisee or Inquisitionist is red. I dunno. You confuse me.

———— ◆•◆ ————

Summerhill School
Leiston, Suffolk

October 5, 1955

My dear Reich,

One of my old pupils married a psychoanalyst and I went to the wedding party. Filled with followers of Melanie Klein. Interesting

---

* *The Red Thread of a Conspiracy* (Orgone Institute Press, 1955).

to hear their talk. I mentioned your name as a test; their faces clouded with disapproval which amused me. They can't laugh; Melanie has evidently shown them that humour is a complex which no normal free man should have. To my asking what Klein was doing to prevent complexes there was silence. I said: you can't analyse humanity but you can attempt to get a humanity that won't need analysis. No answer. *Gott*, they were a dull crowd. I couldn't help comparing them with the life and energy of the Orgonon conferences. They depressed me . . . rather like talking to communists with a blank curtain that you can't penetrate.

Am having a difficult time in the school. Can't get a necessary teacher; they won't come for the small salary and I can't pay more. So I have to teach all the time myself, and at 72 it is no fun to teach children how to count 2 and 7.

I am hoping that by next summer the U.S.A. will have relaxed their visa policy.

I haven't heard from you for some time. Now that Ilse has gone you seem to have to write by hand. She writes sometimes from Sheffield.

1956

January 13, 1956

My dear Reich,

Your Xmas card arrived today stamped "insufficiently stamped for air mail." I was wondering at my end what had happened to you, not hearing from you. For myself I've been stagnating, vegetating for weeks with little interest in anything. I feel so out of touch with what you are doing. The orgone field has receded from my view.

Some weeks ago I wrote to the U.S.A. embassy asking if my ban was perpetual, for if not I'd like to make a trip to U.S.A. next summer to see my co-workers. They replied that I should come and have a talk with the consul "to see if you can qualify for a visa." I resent the word qualify, but I'll go. It would sure be great to see you again, my friend, and so many others, but I don't know how I can get anything organised. For of course without earned dollars I can't come. I'd have to have lectures, conscious of the fact that I have nothing new to say these days.

I am beginning to find life rather sad. Partly the time of the year, the dark damp days of an English January; I hope that hope will return with spring. I get much more easily worried about shortness of cash too. To work for so many years and see red ink in the bank all the time is depressing.

We should never be proud of our children. Zoë now nine will eat nothing but bread and potatoes, refuses all greens and most fruits. *Bockbeinig* [Pigheaded] about it too. She gets catarrh and ear trouble and looks pasty-faced . . . and one can't do a damn thing about it. Self-

401

regulation! But I hope it is just a necessary phase, when the growing body needs mostly starch and sugar. I dunno.

What are you doing in Washington?* I have reluctantly rejected the fancy that Ike sent for you saying: "This coronary business, Reich, is upsetting. I need you to stand by to take my place for a bit." That would be attributing to Ike more sense than he has.

How are you? I have no news, only rumours . . . that you were alone with a dog and Tom Ross at Orgn., that you were madder than ever . . . after trying to understand your orgone writings I think that they are probably right, that you are mad, for if a madman is a guy that ordinary folks don't understand, then, sure, you are one! But men like you make it awfully dull for us so-called sane people . . . oh how dull we can be especially at educational conferences.

Dunno what Ritter is doing. He wants me to write a preface to his book on Self-Regn.; I said I would read the ms. and write one only if I thought the book had any value. He won't accept my view that you can't preach a prophet's words as long as he is alive. Best to wait till he is dead and then corrupt his message à la the Freudians.

Life goes on in a rut really here, the same daily round with too many dull visitors who take all the time and have nothing to give.

———◆◆◆———

[*Telegram*]

JAN 18, 1956

LT.† ALEXANDER NEILL
ANY HELP RENDERED BY YOU TO PAUL RITTER WILL GRAVELY DAMAGE MY WORK AND REPUTATION. P R MOST LIKELY VICTIM-HOST OF RED FASCIST EMOTIONAL TAPEWORM. LETTER FOLLOWS.

———◆◆◆———

---

* Reich lived in Washington during the winters of 1956 and 1957.
† Reich considered himself to be at war and regarded Neill as one of his lieutenants.

[1956]

Alban Towers
Washington, D.C.

January 18, 1956
My dear Neill:

It was a great pleasure, indeed, to hear from you again. It was sad to notice that you are not quite happy. I understand fully why. It would be splendid if you came to the U.S.A. this summer. You could stay in my summer house as my guest. Though things have greatly changed since 1950, and much new has happened, I am certain we would get along.

According to reports from England and also from your description, your land suffers from DOR, i.e., OR energy gone sour or stale, no matter now what the reason, atomic bombs, space ships or plain a dying atmosphere. But there is little doubt as to the nature of the predicament we are in.

Your sad news about Zoë does not surprise me. I saw it coming. Self-regulation cannot possibly work without its physiological, sex-economic basis. The lack of full application of this basis is the reason for so many failures. I have a very hard time keeping Peter's life going well for reasons which I'd rather not mention at this point. He wants, at present, to become a flier. He was with the expedition in Arizona and he loved the work and what he witnessed there. He had trouble in Hamilton's school since the subject of desert work seems taboo there, Ranger told me point blank that I am a paranoic, and everybody, including Ilse, avoids the subject of my work at present. Can you tell me why they always, instead of simply stating that they cannot understand, as you do, have to cover their ignorance up by malignant slander?

I sent you a telegram about Ritter. We here, sane responsible people who work hard on the atmospheric problem, are convinced that Ritter can only be made comprehensible if one assumes that he is being used by pestilent politicians of whatever kind to discredit my orgone work. He himself knows nothing about it.

You write about what "ordinary folks" are telling you about me. I wish I knew who these people are who spread the rumours as you say. I do not care much, but why do they hide?

My *Function* has been translated into Spanish, French and now also an Italian translation is asked for.

Would you tell me the name of the pestilent slanderer? Would you do it, or will you protect the gossiper? It does not matter really . . .

I have discovered a new way of doing what I have tried so hard to do all my medical life: Getting the poison out of people's character. I think I may make it this time. It is the Medical DOR Buster so-called; many physicians including completely sane ones are working with it in their offices. It is a medical variant of the Cloud Buster which draws energy from the atmosphere.

Let me know what happened to your request for a visa. I shall most likely return from Washington to Orgonon around May.

———◆◆◆———

Alban Towers
Washington, D.C.

January 21, 1956

My dear Neill:

This will be a brief, frank amendment to my letter of a few days ago. I invited you to be with me if and when you come to the U.S.A. in my summer house at Orgonon. However, it had not occurred to me when I put in the invitation, due to my wanting you at Orgonon, that for the past 4–5 years we all had gone through hell at Orgonon because of the atmospheric conditions there. The Observatory is not inhabitable. The lower house is lately, but the charges are high, and whoever lives there has to adjust bio-energetically. Oranur has made many people run: Wolfe, McDonald, Ilse, Eva and many others. I had no one there but had to stay on to do my job. There was no one for years to cook a meal for me or really to take care of me except the faithful Tom Ross who was brave and is still there.

I think it unwise for you to come there without first seeing what it does to you. It may be that I shall be again alone at Orgonon with no one to cook or to clean.

It is such a pity that you are reluctant to understand what really happened at Orgonon and in the world at large. That such exact reports as *Oranur* and *Core* do not seem to make sense to you, that dozens of workers in the new field do not count. I shall not try to say more on this score. At any rate I could not put my invitation into effect unless I am again there and am certain that you would be safe there.

Now about my telegram re Ritter again: Neill, there is agreement here that the man is being used as a tool by people of the extreme left to discredit my work. He and his kind are trying hard to "get in" in many ways, as students, as patients, etc. We know them now and we do not permit them to come in. We require utter scientific discipline and in every case certainty that Moskau political Higs are not associated—this goes for any kind of HIG (Hoodlum In Government). The whole FDA affair was running in this framework. It would be most regrettable if they succeeded in getting your name involved. I would have to react against it immediately in public. They are now trying to break into my fortress through your liberal attitude toward the Moskau Higs. I have not fought an American Government agency which was governed by Higs only to get an English Hig into my domain. All this is very serious, Neill. I hope you understand.

I assume you are aware that so very much has changed here since 1950 that many think of it all in terms of a "Second American Revolution" in the making, as it were.

Would you think all this over and let me know soon how you decide. It would certainly be grand to have a few of those great talks again.

To sum up: If you come, do not be surprised that a whole world of the past lies in fragments, psychoanalysis, marxism of the political type, a great deal of wrongly applied liberalism, that desert development has entered upon the human scene, that we learned how to recognize and to fight the pestilent character, the carrier of the Emotional Plague, as one fights rats who transmit the black bubonic plague; that national and political boundaries have collapsed; that boundaries in science have basically collapsed, that our world is full of problems of space and space travel, that the primordial cosmic energy has been discovered, that a new kind of industrial use of a noiseless energy is in the process of being born; that we begin to learn how to handle the climate, etc. etc.

Is this too much? I do not think so. It is rather too late, possibly, since the obstruction by prejudice and obscurantism and a false sense of "love thy neighbor" the wrong way has for so long held up what could have been done maybe 40 to 60 years ago already.

All this is only a prelude to our possible meeting in summer 1956. Let me hear from you.

(Would you be willing to sound a warning about the difficulties of "self-regulation" in education to all you can reach. It is very necessary to kill a new false religion of easy-going heavens before it is too late . . . Will you? Especially into Israel?)

Summerhill School
Leiston, Suffolk

January 29, 1956

My dear Reich,

I got your cable re Ritter. Luckily I have no conflict about his book because his view of self-regn. is far too local with too many irrelevant details that can't interest the outside reader. So I won't write any preface for him.

At the same time I think you have not been wise about the guy. He still thinks that you approve of him and only your disciples are against him. I could not disillusion him because I could not betray your private opinion as given in your letters to me. I really think to settle the question for all time you should send him a letter saying that you do not want him to interpret your work. That would be the kindest way. I never understand your saying that he is a victim of red fascism; my own view is the simple one, that he is quite sincere in his belief in orgones and self-regn., only that he is misguided into thinking he understands more than he is capable of.

If I go to the U.S.A. consul now he will ask what invitation I have to go to America. With none he will say that there is no point in asking for a visa. If a friend on the *N.Y. Times* is to be believed, 90% of the immigration staff are Irish Roman Catholics.

My health is all right but I have sleepless nights nowadays. Finance trouble. Too few pupils and rising prices . . . just been told that my electric wiring is out-of-date and it must be renewed at once. Possible cost £500. And to think I have £800 book royalties frozen in Tokyo!

I hear so little about your work these days. I only hear the opposition side, for instance that flying saucers have been proved to be nonsense. I read of rainmaking but never a word about yours. So I feel rather lost and far away from sources.

Zoë has bad tonsils but I don't want them taken out, believing that what is there by nature has some permanent purpose in the body. She eats too much starch and how to make her eat balanced food is our problem.

Sorry that this letter isn't too cheerful. Maybe because a neighbour bored me with his conversation for over twenty years. I was at his funeral yesterday. He has left a large fortune to his relations whom he never spoke to . . . and not a penny to me. *So ist das Leben* [Such is life] or rather *das Sterben* [dying].

Write soon and tell me what you are doing now. Relaxing I hope, but I can't picture you not working.

———◆•◆———

Alban Towers
Washington, D.C.

February 3, 1956

Dear Neill:

I have received your last letter. Unfortunately I am in no position to send you an invitation; you will know the true reason in a year or two.

Regarding Ritter I suggest that you tell him that his paper has nothing to do with the term Orgonomic Functionalism and the best thing for him to do would be just simply to drop that term from the title. You may also indicate my belief that he is a victim of Red Fascists, who are using for their own evil purposes his strong identification with me.

I am sending along a book on an official account of flying saucers. This book will show you what malignant blabber of little frightened souls around me amounts to.

I would expect from you as a friend that you reveal the identity of the person or persons who are supplying you with all the nice rumours.

———◆•◆———

Summerhill School
Leiston, Suffolk

February 22, 1956

My dear Reich,

I gave Ritter your message two weeks ago but got no answer. I have very little to write about today. You ask me as a friend to tell you where the rumours are coming from. I simply don't know. You are much spoken about over here by admirers and their opposites, but what is said is so *unbedeutend* [unimportant] that one forgets who said which. But I think my mentioning the rumours to you was a spot of plague on my part, for I ought to have remembered that your attitude to gossip and mine differ widely. I don't care a damn what they say about me . . . I don't care because the gossipers don't mean a thing to me and because they aren't true. In your case it may be true that you were alone in

Orgonon for a bit (what the hell anyway if you were?) but since you aren't mad I can't think what it matters if a hundred plague merchants say you are. I ought to have remembered that though, and I guess it was plague on my part . . . *warum ich weiss nicht* [why, I don't know]. Maybe annoyance at getting news (real news not gossip) of you second-hand, *z.B.* [i.e.] Hoppe, Raknes, who both told me about the new application of orgones to disease which I hadn't heard of and still know nothing about.

I don't think I'll try for a visa. U.S.A. doesn't know me and doesn't want me. But maybe that is all rationalization; maybe I feel that the old links are broken and I can't face new ones. I never understood your orgone work really; too old, too set, too conditioned. But you as a personality and friend I shall value as long as I live.

You carry on from old to new. I can't. My work has been done and I am discovering nothing new. I should retire but know that if I did I'd die. Yet I feel like starting again in a new line; I want to write a play or two if I can.

My father used to say that age brings loneliness; I begin to feel it too. Lately so many of my contemporaries have died. If I sometimes think: I can't have many more years now, it isn't a thought that alarms me. I don't fear death; I fear ceasing to live and of course the method of dying.

Nay, Reich, one can't put the clock back. The Hamiltons' seminars, the happy time with you in Maine; I can't think that another visit would be half as good.

If I sound rather depressed blame the cold for we have had three weeks of the coldest weather known in England within living memory, and all our pipes are frozen and our feet like ice.

P.S. An unknown factor in life is the result when age gets past the sexual urge. Am I useless now in work because sex has no more meaning? There is room for a valuable essay on this aspect. I suppose that one could dig out much evidence that the dying of sex does not affect the creative urge. Would make a very interesting book this topic, but it would mean so much research.

Alban Towers
Washington, D.C.

February 29, 1956

My dear Neill:

I was deeply touched by your letter of Feb. 22nd. You are one of the very few honest ones.

I hope you have received the book on Space Ships by Ruppelt.* Let me know what you think about it.

It would be most helpful if you could dampen somewhat the enthusiasm of the Jews in Israel about the present possibilities of self-regulation. Would you tell them how tough the problems involved really are. Otherwise a new disastrous religion of "Self-regulation" *without* true *change* of the *deep structure of man* will result and will continue killing for another 2000 years.

Your decision not to come to the U.S.A. at the present time seems rational to me. I do not believe that you would enjoy it or that your liberal attitude would be appreciated. Liberalism itself has come under sharp public scrutiny as to its true function in society. I personally would love to have you at Orgonon, but Oranur has destroyed its peacefulness and liveability.

———◆•◆———

[The following letter was never sent.]

Alban Towers
Washington, D.C.

March 3, 1956

My dear Neill,

After having mailed my last letter to you I received a letter from Paul Ritter. Somehow in my mind a connection was established between the test liberalism is undergoing at present and the Ritter case.

I shall use his case in a planned publication under the title "Crossroads Ahead" where I shall attempt, concluding from past experiences, to sound a few warnings against continuation of a many-folded stupidity, including my own. I wonder whether it has become clear to you that it

---

* *The Report on Unidentified Flying Objects,* by Edward J. Ruppelt (Garden City, New York: Doubleday, 1956).

is disastrous to any kind of human endeavor to confuse the liberal principle of the dignity of man, to which I subscribe, with being liberal toward crackpots and potential future murderers. I know from past discussions with you that you basically agree with the following: distinguishing authoritarian discipline for the sake of cruelty from the naturally given work democratic discipline of work processes. Human operations require a natural discipline crucial to any professional activity. Looking back I find that though you have clearly distinguished between license and freedom you have not clearly enough emphasized the requirement for a natural disciplined way of procedure in any type of human natural work. In the Ritter sense, I have never been a rebel, never a revolutionary, but an orderly, well-organized, professionally disciplined man of science and medicine. In this respect I always have been conservative in the good sense and I hope to remain so the remainder of my days. In other words, nature is functioning in a work democratic manner but not in a libertine sense of democracy.

To return to the example of social pathology in Ritter, he is mad because I don't accept him as a work democratic partner. He doesn't understand, and never will, that before an organ is functioning work democratically in an organism it had to integrate itself into the totality of the specific organismic function. It had to grow slowly, carefully, and patiently in continuous well ordered and, if you don't mind, *"disciplined,"* coordination, and cooperation with the total purpose. Orgonomists, as any other specialist, have to go through training. We are training our workers in a free way respecting their personalities, letting them choose their own ways to the common goal, but we are training them in a disciplined manner in the above sense, just as a pilot has to be trained carefully and strictly to get his airplane safely from New York to London.

Nothing shows up the psychopathic crackpot better than the fresh remark that "Birth is NOT a shock, the baby works for it with involuntary movement and then it purrs with delight. . . . Not a shock, please—that makes nonsense of life—but an orgasm for mother and child." The idiot wants to be equal with me, does not realize and forgot what he has read, namely that most uteri have for ages been spastic and therefore the births have been painful. Neill, whether you like it or not, agree or not, I'm ready to teach. But the world of the Barakans and the Ritters has nothing to do with learning. In that world grew all the misery through the ages.

It is up to you and at your responsibility what you want to tell him about the content of this letter.

————◆◆————

Alban Towers
Washington, D.C.

March 8, 1956

My dear Neill:

I'm enclosing a photostat copy of a letter I received from Ritter. The poor fellow is in the throes of his alleged friend Boadella.* His remark with regard that birth is not a shock shows his abysmal ignorance and charlatanism.

In spite of my 35 years of high-pitch psychiatric skill I'm still poor in handling such minor things as the case of Ritter.

I do not write him directly since he is only waiting for a letter from me to entangle me endlessly.

————◆◆————

Summerhill School
Leiston, Suffolk

March 9, 1956

My dear Reich,

Ruppelt's book arrived just as I took to my bed for a week with bad influenza. So that it came at the right moment. Many thanks. The guy is typical of the stiff-stomached breed, full of fears and doubts and tied to an anchorage. Yet the book has one merit at least . . . it does debunk some of the more phantastic claims made for saucers . . . The satisfying feature is that even Ruppelt has to admit that a percentage can't be explained away. My own doubts about space ships arise from the fact that there has never been any proof of a landing or any wreckage, which means that another planet has reached the stage of 100% safety which is hard to believe. Another doubt is why most of them over U.S.A.? Some say because of the atomic energy plants, but it

---

* An English university student who learned of Reich through Neill's writings. To Reich's extreme indignation, he had taken it on himself to describe Reich's work in a lecture about flying saucers.

would be just as reasonable to say that they came because of Orgone energy plant. The descriptions given appear to be nearer Orgone than atomic energy anyway. Ruppelt's book forces on us the question you have so often put: Is seeing and experiencing by a scientist enough when his soul and body are rigid?

The New Education Fellowship has a monthly journal, the *New Era*. I was editor in 1920. The present editor writes me asking if she had any chance of an article by Reich. I said I didn't think she had, for you are too busy a man. But since the journal is world-wide and most of its readers are "progressives" which means frightened sitters on the fence, I think it would be worthwhile to read what a live educationist had to say. "The Source of the Human No"* would make em sit up and take notice. Would you allow a reprint of the article?

A big question mark???????

If you can produce rain why is humanity playing with throwing chemicals into clouds? If the Devil himself could make it rain even the most devout Christians would use his methods (after first announcing that the Devil stole them from the genuine God of course), but they would use 'em. It is a melancholy thought that if human rigidity can prevent seeing, there seems no hope for humanity in a million years. Someone said to me that you got grass to grow in Arizona where no grass was known within living memory. Then why did not every farmer there shout all the way to the White House . . . "We demand Reich's rainmaker?" I can never think of a good enough reason for this mystery.

Ilse wrote some months ago saying she was bringing Peter to England this summer. That would be fine to see him again. Often people say to me: "Can't you persuade Reich to come over and give a lecture tour?" I sigh sadly and answer No.

Everything good to you, friend.

———————◆•◆———————

* A commentary on the agony experienced by the newborn child. First published in *Orgonomic Medicine*, 1955; later included in *Reich Speaks of Freud*, 1967.

Alban Towers
Washington, D.C.

March 12, 1956

My dear Neill:

Thanks for your good letter of March 9th. You seem to catch on, slowly, to the basic issue of my existence of the past 6 to 8 years. I got into the UFO problem long before I knew I was in. The spacemen doubtless use OR[gone] energy and mess up our planet with the offal of their machines. I had discovered and worked with OR energy for many years without an inkling of UFO technology.

Your big question mark is answered in the following way. The NO that is being implanted in all newborn ones all over the planet structures them in such a manner that they lose the ability to feel and live OR[go-nomically] or they develop as grown-ups in many different ways sharp NO's against any rediscovery of what was denied them so early in life. From here all killing of life stems. Did you ever read the *Murder of Christ*?

My success in Arizona was very great. There, I learned truly the ways of self-regulation *in nature*: once you remove the deadly black DOR clouds from the atmosphere nature helps itself. One must only reach a certain point of freeing the soil from DOR, until the soil and the atmosphere take over. This happened in Arizona, but only experimentally, with a radius of about 50 miles. There is an awful lot which has to be learned yet. But the breakthrough has been accomplished.

The task ahead of mankind is tremendous, full of pitfalls, dangerous, and proceeding in a realm of natural science which is entirely new with most of the realm still in the dark. We have doubtless entered the Cosmic Age, *not* with atomic energy of course.

Do you remember the work in 1948, with Bill Washington?

I have so very much to do that it is quite unthinkable for me to add lectures to my burden. One cannot say much in an hour or two anyhow. But I would love to appear before large audiences again. My last one was in June 1938 before 600 students of medicine and others in Oslo on bions and cancer.

The Salk Vaccine is being studied by us here now. It belongs to the old world dying.

With regard to why people don't "demand Reich"? Neill, you should know by now????

Peter told me that he does not really want to go to England this summer. He is my best "little" friend. He visited me twice here in Wash.

He partook fully, consciously and enthusiastically in our desert work in Arizona. He knows much already about natural science and about DOR emergency.

You may of course have my "NO" paper and other things reprinted. Those who have it should pay a royalty to me.

———————◆◆◆———————

Summerhill School
Leiston, Suffolk

April 3, 1956

My dear Reich,

Steig sent me an article on cloud busting, etc. [for *The New Era*]. I asked him if I could keep the article meantime for it says so much in so little space.

Poor Judith Bogen is very ill with cancer. The doctors are treating it with radium which makes me see red, for they must know by now that radium never cured cancer and never will. A dear sister of mine died of the same disease and the radium needles simply added to her long agony. I have told her to use the Box as a means of reducing pain. Poor Judith, such a damned shame, for she was so kind and gentle.

Just off to a co-ed school conference which will be very moral and good and asexual, but the meeting place is a club with a licence and it will be easier to listen to the speeches over a glass of whiskey. Then I go on to Bournemouth to lecture to a conference on the maladjusted child . . . title, "The Therapy of Freedom." In both conferences I'll meet as usual a few people who want to know all about that man Reich. An Indian visitor yesterday said to me: "Is it true that Reich is mad?" "Absolutely," I answered, "mad. The rest of us are all sane . . . hence the world of today." But it is becoming monotonous this futile ignorance about your work. Yet I meet folks who read you and understand and are enthusiastic.

I am rereading the *Murder of Christ*. You've said it, brother. No appeal from that verdict. And how right you were about Stalin. His exposure has done great harm to communism in the West.

Sometimes one says to me: "How does this cancer of the lung from smoking fit in with Reich's theory of cancer?" Not knowing the answer I say: "It may be that the smoking only determines where the cancer is to be, and that the guy who takes it in the lung would take it in the stomach if he didn't smoke." I dunno if that is near the true answer or not.

———◆•◆———

Alban Towers
Washington, D.C.

April 12, 1956

My dear Neill:

I was shocked to hear the bad news about Judith Bogen. However I had known for 20 years that she would end up that way.

Thank you for your remark on my book on Christ.

With regard to Stalin, I am wondering why you believe it now, but were unable to see it when I told you about it a decade or so ago.

Your note on cancer of the lung is correct; smoking is what we call an *accidental* cause as distinguished from a specific cause, which in the case of the cancer is putrefaction and shrinking of the Life system.

You did not write whether my note on the NO in infants will be printed. Your answer to the Indian visitor was the right one.

———◆•◆———

Scotland

April 21, 1956

My dear Reich,

I am having a rest here for two or three weeks. Steig sent me an article on your work. He says the trial is on April 30th. What trial? Have you been ignoring the Court *Verbot* [ban]?*

Stalin. Why didn't I see it 10 years ago? I don't know. Maybe lack of sufficient evidence. Maybe reluctance to believe the ideal of brotherhood had failed. But more on this when I get back to my typewriter.

---

* During Reich's desert trip, Dr. Silvert had remained in New York to take care of the mail and minor administrative matters. Without Reich's knowledge, he had had some books and accumulator parts shipped from Orgonon to New York; i.e., across state lines. This violated one of the provisions of the injunction and brought on contempt proceedings against both Reich and Silvert.

Constance writes from Oslo saying that Judith has had an operation and is cheerful now. Poor woman.

I'll write you when I go back to Summerhill.

———— ◆◆ ————

Summerhill School
Leiston, Suffolk

May 23, 1956

My dear Reich,

I did not write because I knew you had so many things to think of. I hear that you and Silvert will be sentenced tomorrow,* but whatever the sentence nothing on earth can destroy the importance of your work.† You have often written me about the wonderful democracy of the States, but I cannot imagine any scientist in England being sentenced for his work. No law court here could possibly order a scientist to stop publishing what he believed, and certainly no court here ever has the power to decide whether anything is dangerous or not. I think that American democracy has a hell of a lot to learn especially about tolerance and real freedom. Over here we all know that you were prosecuted, not because you invented Orgone Accumulators, but because your work in general has stirred up all your enemies. That is clear; what isn't so clear to us is why the U.S.A. laws allow a vendetta against a man of new ideas. The Statue of Liberty ought to have a very red face these days.

Steig writes me that funds are low and can I do anything to assist. For myself I am always in the red and make no profit at all . . . But what a dreadful waste if money has to go to legal expenses instead of to new apparatus for research.

I wonder if a letter signed by several names protesting against your sentence would help. I think that England ought to know the truth about scientific research in U.S.A. I would try to get people who might not believe in your work like Bertrand Russell who maybe never heard of you. I forget who it was who said to an opponent: "I hate what you say but I am ready to go to the gallows in support of your right to say it."

---

* For contempt of court.

† Reich was sentenced to twenty-four months in jail; Silvert to a year and a day, and his license to practice medicine was revoked. He committed suicide five months after he was released.

I do feel most strongly and most sadly that your life has had far too much of enemy attack, but *Gott sei Dank* you got your message . . . nay messages through in spite of them all. So today, even if they put you in prison you and what you have given the world will triumph in the end. But perhaps there isn't much fun in being recognised five hundred years after your death.

Whatever the future, my old and dear friend, I and many others will never lose faith in your work and yourself.

Ena joins me in sending her sympathy and congratulations on refusing to be bullied.

———————◆•◆———————

[*While on a lecture tour in Norway, Neill was told by a mutual friend that Reich considered him unreliable.* He responded to the charge directly.*]

Oslo, Norway

October I, 1956

My dear Reich,

So our long friendship has come to an end because you consider me unreliable and on the side of Ritter and Co. How very sad. Just at a time when you require every friend you can have too. I think you have had few friends; disciples yes, enemies yes, but few who stood as it were outside and were objective. Maybe Sigurd Hoel and I were of the few who were not yesmen. I was a friend who loved you, who recognised your genius and also the Little Man in you, but I never was a "Reichian" who accepted all you said and did. Thus I was genuinely concerned about Peter and his fears of overhead planes† and his grown-up-ness which is not real, for he wants to be childish and play a lot all the time. I could speak to you of him where one of your disciples could

---

* Neill and several of Reich's Norwegian friends sent him a joint telegram of affection and support. Reich cabled his thanks to one of the friends, with an emphatic warning that "Neill is unreliable, tapewormed because of Boadella and Ritter."

† American planes routinely flew over Summerhill from the U.S. Air Force base nearby. During the summer, Peter had spent some time at the school and, while there, had said that the planes were sent to protect him against Reich's enemies. Neill tried to laugh him out of the notion—which Peter then reported to his father.

not. I think you have suffered through too many people being afraid to challenge you in any way. I think you lost perspective, *z.B.* [i.e.] in seeing a danger in an ordinary Mensch like Ritter who has not the tact nor the knowledge to challenge your work. I think you have worried far too much about folks who were *unbedeutend* [insignificant].

I wonder if you know how much you mean to many of us, and I don't mean in your work; I mean emotionally, humanly. The other day sitting with Sigurd and Raknes and Grete and Lilian Bi the warmth of their love for you, the fears for your future showed me that they cared more for Reich the man than Reich the discoverer. They are *bedeutend* [significant] while the Boadellas and Ritters etc. aren't. We all felt strongly the sad fact that we were all 3000 miles from you at this anxious time of your appeal.

Often I have heard you say: Everyone is right in some way. Now I say to you that everyone is wrong in some way also. I say that you are wrong about Peter. He looks too anxious. I think he is trying to live a part . . . "I am the only one who understands what Daddy is doing." He may understand but his emotions are all mixed up. He isn't Peter Reich; he is Peter Reich plus Wilhelm Reich. And, dear old friend, call this emotional plague or what you will. To me it is just plain truth.

I wish you every success in your appeal against an unjust sentence. I wish you many years to continue your work.

Goodbye, Reich, and bless you,

—◆◆—

Summerhill School
Leiston, Suffolk

October 22, 1956

My dear Reich,

Your short letter made me cry. It seemed to symbolize your loneliness, your misery in this abominable martyrdom, yet it conveyed your courage, your belief in your faith and work. Damn this 3000 miles separation. I know only a bit of your reality over there, and can have no perspective. Yet IF you didn't attend the second summons because someone said the summons wasn't properly signed, then I am sure you got wrong advice. Such a point cannot fight a battle whereas your original trumpet call: No court has the right to judge a matter of science, was right and powerful.

Can no one counteract the wrong publicity you are having? I saw a copy of a Washington paper with an article about Eva's application to practise orgone therapy. If Eva said the half of what they say she said I simply stand speechless. They quote her as saying that your road to therapy is by orgasms. What the hell?

Reich I love you. I cannot bear to think of your being punished by an insane prison sentence. You couldn't do it and you know it. I wish to God that you'd simply let some good lawyer take up your case from the legal angle. Why should anyone waste breath and time trying to explain to a judge and jury what your work is? They can't possibly understand and the reporters will make a travesty of it all in a Brady way. I think you are all wrong in thinking that the trials are instigated from Moscow.

The *Tatsache* [fact] is that you are being crucified fundamentally because you are the first man in centuries who has preached pro-lifeness, because you were the one and only man to assert the right of adolescence to love completely. The majority in U.S.A., Britain, Russia, in the whole world are anti-life, so that you do not need to look for specific enemies like the FDA; they are only the shot that was fired at Sarajevo, not the basic cause of the attack on you. In any court your defence should be in big letters I AM FOR LIFE AND LOVE, not I am the victim of Russia or red fascism or anything else. I confess to a feeling that you have imagined motives when the big motive of hostility was there plain to be seen. You haven't enough normal people around you to argue the point with you. To think that the great man who has advocated rationalism all his life would now embrace irrationalism is a terrible thought. Terrible because when you are up against the hard rationalism of law courts you must be super-rational to win.

Sorry to lecture like this but I am concerned about you, very much so. Get that lawyer and fight them with their own legal weapons, for your weapons are invisible to them.

My love and concern and blessings.

1957

Summerhill School
Leiston, Suffolk

January 29, 1957

My dear Reich,

I haven't written for a long time simply because I did not know what to say to you. I have heard via Raknes of the failure of your appeal, also that you can appeal to the highest court. You said in your last letter that I should read the whole legal case, *aber wie* [but how]? Is it published?

I have more than once wondered why you did not call cured patients to the witness stand. I guess it is too late now, but if a dozen benefitted patients had got up at the first trial and sworn that O. Energy helped them to health, the FDA would have found it difficult to discount their evidence.

But what now? There seems to be a conspiracy to *totschweigen* [kill by silence] the whole affair. I signed a letter along with Sir Herbert Read and others protesting against the scandal of your martyrdom, but no paper would take the letter. We tried the *New Statesman* and *Nation* and also the *Manchester Guardian*. Our impotence is appalling, partly because of our ignorance of what is going on.

We do not know on what grounds your appeal was dismissed. I have some fear that the highest court will support the lower ones since the affair now seems to be strictly the legal one of contempt of court. Lawyers like doctors are a closed corporation backing each other up. As Shaw said: Every profession is a conspiracy against the layman. In your case the layman being the skilled doctor who would not follow the vested interests of the profession. Alas it isn't much consolation to

421

know that years later you will be recognised as the victim of vast suppressive anti-life forces. And, Reich, since old friends like myself cannot possibly follow you in your deep thinking and knowledge, it is hardly likely that any judge or jury will do so.

I wish I could help you . . . but independent men are difficult to help. To think of your going to prison is a great tragedy, yet almost as great a one is that you have had to fight the Philistines and waste all the wonderful energy that should have been going into more and more scientific discovery.

We are all well. I was going to lecture in Israel in October but had to cancel the trip when the Nasser thing* began. I wish I could have some optimism about the future of mankind. The H bomb in the hands of haters is a terrible thought.

———◆•◆———

Washington, D.C.

February 3, 1957

My dear Neill:

I have your letter of January 29th. It is impossible for me at the present moment to answer it in any way satisfactory to you or other friends. I am engaged in a deadly and quite decisive battle with the Enemy of Man. Anything may happen one way or the other.

This case is coming up before the Supreme Court. The legal material is contained in some seven volumes of public record. These volumes may be had against compensation from the Core Pilot Press, c/o William Steig, 5 West 8th Street, New York, N.Y., with the exception at present of two of these volumes. I do not know whether you are really interested in going into all that material.

Be patient, please, if I keep silent or do not answer promptly. I am extremely busy.

———◆•◆———

* The nationalization of the Suez Canal, which precipitated a short-lived Anglo-French invasion.

[*In May 1956, Reich had been sentenced to two years in prison for contempt of court. All appeals having failed, he filed to have the sentence reduced or suspended. The hearing was held on March 11, 1957, in Portland, Maine. Reich's motion to have the sentence suspended was denied, and Reich was led from the courtroom in handcuffs. He was imprisoned in the federal penitentiary in Lewisburg, Pennsylvania. On November 3, 1957, he was found dead in his cell. The diagnosis was massive heart failure.*]

Index

DATE DUE